Landscapes of Fraud

LA FRONTERA: PEOPLE AND THEIR
ENVIRONMENTS IN THE U.S.-MEXICO
BORDERLANDS

Series Editor: Thomas E. Sheridan, Ph.D.

Landscapes of Fraud

MISSION TUMACÁCORI,

THE BACA FLOAT,

AND THE BETRAYAL OF

THE O'ODHAM

Thomas E. Sheridan

The University of Arizona Press   Tucson

The University of Arizona Press
© 2006 The Arizona Board of Regents
All rights reserved

First paperback printing 2007
ISBN 978-0-8165-2749-6 (pbk. : alk. paper)

Library of Congress Cataloging-in-Publication Data
Sheridan, Thomas E.
Landscapes of fraud : Mission Tumacácori, the Baca Float, and
the betrayal of the O'odham / Thomas E. Sheridan.
p. cm.
Includes bibliographical references (p.   ) and index.
ISBN-13: 978-0-8165-2513-3 (hardcover : alk. paper)
ISBN-10: 0-8165-2513-7 (hardcover : alk. paper)
1. Land tenure—Santa Cruz River Valley (Ariz. and Mexico)—History.
2. Land speculation—Santa Cruz River Valley (Ariz. and Mexico)—History.
3. Fraud—Santa Cruz River Valley (Ariz. and Mexico)—History. 4. Tohono O'odham
Indians—History. 5. Jesuits—Missions—Arizona—History. 6. Land settlement—
Santa Cruz River Valley (Mexico and Ariz.)—History. I. Title.
HD1251.S54 2006
979.1004'974552—dc22
2005024584

Publication of this book is made possible in part by grants
from the Southwestern Mission Research Center and
the Charles Redd Center for Western Studies at
Brigham Young University.

Manufactured in the United States of America on acid-free,
archival-quality paper containing a minimum of 50% post-consumer
waste and processed chlorine free.

12   11   10   09   08   07   7   6   5   4   3   2

This work was initially sponsored by the National Park Service.

To Deezie, David, and, as always,

To Chris

contents

List of Maps / ix
List of Figures / ix
Acknowledgments / xi

1 The Production of Space in the Upper Santa Cruz Valley / 3

PART I   Landscapes of community

2 The O'odham World and the Jesuit Intrusion / 19

3 The O'odham and the Franciscans / 55

4 Hispanic Settlement and the Final Displacement of
   the O'odham / 82

PART II   Landscapes of fraud

5 Early Anglo Speculation and the Tumacácori Land Grant / 107

6 Fictitious Capital and Fictitious Landscapes / 138

7 The Bottom of the Bottle / 172

8 Rio Rico and the Great Arizona Land Rush / 195

9 Buried Landscapes / 227

Notes / 243
Glossary of Spanish Terms / 271
References / 273
Index / 293

Maps

1 O'odham rancherías in Upper Santa Cruz River Valley,
   late 1600s / 27

2 The Upper Santa Cruz River Valley, late Spanish colonial times / 67

3 The Tumacácori-Calabasas land grant and Baca Float No. 3 / 149

4 Rio Rico and modern Upper Santa Cruz River Valley / 206

Figures

1 Mission Tumacácori, looking east, 1929 / 7

2 Interior of Mission Tumacácori, 1946 / 9

3 Calabasa, Santa Cruz Valley, Sonora / 121

4 Calabasas Land and Mining Company, Arizona / 126

5 Aztec Mining District, Pima County, Arizona / 150

6 Tohono O'odham potter preparing to fire pottery / 236

Acknowledgments

I would like to thank the following colleagues for their assistance in the research and writing of this book. Paul and Suzanne Fish, Bernard Fontana, Don Garate, Sallie Marston, and Bob Spude read and commented on portions of the manuscript. Debbie Newman at the Arizona Historical Society in Tucson, Axel Holm at the Pimería Alta Historical Society in Nogales, and above all, Mary Bingham at the Tubac Historical Society, who went out of her way to alert me to hidden sources and unpublished manuscripts, helped me explore the archives of their institutions and follow the often elusive spoor of the Tumacácori Land Grant and Baca Float No. 3. Nick Bleser and Birdie Stabel of Tubac offered me friendship, food, and a place to stay on overnight forays to Santa Cruz County.

Mintai Kim and Dai Shi prepared the maps. Deezie Manning Catron generously shared her memories of Canoa Ranch and the characters of "Santa Booze Valley" during its heyday in the 1940s and 1950s. Hydrologist Philip Halpenny, who knows the Upper Santa Cruz Valley better than anyone I know, gave me a guided tour of many of the sites mentioned in this book and taught me about its water history and politics. Steve Auslander, formerly of the *Arizona Daily Star,* informed me about Rio Rico and the Great Arizona Land Rush. Finally, the staff of Tumacácori National Park—particularly Superintendent Ann Rasor, Historian Dan Garate, and Historic Preservation Specialist David Yubeta—welcomed me into their extraordinary professional family and gave me access to documents, photos, and their knowledge of Tumacácori Mission itself. Their dedication, creativity, and passion exemplify the stewardship of the National Park Service at its best.

The research and writing of this book were partially supported by the United States Department of the Interior, National Park Service, through a Cooperative Agreement (#1443CA125097017) between the Southwestern Mission Research Center and the National Park Service.

Landscapes of Fraud

1

The Production of Space
in the Upper Santa Cruz Valley

The book you hold in your hands is a "history" in the sense that it chronicles and interprets social change through time, in this case the creation and destruction of human communities in the Upper Santa Cruz River Valley of southern Arizona from Mission Tumacácori to Rio Rico. Time, after all, has long been the primary analytical axis of our relentlessly teleological Western civilization. Whether we talk about Christian theology, evolutionary psychology, dialectical materialism, or modernization theory, our story lines demand change, evolution, progress. We are advancing toward something, a goal, an end, a culmination. The cultural webs we spin are linear, not cyclical. Even critical theorists who challenge deterministic ideologies embrace history. "It is precisely the critical and potentially emancipatory value of the historical imagination, of people 'making history' rather than taking it for granted, that has made it so compulsively appealing," geographer Edward Soja writes. "The development of critical social theory has revolved around the assertion of a mutable history against perspectives and practices that mystify the changeability of the world" (Soja 1989:14).

As Soja points out, however, our scholarly obsession with time "submerges and peripheralizes the geographical or spatial imagination" (Soja 1989:15). The spatiality of social life is often overlooked by our linear focus upon sequence and cause and effect. "Space was treated as the dead, the fixed, the undialectical, the immobile," Michel Foucault, talking about Western intellectual traditions, noted in an interview. "Time, on the contrary, was richness, fecundity, life, dialectic" (Foucault 1980:70).

To restore balance, critical geographers shift attention from time to the other defining axis of human social life: space. "The constitution of society is spatial and temporal, social existence is made concrete in geography and history," Soja (1989:127) notes. Such a statement seems straightforward and intuitively appealing. But when Soja and others talk about the "production of space," a major theme in critical geography since the publication of Henri Lefebvre's seminal work of the same name in 1974, they confound our commonsensical assumptions. Space, after all, is a void to be filled or a gap to be bridged. We can study *things* in space, but how can space itself be produced? It sounds like a question for physicists, not social scientists.

Let us begin to answer that question by taking a drive from Tucson to Nogales, Arizona, through the Upper Santa Cruz Valley, the geographical and intellectual terrain of this study. First, we are traveling by car, a manufactured space that surrounds and separates us from the natural environment. Whether we are aware of them or not, our automobile enmeshes us in a complex web of global interrelationships ranging from holes in the ozone layer to wars in the Middle East. No other technological invention since the railroad has transformed space in the American West more profoundly. Automobiles dictate the shape and density of our cities, the quality of our air, the spatial patterns of our neighborhoods, and the location of our workplaces. Originally, the floodplain of the Santa Cruz River bisected the Santa Cruz Valley in a roughly south-to-north direction. The floodplain still exists, even though flow in the river is largely artificial, fed by wastewater from Nogales. But the most important bisection now is Interstate 19, which speeds us back and forth between Tucson and Ambos Nogales (Nogales, Arizona, and much larger Nogales, Sonora), usually in air-conditioned isolation with the sounds of norteña, hip-hop, or country-western immersing us in worlds far removed from the desert landscape receding away from us.[1]

Once we reach Nogales, the freeway intersects with another social construction of space, the international border between Mexico and the United States. That border surges with unimaginable energy, the pent-up frustrations and aspirations of Latin America slamming against the barriers of surveillance that try to contain them. The natural unity of the Upper Santa Cruz watershed has been drawn and quartered, first by an imaginary line signifying conquest and national sovereignty, second by an artery of transportation designed to link the two nations together, at least economically. These two perpendicular constructions, both projections of state power, overwhelm any natural feature of the valley itself.

The border and the freeway also express and enable the relentless power of capital to fragment and reconnect, create and destroy. If you were to compare aerial panoramas of the Santa Cruz Valley in 1950 and 2000, the contrasts would astound you. The differences would be particularly dramatic between Sahuarita and Canoa Ranch, a stretch of the valley striking in its spatial schizophrenia. On the west, partially obliterating the Sierrita Mountains, great mounds of overburden rise like Aztec pyramids. Behind them, hidden from view, huge machines searching for tiny traces of copper spiral deeper into the earth, disgorging the subterranean. The mounds did not begin to pile up on the western horizon until the 1950s, a decade when Arizona barreled from its extractive past into its urban future with accelerating speed. Nonetheless, the mounds stand as mute testimony to relations of production rooted in an era when extractive industries like copper mining, cattle ranching, and cotton farming dominated the state (Sheridan 1995).

To the east, in contrast, islands of red-tiled roofs creep up the *bajada* (lower slopes) of the Santa Rita Mountains. Green Valley is one of the most successful examples of an entirely new social space—one not even envisioned until the late 1950s. The postwar economic expansion of the United States intersected with the aging of America's population to create a new class of consumers—"active seniors" freed from the constraints of living out their old ages near their children. Responding to this latent demand, retirement communities like Green Valley sprouted fully formed, age restricted, architecturally uniform. This peculiarly American phenomenon—one symbiotically associated with the country club and golf course—flourished in the Arizona sunshine precisely because the invention of air-conditioning kept the desert heat at bay in homes, businesses, and automobiles. The industrial spaces of the modern copper industry and the residential and recreational spaces of Green Valley—not to mention the cool green of Farmer Investment Company's (FICO) pecan groves, the largest pecan farm in the United States—form a startlingly dissonant geographic ensemble that embodies many of the most dynamic trends of capitalist development in Arizona during the past century.

When we drive south from Green Valley, however, the natural landscape is less fragmented, the social spaces sloppier and more jumbled. The arts and retirement community of Tubac does not have the same architectural homogeneity of Green Valley, although it clearly aspires to Santa Fe status with a dash of Sonoran style. Just to the south but difficult to see from the freeway, Tumacácori National Historical Park appears as an anachronistic oasis amidst a floodplain cluttered with houses, trailers, and small stores. The small community of Carmen has a messy, lived-in feeling missing from Tubac or Green Valley. No dominant entities or enterprises stitch this stretch of the Upper Santa Cruz Valley together. Even the real estate development of Rio Rico, with its network of eroding roads and scattered houses climbing the foothills of the San Cayetano Mountains, conveys little sense of grandiosity or hubris. The swampland swagger of Gulf American and GAC (formerly General Acceptance Corporation), its original developers, dried up and blew away decades ago.

Hidden by this hodgepodge are more than three centuries of speculative failure, of grand designs that never amounted to much but dispossessed people in their wake. One of the major goals of this book is to excavate those failures, to examine the new social spaces they struggled to create and the existing social spaces they destroyed. Lefebvre argues that every society produces its own space containing both the social relations of reproduction and production (Lefebvre 1991). And when a society imposes itself on another, the spaces it produces interpenetrate, shove aside, or shatter the spaces of the people already living there. The production of space, then, is as much about the production, reproduction, and destruction of relations of power as it is about the physical manifestations of those relations between people, legal systems, and nations.

By way of illustration, let us briefly consider the first grand design explored in this book. Before it became a romantic icon of the past, Mission Tumacácori was a theocratic vision of communal order imposed upon the O'odham Indians living in the Upper Santa Cruz Valley. That vision of Jesuit and Franciscan missionaries was accompanied by the endeavors of Hispanic frontiersmen striving to create their own social spaces of ranchos and presidios within a hierarchical and bureaucratic colonial system. Apache hostilities prevented the Spanish frontier from expanding beyond the Santa Cruz Valley, making the colonial enterprise a tenuous affair, a series of advances and retreats, expansions and contractions (Officer 1987). Meanwhile, the Western and Chiricahua Apaches

Figure 1. Mission Tumacácori, looking east, 1929. (Courtesy Tumacácori National Historical Park)

were aggressively pushing southward, generating their own spaces of raiding corridors and refuges in the surrounding mountains. Contesting geographies overlapped as Athabaskan speakers from the north and Hispanics from the south collided in O'odham territory. Viewed from the perspective of the Spanish empire, you could say that the colonial production of space in Arizona was continually being shot full of holes.

Nonetheless, the creation of mission, ranches, and presidios fragmented O'odham society along axes of both space and time. In Chapters 2 through 5, I discuss how the O'odham world of autonomous communities moving across the landscape in seasonal rounds was reduced to a mission world of subordination and circumscription. O'odham hunting and gathering were discouraged. O'odham ritual space was suppressed. O'odham fields were divided into individual fields and mission fields, where the O'odham were supposed to labor three days a week to produce surpluses controlled by the missionaries, not them. The very concept of "week" itself was a foreign construction, a European partition of time that reflected missionary demands, not natural cycles. As Lefebvre notes, "The adoption of another people's gods always entails the adoption of their space and system of measurement" (Lefebvre 1991:111).

Lefebvre (1991) offers a "conceptual triad" consisting of *spatial practice, representations of space,* and *representational spaces.* Let us apply that triad to Mission Tumacácori, starting with the representations of space Jesuit and Franciscan missionaries brought with them to the Arizona frontier. The spatial practices they struggled to instill among the O'odham reflected a vertical ideology of sacred power based upon Roman Catholic theology and Western European absolutism. Fundamental was the concept of Ambos Majestades—Both Majesties, God and king. Ritual and political authority flowed from the top down through a social hierarchy ordained by God. The O'odham, in contrast, believed that authority emanated from the community through consensus, not coercion.

I tell my students never to confuse missions with churches, because missions were all-encompassing programs of directed culture change designed to transform the ways native peoples lived as well as how and where they worshiped. But the mission church of Tumacácori—a representational space according to Lefebvre's triad—embodied and enshrined the ideology of power permeating every daily practice of mission life. The master builders and their Franciscan overseers operated according to a representation of space that guided the planning and construction of the church itself. Based upon geometric principles that had been passed down as esoteric knowledge for six thousand years, their representation provided a template determining the proportions of the building, the relation of parts to whole. Those proportions, rooted in ancient astronomical observations, reflected the divine order of the universe. All details from the width of the nave to the arrangement of the façade in churches were charged with sacred meaning (Schuetz-Miller 2003).

A chronic shortage of funds and skilled artisans repeatedly compromised the building of San José de Tumacácori. As a result, the church fell short of the Neoplatonic ideals lodged in the minds of its builders. But the structure still draws your attention forward and upward, as it was designed to do. As the O'odham neophytes entered through the church's portal and walked into the nave, where they would have stood or kneeled, the sanctuary at the other end of the church would have captured their attention. The focal point of any Catholic church, the sanctuary with its

Figure 2. Interior of Mission Tumacácori from the sanctuary, 1946. (Courtesy Tumacácori National Historical Park)

statuary and candles is the most sacred of interior sacred spaces, the section of the church where the priest presides and the consecrated hosts reside in the tabernacle above the altar. The *retablo*, or carved wood altarpiece, long ago dismantled or destroyed, would have swept the gaze of the O'odham heavenward into the celestial space created by the dome above the sanctuary.[2] The original plan called for a cruciform church with vaulted transepts and a vaulted nave as well, but those plans had to be simplified as the missionaries ran out of money (Pickens 1993; Officer, Schuetz-Miller, and Fontana 1996). Nonetheless, no other colonial space in the Upper Santa Cruz Valley better symbolized the hierarchical cosmos the O'odham were being forced to embrace.

But the production of space at Mission Tumacácori extended far beyond the mission church and its immediate grounds. Another representation of space the missionaries carried with them was what anthropologists call the peasant corporate community. Throughout the world at various times and places, groups of farmers and stock raisers have joined together to hold certain resources, usually pastures, woodlands, and flowing surface water, in common (Wolf 1955, 1957; Netting 1981; Sheridan 1988b). These peasant resource-holding communities still survived on the Iberian peninsula during the seventeenth and eighteenth centuries (Vassberg 1974, 1980, 1984). They provided one of the most widespread and enduring models for the reorganization of Native American societies throughout the Americas after the Spanish conquest.

Most missions, including Guevavi and Tumacácori, patterned themselves after peasant corporate communities, with one important difference. The missionary, not the Indian community, was in charge of making all the important economic as well as religious decisions, including the distribution of surplus from mission fields and herds. Nevertheless, resources belonged to the community, not to individuals or to the Jesuit or Franciscan orders. Membership, usually through birth or marriage, entitled an *hijo/a del pueblo* ('son/daughter of the pueblo') to use community resources and to pass on that access to heirs. Households cultivated their own fields, irrigating them from mission *acequias* (canals). They also ran livestock, gathered firewood, and collected wild plants on mission uplands. But land and water could not be sold, mortgaged, or otherwise alienated because they were held in trust for future generations. The only way a community could legally lose its resources was by failing to use them. If the community moved or disintegrated, its land and water reverted back to the Spanish crown.

At Tumacácori National Historical Park, we can glimpse remnants of that corporate spatial identity—the lime kiln, the granary, a stretch of the acequia that diverted water from the Santa Cruz River onto mission fields. As the park expands, an orchard and fields will be planted with heirloom crop varieties introduced into the region by missionaries and Spanish settlers. But the park will never recapture the boundaries of the mission lands as they were surveyed and confirmed under the Tumacácori land grant of 1807. As this book makes clear, that social space was stolen from the O'odham by a Mexican *caudillo* (military strongman) in 1844. Then it was sold to an Anglo speculator, negated by the U.S. Supreme Court in 1898, and swallowed up by a fraudulent land grant known as Baca Float No. 3, which the Supreme Court confirmed, despite opposition from the Department of the Interior, in 1914.

Throughout these legal maneuverings, these contestations of paper titles, missionaries, ranchers, and speculators carved the natural landscape of the Upper Santa Cruz Valley into smaller and smaller pieces. The penetration of the evolving capitalist world system transformed this isolated frontier from a landscape of open access, as it had been for the O'odham before the Spaniards arrived, into increasingly subdivided social spaces of mission, presidio, and private ranches. During the colonial period, however, those divisions were visible only along the floodplain, where the fields of communities like Tubac, Tumacácori, Calabasas, and Guevavi had boundaries. The uplands, in contrast, were open range, even though boundary markers unobtrusively signified where private ranch land ended and mission lands began. Moreover, the primary purpose of land and water was to reproduce human communities rather than to generate profit. The Upper Santa Cruz Valley therefore remained a *landscape of community* throughout most of the colonial era.

Nonetheless, "land"—a social construction as well as a physical entity—was slowly being converted into a commodity to be bought and sold regardless of social impact. This, of course, was a fundamental stage in the development of capitalism across the world: the severance of labor from the land. As Marx pointed out in *Theories of Surplus Value*, the emerging bourgeoisie had to ensure that "land should not be common property, that it should confront the working class as a condition of production not belonging to it" (Marx 1969 Part 2:44). Private ranchers would not begin to fence off the open range until barbed wire made the project economically feasible in the late nineteenth century. Nonetheless, Spanish and Mexican ranchers laid the legal foundations much earlier when they established claims to both floodplain and upland surrounding Mission Tumacácori.

Those ranchers viewed land as a means of production—a space where "nature" produced the grasses and forbs that another means of production, livestock, converted into beef, hides, tallow, mutton, wool, milk, and cheese. At the same time, miners staked their claims to subterranean spaces where traces of gold, silver, and copper could be extracted. Their subdivisions of space were smaller but deeper, their investments of capital much greater per unit area of land. Mining was the first industry that attracted speculators to the southern Arizona frontier. As Chapter 6 demonstrates, Judge John Watts and William Wrightson conceived Baca Float No. 3 as a mining, not a ranching, venture.

None of these speculative grand designs—the Sonora Exploring and Mining Company, the Calabasas Land and Mining Company, or the amended location of Baca Float No. 3—turned a profit, much less made a killing. Colonel C. P. Sykes's Calabasas was the most grandiose, portraying an intermittent stream as a navigable river deep enough for sailing ships. But as these schemes clawed their way to the U.S. Supreme Court, they obliterated two land-based communities: the O'odham at Mission Tumacácori in the 1840s and the homesteaders along the same stretch of the floodplain during World War I. The production of space was commodified. Landscapes of speculation devoured landscapes of community during the nineteenth and early twentieth centuries.

There were interludes. Between the Great Depression and the postwar boom, Baca Float No. 3 became a plaything of oilmen, movie stars, and retired executives from General Motors. Gentlemen ranchers like Tol Pendleton may have raised blooded stock, but their money came from industrial, not agrarian, enterprises. In a sense, they kept the landscape of the float intact for future speculators by sinking surplus capital into their showcase ranches with little need for short-term profit in return.

From its inception, however, Baca Float No. 3 escaped any real moorings as a means of production. Instead, it functioned largely as a form of "fictitious capital"—real estate bought and sold by speculators for its future value, not for what it could produce in the present. As Arizona became an overwhelmingly urban state, the showcase ranches of "Santa Booze Valley" disintegrated and reformed as subdivisions, especially the real estate development of Rio Rico. Those developments sank more surplus capital into the speculative landscape. Under such conditions, according to geographer David Harvey, "the land market functions simply as a particular branch—albeit with some special characteristics—of the circulation of interest-bearing capital" (Harvey 1999:347).

Thousands of unwary buyers across the world bought the dreams salesmen from Gulf American and GAC were peddling. When they tried to cash in or make the dreams materialize, however, many of them found that their lots at Rio Rico were little more than paper fictions. Some had not even been surveyed yet. Thousands of others had no basic utilities and would not have them for ten years or more. Gulf American and GAC were not as flimsy as dozens of other land companies that feasted on the unwary during the postwar Great Arizona Land Rush. Nonetheless, they made claims that were not true and promises that could not be kept to servicemen in Saigon, little old ladies in Las Vegas casinos, and plane-loads of Midwesterners flown in to visit Rio Rico and get the hard sell. For almost two decades after GAC went bankrupt in 1975, Rio Rico was a resort, a few scattered homes, and hundreds of miles of roads that led nowhere—a far cry from the four satellite cities of 250,000 people its promoters envisioned.

When I was searching for a way to phrase the major theme of this book—to capture the interplay of both time and space—I found the following quote from an essay by critical geographer David Harvey. "Capitalist development must negotiate a knife-edge between preserving the values of past commitments made at a particular place and time, or devaluing them to open up fresh room for accumulation. Capitalism perpetually strives, therefore, to create a social and physical landscape in its own image and requisite to its own needs at a particular point in time, only just as certainly to undermine, disrupt and even destroy that landscape at a later point in time," Harvey argues. "The inner contradictions of capitalism are expressed through the restless formation and re-formation of geographical landscapes. This is the tune to which the historical geography of capitalism must dance without cease" (Harvey 1985:150).

That tune as it was played in the Upper Santa Cruz Valley cannot be heard through the approaches of conventional environmental history alone. I am more interested in capital flows and relations of power than I am in the impact of climatic variability or the ways in which the production of space transformed plant and animal communities across the landscape. Natural forces recede into the background as my focus upon the role of capital grows stronger.

Even water, the ultimate limiting factor on human society in arid and semiarid lands, never played much of a limiting role in the development of the Upper Santa Cruz Valley until the late twentieth century, after Rio Rico's bankruptcy. The Santa Cruz River originates in the San Rafael

Valley of southeastern Arizona and flows south into Mexico. Then it makes a great loop and heads north across the international border. There were stretches of perennial flow from Guevavi to Tubac. North of Tubac, however, the mountains on either side drop away and the river empties into the Tucson Basin, a deep alluvial plain. Flow ceased except during floods until bedrock forced water to the surface once again at Martínez Hill south of Bac.

The stretch of the Santa Cruz relevant to this history draws its water from four subbasins upstream of the Tucson Basin: (from south to north, the direction of the river) Nogales, Rio Rico, Tubac, and Amado (Gettings and Houser n.d.). Perched upon and pinched by the bedrock of surrounding mountain ranges—the Patagonia, San Cayetano, and Santa Rita Mountains to the east, the Pajarito, Atascosa, and Tumacacori Mountains to the west, these subbasins are narrow and relatively shallow (three thousand feet or less). They do not hold huge quantities of water, and their water tables drop quickly if overpumped. But they recharge rapidly from rainstorms and periodic floods. "This became evident most recently during the 1999 summer monsoon season," writes environmental historian Michael Logan. "The preceding winter had been very dry and the wells in the Santa Cruz River and tributary canyons started to diminish in output. Then the summer rains came in abundance, delivering eighteen inches of rain to the upper basin, and the aquifer quickly recovered to its full potential" (Logan 2002:238).

To narrow the focus even further, the aquifers that sustained human communities from Mission Tumacácori to Rio Rico saturated the subbasins of Tubac and Rio Rico, which is separated from the Nogales subbasin by Eagan Narrows, a bedrock intrusion that constricts subsurface as well as surface flow. The Rio Rico subbasin is wider and deeper and holds more water than the Nogales subbasin upstream. It underlay the mission *visita* (visiting station) and *estancia* (stock ranch) of Calabasas, recharged not only by the flow of the Santa Cruz but by Sonoita Creek as well. It constitutes the aquifer from which modern Rio Rico drinks.

Moreover, groundwater downstream from Nogales and Guevavi is supplemented by the Nogales International Waste Water Treatment Facility (NIWWTF) at the confluence of Nogales Wash and the Santa Cruz River. NIWWTF has the capacity to process more than seventeen million gallons of effluent a day from Nogales, Arizona, and Nogales, Sonora (Ingram, Laney, and Gillilan 1995). This treated effluent waters the golf courses of the Rio Rico and Tubac country clubs, and has recreated the lush riparian oasis along the floodplain from Calabasas to Tubac. Water scarcity and water politics will play an increasing role as more people and industry pour into Rio Rico and Ambos Nogales. Responses to scarcity will be complicated by the need to coordinate not just competing municipalities but the demands of two nations (Ingram, Laney, and Gillilan 1995). But from Spanish colonial times through Rio Rico's first incarnation, water use upstream did not significantly affect the water supply from Calabasas to Tubac, where most of this history takes place.

My focus on capital, not natural constraints, therefore reflects the accelerating importance of economic and political forces, particularly after the region became part of the United States with the ratification of the Gadsden Purchase in 1854. As landscapes of speculation consumed landscapes of community, the production of space became less and less grounded in the materiality of the upper Santa Cruz River Valley itself. The historical geography of the region danced more and more to a paper shuffle rather than an agrarian waltz.

Before I conclude, I need to clear up one common misconception: the conflation of space with nature. In the American West, we talk passionately about the "wide, open spaces," a powerfully ambiguous phrase that conjures up sweeping natural vistas free of human clutter. Yet this aesthetic vision of nature often obscures the dynamic interplay of human and nonhuman forces that shape so-called "natural" landscapes. As historian William Cronon notes, "the boundary between human and nonhuman, natural and unnatural is profoundly problematic" (Cronon 1991: xix). Cronon goes on to say, "Just as our own lives continue to be embedded in a web of natural relationships, nothing in nature remains untouched by the web of human relationships that constitute our common history" (Cronon 1991:19).

But Lefebvre and other critical geographers are pursuing a concept more radical than the recognition that the human and natural are inextricably intertwined. When they talk about the production of space, they are talking about the social construction of nature as well as the social construction of human society. Lefebvre even anticipates the eventual destruction of nature as human labor extends its reach.[3] One can argue that as global warming and increasing water consumption suck aquifers dry, "Nature" may indeed "Bat Last!" as the old Earth First! bumper sticker proclaimed. But as far as Lefebvre is concerned, the point of departure for a history of space "is not to be found in geographical descriptions of natural space, but rather in the study of natural rhythms, and of the modification of those rhythms and their inscription in space by means of human actions, especially work. It begins, then, with the spatio-temporal rhythms of nature as transformed by a social practice" (Lefebvre 1991:117).

In the Upper Santa Cruz Valley, those natural rhythms were transformed and eventually ignored as land made a surreal odyssey from means of reproduction to means of production to fictitious capital. In the process, land was alienated not only from labor but also from production itself. "There is, it seems, something perverse in trying to create physical conditions favourable to accumulation," Harvey points out, "by giving free reign to the *appropriation* of surplus value by landlords, developers, financiers, and the like (none of whom, with the exception of builders, organize the real production of surplus value)" (Harvey 1999:397).

That perversity—the "logic" of speculative capitalism uprooting, devouring, and burying the communities that made a living off the land before the speculators triumphed—is the greedy beating heart of this book.

PART I

Landscapes of Community

The O'odham World
and the Jesuit Intrusion

In the spring of 1935, during the depths of the Great Depression, three
men met for several nights in the village of Snaketown just north of the
dry carcass of the Gila River. One was Julian Hayden, a young archaeologist working on the excavation of the Hohokam site at Snaketown under
the direction of Emil Haury. Another was William Allison Smith, the
foreman of the digging crew, an Akimel O'odham who spoke English and
was a Presbyterian deacon in the Snaketown church. The third was Juan
Smith, one of the last narrators of the full Pima version of the O'odham
creation story (Bahr et al. 1994). There, in an old mesquite-roofed adobe
storeroom, Smith recited the thirty-six stories that reveal O'odham history from the creation of the universe to the end of the Apache wars.
Allison Smith translated Smith's Pima narration into English. Hayden
scribbled furiously to record the word-for-word transcript. One evening,
Hayden also snapped a picture of Smith by the light of a Coleman lantern.
Smith is seated in front of a jumble of wagon wheels leaning against an
adobe wall. His broad face, framed by a shock of black hair, is patient and
intent. You can almost smell the dry, dark earth enclosing the three men.

The text, in English with a sprinkling of Pima words, is one of the
most complete glimpses we have into the O'odham world before the Europeans arrived. The first part is a Pima Genesis. A pure spirit named Jeoss
creates the heavens out of darkness.[1] Then he makes Earth Doctor—
Jewed Ma:kai—who fashions another being, Siuuhu. Earth Doctor and
Siuuhu take clay, shape a man, and breathe life into him. They do the
same to produce a woman. These two first humans become the original
ancestors of the O'odham. Earth Doctor and Siuuhu then create the dawn,
sun, deer, jackrabbit, windstorm, clouds, and rain. Grasses spring up after
the rain. "The woman went out and picked some of the grass and took it
and cooked it and ate it," Smith recited. "When through eating, the man

went out with bow and arrow and killed a deer, and they had it for supper that evening. At that time, the sun went down, and darkness fell over the earth, as it had been before. This was the end of the first day" (Bahr et al. 1994:49).

Creation continues with the making of the moon, Coyote, the Milky Way, and Buzzard, who shapes the mountains. A great flood destroys this first creation. In other versions of the narrative, the flood is caused by the tears of a baby born from the penis of a promiscuous young man. Only Earth Doctor, Siuuhu, and Coyote survive. Earth Doctor returns to the heavens, but Coyote and Siuuhu take refuge in a flute and a house. Siuuhu emerges first and begins to be called S-e'ehe, or Elder Brother. Later in the narrative, he is also called I'itoi.

This is where the creation narrative leaves the realm of mythology and enters "prehistory." In Smith's account, the first people all die. In others, however, they take refuge in the underworld after Earth Doctor opens a passage into the earth with his cane. Siuuhu then makes more people, including the O'odham, whom he teaches how to cultivate a variety of crops, including corn, cotton, and tobacco. A series of stories follows with two interwoven themes: the domestication of plants and of sexual relations. The people also learn to make saguaro wine and to irrigate their fields from canals.

Anthropologist Donald Bahr (Bahr et al. 1994) calls these tales the "Hohokam chronicles" because they tell the story of the people who built the great platform mound communities like Casa Grande along the Salt and Gila Rivers. As these people's mastery of canal irrigation grows, their societies become more complex. The origins of turquoise and parrots—two highly prized items that linked the Hohokam in trade networks extending from the Four Corners to Mesoamerica—are explained. Warfare breaks out and Siuuhu pioneers the four-day ceremony to purify warriors after they have killed. The Hohokam grow so arrogant they kill Siuuhu himself.

It is here in the narrative that "history" begins. After four years of death, Siuuhu resurrects himself and contacts the people Earth Doctor either created or saved. They agree to join him in making war against his killers. The people who accompany Siuuhu are called Wooshkum or Vupshkam (Wu:skam), which means "Emerger" or "Emergent." They arise from the underworld far to the east. Medicine men among both the Hohokam and Wu:skam have visions about the impending conflict. Hohokam medicine men try to conceal their communities. Wu:skam medicine men attempt to divine their locations. Finally, however, battle is joined. The Wu:skam send an owl to frighten the Hohokam, a gopher to chew up their weapons, and a rattlesnake to bite and kill a powerful Sivañ (chief). Then they descend upon a series of communities with Great Houses (Vahki) beginning with Casa Grande, killing the medicine men chiefs and routing their followers. In addition to Casa Grande, Smith's narrative and the more fragmentary narratives recorded by others mention communities that can be identified as Sweetwater, Casa Blanca, Lower Santan, Upper Santan, Los Muertos, Los Hornos, and Pueblo Grande, ruled by the powerful priest-chief Yellow Buzzard (Teague 1993; Bahr et al. 1994). According to archaeologist Lynn Teague, "The settlements identified in the oral traditions are an archaeologically accurate inventory of the late Classic period platform mound sites along a lengthy segment of the Gila River. Further, it can be shown that the ethnohistoric reports provide an account of these settlements too accurate and detailed to have been simply a tale created to explain the existence of numerous sites in the region" (Teague 1993:440).

In other words, O'odham in the twentieth century possessed a detailed oral tradition that their ancestors conquered the Hohokam living in the same area four to five hundred years earlier. According to the creation narratives, Hohokam rulers and some of their followers died whereas others fled west to the Colorado River or north to Zuni country and the Hopi mesas. But others were incorporated into O'odham society, perhaps into the Buzzard moiety (Hayden 1970). As such, the creation narratives contain tantalizing slivers of evidence about the antiquity of the O'odham in Arizona and their relation to the Hohokam.

The Piman-Hohokam Continuum

The nature of that relationship remains a matter of debate. Most archaeologists believe in some variant of the Hohokam-Piman continuum, which contends that the Upper Pimas (O'odham) of Arizona are biological and cultural descendants of the Hohokam. After Hohokam civilization collapsed because of social conflict, environmental degradation, or perhaps even the devastation of Old World epidemic diseases, the Pimas were the remnants who survived (Haury 1945, 1950, 1976; Simpson 1946; Gumerman and Haury 1979; Doyel 1979, 1991; Reff 1991; Dobyns 1988; Ezell 1963). Charles DiPeso, in comparison, argued that the Hohokam intruded upon the O'odham, who had been living in the northern Sonoran Desert since Archaic times (DiPeso 1956, 1979; see also McGuire 1991). A third scenario, advanced by ethnohistorian Bernard Fontana (1976) and ethnobiologist Amadeo Rea (1983, 1997), views the Upper Pimas as relatively recent newcomers who moved into the region as Hohokam civilization was disintegrating. Because they had no public architecture that rivaled the platform mounds of the Classic Hohokam, buried rather than burned their corpses, and relied upon small-scale rather than massive irrigation systems, Rea argues that the Upper Pimas were too different from the Hohokam to be "the degenerate remnants of a pre-existing Puebloan or puebloid desert culture" (Rea 1997:8).

The debate is complicated even further by the so-called "Tepiman connection." People speaking Piman languages within the far-flung Uto-Aztecan language family extend from central Arizona to northern Jalisco. They include the Upper Pimas (Akimel and Tohono O'odham), who occupied most of southern Arizona and northern Sonora when the Europeans colonized the Pimería Alta in the late 1600s. They encompass the Lower Pimas of central Sonora: the Névome, who lived along the middle Río Sonora and Río Yaqui; the Mountain Pimas, who occupied the western foothills of the Sierra Madre Occidental; and a number of poorly understood groups such as the Cocomacaques, who ranged across the desert north and west of modern Hermosillo. Tepiman speakers also comprise the Northern Tepehuan of Chihuahua, the Southern Tepehuan of Durango, and the Tepecano of northern Jalisco. This long, broken S-shaped curve of Piman speakers snakes for a thousand miles across the deserts and mountains of North America.

The languages of these people, who call themselves O'odham, O'odaam, Ootoma, and Odami, are so closely related that linguists Kenneth Hale and David Harris state, "It is somewhat misleading to speak of time-depth within Piman; it is more probable that, until very recent times, Piman represented a more or less continuous chain of dialects belonging to a single language" (Hale and Harris 1979:176). Linguistic anthropologists David Shaul and Jane Hill (1998) note that the various Tepiman languages share cognate densities of 74.4 percent to 86.4 percent, suggesting that they split from one another a millennium ago; a rough glottochronological rule of thumb is that cognancy of 80.5 percent represents a divergence of about one thousand years. "Glottochronological dates should, of course, be used only with great caution," they observe, "but the fact that the lowest percentage of shared cognancy within Tepiman (between Southeastern Tepehuan and Tohono O'odham) is 73 percent is consistent with a hypothesis that the proto-Tepiman speech community existed sometime during the first millennium A.D., well within the Hohokam period" (Shaul and Hill 1998:379).

Shaul and Hill (1998) contend that the center of maximum linguistic diversity in Tepiman is in the north, suggesting that Proto-Tepiman may have originated there. They also examine both phonological and lexical borrowing between Yuman and Tepiman languages, expanding upon arguments made by Shaul and Andresen (1989). The Proto-Tepiman word for water, *suu-dagi*, for example, is found in some form in all Tepiman languages. The Proto-Uto-Aztecan root for water, in comparison, is **pa-*. The Tepiman languages retain that Proto-Uto-Aztecan root as *va- only in combining forms (for example, wa:k, "reedy place," in Tohono O'odham). The words for water itself probably derive from River Yuman words for "blue, green" including the sequence hava:sú, which the Tepimans may have interpreted as "their-water-green/blue" and may have used in ritual contexts. Because some form of the element -su is found in all Tepiman languages, the borrowing from Proto-Yuman to Proto-Tepiman must have occurred where the two groups were in contact, that is, in the northwestern Sonoran Desert near the Colorado River. Shaul and Hill (1998) point out that Upper Piman dialects exhibit phonemic borrowing from Yuman as well.[2] According to their reconstruction, Proto-Tepiman and River Yuman groups lived in close association with one another in southwestern Arizona for several centuries around 1000 AD. "Speakers of Proto-Tepiman and Proto-River Yuman were probably in a sufficiently intense contact with one another for a substantial population of bilinguals to exist, among whom convergences developed in the sound system, the morpho-syntactic system, and to a limited degree in the lexicon of the two languages," Shaul and Hill (1998:392) postulate.

Proto-Tepimans, Proto-River Yumans, and probably some Zunis were part of the Late Classic Hohokam system.[3]

Shaul and Hill do not make the same claim for speakers of the modern Upper Piman languages, Tohono O'odham and Akimel O'odham. The most innovative modern dialect of Tohono O'odham—Aji/Totoguañ, which dominates most of the Papaguería, including areas where Hohokam archaeological remains are located—may instead reflect people who "spread into abandoned Hohokam regions in the late prehistoric period. This is also consistent with Aji-Totoguañ oral tradition that they represent a later emergence from undergound, which resulted in their displacing autochthonous peoples—the Hohokam—in their region" (Shaul and Hill 1998: 391). In other words, the ancestors of the modern O'odham may indeed be Rea's invaders from the south.

Archaeological surveys and geomorphological studies on the Gila River Indian Community may also shed some light on Proto-Tepiman migrations. According to Waters and Ravesloot (2003), regional climatic changes between AD 1020 and 1160—a time of major change among the Hohokam—caused the entrenchment of river channels throughout the Southwest. Channel widening and cutting were particularly severe along the middle Gila River from its confluence with the Salt to at least 110 kilometers upstream. One response was a shift in settlement and subsistence patterns as fields were washed away or some stretches of canals had to be abandoned. Communities dispersed and "more diversified agricultural and plant harvesting strategies" had to be pursued (Waters and Ravesloot 2003:404). Perhaps these catastrophic floods forced some Proto-Tepiman groups to migrate south.

As the Classic Period (1150–1450) progressed, however, the Hohokam expanded their canal systems and constructed large "big houses" like Casa Grande on platform mounds. These imposing public structures may have been controlled by elites who organized Hohokam labor to maintain their extensive irrigation systems, the largest in pre-Columbian North America. No widespread evidence of warfare has been found at Classic Hohokam sites. Yet the presence of big houses and platform mounds suggests hierarchy if not conflict as the Hohokam came together in fewer but larger communities than they had during the Preclassic Period. "Monumentality, for instance, always embodies and imposes a clearly intelligible message,"

Henri Lefebvre notes. "It says what it wishes to say—yet it hides a good deal more: being political, military, and ultimately fascist in character, monumental buildings mask the will to power and the arbitrariness of power beneath signs and surfaces which claim to express collective will and collective thought" (Lefebvre 1991:143).

Why the Hohokam abandoned their massive canal systems and big house communities in the 1400s or early 1500s remains a matter of intense debate. In contrast to the channel cutting of the late Preclassic, Waters and Ravesloot (2003) find no geomorphological evidence of major landscape change at the end of the Classic, when Hohokam civilization collapsed. They conclude that cultural rather than environmental factors must have been responsible for the disintegration of Hohokam society.

None of this evidence is conclusive. When all the strands are woven together, however, one possible scenario emerges—a scenario that incorporates the insights of Rea as well as Shaul and Hill. A thousand years ago, Proto-Tepimans lived in close proximity to River Yumans and may have participated in the Preclassic florescence of the Hohokam. As irrigated agriculture in the Hokokam heartland became more difficult because of eroding floodplains, some of those Proto-Tepimans moved south through the Sonoran Desert and into the foothills and upland valleys of the Sierra Madre Occidental. Gradually, linguistic and cultural distinctions emerged. Sometime in the fifteenth or sixteenth century, the ancestors of the Akimel O'odham and the Tohono O'odham who speak the Aji-Totoguañ dialect turned northward once again and entered Hohokam territory from the southeast, perhaps along the San Pedro or upper Santa Cruz drainages. These O'odham helped overthrow the Hohokam elites controlling the platform-mound communities along the Gila River.[4] Whether the conquerors were seizing new territory or reclaiming ancestral homelands remains to be determined. Nonetheless, the modern Akimel O'odham and Tohono O'odham do not appear to be the biological or cultural descendants of the Late Classic Hohokam elites themselves.

First Encounters

Conflict continued to divide the people of southern Arizona when Europeans first settled there in the late 1600s, two centuries after Hohokam civilization disintegrated. When Jesuit missionary Eusebio Francisco Kino crisscrossed the Pimería Alta in the early 1690s, he and his frequent traveling companion, Juan Mateo Manje, distinguished among different groups of O'odham, including the Sobas along the Río de la Concepción and the Papabotas (Papagos) between the Tucson Basin and the Colorado River (Fontana 1996; Sheridan 1988a). The distinction between those they called *Pimas* and those they named *Sobaipuris*, a term with no known etymology, is less clear. According to historian Herbert Bolton, "In the southeastern portion of the area, nearest the Spanish settlements, were the people then regarded as the Pimas proper. They lived on all the slopes of the watershed which zigzags roughly westward from Huachuca Mountain to Nogales, having villages on the upper waters of the south-flowing Sonora, San Miguel, and Cocóspora [*sic*; Cocóspera] rivers, on the west-flowing San Ignacio and Altar, and on the north-flowing San Pedro and Santa Cruz" (Bolton 1984:247). He goes on to say, "North of the Pimas proper lived the Sobaípuris (Sobajípuris). A line drawn eastward from Tubac through Fairbank approximates the old boundary between the two peoples. Of the Sobaípuris there were three groups: one living all down the San Pedro River northward from the vicinity of Fairbank; another on the middle Santa Cruz between San Xavier del Bac and Picacho; a third on the Gila River from the Casa Grande westward nearly to the Bend of Gila River" (Bolton 1984:247).

Kino mentioned two cases of warfare among the O'odham themselves. The first pitted the western Sobas of the Río de la Concepción drainage against the eastern Pimas of the Dolores Valley, who sought revenge because the Sobas had killed Podenco, headman of Dolores, a decade or so earlier. The second matched Sobaipuris under Coro in the middle San Pedro Valley against Sobaipuris under Humari along the lower San Pedro. Meanwhile, nomadic groups identified as Sumas, Mansos, Janos, Jocomes, and Apaches raided O'odham living along both the San Pedro and the Gila. The region was no more stable in the late seventeenth century than it had been in the fourteenth and fifteenth centuries.

The political dynamics of the 1500s and early 1600s are less clear. Álvar Núñez Cabeza de Vaca and his fellow *náufragos* (shipwrecked ones) may have nicked southeastern Arizona in the 1530s, but recent ethnobotanical evidence suggests they traveled across northern Mexico, not

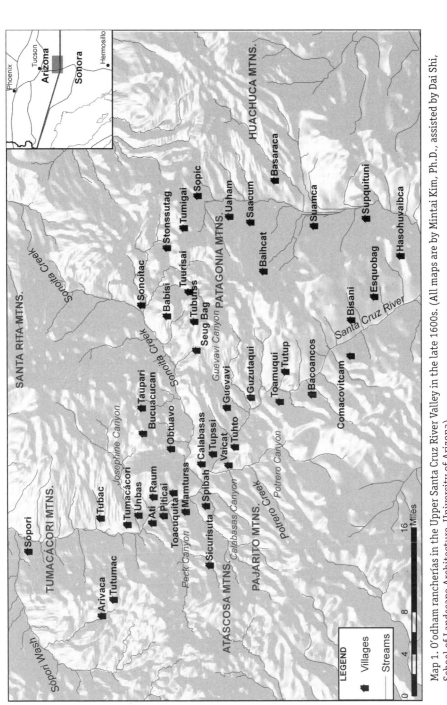

Map 1. O'odham rancherías in the Upper Santa Cruz River Valley in the late 1600s. (All maps are by Mintai Kim, Ph.D., assisted by Dai Shi, School of Landscape Architecture, University of Arizona)

the southwestern United States (Olson et al. 1997).[5] The expedition of Francisco Vásquez de Coronado passed to the east, perhaps through the San Pedro Valley, but neither Coronado nor his chroniclers had much to say about that stretch of their journey. Not until the advent of Kino in 1687 do the O'odham of southern Arizona begin to take shape on European paper. The descriptions of Kino and his companions, particularly Juan Mateo Manje, provide our first indisputable window into the O'odham world. Unfortunately, that window opens more than a century after European influences, including European diseases, may have buffeted O'odham society and culture (Reff 1991).

When Kino first entered the Upper Santa Cruz Valley in January 1691, he only described two settlements in the Upper Santa Cruz Valley north of the modern international border—Guevavi and Tumagacori (Tumacácori), which he called "rancherías" rather than pueblos. Other communities noted by later observers were not mentioned (Map 1). Kino did not give population figures for the two communities but did note that Tumacácori consisted of "more than forty houses close together" (Bolton 1919 1:120). Kino also observed that the O'odham prepared three ramadas for Kino, Salvatierra, and their entourage—"one in which to say mass, another in which to sleep, and the third for a kitchen" (Bolton 1919 1:119–20). Consummate diplomat that he was, Kino relied upon friendly persuasion and gifts of food to convert the O'odham. He also attempted to keep the worst excesses of the Spanish empire at bay by obtaining a royal decree exempting the O'odham for twenty years from paying tribute or serving on the labor drafts (*repartimiento*) so often abused by Spanish miners and hacendados.

Despite his charisma and diplomacy, however, violence scarred the early Spanish settlement of the Pimería Alta. Spanish miners and ranchers were pressing north into O'odham territory at a time when the Spanish frontier to the east was convulsing because of widespread Indian resistance and rebellion. The convulsions began with the Pueblo Revolt of 1680, which drove all Spanish settlers from New Mexico. Almost three thousand refugees fled south to El Paso, accelerating competition for land, water, and Indian labor in the El Paso and Casas Grandes areas. Those demands triggered the Suma Revolt in 1684. Meanwhile, raiding by Janos, Jocomes, Mansos, and Chinarras intensified as Apache bands pushed south beyond the Gila River (Naylor and Polzer 1986; Sheridan n.d.). Because of these convulsions, Spaniards were quick to imagine pan-Indian confederacies and conspiracies. They accused the O'odham, particularly the Sobaipuris along the San Pedro River, of allying themselves with the Janos, Jocomes, Apaches, and even the Tarahumaras, who mounted a series of rebellions of their own beginning in 1690.

One response was to militarize the frontier. The Spanish crown established the new presidios of Nuestro Señor del Pilar y Glorioso San José del Paso del Norte at El Paso (1683), San Pedro del Gallo north of the Río Nazas (1685), Concepción del Pasaje de Cuencamé northeast of Durango (1685), San Francisco de Conchos on the Río Conchos (1685), San Antonio de Casas Grandes (1686), which was soon moved to San Felipe y Santiago de Janos, and the Presidio de las Fronteras de la Provincia de Sonora (1689), which served as a flying company (mobile, without a fixed location) for about a decade until it settled at Santa Rosa de Corodéguachi in northeastern Sonora (Naylor and Polzer 1986; Moorhead 1975).

Unlike Kino, who sought to create alliances with the O'odham, some of the new military commanders drew their swords first and negotiated later. The first act of violence was the massacre of the O'odham ranchería of Mototicachi along the Río Bacoachi north of Arizpe. In 1688, Spanish soldiers led by Nicolás de Higuera, *cabo* of the presidio of Sinaloa, killed seven Pimas accused of being spies for the Janos and Jocomes. When other men in the settlement resisted, Higuera slaughtered forty-two others and took the women and children captive. Higuera was tried and sentenced to death but escaped and rejoined the military, suffering nothing more than a reduction in rank from captain to corporal (Naylor and Polzer 1986; Burrus 1971). Mototicachi became the first bloody symbol of Spanish treachery among the O'odham, who committed scattered acts of vengeance in response.

More widespread rebellion broke out in the western Pimería Alta in 1695. Again, the uprising was preceded by violence perpetrated by the Spanish military. In 1694, Lieutenant Antonio Solís killed three Sobaipuris drying meat on a rack. He thought the meat was horseflesh stolen from missions further south. It turned out to be venison. As historian Herbert Eugene Bolton (1984:289) wryly points out, "The Sobaípuris were exonerated, but the three dead men remained quite dead." Later that year, Solís and thirty troops rode to Tubutama in response to a plea for help from Father Daniel Januske. Januske accused two O'odham of stirring up his congregation by giving *tlatoles*—a Nahuatl term the missionaries and Spaniards used to describe Indian incitements to rebellion. Solís quickly executed the leaders. O'odham sought to demonstrate their loyalty to the Spaniards by accompanying Solís on expeditions against the Janos, Jocomes, and Apaches in the fall of 1694. But suspicions about the Pimas persisted.

Those suspicions bore bloody fruit on March 29, 1695, when O'odham at Januske's mission of Tubutama killed an Opata Indian overseer who had knocked down one of their fellow villagers and was slashing him with his spurs. Then the O'odham turned on two other Opatas, killing them, burning Januske's church and *convento*, and butchering Tubutama's cattle. The rebels continued downstream, gathering O'odham from Oquitoa and Pitiquito until they confronted Fr. Francisco Saeta at Caborca on April 2, Holy Saturday. Piercing Saeta with arrows, they also killed Francisco Pintor, the famous Lower Pima interpreter from Ures, and two more Opatas.

These initial actions appeared to be more a spasm of resistance than coordinated rebellion. They also manifested characteristics of what historian Susan Deeds (1998:45) calls "first-generation rebellions." First-generation rebellions broke out when Indians who had grown up during preconquest times attempted to restore pre-Hispanic rituals and ways of life. We do not know if there were messianic or millenarian elements to the uprising as there were among the Acaxees of the Sierra Madre in 1601 or the Tepehuanes in 1616. Nonetheless, Padre Luis Velarde, arguing that Saeta should be considered a true martyr, wrote, "According to what the Indians declared, according to what was done with the sacred vestments, holy oils, altars, chalices, and patens, which were the same excesses as those committed in Tubutama, along with other motives and circumstances, I do not doubt they killed him *in odium fidei* [through hatred of the Faith]" (my translation of González Rodríguez 1977:71). Some O'odham undoubtedly were beginning to see Roman Catholic beliefs and mission life as a threat to their own Uto-Aztecan philosophies about the order of the universe and human society.

The Spaniards gathered up Saeta's remains and bore them in solemn procession to Cucurpe. There Domingo Jironza Petris de Cruzate, captain of the newly created flying company of Sonora and *alcalde mayor* of the province, demonstrated his reverence for the martyred missionary by dismounting from his horse. Taking the mule carrying Saeta's bones by the bridle, Jironza shouldered the slain missionary's remains and carried them to the path leading up to the pueblo, where Father Rector Marcus Kappus met him with solemn fanfare and salvos from harquebuses. Kappus sang a requiem mass and buried Saeta on the epistle side of the main altar (González Rodríguez 1977). The military and religious authorities of the frontier were trying to impress upon the Eudeve and O'odham Indians crowding into the church that the sword and the cross were one.

Kino immediately went to work to repair his fledgling alliance between Spaniards and O'odham. He convinced Spanish officials to allow O'odham who wanted peace to bring the killers of Saeta to justice. But Jironza hedged his bets, dispatching Solís to harry the rebels at Tubutama and Oquitoa while Kino arranged a peace conference at El Tupo, a *ciénega* (marsh) fed by springs in a broad valley west of San Ignacio. The O'odham trusted Kino and came to the rendezvous. They also left their weapons behind as they approached the camp of Solís and his troops, who included Tepoca Seris. As they entered the circle of mounted soldiers, however, the surrender of the guilty went terribly wrong. The O'odham governor of Dolores grabbed one of the leaders of the revolt by the hair and said, "This is one of the murderers." Solís slashed off his head. Guilty or innocent, the O'odham bolted as the Seris drew their bows and the Spaniards opened fire. When the slaughter was over, the bodies of forty-eight O'odham sprawled across the marshy ground. El Tupo became La Matanza—The Killing Ground.

For a brief time that bloody summer, the massacre at El Tupo threatened to turn a minor outbreak into a major rebellion. The number of rebels rose from forty to three hundred. First they burned Tubutama and Caborca. Then they attacked Father Agustín de Campos's *cabecera* (mission headquarters) at San Ignacio and his *visitas* at Magdalena and Imuris. Forewarned by the O'odham leader of Cíbuta, Campos fled across the pass of El Torreón to safe haven at the Eudeve mission of Cucurpe. Rumors flew that the rebels were even planning to attack Kino's own cabecera of

Dolores. Alarmed at the prospect of another regional conflagration, Jironza summoned forces dispatched on a campaign against the Janos, Jocomes, and Apaches. But the O'odham were too scattered, too autonomous, and too divided to sustain the uprising. As soon as the Spaniards made a show of force, attacking Tubutama and Sáric, support for the rebels dissipated into a series of peace negotiations. By the end of the summer, most of the O'odham had returned to their communities along the Río Magdalena-Altar-Concepción drainage system. Wary peace had been restored to the Pimería Alta.

Violence never flared along the Upper or Middle Santa Cruz. Nonetheless, Mototicachi and El Tupo must have caused many O'odham to retreat, either physically or psychologically, from the new imperial order slowly taking shape on the northwestern frontier. Missionaries and Spanish settlers would not be killed again in large numbers for more than half a century, but the O'odham's affection for the charismatic Kino was tempered by memories of bloodshed and betrayal. With the exception of Campos, the Jesuits who followed Kino to the Pimería Alta often met with resistance that stopped short of violence but included evasiveness, witchcraft, foot-dragging, and retreat into the desert or mountains—tactics that political scientist James Scott (1985) calls the "weapons of the weak." Only Campos, who may have grown more O'odham as he grew older, won and held their trust.

"No one to Distribute the Bread"

Direct Jesuit influence upon the O'odham of the Upper Santa Cruz Valley was sporadic during Kino's lifetime. Kino and his superiors decided to make Guevavi the cabecera with visitas at Tumacácori and Coro's Sobaipuri resettlement at Sonoita. But Father Juan de San Martín, a thirty-one-year-old Jesuit from Caravaca, Spain, remained at Guevavi for less than six months in 1701 before abandoning the mission. Father Francisco Gonzalvo, assigned to Bac the same year, did not survive the Pimería Alta. In the summer of 1702, he had to be carried back to San Ignacio, where he died of a fever.

For the next three decades, Campos was the nearest resident missionary. Catholic ritual and doctrine must have been limited to an occasional festival or sacrament when the hard-riding Campos visited the simple adobe churches surrounded by the *kis* (brush houses) of Guevavi and Tumacácori. Jesus, Mary, saints—baptism, marriage, and last rites—drifted through O'odham life and thought like smoke from a campfire, pungent but elusive. The O'odham along the Upper Santa Cruz hovered on the periphery, not quite outside the Spanish empire but not yet incorporated into it. They were still free to practice their own rituals, consult their own diagnosticians and healers, and follow the seasonal rounds that drew them away from the river at certain times of the year. Neither Jesuit priests nor Spanish officials had the manpower to produce the mission spaces of church and communal fields and herds—of missionary discipline and surplus production—that would have forced them to change their daily lives. In the words of Father Luis Velarde, "There is no doubt that many souls are lost because there is no one to distribute the bread which they so anxiously ask for and desire" (quoted in Kessell 1970:17).

Nevertheless, their lives did change as the ecological revolution that biological historian Alfred Crosby (1972) calls the Columbian Exchange washed through their bloodstreams and digestive systems. Despite the fact that no missionaries lived among them, the O'odham of the Upper Santa Cruz Valley suffered periodic epidemics of Old World contagious diseases. In his 1716 *relación*, Father Luis Vellarde, describing the bravery and haughtiness of the O'odham, wrote, "And truly it has been the particular providence of Our Lord that this nation has diminished so much because of continual epidemics; due to their arrogance, there is no lack of troublesome and seditious spirits among such a multitude" (my translation of González Rodríguez 1977:62). Almost a decade later, in the winter of 1724, Campos baptized 157 people, many of whom were probably dying, in the Santa Cruz and San Pedro Valleys during a smallpox epidemic (R. Jackson 1994).

Unfortunately, no systematic population figures were recorded during this early period, so it is impossible to assess population trends during the late 1600s and early 1700s. Geographer Carl Sauer (1935) estimated that fifty-five hundred O'odham lived along the Santa Cruz at contact, whereas anthropologist Henry Dobyns (1963) concluded that twenty-four hundred O'odham occupied the middle stretches of the valley from Punta de Agua on the north to what is now the U.S.-Mexican border on the south. In 1732, there were an estimated forty-two hundred O'od-ham living in the Santa Cruz Valley, but that figure apparently included Sobaipuris from the San Pedro Valley as well (R. Jackson 1994:61). The magnitude of O'odham depopulation during the early Jesuit period re-mains unclear.

o'odham subsistence patterns

More light can be shed on the revolution in O'odham subsistence pat-terns. Before Kino and his companions rode down the Santa Cruz, O'od-ham wove their lives into desert rhythms with an intimacy we can barely imagine. Family groups broke apart and came together according to the pulse of seeds they buried in the ground or gathered from floodplain, bajada, and mountain slope. Those living along the few rivers and streams of the Sonoran Desert pursued three complementary subsistence strat-egies, all of which depended upon an intricate knowledge of plants, animals, and climate. During the spring and summer, they farmed flood-plain fields or arroyo deltas. Throughout the year, they harvested wild plants and hunted wild game (Rea 1997). When rains were abundant, washes ran and rivers flowed, watering their desert cultigens. When heat and drought withered crops, the O'odham relied entirely upon the seeds, fruit, roots, and caudices produced by the desert itself.

Their agriculture was based upon three thousand years of accumu-lated knowledge about plant physiology and microclimates in the Sonoran Desert. O'odham in the Santa Cruz, San Pedro, and Magdalena-Altar-Concepción watersheds practiced irrigation agriculture, constructing brush weirs that diverted water into earthen canals that led to their fields. O'odham along the Gila River, in contrast, may not have been irrigating their fields in the late 1600s when the Jesuits first visited them. After the platform-mound communities disintegrated and population densities de-creased, Gileños may not have needed to expend the energy to build weirs and canals. Instead, they simply may have planted their seeds in swales and islands after the Gila's seasonal floodwaters receded (Winter 1973; Doelle 1975).

O'odham also cultivated fields on the deltas of arroyos that captured the surges of water spit forth by desert storms. These silty, nutrient-rich torrents coursed down the washes (*a'akĭ*), dissecting the bajadas until they spread out across valley floors (*chiñ*; at the "mouth" of the wash; *akĭ chiñ* agriculture). And whereas O'odham agricultural technology may have been simple, consisting of little more than wooden digging sticks (*eskuḍ*) and weeding sticks (*giikĭ*), the farmers themselves were consummate plant breeders. According to Rea (1997:44), "The Pima had selected for fast-maturing, drought-resistant crop varieties that produced a minimum of foliage and a maximum of seed." In both floodplain and *akĭ chiñ* fields, they planted at least seven varieties of sixty-day maize (*huuñ*), as many as forty-six varieties of tepary beans (*bavĭ*; *Phaseolus acutifolius*), common beans (*muuñ* or *muuñĭ*; *Phaseolus vulgaris*), squash (*haal*; *Cucurbita* spp.), grain amaranth (*ki'akĭ*, *giád*; *Amaranthus hybridis*), grain chenopod (*kovĭ*; *Chenopodium berlandieri*), and possibly lima beans (*havul*; *Phaseolus lunatus*) (Rea 1997). Sobaipuris along the Santa Cruz, San Pedro, and Gila also grew cotton (*toki*; *Gossypium hirsutum*), which they skillfully wove into red- and yellow-died mantas. Their agriculture was superbly adapted to heat and drought. Teparies, for example, yield four times as many seeds as common beans with only one or two waterings.

The O'odham also gathered a wide variety of wild foods growing along a gradient from floodplain to mountain slope. Perhaps the two most important were mesquite pods and saguaro fruit. Great *bosques* (forests) of mesquite grew along the Santa Cruz and its tributaries, with trees occasionally reaching thirty to fifty feet in height. *Kui*, the O'odham name for velvet mesquite (*Prosopis velutina*), usually produces both an early seed crop that matures in late June and a late summer crop that ripens in mid-September. After the pods (*vihog*) enclosing the seeds dried and fell to the desert floor, O'odham harvested enormous quantities, grinding them on metates to make a protein- and carbohydrate-rich flour from the soft mesocarp surrounding the seeds. This flour, often quite sweet, was baked into hard loaves called *komkĭcheḍ* (turtle or tortoise) because of their shape. The flour was also mixed with water to make puddings or a sweet drink called *vau*. Mesquite was such an important part of the O'odham diet that two months of their calendar reflect its annual growth cycle: *kui i'ivagĭdag mashad* (mesquite leafing-out moon; ca. April) and *kui hiósig mashad* (mesquite-flowers moon; ca. May) (Rea

1997). Because the so-called foresummer of the Sonoran Desert (April-May-June) was the leanest time of the year—a time when stored foods sometimes ran out and field crops had not yet matured—the early summer mesquite crop occasionally meant the difference between starvation and survival for the O'odham and other desert peoples. For that reason, ethnobotanist Amadeo Rea calls velvet mesquite the O'odham "tree of life" (Rea 1997:184).

Saguaro fruit, which ripened about the same time as the first mesquite harvest, were another important source of food during the foresummer. The O'odham employed saguaro-rib poles (*ku'ipaḍ*) to knock down the fruit from the *haashañ*, or saguaro, eating it fresh or drying and storing it. They also boiled down the pulp to make a syrup called *sitol*, which could keep for months and even years if sealed in small earthen jars buried underground. And finally, the O'odham ground saguaro seeds (*haashañ kai*) on metates and mixed them with other foods. The waxy white flowers pollinated by white-winged doves and long-nosed bats, the bright red fruit splitting open on green trunks, offered the promise of abundance during a time of want.

That promise gave the saguaro a ritual significance even greater than its dietary importance. The first month of the O'odham new year was *haashañ bahidag mashad* (saguaro harvest moon) beginning in late June. At that time, O'odham villages fermented some of the *sitol* (saguaro syrup) into saguaro wine (*navait*). By the twentieth century, when anthropologists like Frank Russell began to systematically record the rituals and beliefs of the Gila Pima, the wine feast had lost much of its sacred ceremonial character. Nonetheless, Rea believes that the Akimel O'odham used to consume saguaro wine to call the wind and rain, just as their Tohono O'odham brethren to the west still do (Underhill et al. 1997; Sheridan 1996b). Even though their well-being did not depend as directly upon the summer rains as the Tohono O'odham, Akimel O'odham realized that rain meant abundance and drought scarcity. On an intermittent stream like the Santa Cruz, strong monsoons transformed the trickle of the foresummer into enough flow to irrigate everyone's fields. During years when the heavy black thunder clouds did not build to a crescendo of rain, O'odham farmers, like the Hispanic farmers who followed them, had to wait longer for the water that kept their corn, beans, and squash from withering under the relentless sun.

For the O'odham of the Upper Santa Cruz, agaves (*a'u[d]*) must have been a major food source as well. Far more agaves studded the slopes of the Santa Rita, Patagonia, Tumacacori, and Atascosa mountains than the low desert ranges of Gila Pima country. O'odham from Tumacácori, Guevavi, Suamca, and other settlements climbed the bajadas to pry the caudices (the basal portion, also known as "heads" or "hearts") from the rocky soil and roast them in rock-lined pits. When Father Visitor Jacob Sedelmayr inspected San Xavier del Bac's visitas of Tucson and "Ohia" in late February 1751, he found not "a single soul since all of them were out gathering mescal [agaves] in the mountains to the east" (Matson and Fontana 1996:45). And even though no historic description of agave cultivation in the region has yet been found, Hohokam peoples to the north were growing as many as one hundred thousand plants at one time in rock pile fields in the western foothills of the Tortolita Mountains (Fish, Fish, and Madsen 1992). Whether O'odham at contact were cultivating *Agave parryi*, *Agave murpheyi*, or other species remains to be determined.

In addition to mesquite pods, saguaro fruit, and agave hearts, the O'odham gathered cholla buds, prickly pear fruit, yucca fruits and shoots, acorns, and *chiltepines*, the tiny, fiery wild chiles that reach their northern range in the mountain canyons of the Upper Santa Cruz watershed. They also harvested numerous species of wild and semidomesticated greens. Ethnobotanist Frank Crosswhite (1981:64) argues that O'odham fields included a "second garden" where tailwaters from irrigation or runoff-diversion supported dense stands of amaranth, chenopodium, and other vitamin- and mineral-rich greens. The line between domesticated and wild blurred in O'odham fields, where diversity was more valued than yield per unit of land.

Finally, the O'odham hunted large and small game, including rodents, jackrabbits, cottontails, mule deer, whitetail deer, pronghorn, and bighorn sheep. Javelina, expanding northward out of the tropics, may not yet have reached Arizona. In his 1716 *relación*, Father Luis Xavier Velarde lists the wild animals of the Pimería Alta—"jaguars, mountain lions, bears, bobcats, wolves, foxes, coyotes, bighorn sheep, deer, jackrabbits, cottontails, and others"—but does not mention peccaries, which undoubtedly would have been hunted by the O'odham if they had been abundant (González Rodríguez 1977:52).

Hunting was both organized and individual. The weedy margins and living fencerows of O'odham fields and canals provided habitat for rodents, rabbits, and birds, which were trapped or taken by men, women, and children as they carried out their agricultural tasks. Women and children also collected cicadas and caterpillars. The *tobdam*, the town crier and hunt leader, organized several types of communal hunts. One was the *shaada*, in which the men of a village would form a large circle and drive jackrabbits, cottontails, and rodents toward the center to be clubbed or shot with arrows. Another was the *kuunam*, or fire drive, which was carried out in grasslands or swales where there was enough vegetation to carry a blaze. Certain men, in contrast, devoted themselves to solitary big-game hunting, which Rea says "was almost a religious vocation, like shamanism" (Rea 1997:45).

Wild plants and animals, particularly mesquite, saguaro, and agave, constituted at least half the O'odham diet during good years when there was enough water in the Santa Cruz to irrigate their fields. During drought years, wild foods kept famine at bay. But O'odham subsistence also confronted iron limits imposed by the seasonality of desert rains and the plants and animals that depended upon them. Late spring and early summer were often times of severe hardship—day after long, hot day when people waited with hungry bellies for the clouds to form, the mesquite pods to ripen, and the corn and bean plants to mature.

The columbian Exchange in the pimería Alta

Old World crops and livestock loosened those limits, enabling the O'odham to farm more intensively and to turn more wild plants into food and fiber. The introduction of Old World livestock was the most dramatic transformation of the landscape. When herd animals domesticated in Eurasia lumbered into the Upper Santa Cruz Valley, nonedible grasses and forbs could be converted into beef, mutton, *cabrito* (roast goat), milk, cheese, and *menudo* (tripe stew), not to mention rawhide, wool, and tallow. For people whose animal protein came from rabbits, rodents, and an occasional deer or bighorn sheep, cattle, goats, and sheep must have offered an incredible bounty.

Kino's introduction of livestock into the Pimería Alta was systematic and sustained. "On January 13, 1697, I traveled in to the Sobaípuris of San Xavier del Bac. We drove cattle, sheep and goats (*ganado mayor y menor*), and a small herd of mares," Kino wrote. "The small ranch of San Luís de Bacoancos (Bacuancos) was begun with 60 head of cattle. There also were sheep and goats at San Cayetano, which the loyal children of the Venerable Father Francisco Xavier Saeta had brought, rounding them up at Concepción during the time of the disturbances of 1695" (Kino 1989:55). Kino increased those small mission herds and established two cattle ranches as well—one at Bacoancos on the Santa Cruz mentioned above, the other at San Simón y San Judas de Síbuda (Cíbuta) on an upper tributary of the Río Magdalena. Kino's January 1697 expedition marked the beginning of cattle ranching in southern Arizona.

The herds at Cíbuta and Bacoancos flourished. In March 1701, Manje reported four hundred cattle and two hundred sheep at Bacoancos. On that same visit, Kino ordered his Indian cowboys to brand seven droves of mares and one thousand cattle at Cíbuta while he took twenty pack animals for his expedition to the Gulf of California. The grasslands and oak woodlands of the Upper Santa Cruz and Upper Magdalena drainages were prime cattle country.[6]

The O'odham also received Old World crops. Melons apparently reached the O'odham before Kino entered their territory. But he introduced many other Eurasian domesticates, particularly wheat, to the Pimería Alta. Kino concluded his description of his January 1697 expedition to the O'odham of the Santa Cruz Valley by noting, "The word of God was spoken to them [the people of San Xavier del Bac], there were baptisms of children and the beginnings of good sowings and harvests of wheat and maize for the father minister whom they asked for and hoped to receive" (my translation of Kino 1989:55).

Another ecological revolution had just been launched. Because it tolerated frosts, wheat, *pilkañ* in O'odham, filled a largely empty niche in the agricultural cycle, growing during the winter months when corn, beans, and squash would have withered. O'odham could now double-crop their fields, planting wheat in November or December after their summer corn and beans had been harvested. *Pilkañ* matured in May or June at a time when mesquite pods had not yet ripened and spring maize and bean plants were still struggling to grow. Within a century, O'odham throughout the Pimería Alta, even the Gila Pimas, who were never missionized by the Jesuits or conquered by the Spaniards, were growing more wheat than corn. Like Old World livestock, wheat affected many O'odham more profoundly than Catholic rituals and beliefs. When Father Felipe Segesser reoccupied the abandoned mission of San Xavier del Bac in 1732, he noted that the O'odham there knew nothing of God, heaven, or hell but a great deal about cattle, horses, and wheat.

Kino introduced the O'odham to other Old World cultigens as well, including peaches, pomegranates, figs, pears, quinces, grapes, sugar cane, chickpeas, lentils, bastard chickpeas, cabbage, lettuce, onions, leeks, garlic, cilantro, anise, and perhaps mint. O'odham reliance upon agriculture intensified, even though they apparently did not yet adopt the plow (Officer 1993). O'odham settlements also grew larger and more concentrated in response to Apache and Yavapai hostilities (Ezell 1961; Doelle 1975; Sheridan 1988a). Hooved stock and handfuls of seed transformed O'odham society, deepening their dependence upon domestication. An agropastoralist economy, based on Old World animals and an Old World grain, was taking root along the Santa Cruz River.

We have few glimpses of this transformation in its early stages. The most systematic chronicler of the Pimería Alta after Kino died in 1711 was Father Luis Xavier Velarde, a Spaniard from Valladolid who succeeded Kino at Mission Dolores in 1714 and remained there until his death in 1737. Tall, deaf, and prone to heat stroke, Velarde was not much of an explorer. Because his health did not permit him to take to the saddle as often as Kino or Campos did, he had more time to record daily life in the Pimería Alta.

His earliest *relación*, written in 1716, notes the agricultural fusion of New and Old World plants in O'odham fields. "The other fruits of this Pimería are: maize, a small bean called *tépari*, and other seeds that, in their seasons, the Pimas harvest and store for their sustenance," Velarde observed. "And after they came into contact with the Spaniards, and the padres entered [their territory], they harvest a considerable amount of wheat, especially those of the west; beans of all kinds, fava beans, lentils, squash of various kinds, watermelons, and melons. And the missions yield abundant grapes, peaches, figs, pears, quinces, pomegranates, sugar cane, and other fruits, along with vegetables as in any other area" (my translation from González Rodríguez 1977:51–52).

Velarde also described the extensive cultivation of cotton among "the Sobaipuris and others to the north" (González Rodríguez 1977:52). Old World grains and broad beans (favas and lentils) greened O'odham fields during the cooler months when frosts were a danger. The New World triumvirate of maize, beans, and squash continued to dominate the spring and summer planting seasons. Meanwhile, Old World orchard crops graced mission gardens. The agricultural repertoire of the O'odham had expanded enormously.

O'odham cuisine reflected this vibrant fusion. "Many of the new crops were additive," Rea notes, "but wheat largely eclipsed maize as the basic crop. Wheat tortillas became the staple at most meals; even the oldest people today cannot remember anyone making corn tortillas. Wheat replaced corn and mesquite flour in many preparations as well. Wheat pinole (parched and finely ground wheat) became a staple for both those traveling and those at home. It needed only to be mixed with water to make a hearty cereal drink" (Rea 1997:72–73).

Despite wheat's importance, however, the O'odham often combined it with aboriginal foods, particularly mesquite flour. Mesquite and wheat flour were blended to make a sweet pudding called *vihog hidoḍ*. The O'odham also made a dish called *ka'akvulk* (hills made), wheat tortillas alternating with layers of mushy mesquite. O'odham men carried *ka'akvulk* on hunting trips or revenge raids against the Apaches. Mesquite flour (*vihog weenagim chu'i*) sweetened wheat pinole whereas whole wheat dumplings (doves) simmered in mesquite juice (*hooi-wichda*; mourning doves done in imitation) (Rea 1997). Old World foods did not obliterate New World fare.

Pre-Hispanic O'odham cultural patterns also persisted. According to Velarde, the O'odham were still raising macaws (*guacamayas*) "for their red feathers, and other colors, almost like those of the peacock, which they pluck in the spring for their adornment" (my translation of González Rodríguez 1977:53). Perhaps macaw feathers were among the items Sobaipuris traded to the Hopis when the "moquinos" came to Jaibanipita in the San Pedro Valley for "fairs" (González Rodríguez 1977:64). According to elderly O'odham, those fairs had been suspended after the Sobaipuris killed a large number of Hopis. Perhaps during those exchanges at some time in the past, O'odham adopted the *wi:gida*—a ritual with Pueblo-like masked dancers wearing turkey tail feathers that spread as far west as Quitovac, where the Hiá ch-eḍ O'odham still perform the summer version (Hayden 1987; Sheridan 1996b). Velarde's *relación*, as biased as it is with ethnocentric preconceptions and dismissals, offers us a glimpse into a pre-Hispanic world where people journeyed back and forth between the Colorado Plateau and the southern deserts before Old World epidemics and Apache raiding rent the region asunder.

The Jesuit "Mission" of 1732

While Campos and Velarde were struggling to maintain a presence in the Pimería Alta, tensions escalated between the Jesuits and Spanish settlers, who resented missionary control over Indian land and labor. A powerful faction dominated by Gregorio Alvarez Tuñón y Quirós, the corrupt but ever-resourceful captain of Fronteras presidio, advocated the removal of the Jesuits and the secularization of the Sonoran missions. The Jesuits countered their critics in a series of polemics, the most eloquent of which was the *informe* of Father José María Genovese, the Sicilian *visitador* of the Sonoran missions (González Rodríguez 1977; Polzer and Sheridan 1997).

The Jesuits were not without allies, however. Opposed to Alvarez Tuñón y Quirós and his confederates were a tight-knit group of Basque merchants and military men—*vizcainos* who venerated the Society of Jesus because it had been founded by one of their own, Ignatius of Loyola. The Jesuits won the battle, at least temporarily, when Inspector General Pedro de Rivera Villalón removed Alvarez Tuñón y Quirós from office and replaced him with a vizcaino, Juan Bautista de Anza, in 1726. Rivera went on to laud the Jesuits in his official reports, and Anza remained a staunch supporter of the missionaries until he was ambushed and killed by Apaches in 1740 (Naylor and Polzer 1988; Polzer and Sheridan 1997).

None of these struggles meant much to the O'odham of the Upper Santa Cruz, even though Jesuit ascendancy may have protected them from land grabs and labor drafts at the hands of the settlers. In 1732, however, the O'odham world changed forever. Two years earlier, a "mission" of twenty-six Jesuits sailed from Cádiz for the Indies. Three of those Europeans—Johann Baptist Grazhoffer from Austria, Phelipe Segesser from Switzerland, and Ignaz Xavier Keller from Moravia—were assigned to the Pimería Alta. These "German" Jesuits ended the isolation of the Santa Cruz O'odham. After several months of orientation on the northern frontier, they took up their missions in the spring of 1732: Segesser at San Xavier del Bac, Grazhoffer at Guevavi, and Keller at Santa María Suamca. Grazhoffer died a year later—his fellow Jesuits accused the O'odham of poisoning him—but Keller remained at his post for twenty-seven years. Segesser replaced Grazhoffer at Guevavi; Gaspar Stiger, another Swiss, was transferred from the Tarahumara missions to Bac. The O'odham of the Upper Santa Cruz would not be free of at least one resident missionary for the next century.

You can read the rumblings of the O'odham between the lines of the missionaries' letters and reports. An old O'odham man confessed to poisoning Grazhoffer, although the missionary was already suffering from a fever when he reached Guevavi. Segesser, who almost died from what may have been malaria, blamed his own illness on Guevavi *hechiceros*, the Spanish term for Indian shamans. Stiger claimed that he had been cursed three times by shamans at Bac. Then, in 1734, O'odham at Suamca, Guevavi, and Bac deserted their missions. At Guevavi, they drove the mission's herds of horses and cattle into the mountains. At Bac, they ransacked Stiger's house and stole all belongings, "including the new, beautiful, and precious vestments in five colors and all appurtenances which our viceroy had given us when we were sent to these new missions" (Segesser in Treutlein 1945:164). Anza quickly restored order, but the O'odham of the Upper Santa Cruz clearly did not appreciate missionaries who came to stay (Kessell 1970).

And stay they did. Segesser left Guevavi in 1734 because of poor health. In 1737, however, blond-haired, blue-eyed Father Alexandro Rapicani took up the post and remained there until the fall of 1740. He was followed by Father Joseph de Torres Perea, who served until 1744, and by Father Ildefonso de la Peña, who stayed less than a year. Then, in 1745, Father Joseph Garrucho arrived for almost seven years of proselytizing and church building. Beginning in the 1730s, resident Jesuits mounted a sustained assault on O'odham beliefs and cultural practices they considered savage or idolatrous. Polygamy, shamanism, the saguaro wine feast —all had to be rooted out if the O'odham were to be turned into proper Christians.

At the same time, the discovery of huge chunks of silver at Arizonac, southwest of modern Nogales, drew hundreds of prospectors—Spaniards, *mestizos*, mulattoes, Yaquis, Opatas—into the region. During the 1720s, Spanish ranchers had already recolonized the San Luis Valley south of Guevavi where the Santa Cruz makes a great bend. By the 1740s, there were sizeable populations of Spanish settlers at Arivaca and Tubac as well. Jesuit missionaries and Spanish settlers were slowly but surely contracting the O'odham world.

We can only infer how the O'odham perceived these mounting pressures. Modern readers often dismiss the frequent references to Indian hechiceros in Jesuit documents as boilerplate religious rhetoric. But as anthropologist Daniel Reff (1998) points out, Jesuit ideas about how the world worked converged more closely with O'odham sensibilities than with those of our own. "At a time when rationalism and nominalism were flowering in Europe, the Jesuits and other religious retained what was essentially a medieval epistemology and worldview, championing the idea of a mysterious God who constantly intervened on earth to change the course of events and to combat Satan (Moore 1982)," Reff writes. "Jesuit 'supernaturalism,' particularly the idea of the inseparability of the natural and invisible worlds, was consistent with the aboriginal beliefs of their Native American converts (Moore 1982:197; Rubert de Ventos 1991). Although the Jesuits and their converts may have disagreed about who was responsible for the supernatural events, neither doubted reports of flying shamans, talking stones, or altar cloths that mysteriously began to bleed (Reff 1995)" (Reff 1998:28).

Jesuits believed that shamans in league with the Devil were continually trying to prevent the conversion of their people and inflict illness or death on the missionaries themselves. In a sense, the Jesuits may have been right. Shamans have been central figures in O'odham society since pre-Hispanic times. Today, the primary function of an O'odham shaman (*má·kai*) is to define and diagnose disease in a night-long session called *dóajida*. In the past, however, their magic pervaded all aspects of O'odham life and thought. "While the shaman played a minor role in organizing the ceremonial life, his experience, as celebrated in song, drama, and oratory, dominated the content of every ceremony," anthropologist Donald Bahr observes. "The ritual oratory, for example, was a poetic form based on the idea of shamanic journeys from the earth to the sky or underworld and back to the earth again" (Bahr 1983:193). O'odham believed certain individuals had the power to make crops grow, to bring rain, to divine the location of enemies, and to cast spells over them, as well as to diagnose and cure disease. The black-robed priests with their elaborate rituals must have been seen as direct threats to the power of the shamans—competitors who had to be eliminated if the old ways were to be restored.

And since missionization was being carried out in what Reff (1998: 31) calls a "disease environment," the role of O'odham shamans must have been even more fraught with tension than it is now. There are entries on nineteenth-century O'odham calendar sticks of villagers killing shamans during outbreaks of disease (Russell 1975). Imagine the ambivalence with which O'odham must have viewed their religious practitioners as they watched their children die from illnesses their bodies had never been wracked by before. The pustules, rashes, hemorrhages, fevers, bloody stools, and "black" or "yellow" vomit brought on by epidemics of smallpox, measles, malaria, dysentery, and typhoid posed terrible challenges to O'odham shamans. During the first two decades following the refounding of the Santa Cruz missions in 1732, at least five major epidemics swept through the Pimería Alta (Dobyns 1959). Many O'odham undoubtedly turned to the missionaries, at least at first, hoping against hope that the waters of baptism, the holy oils of extreme unction, the processions, benedictions, and ritual invocations of the mass would heal their bodies and restore order to their universe. Later, when they continued to die, some O'odham came to associate baptism and even the tolling of mission bells with the spread of disease.

Luis Oacpicagigua and the 1751 Upper Pima Rebellion

But it was a military leader appointed by the Spaniards, not a shaman, who led the O'odham rebellion that brought Jesuit dreams of northward expansion crashing to the desert ground. Luis Oacpicagigua of Sáric was an accomplished war leader who had carried out numerous campaigns against the Apaches. In 1750, Governor Diego Ortiz Parrilla requested his help against the Seri Indians, who had taken refuge on Tiburón Island in the Gulf of California. When Ortiz Parrilla invaded Tiburón in September, Oacpicagigua commanded 443 O'odham warriors—by far the largest contingent in Ortiz Parrilla's force (Sheridan 1979, 1999).

The O'odham leader may also have prevented a mutiny. Waging a desperate war of thirst, Seris killed two horses left behind by a Spanish reconnaissance force and threw their decomposing bodies into water holes on Tiburón. Unable to drink, the presidial soldiers and Spanish militia chafed under their heavy leather armor and stared at the crags of the Sierra Kunkaak, where they envisioned Seris waiting to ambush them with their legendary poisoned arrows. Ortiz Parrilla exhorted them to move forward. They refused. He promised them money and military honors. They remained where they were. Then, in desperation, the governor turned to Oacpicagigua. The O'odham leader responded that the Pimas had come from very far away to kill the Seris, "who wandered through the wilderness doing harm. Until now, however, they had done nothing but eat, and they wanted to go into the mountains to look for the Seris" (Sheridan 1979:330; 1999). Shamed by the O'odham leader, the Spaniards grudgingly took up their arms, but the O'odham proved to be more effective fighters on Tiburón's rugged terrain. Oacpicagigua must have come away from Tiburón with an abiding contempt for Spanish military prowess.

He still might have remained an ally of the Spaniards, however, if tensions had not escalated between missionaries and Spanish officials. Soon after the expedition to Tiburón, Ortiz Parrilla appointed Oacpicagigua governor and captain general of the northern O'odham, an office that had no analogue in O'odham society. The Jesuits bitterly resented Oacpicagigua's elevation in status. They believed that it was their right and responsibility to appoint Indian officials. Ortiz Parrilla was usurping their authority, weakening their control over people who had rebelled against them in the past. "What we are seeing is that during the [Seri] campaign he [Ortiz Parrilla] flattered them greatly and they now return most haughty and averse to the Padres," Father Gaspar Stiger complained (quoted in Kessell 1970:103).

The tipping point occurred in early fall, 1751. Assembling a large force of O'odham warriors to campaign against the Apaches, Oacpicagigua marched north to rendezvous with Santiago Ruiz de Ael, captain of the presidio of Terrenate. At Guevavi, Father Joseph Garrucho fed the O'odham for three days and gave them fifteen head of cattle to take with them. At Soamca, in contrast, the irascible and alcoholic Ignaz Keller publicly humiliated the O'odham leader.[7] When Oacpicagigua arrived dressed as a Spanish officer to ask Keller where Ruiz de Ael had gone, Keller snarled, "You are a dog to come here and ask me that. You can go wherever you want, or not go at all. It would be better if you remained behind. You act like you are trying to be a Spaniard by the arms you are carrying. You are not worthy to go about in this manner. You should be in a breechcloth with bows and arrows like a Chichimeco" (Garate n.d.:24).

According to Pedro de la Cruz, the son of an O'odham father and an Opata mother who was executed as a spy soon after the revolt broke out, Keller's affront was the last straw. "Brother, I am possessed with this evil of serving in this charge that was conferred upon me by the Father Visitor and confirmed by the Lord Governor in the name of the King," Oacpicagigua reputedly told de la Cruz. "I accepted it in order to be Captain General of my nation and because the Fathers could not now scorn me in any way, since they would have to do as the King commanded. But because the Fathers detest us we are already lost. So don't say anything to me about how we should love the laws of God. It is better that we should live with our liberty. Already, I do not want these arms or this uniform. Now I will betray all the Spaniards" (Garate n.d.:25).

Other witnesses, including Santiago, an O'odham official at Santa María Suamca, declared that Oacpicagigua had been planning the revolt for more than a year and was only looking for excuses to start it (Garate n.d.). Luis of Pitic (Pitiquito), one of Oacpicagigua's allies, even confessed that on their way home from the expedition to Tiburón, they had stopped at El Tupo, site of the 1695 massacre. There Oacpicagigua had asked Luis of Pitic if he remembered how their ancestors had killed the missionary at Caborca in retaliation (Kessell 1970). Memories of Spanish outrages more than half a century before may have stoked Oacpicagigua's anger in 1751.

Whatever his motives, Jesuit contempt for O'odham leaders they did not control certainly seemed to poison an already perilous atmosphere. While he was being interrogated in chains, Pedro de la Cruz wailed, "I am not the cause of the rebellion. Those who have caused it are Fathers Jacobo Sedelmayr, Ignacio Xavier Keller, and Joseph Garrucho, because of the severity with which they and their *mayordomos* treat the Indians" (Garate n.d.:24). When Pedro himself arrived in Guevavi carrying the *bastón* (cane of office) he had been given as Oacpicagigua's sergeant, Father Garrucho snatched it away, saying, "You are a dog because you are carrying that bastón. Don't come here disturbing the people. If it was not for the day that this is, I would have given you a hundred lashes with a whipping stick" (Garate n.d.:25).

If Oacpicagigua had risen to prominence a generation later, he might have become an officer in the Spanish military. But Keller and Oacpicagigua were transitional, even tragic, figures. During the mid-eighteenth century, New Spain's northern frontier was in the throes of a political and philosophical revolution. As Indian rebellions and Apache attacks wracked the Northwest, many Spanish officials concluded that militarization, not missionization, was the best way to pacify the region. Following the 1740 Yaqui revolt, the Spanish crown established two new presidios in Sonora: one at Pitic on the outskirts of Yaqui, Seri, and Lower Pima country, another at Terrenate in the Pimería Alta. After the 1751 Pima rebellion, two more garrisons were added—one at Tubac (1752), another at Altar (ca. 1755) (Polzer and Sheridan 1997).[8] The guerrilla warfare of the Seris and their Lower and Upper Pima allies triggered the creation of the presidio of San Carlos de Buenavista in 1765. Two years later, Carlos III expelled the Jesuits from Spain and all of its dominions.

While this transition was taking place, more and more Indians articulated with the Spanish empire as military allies rather than mission neophytes. This process culminated in the formation of all-Indian presidial companies at Bavispe (Opatas, 1779), Bacoachi (Opatas, 1784), and Tubac (O'odham, 1787) (Moorhead 1975).[9] Military service became an avenue of upward mobility for many O'odham and Opatas. It also accelerated the process of *mestizaje*, or racial mixing, which weakened ethnic boundaries in Sonora during the late eighteenth and early nineteenth centuries (Radding 1997).

In 1751, however, the transition from missionization to militarization was still in its early stages. Moreover, the Pimería Alta, unlike the Hiakim (Yaqui homeland), was the frontier of a frontier, surrounded on three sides by the territories of peoples who had never been conquered by the Spaniards. O'odham like Oacpicagigua could still dream of complete independence from Spaniard and Jesuit alike.

Those dreams proved more feverish than real. On Saturday, November 20, Oacpicagigua panicked his Spanish neighbors and their servants into taking refuge inside his house at Sáric under pretext of Apache attack (Ewing 1934). Then he and his confederates set the dwelling on fire and clubbed anyone who tried to escape. Similar assaults flared that night or the next morning in Caborca, Pitiquito, Oquitoa, Atil, Tubutama, Sonoita, Busani, Agua Caliente, Baboquivari, Arivaca, and Tubac. By Sunday evening, 109 people—most of them Spaniards—had been killed (Garate n.d.).

The terrified Spanish families of the Upper Santa Cruz Valley fled to safety at Terrenate presidio. Meanwhile O'odham residents of Guevavi, Tubac, and Tumacácori who did not join the rebellion took refuge in the Santa Rita Mountains or at Tres Alamos on the San Pedro River. Rebels sacked the mission churches at Guevavi and Bac, and for a few brief weeks that winter, Spaniards feared that the Pimería Alta, like New Mexico in 1680, would be lost.

After Bernardo de Urrea and his militia routed Oacpicagigua at Arivaca on January 5, 1752, however, the revolt quickly dissipated.[10] Oacpicagigua retreated to the Santa Catalina Mountains and entered into negotiations with Ortiz Parrilla, much to the disgust of the Jesuits. One of his demands was the removal of Father Keller. On March 18, 1752, Oacpicagigua surrendered to Captain Joseph Díaz del Carpio at Tubac, where he was granted amnesty. By April, there were sixty-six O'odham at Guevavi, forty at Tubac, eighteen at Sópori, ninety-seven at Sonoita, and ninety-eight at Suamca (Garate n.d.:46–48). After defending himself before the viceroy in Mexico City, Keller returned in triumph to Suamca in the spring of 1753. Meanwhile, Oacpicagigua performed obligatory rituals of abasement before Spanish and missionary audiences, dying in prison at Horcasitas in 1756.

"A Live Flame Covered with Ashes": Resistance and Reducción

But resistance still simmered. Even though a new presidio was established at Tubac in 1752, some of Oacpicagigua's followers, including two of his sons, fought on. Known as Piatos to the Spaniards, they allied themselves with Hawani Mo'o (Raven's Head), an O'odham war leader from the Gila River who attacked San Xavier del Bac and looted its church in 1756. Papagos and even some O'odham residents of Bac joined in the pillage. They even tried to kill their missionary, Father Alonso Espinosa, perhaps because he attempted to suppress their traditional fall harvest festival (Kessell 1970).

The Piatos also joined forces with Seris and Sibubapas—Lower Pima rebels from the mission communities of Cumuripa, Tecoripa, and Suaqui. Together and apart, these loose bands of resistance fighters attacked mines, ranches, and pueblos from the Pimería Alta to Ostimuri during the 1750s and 1760s.[11] In the Upper Santa Cruz valley alone, Piatos ran off mission and presidial livestock and mounted major assaults on Guevavi during Holy Week in 1758 and on Sonoita the following year (Kessell 1970). It took the largest professional military force in the history of northwestern New Spain—the Sonoran Expedition led by Colonel Domingo Elizondo—to wear the rebels down and bring a tenuous peace to the region (Sheridan 1999). The last two decades of Jesuit missionization in the Pimería Alta were years of wary retrenchment, not expansion. In the words of Father Visitor General Ignacio Lizasoáin, "Experience has shown that the peaceful state of many of these Upper Pimas and Papagos, seemingly so untroubled and tranquil, has been a live flame covered with ashes, ready to show itself for what it truly is at the slightest wind" (Polzer and Sheridan 1997:449).

That "live flame covered with ashes" smoldered on pox-ridden corpses and deserted villages. For the O'odham, their final years under the Jesuits were years of territorial contraction and population decline. O'odham from the ranchería of Sópori began moving to Guevavi in 1747. By 1762, the ranchería was abandoned. In the late 1740s, Luis Oacpicagigua himself convinced O'odham from Concuc and Upiatuban to reduce themselves to Guevavi as well (Dobyns 1959). Father Francisco Pauer, who took over Guevavi after the 1751 revolt, relocated all seventy-eight residents of the ranchería of Doacuquita or Toacuquita to a place he christened San Cayetano de Calabazas in 1756. Despite these and other newcomers from the Papaguería, however, the population of O'odham communities along the Upper Santa Cruz continued to drop, primarily because of periodic epidemics.

To reinforce their declining missions, Jesuits convinced Spanish authorities to undertake the most ambitious *reducción* of them all. In 1757, two young German Jesuits, Francisco Hlava and Miguel Gerstner, attempted to missionize the Sobaipuris of the San Pedro. The Sobaipuris quickly drove them away, threatening to kill any missionary other than Keller. According to one observer, "In a word, they want to be baptized, but to live as they wish, to be Christians only in name" (quoted in Kessell 1970:146). Five years later, however, interim Governor Joseph Tienda de Cuervo ordered the resettlement of the San Pedro Sobaipuris after consulting with Visitor General Lizasoáin. Captain Francisco Elías González de Zayas, captain of Terrenate presidio, carried out the order in 1762. Two hundred fifty Sobaipuris—O'odham frontiersmen who had buffered the communities of the Santa Cruz Valley against the Apaches for at least three generations—abandoned the San Pedro and settled at Soamca, Sonoita, and Tucson.

Spanish authorities soon learned to regret that decision as Apache attacks intensified. A year later, Spanish settlers in the San Luis Valley asked Captain Juan Bautista de Anza, captain of Fronteras presidio, for permission to move downstream, closer to the presidio of Tubac. Soon the ranches of San Luis, Buenavista, and Santa Bárbara were also deserted. In 1768, Soamca itself had to be abandoned after Apaches set fire to the homes of the thirteen O'odham families living there and punched a hole through the wall of the church, defiling its statues (Kessell 1970, 1976; Hadley and Sheridan 1995). Through disease and assault, the Pimería Alta was collapsing inward upon itself.

o'odham Divisions

Oacpicagigua and his confederates may have thought they could drive the Spaniards from the Pimería Alta, but the course of the rebellion revealed how deeply divided the O'odham were. This was due in part to the autonomous nature of O'odham society at contact. No overarching tribal organization linked Sobaipuris to Sobas, Gileños to Himeris (O'odham living along the Río Dolores in northern Sonora). Spanish administration and Jesuit missionization may have imposed a certain degree of unity on O'odham communities through institutions such as the captaincy general, but those institutions did not endure. Moreover, the appointment of O'odham to offices of European origin—*gobernador*, *alcalde*, *fiscal*—factionalized O'odham society, generating cultural and political tensions among and within individuals. Although it would be hard to demonstrate, missionaries may have favored families sympathetic to Jesuit control with better lands and greater access to mission goods and surpluses.

The very act of dividing mission lands themselves ruptured pre-Hispanic O'odham relations of production. Before the blackrobes arrived, groups of families related through male lines enjoyed customary use rights to arable stretches of the floodplain and areas along arroyos where runoff agriculture could be practiced. Family groups may also have returned year after year to places where mesquite, saguaros, agaves, or acorns were abundant. But land was not considered the property of individuals or even family groups. Village councils composed of adult males made sure that households had access to the land they needed and resolved disputes when they arose. If a family line died out, the council would distribute its land to another family in the village. Because desert resources were scattered across the landscape, sharing and consensus were the governing principles of O'odham land tenure (Underhill 1939).

It is always a little treacherous to draw assumptions about past values and behaviors from ethnographic research carried out in the twentieth century. Mounting evidence of conflict among the Hohokam in the Late Classic Period indicates that cooperation and consensus may not always have governed O'odham resource use. Hohokam elites probably did extract surplus from Hohokam commoners. By the late seventeenth century, however, there is little evidence of pronounced social stratification among the O'odham. An ideology of exchange seems to have replaced a hierarchical ideology of accumulation as evidenced by the platform mounds and mortuary practices of the Late Classic.

O'odham perceptions of the landscape—and their right to exploit it—also differed in fundamental respects from those of the Jesuits trying to change them. According to ethnobiologist Amadeo Rea, "From myth to medicine, the Pimas' metaphor of themselves was as part of the desert, a component of it rather than something separate—and especially not superior to it. Personal and community health were viewed as part and parcel of the larger natural community" (Rea 1997:42).

The Jesuits attempted to impose the notion of a surplus-generating theocratic community upon this "natural" community. Jesuit ideals were based in part on the peasant corporate communities that continued to survive throughout Europe in the sixteenth and seventeenth centuries. Land, water, and natural resources of the landscape such as timber, fuel wood, stone, and wild plants belonged to the community, not individuals or households. *Hijos del pueblo* (natives of the community) enjoyed birthrights to those resources, but those birthrights were usufruct rights, not private property rights. Arable land was divided into plots assigned to individual households. Nonarable land was accessible to all hijos del pueblo to graze their livestock, gather firewood, harvest wild plants, hunt game, and collect building material.

In contrast to peasant corporate communities, however, the Jesuits ran mission herds and reserved part of the arable land base as a *común*. Each household was supposed to labor on that común or care for mission livestock a certain number of days each week. The crops and livestock from mission fields and mission herds were stored in mission granaries for hard times or traded to obtain goods, especially cloth, that the Indians of the mission could not produce themselves (Radding 1997).

Missionaries, not Indians, controlled such surpluses. Radding (1997) argues convincingly that the coercive power of the missionaries was rarely absolute. She points out that Indians resisted labor on the comunes and rarely cultivated more than a fraction of mission lands. If mission discipline grew too onerous, Indians fled to the *monte* (wildlands) or migrated to work on Spanish mines and haciendas. Radding's analysis of sales and expenditures for Opata and Eudeve missions also suggests that Indians were able to negotiate substantial gifts of cloth from the Jesuits in return for their labor. Jesuit missions were not the self-sufficient, smoothly running theocracies romanticized by Herbert Eugene Bolton and his students.

Nonetheless, European lines were being drawn across the O'odham landscape, dividing fields within missions, dividing one mission from another, carving Spanish *ranchos* out of O'odham territory. These divisions of space were accompanied by divisions of time—three days a week of labor, at least in theory, in mission fields or *estancias* (stock ranches), three days a week in household fields. These were critical first steps in the commodification of both land and labor in the Upper Santa Cruz Valley. The contraction of the O'odham world was therefore occurring at the same time as the subdivision of the O'odham world along axes of both space and time.

3

The O'odham and the Franciscans

In May 1768, after ten months of confinement, fifty Sonoran Jesuits sailed south from the sun-bleached port of Guaymas. After a hellish voyage down the Pacific coast, they landed at San Blas and were forced-marched across Mexico from Tepic to Vera Cruz. Those who survived were shipped to house imprisonment in Spain. Almost two centuries of evangelization on the northwestern frontier came to an abrupt end as the ultramontane Society of Jesus fell victim to European intrigue, Enlightenment ideas, and the triumph of mercantile capitalism embodied in the Spanish crown's Bourbon reforms.

José de Gálvez and his fellow architects of the new colonial order then toyed with the idea of turning all missions into secular parishes once and for all. The realities of ethnic politics and ecclesiastical resources soon intruded. The reformers had to concede that there were not enough secular priests to transform thousands of Indian neophytes into tithe-paying parishioners. They arm-twisted the oldest missionary order on the frontier—the Order of Friars Minor, or Franciscans—into taking over the missions of Sonora and the Pimería Alta. Baja California—Kino's dream and Salvatierra's bone-dry reality—became the responsibility of the Dominicans.

But even though the reformers could not dispense with missionaries, they severely curtailed their power. Initially, Spanish officials granted the Franciscans only spiritual control over the missions. Civil commissioners (*comisarios*) took over the temporal management of mission fields, herds, and storehouses. Moreover, Viceroy Marqúez de Croix gave mission Indians more autonomy as well. "Under no circumstances are Indians to be deprived of civil intercourse, communication, commerce or residence with Spaniards," he instructed, "no less the possession in individual and private domain of their property, goods, and the fruits of their labor" (quoted in Kessell 1976:17). The old utopian vision of self-sufficient missions isolated from Spanish vices was crumbling. In its place rose a new vision—King Charles III's blueprint for a streamlined empire where ecclesiastical privileges were subordinated to royal power and the forces of production were freed from medieval constraints like the corporate control of land.

The transition proved chaotic. Civil commissioners administered the missions for more than a year before the Franciscans arrived. The economic state of the missions therefore depended upon the scruples of the Spanish settlers appointed to those offices. In Guevavi, Captain Juan Bautista de Anza of Tubac had to intervene after Comisario Andrés Grijalva handed over the keys to the granaries to the O'odham and told them "they were the absolute owners of the missions' goods and that as such they might dispose of them as they saw fit." "In just a few days they must have consumed at Tumacácori more than fifty fanegas [more than forty-one hundred pounds, probably of wheat] without accounting for it," Anza reported. "The same thing was happening with the horses, cattle, etc. Everything would have been finished off within a few days. For this reason on my own initiative I have taken back the keys, leaving out enough provisions for their normal needs . . . until such time as the *comisario* appears, when I shall warn him not to proceed in such a disorganized state" (quoted in Kessell 1970:189–90).

The Demise of Guevavi

By the time Franciscans entered the Upper Santa Cruz Valley a year later, Guevavi—the Jesuit cabecera—was dying a lingering death. At its height during the Jesuit period, about three hundred O'odham families farmed the floodplain of the Santa Cruz at Guevavi and its visitas of Calabasas, Sonoita, and Tumacácori. When the Franciscan grayrobes replaced Jesuit blackrobes, only sixty-two to seventy-one families remained (Kessell 1976:38).

The first friar was Juan Chrisóstomo Gil de Bernabé, a tall, eloquent Aragonese who epitomized late-eighteenth-century Franciscan fervor at its most exalted and penitential. Soon after he was ordained, Gil forsook the relative comforts of the Franciscan *convento* in Zaragosa and confined himself in the mountaintop monastery of Monlora. Then, in 1762, he answered the call to mission in the Americas, surviving a shipwreck on the Yucatán peninsula to preach home missions—Catholic revival meetings—in the countryside around the Franciscan apostolic college of Querétaro.

Five years later, Gil volunteered for the Sonoran missions along with his frequent traveling companion, the much earthier Francisco Garcés. Gil's stay at Guevavi almost killed him. In the spring of 1771, half paralyzed, he had to be carried south to the hot springs near Aconchi in the Sonora River Valley (Kessell 1976). His zeal—soaring and self-scourging—won him a martyr's death two years later, when he tried to establish the mission of Carrizal on the salt flats east of modern Bahía de Kino. The Seri Indians proved even more resistant to his message than the O'odham (Kessell 1975; Sheridan 1999).

By then, Gil's former mission of Guevavi had withered to nine families (Kessell 1970). O'odham abandoned it completely in 1775. Tumacácori now served as the cabecera. This was not the older settlement of the same name east of the river, however, but a new *reducción* west of the Santa Cruz. Tumacácori contained O'odham from the earlier village, O'odham displaced from nearby Tubac after the presidio was established there in 1752, and Tohono O'odham from the western deserts. A 1774 census revealed a population of 236 Indians and 19 Spaniards. Calabasas was its only visita, with an amalgamated population of 138 living in 3 separate rancherías—the inhabitants of Calabasas and refugees from Guevavi and Sonoita (Kessell 1976). Apaches had driven the O'odham from Soamca in 1768, and they did the same to the remnants of Sonoita and Guevavi the following decade.

"The Indian is so attached and so passionately devoted to his land and his country," one Franciscan noted, "that to take him from the place of his birth—even if it is no more than the shade of a mesquite—is to take his life or at the least his most cherished possession" (quoted in Kessell 1976:89). But Apache expansionism took a terrible toll. O'odham in the Upper Santa Cruz Valley were like an intermittent stream drying up during a prolonged drought. Pools remained, but the flow that may have routed Hohokam elites in the fifteenth century was not even a trickle three hundred years later.

Mission and Presidio

Meanwhile, the debate over missions continued to rage. Juan Bautista de Anza, born and bred on the frontier and a Basque *criollo* raised to revere the Jesuits, sided firmly with the Bourbon reformers. Captain of Tubac presidio since 1760, Anza argued that mission Indians should not have to work three days a week at mission tasks. On the contrary, they should till their own fields and dispose of their own produce. "When they have real property, we shall be free of uprisings or fears of them," he contended (quoted in Kessell 1976:85).

Despite these polemics, however, the realities of frontier life encouraged cooperation between the presidio and mission. Anza allowed civilian and mission livestock to run with the presidial horse herd under presidial guard. At times the combined herd numbered more than a thousand animals. Even though the Marqués de Rubí criticized Anza for this practice when he visited Tubac on his inspection of the northern presidios, it undoubtedly reduced the losses to mission and civilian herds.[1]

Anza also managed the irrigation systems of Tubac and Tumacácori together. During times when water was scarce in the Santa Cruz, all water was diverted onto the fields of the O'odham at Tumacácori for one week and onto the fields of the Tubaqueños the following week (Dobyns 1959). This was common practice along streams in the Sonoran Desert, where flow often slowed to a trickle during the parched "foresummer" of April, May, and early June. Water judges (*jueces de agua*) in the *municipio* of Cucurpe, Sonora, still enforce such diversions today (Sheridan 1988b).

If the presidio had remained in Tubac, Tubac might have overwhelmed Tumacácori. In 1775, however, Comandante Inspector Hugo O'Conor—one of the Catholic "Wild Geese" who fled occupied Ireland to fight for England's enemies—ordered the presidio to be moved to Tucson forty miles downstream. Anza had already bled away twenty soldiers from the garrison for his expedition to California early in 1774. In order to protect the new land route he blazed between Sonora and Alta California, the rest of the presidio rode north sometime in 1776. Many settlers followed suit, seeking the protection of their neighbors and kinsmen. Tubac's population dropped to 40 families, or about 150 people (Dobyns 1959).

Those who remained complained bitterly about the loss of the garrison. In October 1777, the Apaches ran off all their horses and cattle. In November, the raiders even had the temerity to pasture their stolen horses near the beleaguered pueblo for three days while they stripped its fields of maize. At the same time, O'odham and non-Indian settlers at Tumacácori were diverting more upstream water onto their own fields, making it difficult for the Tubaqueños to irrigate their spring and summer corn crops (Dobyns 1959). In response to their complaints, Captain Pedro Allande, the new commander of the Tucson presidio, instructed them to return to Anza's system—one week of water for Tumacácori, one week for Tubac—during the dry season. He also stationed a small detachment of soldiers in Tubac to protect both the pueblo and mission (Dobyns 1959).

But even though Tubac lost its garrison, there was now a permanent community of Spaniards, *coyotes* (of Indian and Spanish blood), mulattoes, Yaquis, and Opatas living in O'odham territory. The San Luis Valley to the south had long been dominated by Spanish ranchers. Tubac provided an even stronger nucleus of non-Indian settlement. Tubaqueños and O'odham at Tumacácori shared the same irrigation water and herded their livestock together. Soldiers and settlers also served as godparents for O'odham children when they were baptized in the mission church. The power of the *santos*—the Catholic saints—was growing as fewer and fewer people listened during the four cold nights of the winter solstice to the Creation Story and the triumph of Siuuhu. Cultural differences blurred between O'odham and non-O'odham as Spanish Sonora leapfrogged north.

The Militarization of the Frontier

The goal of most missionaries, both Jesuit and Franciscan, was to isolate their neophytes from the corrupting influences of Spanish frontier society. Antonio de los Reyes, the conniving Franciscan reformer who became the first bishop of Sonora, promulgated a set of instructions that forbade Spaniards and *gente de razón* (people of reason; non-Indians) from living in mission communities even if they worked for the missionaries. Missionaries were instructed to keep their Indians from leaving the missions and to make sure that all males worked in mission enterprises two days a week in three shifts. Then, and only then, would they be allowed to depart for the mining camps in groups led by one of their *justicias* (deputies) (Kessell 1976).[2]

The militarization of the frontier eviscerated these desperate measures to recover mission autonomy. O'odham from the Upper Santa Cruz Valley had fought as allies and auxiliaries of Spanish soldiers and militia for nearly a century. In 1782, however, Teodoro de Croix, the first *comandante general* of the newly formed *provincias internas*, created a formal company of O'odham soldiers and assigned it to Mission San Ignacio. Known as the Compañía de Pimas or Compañía de San Rafael de Buenavista, the company consisted of eighty soldiers and four officers.[3] In 1783, sixty-seven of the soldiers were Pimas Altos whereas four were Pimas Bajos, six Opatas, and three Yaquis. The four officers were Spaniards. Sixteen of the O'odham were from communities along the Santa Cruz, including Tumacácori and its visita of Calabasas (Kessell 1976).

Paid 137 pesos a year, less than half (290 pesos) of what a non-Indian soldier made, these Indian soldiers reported to their commanders, not their missionaries. Along with the Opata companies at Bavispe and Bacoachi, they were professional soldiers, not auxiliaries, even though they at first fought on foot and carried bows and arrows. Reassigned to Tubac in 1787, the O'odham received regular wages and reoccupied the old presidio. Eventually they were issued firearms as well. The military became an attractive alternative to mission life and an avenue of upward mobility. In 1818, the O'odham lieutenant of the Tubac presidio even married his commander's daughter, a Spanish woman named Manuela Soto (Officer 1987). Class and race still mattered on the frontier, but the professionalization of the military weakened ethnic boundaries in communities like Tubac, where O'odham, Spaniards, coyotes, mulattoes, Yaquis, and Opatas lived side by side.

Indian presidios—Bavispe (1779), Buenavista/Tubac (1782), and Bacoachi (1784)—were only part of a series of innovations that represented a major change in northern New Spain's philosophy of conquest. Reyes pontificated that the Apaches could be conquered by more missionaries, not more soldiers. "The reduction of Indians and the possession of these kingdoms is the business of ministers of the Gospel," he argued (quoted in Kessell 1976:160). Spanish officials disagreed. "By the 1760s, when the marqués de Rubí made his tour of inspection, the military had become the dominant institution on the frontier," historian David Weber observes, "and war rather than 'pacification' had become the prevailing mode of subduing intractable nomads" (Weber 1992:214). Except for Alta California, where the Spaniards did not have to face mounted enemies like the Apaches or Comanches, the military, not the missionaries, hammered out the policies that determined Spanish-Indian relations for the rest of the colonial period.

Rubí's solution, embodied in the Regulations of 1772, was a uniform line of presidios—one hundred miles apart—stretching from Louisiana to Sonora along the thirtieth parallel. Hugo O'Conor rode ten thousand miles to turn Rubí's blueprint into reality. He moved presidios forward like chess pawns, particularly in Sonora: Tubac to Tucson, Fronteras to San Bernardino, Terrenate to an exposed and isolated position on the west bank of the San Pedro River. But the Apaches refused to fight a European war, slipping through this supposedly impregnable cordon of defense with impunity. In less than a decade, Teodoro de Croix returned San Bernardino to Fronteras and pulled Terrenate back to Las Nutrias a few miles southeast of its original location. The hard lessons learned by the Sonora Expedition against the Seris and Lower Pimas in the late 1760s had to be learned again by Croix. European military tactics did not work on the northern frontier. To defeat guerrilla enemies, you had to wage a guerrilla war (Weber 1992; Sheridan 1999).

War with England forced Spanish officials to adopt some French innovations as well. French traders in Louisiana had mastered the art of diplomacy and trade with the sophisticated Indian nations of the Southeast and the Caddoan peoples of Texas. Learning from these teachers, Spanish officials like Viceroy Bernardo de Gálvez, who had served as acting governor of Louisiana, developed a three-pronged strategy articulated in his famous Instructions of 1786. Coordinated offensives were to be mounted against the Indian enemies of the *provincias internas* (interior provinces), particularly the Apaches. At the same time, however, alliances were to be forged whenever possible. "The vanquishment of the heathen consists in obliging them to destroy one another," Gálvez noted with characteristic realpolitik cynicism.

Juan Bautista de Anza, governor of New Mexico from 1777 to 1787, was perhaps the most successful practitioner of this second prong. He negotiated peace treaties with the Comanches and Navajos while preserving alliances with the Utes and Jicarilla Apaches. That put enormous pressure on the Western, Chiricahua, Mescalero, and Lipan Apaches. By the 1790s, several thousand Apaches had settled in *establecimientos de paz*, or Apache peace camps, near presidios like Janos, Fronteras, and Tucson. There they received weekly rations of meat, corn, tobacco, and brown sugar in return for not raiding Spanish settlements (Weber 1992; Griffen 1988; Officer 1987). Institutionalized bribery—the third prong of Gálvez's peace policy—filled hungry bellies and gave Apaches an alternative to constant war. Although Apache raiding did not completely come to an end, a new era of relative peace and prosperity reigned—one negotiated by the state, not the Church. Missions no longer were instruments of expansion. Instead, their primary purpose for the rest of the colonial period was to maintain what historian Cynthia Radding (1997, 1998) calls the "colonial pact" between mission Indians and the Spanish empire.

The colonial pact and the Ascendancy of private property

According to Radding, the colonial pact was a moral compact, not a legal contract, between Indian communities and the Spanish Crown. "Indigenous community leaders understood this relationship as being regulated by a reciprocal arrangement through which Indians provided labor for Spanish enterprises and auxiliary warriors for military defense in return for protection from enslavement and the loss of village lands" (Radding 1998: 52–53). The corporate control of those lands, including floodplain *milpas* (irrigated fields), side-canyon *temporales* (runoff fields), and upland pastures, was the foundation of the colonial pact (Sheridan 1988b). Without their corporate land base, Indian communities would wither away.

After the Compañía de Pimas was stationed there in 1787, Tubac once again flourished. The few remaining O'odham families at Calabasas, in contrast, abandoned their visita and moved north to Tumacácori. As a result, Tumacácori and Tubac relied upon one another even more than they did when Anza commanded Tubac's non-Indian presidio. Father Baltazar Carrillo, Tumacácori's missionary, ministered to both communities. Tubac's payroll of 13,098 pesos provided Tumacácori's largest market for produce and livestock. O'odham from Tumacácori enlisted in the Compañía de Pimas and Indian soldiers from the presidial company married women from the mission. Meanwhile, more Spaniards and gente de razón settled along the Santa Cruz near both mission and presidio. Ties of compadrazgo—the relationship between godparents and parents of a child receiving a sacrament, particularly baptism—wove the communities together and pulled the O'odham deeper into the Hispanic world.

Tubac's second incarnation also set in motion the slow but inexorable commodification of land along the river. One of the goals of the Regulations of 1772 was to encourage civilian settlement around presidios. Vecinos who agreed to serve as militia and provide their own horses and weapons were to be given town lots and farmland (Moorhead 1975). In 1789, twenty-eight-year-old Toribio Otero applied for such a grant—the earliest land grant in Arizona. He received a town lot in Tubac and four plots along the Santa Cruz north of the pueblo. Otero was the brother of Ignacia Otero de Villaescusa, wife of Lieutenant Pedro Sebastián de Villaescusa, the first commander of the Compañía de Pimas. Otero's descendants retained control over the grant until the 1940s, long after the Spanish empire had crumbled and Arizona had become a part of the United States (Dobyns 1959; Officer 1987).

Unlike later Mexican land grants in Arizona, Otero's grant entailed restrictions and responsibilities. Otero had to reside on the grant four years before he received full title. During that period, he could neither alienate nor mortgage the land, nor could he ever sell it to the Church. He also had to build a house within two years and plant fruit trees or other useful plants. And, as stipulated in the Regulations of 1772, he had to maintain his own horses and weapons and serve in the militia when called to arms (Dobyns 1959). Otero's grant was a pact between him and the frontier society he was moving into, one designed to attract permanent settlers, stimulate agricultural production, create a civilian militia capable of defending its own community, and limit the economic power of the Church. Land had not yet been completely shorn of community obligations in the late eighteenth century.

Despite these restrictions and responsibilities, however, Otero's grant was more than a grant of usufruct, or use-rights. In 1804, a drought reduced flow in the Santa Cruz, forcing Otero to move downstream where water was more abundant. After he vacated his fields, several other vecinos from Tubac received permission from Tubac's commander, Manuel de León, to cultivate Otero's land. Three years later, Otero petitioned Alejo García Conde, intendant-governor of the Intendancy of Arispe, for the return of his fields.[4] If the present users were allowed to keep them, he asked that he be reimbursed for his improvements, including the diversion dam and network of *acequias* (irrigation canals) that brought water to his fields (Dobyns 1959).

García Conde ordered León to inform him of the situation. León responded that Otero had loaned part of his fields to another vecino during the drought. When the drought broke and flow in the river increased, León allowed another settler to farm Otero's land. Fields were to be tilled, not left vacant. But León also told the settler that Otero retained title, thereby confirming that Otero did indeed own the land. León recommended that Otero be paid for his improvements, implying that the vecinos currently cultivating the land not be evicted. Otero was living in Arispe at the time, where he taught school. His standing as a vecino in Tubac was therefore compromised, at least temporarily. Land was still a community resource, one that could be redistributed to other members of the community if the present occupier let it lie fallow or left the community. That ancient Iberian principle had not yet been obliterated by private property rights (Vassberg 1974, 1984).

García Conde tried to accommodate both custom and the new order. He recognized Otero's title but stated that the present cultivators could remain as long as they paid Otero for the improvements. Apparently, the other vecinos did not do so, because Otero and his heirs remained in possession of the grant. And even though the Otero grant was considerably smaller than later grants, it signified a new era in the occupation of the Upper Santa Cruz Valley. Other members of the frontier elite like the Romeros and Juan Bautista de Anza had established ranchos in the watershed but Otero was the first to receive formal title to his land. Legalism began to challenge custom. The ascendancy of private property championed by the Bourbon reforms was already rearranging the political and legal landscape in Sonora (Radding 1997; Río 1996).[5] Now those reforms were embedding themselves in the rich alluvial soil of the Santa Cruz floodplain.

The Tumacácori Land Grant

To protect themselves, the O'odham of Tumacácori decided to seek a grant of their own. In 1806, Governor Juan Legarra and four other O'odham from Tumacácori traveled to Arispe to present their petition to García Conde.[6] There they acquired the services of an attorney, Ignacio Díaz del Carpio, who drew up the petition itself. Díaz del Carpio stated that the "original instruments" allotting the lands of the mission had been lost. Consequently, neither the "limits" within which the original allotments had been made nor the mission's "legitimate and true holdings and boundaries" were known.[7]

The petition requested a *fundo legal*, the standard grant of municipal property that customarily comprised four square leagues or their equivalent depending upon the nature of the terrain.[8] In this case, the petition asked for four square leagues "of land most useful for the sowing of our fields." It also requested an *estancia*, or stock ranch, comprising "Guevavi and the lands pertaining to it" because it was "most suited and best accommodates our needs to maintain the livestock of our mission of Tumacácori and to achieve there the preservation and, better yet, the increase of those animals that are multiplying considerably." The petition went on to establish both a legal and moral claim to Guevavi by pointing out that it was one and the same mission—Guevavi used to be the cabecera of Tumacácori—and that Legarra was the "actual governor, one of the native sons of that same ancient pueblo of Guevavi." The O'odham delegation asked that a place called la Boca del Potrero be included in the "enunciated *sitios*" of the estancia as well.

The O'odham concluded by imploring García Conde to grant their requests "for the just relief and improvement of the community of natives of our republic" (*común de naturales de nuestra república*).[9] In this case, *común* referred not just to a community of people but a corporate community that persisted through time and held land and other resources in common (Wolf 1955, 1957, Menegus Bornemann 1980, Netting 1976, Sheridan 1988b). República signified the commonwealth of Tumacácori itself, implying that the community was politically and geographically distinct and self-governing.

García Conde granted the petition on December 17, 1806, and

directed Manuel de León to conduct the survey. He instructed León to "measure for those natives one league to each wind or four in whatever direction accommodates the best and most useful lands adjoining their pueblo without prejudice to third parties." He also told León to survey "una estancia de ganado mayor"—a stock ranch of large livestock—encompassing "at most two sitios in the place that best suits those natives."[10]

Two days before Christmas, Father Narciso Gutiérrez wrote another petition to León on behalf of Legarra and the "natives of the community" (*hijos del común*). This second petition stated that the mission of Tumacácori, "through the *rancho* of Guevavi, borders the *rancho* of the Romeros, whose boundary markers still exist beyond Yerba Buena, where a corral that used to hold the stock rounded up by our mission also stands.[11] Along Potrero [Creek], the measurements reached to the point of the cienega."[12] Gutiérrez went on to say that those sitios had been purchased "in past years with money from the common fund of the mission and its natives." The papers of those transactions had been in the possession of Don Manuel Carrera but could no longer be found.[13] The mission community had not pressed its claims in the past but needed to do so now because its "goods" (*bienes*)—in this case, livestock—were increasing. Gutiérrez implored León to "take the sworn statements of the Romeros, Apodacas, Baes, and other old settlers [*vecinos antiguos*] who know about what we have presented to you at the request of the governor and the natives of this mission of Tumacácori."[14]

León immediately honored their request. On December 24, seventy-year-old Juan Nepomuceno Apodaca, a resident of Santa Cruz who had an interest in the rancho of Buenavista, testified at Tubac. Apodaca confirmed the boundaries in Gutiérrez's petition. On the south the mission bordered the rancho of Buenavista, "known as the rancho of the Romeros." "In the direction of Potrero, the boundary markers were placed above the large cienega, and to the east, the boundary markers were placed in the ravine (*cajón*) of Sonoita on a very flat mesa." León asked Apodaca how he had acquired this knowledge. Apodaca responded that he had witnessed mission roundups, listened to the missionaries, and heard about it from the now deceased Manuel de la Carrera. Carrera had been "juez" (judge) for many years and held "the necessary documents" in his home concerning

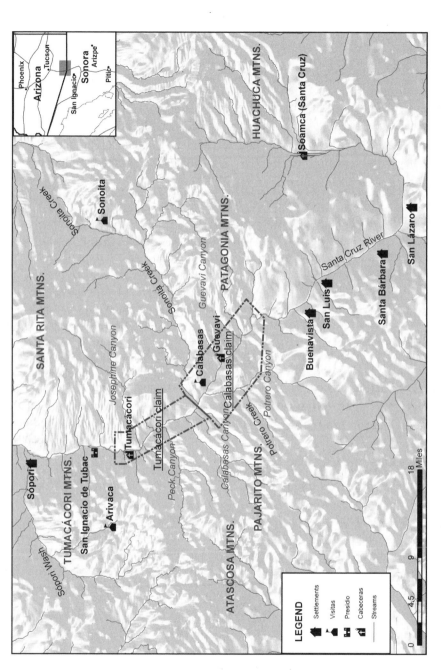

Map 2. The Upper Santa Cruz River Valley during late Spanish colonial times

LEGEND

Settlements
Visitas
Presidio
Cabeceras
Streams

ATASCOSA MTNS.

PAJARITO MTNS.

Potrero Canyon

Potrero Creek

Calabasas Canyon

Calabasas claim

Guevavi

Calabasas

PATAGONIA MTNS.

Guevavi Canyon

Buenavista

San Luis

Santa Cruz River

Santa Bárbara

San Lázaro

Tumacácori claim

Tumacácori

Peck Canyon

Josephine Canyon

Sonoita Creek

San Ignacio de Tubac

Arivaca

TUMACÁCORI MTNS.

Sópori

Sópori Wash

SANTA RITA MTNS.

Sonoita Creek

Sonoita

Sóamca (Santa Cruz)

HUACHUCA MTNS.

0   4.5   9   18
Miles

Phoenix
Arizona
Tucson
San Ignacio
Sonora
Pitic
Arizpe

"not only the lands of the mission but also those of the interested parties, those of the Romeros, Santa Bárbara, and other sitios found not only in the direction of Guevavi but also in the Potrero valley."[15]

On January 7, 1807, León interviewed the second witness, Juan Bautista Romero, sergeant of the Tubac presidio. Romero stated that from an early age, his now-deceased father had carried him around and shown him the borders between the mission and the rancho of Buenavista. Romero affirmed that the boundary markers of the mission stood above the place called Yerba Buena.

The third and final witness was eighty-year-old Pedro Baes, who appeared before León on January 9. Baes lived at the presidio of Tucson but had grown up on the rancho of the Romeros. He remembered the roundups that the mission used to hold along the boundaries of Yerba Buena. He remembered the Romeros riding in those roundups to gather their cows. Corporal Eugenio of the presidio of Tucson, whom Baes raised, learned how to read from the titles to those lands. Baes, who had been born at a time when Spanish ranchers were resettling the loop of the Santa Cruz in the 1720s—who had seen the arrival of the German Jesuits in the 1730s and who had survived the O'odham rebellion of 1751 and the intensification of Apache raids in the 1760s—remembered more details than either of the other two witnesses. The mission lands extended up Potrero Canyon to a place called El Pajarito above the large cienega. They extended up Sonoita Creek to a flat ridge. Fallen-down piles of rocks marked where one rancho began and another ended. In his mind's eye, the old frontiersman conjured up the geography of southern Arizona's first open range.

After taking Baes's testimony, León was ready to reconfirm that geography and enshrine its imaginary lines in new documents. León found no landowners who would be affected by Tumacácori's petition in any direction other than the presidio of Tubac, a league to the north. He therefore appointed his surveying crew, summoned Legarra and the other Indians of Tumacácori, and began to measure off the grant on January 14, 1807. The measuring instrument was "a well-twisted and waxed cord of sisal (*istle*)" fifty *varas castellanas usuales* long, each vara consisting of four *palmos* (ca. 8¼ inches).[16] One hundred lengths of this cord equaled a league (5,000 varas). Attached to two poles of "very hard wood," the cord was what the surveying party stretched across the landscape—through mesquite bosques and up and down arroyos and hills—as they laid out Tumacácori's mission lands.[17]

Legarra and the other Indians of the mission selected the cross in the mission's cemetery as the central point of the fundo legal. The documents do not mention whether this was a symbolic or a pragmatic choice. Catholics might have interpreted it as expressing the community of the living and the dead, even though the Hispanic residents of Tumacácori probably viewed the cemetery with ambivalence—a place where family members rested but where the dead held sway (Griffith 1992).

O'odham ideas about death were even more complex. They buried their dead—except for those killed by enemies, who were cremated to destroy enemy magic—and offered them food and water. But they also exhorted them to "Go! Do not come back. Your place is not here any longer. Your place is with the dead. Do not trouble us" (Underhill 1939: 189). Escorted by ancestors who took the shape of owls, the dead were supposed to travel through a gap to the east until they reached the town of the dead. But ghosts could return as owls and call for relatives to join them. The O'odham tore down the brush dwellings (*kis*) of the deceased to discourage ghosts from returning. They also considered cemeteries dangerous places. Anthropologist James Griffith notes that most O'odham cemeteries "are located outside the villages, with at least a potential source of running water separating them from human habitations. Even more than in the case of Mexican cemeteries, the dead are *there*, a real presence" (Griffith 1992:123). Designating an abode of the dead as the center of a living community's land base may have been an ambivalent act, or a decision made for the O'odham by their missionary.

Whatever its cultural significance, the cemetery cross was never intended to be the center of a standard "pueblo league" grant. Rather than measuring a linear league in each of the four cardinal directions, the surveying party accommodated the desires of the O'odham by marking off almost four linear leagues along the Santa Cruz River, where the Indians could cultivate fertile stretches of floodplain land. This adjustment had apparently been authorized by Juan Claudio de Pineda, governor of Sinaloa y Sonora from 1763 to 1770. With the establishment of the nearby presidio of Tubac, the O'odham of Tumacácori no longer could farm the floodplain of the Santa Cruz for a full league north of their mission. Pineda therefore gave them permission "to make up the difference in the direction that best suited them."[18]

With that in mind, the surveying party began by establishing the northern boundary of the grant, the only direction in which there was an existing settlement. Because Tubac was just a league away, the surveying party measured fifty rather than one hundred cord lengths downstream (north), erecting a pile of rocks at an elevated point (*divisadero*) in the valley between two big cottonwoods and a trail leading to a flat along the river. Then they returned to the cemetery and marked off 332 cord lengths to the south, which brought them to the arroyo (*cañada*) right next to the "sitio called Calabasas." Only eighteen of the four hundred allotted cord lengths remained, so the surveyors "scrupulously" marked off seven cord lengths to the east—from the riverbed, not the cross—which brought them to the foot of a hill in the middle of a mesquite grove. To the west, they measured eleven cord lengths, erecting the fourth boundary marker on a flat ridge at a place called Mesquite Seco.

That concluded the survey of the "*fundo legal y tierra de pan llevar*," a phrase that meant irrigated lands (Radding 1997:176). According to León, the survey included all lands that could be sown (*tierras de sembradura*) along that stretch of the Santa Cruz.[19] The O'odham had maximized floodplain, and minimized "unproductive" (*infructíferas*) acreage above the floodplain. The survey could have given them a fundo legal of four square leagues (17,264 acres). Instead, they selected a narrow ten-mile strip of the river with its bends and pockets of rich alluvial soil.

Next came the estancia. León asked his crew if they wanted to resume the next day, but they decided to press on. Legarra and the other O'odham wanted the stock ranch to encompass Guevavi to the south and the mouth of Potrero Creek to the north. They also wanted the estancia contiguous with the fundo legal.[20] León therefore commanded the surveying party to measure eighty cord lengths from the cairn marking the southern boundary of the fundo legal near Calabasas. The spot they reached—four-fifths of a league from the fundo legal's cairn—became the center of the estancia. Then, as daylight waned, the surveying party marked off another fifty-five cord lengths upstream (south). There, beyond the "ancient pueblo or mission of Guevavi" on a mesa that sloped down to a dry ford on the river, León ordered his crew to pile up the estancia's southern boundary marker as the short January day came to an end.[21]

They continued the next morning. Returning to the center of the estancia, the survey party headed east for twenty-seven cord lengths until it came to a rugged hill called San Cayetano. The hill's escarpment was too steep to scale, so León ordered the crew to place the boundary marker at its base. The O'odham requested that the remaining thirty-eight cord lengths—the linear length of each sitio de ganado mayor was one hundred cord lengths, or one league—be marked off in the direction of Potrero Creek to the west. León obliged. The final boundary marker was erected "on the slope of the highest hill overlooking Potrero." That concluded the survey of "both the tierras de pan llevar as well as the two sitios for the stock ranch." León dispatched the original documents of the survey to García Conde in Arispe that same day.[22]

But Legarra and the O'odham of Tumacácori had laid claim to more than the fundo legal and estancia. Their lawyer in Arispe, Ignacio Diaz del Carpio, presented a final petition "for the lands to the south of the ancient pueblo of Guevavi that border the rancho of the Romeros beyond the place of Yerba Buena, and in the direction of the north and valley of Potrero to the point above the cienega grande, as well as in the direction of the east to the ravine of Sonoita." The petition went on to say, "These sitios and lands belong to us through legal, public, and juridical purchase. And from the original or ancestral owners, since the time of the ex-Jesuits, our mission of Tumacácori, with its fund, has possessed them." "All the respective instruments of sale and transfer" had been in the possession of Manuel Fernández de la Carrera, who held power of attorney, but after he died, the Indians of Tumacácori had not been able to find the documents.[23] Legarra and the other O'odham officials declared that they urgently needed those lands because their livestock (bienes de campo) were steadily increasing and the estancia surveyed by León was not big enough to sustain them.

At this stage in the process, something curious happened. García Conde sent the petition and related documents to asesor Alonso Tresierra y Cano for a legal opinion. Tresierra recommended that the petition be granted. According to Tresierra, however, the Indians of Tumacácori claimed the "land occupied by the abandoned pueblo of Calabasas."[24] No mention was made of Guevavi. Kessell (1976) believes that Tresierra either confused Calabasas with Guevavi or that the documents were altered by later claimants—perhaps agents of Manuel María Gándara—who wanted the Calabasas lands.

Whether by mistake or subterfuge, Calabasas, not Guevavi, wormed its way into García Conde's decree. On March 31, García Conde granted the Indians of Tumacácori the lands they claimed to have purchased as well as the fundo legal and estancia surveyed by León. Those lands were to be "fully enjoyed and freely possessed according to their discretion and desire for their own advantage, in common and individually, and for the decent maintenance of the church."[25] Nevertheless, there were restrictions and stipulations. None of the lands could be alienated. On the contrary, they were to be "always recognized, respected, and maintained by the same republic and community of natives for their requisite affairs alone." Moreover, if "the Indians of the same nation" ever repopulated "the ancient and deserted pueblo de visita of that mission named Calabasas," its lands were to be restored.[26]

García Conde reiterated and expanded upon those stipulations in his official notice of the decree. "To the community [comunidad] of Indians of the pueblo of Tumacácori, located in the district of the Pimería Alta and the jurisdiction of the military barracks of Tubac, I concede, grant, and award to same natives, their children, heirs, and successors the indicated cultivated lands and lands for livestock with all their entrances, exits, usufructs, uses, right-of-ways, woodlands, pasture lands, waters, watering places and other [resources] corresponding to and encompassed within their measurements, demarcation, and boundaries." Then he enumerated the three stipulations. First, the grant was made with the understanding that it affected no other interested party. If anyone else had a claim, it had to be presented "in due time and in the proper manner." Second, if the abandoned pueblo of Calabasas was ever repopulated and reestablished, its fundo legal and estancia had to be restored. Finally, if the grant were ever abandoned for a period of "three complete and successive years," the grant lands could be awarded to the person who denounced them.[27] Possession was clearly tied to production. Title was not a legal abstraction but an active process. The lands had to be inhabited, crops had to be cultivated, stock had to be raised.

The O'odham and Roman Catholicism

And so they were. Despite Napoleon's invasion of Spain in 1808 and the outbreak of the wars for Mexican independence in 1810, Tumacácori flourished. In 1814, 147 Indians and people of mixed race inhabited the mission. Its treasury contained 5,654 pesos while its herd totaled 5,000 cattle, 2,700 sheep and goats, and 750 horses and mules. Downstream, Mission San Xavier ran 8,797 head of cattle. Stock raising in the Santa Cruz Valley had never been more extensive (Kessell 1976:228).

Religious instruction, in contrast, languished. Fray Juan Bautista de Cevallos, who conducted an inspection of the missions in 1814, reported that only two missionaries in the Pimería Alta understood the O'odham language. For their part, few O'odham spoke Spanish or knew much about Catholic doctrine, but they were fluent in the "superstitions of heathendom" (quoted in Kessell 1976:229).[28] More than a century of contact with Jesuits and Franciscans had transformed O'odham fields and provided them with animals to graze the uplands. By 1818, they were raising 150 fanegas of wheat but no maize (Kessell 1976:237). But their philosophical principles and religious beliefs remained largely O'odham, not Roman Catholic. The missionaries won their bellies but not their souls.

Cevallo's successor, Father Joseph Pérez, confirmed his pessimism. Of the O'odham at San Ignacio, Campos's old headquarters, Pérez wrote:

> With regard to Christianity, only God looks into the heart, but from outward effects I am of the opinion that only those who die before the use of reason are safe, and they are many. The grownups are full of superstitions, and no matter how the ministers work they do not believe them because they have more faith in their old medicine men.
>
> Often one catches them in the gatherings they hold in the caves of the hills, burns the implements of their superstitions, breaks their ollas, preaches to them, punishes them—but one observes no change

for the better. It is a peculiar thing that those who make the greatest false show of Christianity prove the most wed to their abuses. Great is their effort to hide these transgressions. Even when they are caught at them they do not want to confess their evil belief, saying only that the Spaniards have their way of curing and the Indians theirs, as they learned from their ancestors. (Quoted in Kessell 1976:236–37)

Pérez was describing a process of both compartmentalization and resistance. By the early 1800s, O'odham in the Santa Cruz Valley realized that violent rebellion was no longer an option. There were too many Spaniards and gente de razón to drive away or kill. The old dreams of restoring a pre-Hispanic past no longer resonated and another uprising like the 1751 revolt would have been suicidal. Instead, the O'odham employed what political scientist James Scott calls the "everyday forms of peasant resistance." Those included "foot dragging, dissimulation, false compliance, pilfering, feigned ignorance, slander, arson, sabotage, and so forth" (Scott 1985:29). Many O'odham understood more Spanish than they let on. By erecting a linguistic barrier between themselves and the Franciscans, they could avoid work or commit small acts of sabotage under the guise of linguistic misunderstanding. Above all, they could protect domains of their culture from Franciscan intrusion. The O'odham carefully hoarded their symbolic capital of ritual knowledge—much of which they believed was instrumental rather than symbolic—while at the same time manipulating the mission system to preserve their land base.

Religious ceremonies—for curing, to promote growth and renewal—were among the domains they shielded most carefully. "It is reasonably clear that the success of de facto resistance is often directly proportional to the symbolic conformity with which it is masked," Scott (1985:33) observes. Instead of rejecting the forms of worship the missionaries imposed, the O'odham carefully separated their rituals and systems of belief from the Catholicism they made a "false show" of embracing. The "gatherings they hold in the caves of the hills" must have included the saguaro wine ceremony to call the summer rains. The ollas Pérez and other missionaries tried to find and break would have contained the fermented syrup of saguaro fruit gathered in June when the fruits ripen. Rather than fermenting the syrup in the communal roundhouses (*o:las ki:* or *váhki*) they constructed before the Jesuits or Franciscans suppressed their ceremonies, however, the O'odham hid the ollas in caves and performed the saguaro wine feast far from prying eyes. To borrow a central metaphor from Scott, the "full transcript" of O'odham religious belief and practice was hidden—discursively, behind dissimulation and feigned ignorance, and spatially, in isolated canyons and caves (Scott 1985, 1990).

But not all of their outward acceptance of Catholicism may have been a "false show." Tohono O'odham Catholicism encompasses several "ways" (*himdag*)—"God way" (*Jios himdag, Jios* deriving from the Spanish word for God, Dios), "Saint way" (*Santo himdag*), and "Devil way" (*Jiawul himdag*, from the Spanish *diablo*).[29] Anthropologist Donald Bahr (1988:133) believes this O'odham "folk Christianization" emerged between 1850 and 1900 after the missionaries departed and much of the Papaguería became part of the United States. But even if Bahr is correct, the Tohono O'odham would have engendered this "self-Christianization" out of elements apprehended in the missions of the Pimería Alta: belief in the power of saints, particularly the reclining statue of San Francisco in Magdalena; incorporation of the Devil and the association of devils with ranches and mines; devotion to rituals tied to the Christian calendar that include both praying (often the rosary) and feasts.[30] These feasts are perhaps the most enduring examples of the Columbian Exchange. All the important foods, particularly beef and wheat flour, originated elsewhere. Native foods like corn, tepary beans, cholla buds, or mesquite pods are nowhere to be found (Bahr 1988).

Bahr (1988:142) argues that the O'odham initially paganized Christianity and then "Christianized their paganism, not by centralizing Jesus, but by centralizing a Jesus-like, murdered man-god figure," that is, I'itoi. Undoubtedly there were supple minds in the missions reinterpreting foreign supernaturals, rituals, and even healing practices into uniquely O'odham conceptions of the universe and the power that pervades it. Today the O'odham compartmentalize diseases into "staying sicknesses" (*ká:cim múmkidag*) and "wandering sicknesses" (*'óimmeddam múmkidag*) (Bahr et al. 1974). Staying sicknesses are caused by dangerous objects whose "ways" and "strengths" harm only O'odham. Only O'odham shamans can diagnose them and only O'odham curers can cure them. The Devil, or devils, is one such class of dangerous objects. The Devil way is a system of curing sicknesses caused by devils through songs taught by particular devils during dreams.[31] The O'odham appropriated a major Christian supernatural, pluralized him, localized him in the landscape, and incorporated him into their traditional system of healing.

Wandering sicknesses like chickenpox, measles, and whooping cough, in comparison, are caused by germs and can be treated by Western medicine (Bahr et al. 1974). Neither the O'odham or the Spaniards knew about "germs" in the eighteenth or early nineteenth centuries, yet the new and terrifying epidemics of smallpox, measles, and influenza that "wandered" from one community to another were apparently never categorized as "staying sicknesses." O'odham shamans and curers were powerless against them, so many O'odham turned to the missionaries and their new sources of supernatural power to protect themselves from these scourges. Such compartmentalization is evident in their reply to Pérez: "that the Spaniards have their way of curing and the Indians theirs, as they learned from their ancestors" (quoted in Kessell 1976:236–37).

The Construction of Mission Tumacácori

It is therefore ironic that the most monumental Catholic sacred structure in the Upper Santa Cruz Valley was erected at a time when the O'odham had learned to selectively hold Catholicism at bay. Fray Narciso Gutiérrez, who resided at Tumacácori from 1794 until his death in 1820, wanted to build a church as splendid as Fray Velderrain's Mission San Xavier to the north. He laid out its foundations in 1802. He even brought in craftsmen and laborers, swelling Tumacácori's population by 70 percent. Like San Xavier, San José de Tumacácori would be cruciform—the church itself a symbol of Christ's crucifixion, the central sacrifice of the faith—with two transepts spreading east and west just below the sanctuary. And it would be oriented north-south, with the convento stretching like a wing to the east. Roofed by domes and a barrel vault and constructed of fired brick, Gutiérrez's Tumacácori would be another architectural triumph proclaiming Franciscan organizational ability and religious zeal.

The historiography of the Pimería Alta bestows far more attention and adulation on the Jesuits than their Franciscan successors. Padre Eusebio Francisco Kino has become a regional culture hero. He is commemorated in statues and the traditions of rural people who attribute many agrarian innovations to him. His bones lie on display in a rotunda on the Magdalena plaza across from the region's most powerful supernatural, San Francisco (St. Francis Xavier), the reclining statue of a Jesuit saint. But nearly all the tangible symbols of missionary endeavor—the magnificent churches of San Xavier or Tubutama, the brooding ruins of Cocóspera —are Franciscan, not Jesuit, creations. The black-robed Jesuits wrote architectural prose, not poetry, out of the materials at hand—baked dirt bricks fashioned in wooden molds, ceilings of *carrizo* or saguaro ribs, rough-hewn mesquite vigas supporting earthen roofs—the width of their churches determined by the size of local trees. There were no master craftsmen to instruct the O'odham in the theory and practice of domes or vaults. Instead, everything was rectangles and right angles—frontier utilitarianism arising from an unschooled labor pool and a chronic shortage of funds. Simple decorations might grace the facades, but the only real flourishes came from the exquisite statuary, the gold and silver ornaments, the oil paintings set in gilt *retablos* (altar pieces) imported from the workshops of central Mexico or Spain.

By the late eighteenth century, however, Apache hostilities had diminished and the Franciscans had more opportunity to elaborate their ecclesiastical spaces. Bac and Tubutama were the first, then Caborca. Gutiérrez, in contrast, could never cobble together enough money to turn his vision into reality. Part of the problem, paradoxically, was the growing prosperity of the region itself. Herds along the Santa Cruz multiplied from the San Luis Valley to the Tucson Basin, glutting the regional market. Within five years, the price of a cow plummeted from ten to three and one-half pesos. Gutiérrez tried to compensate by encouraging the O'odham of Tumacácori to weave woolen blankets and serapes and to raise more wheat. He even managed to lay the foundations of his church with river boulders cemented with mud mortar. But once the wars for independence erupted, missionaries no longer received their annual stipend and royalist forces demanded forced loans. Gutiérrez died on December 13, 1820, alone, without benefit of sacraments, knowing his church was an empty shell (Kessell 1976).

His successors quickly scaled the vision down. The first—Fray Juan Bautista Estelric—enlisted master builder Félix Antonio Bustamente of Zacatecas and expunged the two vaulted transepts, sacrificing the cruciform design. Estelric also took a hard look at mission finances. Tumacácori's fields did not produce enough wheat to feed the 121 Indians and 75 gente de razón living there, so its only liquid assets were livestock, particularly its 5,500 head of cattle. Luckily, this was an era of expansion, as members of the community (*parcioneros*; shareholders) in Santa Cruz and powerful families like the Elías González petitioned the Spanish crown and the Mexican government for grants of land in southeastern Arizona (Hadley and Sheridan 1995; Officer 1987). Lieutenant Ignacio Pérez, whose family owned the mines at Cananea, had just applied for an estate encompassing seventy-three thousand acres in the San Bernardino Valley. Hungry for stock, Pérez, who was related to the Elías González, agreed to buy four thousand cattle from Estelric at three pesos a head: four thousand pesos when the cattle were delivered, two thousand pesos six months later, and the balance within a year and one-half. Suddenly funding for completion of the church seemed at hand (Kessell 1976).

But Estelric's relations with Pérez and the Elías González family quickly deteriorated. Pérez delayed his second payment, prompting an angry letter from Estelric. Soon afterward, Estelric's superiors removed him from Tumacácori because of his flagrant affair with a local woman. Construction halted once again as scandal swirled (Kessell 1976). Estelric's successor—pragmatic Fray Ramón Liberós—completed the project. First he put pressure on Pérez to pay his debt. When Pérez stalled, Liberós appealed to Rafael Elías González, who agreed to guarantee the balance. Then Liberós simplified the church even further. A dome crowned the sanctuary, but Liberós eliminated the brick vault over the nave. Instead, its roof would be flat and made of wood and mud. Moreover, sun-dried adobes replaced fired bricks as the walls rose, with bricks being used only to cap the walls or to serve as decorations. Finally, Liberós abandoned plans for the second of twin bell towers. San José de Tumacácori would never rival San Xavier.

Two years after Gutiérrez died, however, Liberós dug up his remains from the dilapidated Jesuit church and interred them and those of another priest beneath the floor of the new sanctuary on the gospel side.

Tumacácori was not finished but stars no longer glittered overhead. Gutiérrez's vision had finally materialized into a living church.

What the O'odham thought of the church remains unknown. It probably impressed them with its high ceiling and its thick walls, the dark interior illuminated by candles flickering off the images of virgins, saints, and Christs. But their sacred spaces were outdoors—holy places like the Children's Shrine near Ge Aji (Santa Rosa), where four children were sacrificed to keep the world from flooding, or features of the landscape like Baboquivari Peak (*waw kiwulk*; constricted hill), where I'itoi, creator of the O'odham, lives in a cave. Before the arrival of the missionaries, the O'odham had no public architecture other than communal roundhouses where adult males held their nightly councils. They carried out their important ceremonies like the saguaro wine feast or the *wi:gida* with its masked dancers under the desert sky.[32] The platform mounds of the Salt and Gila Valleys were distant cultural memories revived during the annual telling of the creation story—structures attributed to people their ancestors conquered, not their ancestors themselves.

The O'odham were a nonhierarchical people confronting a religion of profound hierarchy, and that hierarchy was embodied in every architectural feature and image in San José de Tumacácori. Roman Catholicism bounded its sacred space within walls, towers, and domes. Even though medieval Catholicism embraced processions and other rituals outside churches, those rituals culminated within the church itself, drawing the community of faithful into the consecrated interior. Once inside, the congregation stood or knelt in the nave. The priest, in comparison, presided in the sanctuary, which was set off from the nave by an arch and often raised. Finally, over the altar, was the tabernacle where the consecrated hosts—the body of Christ—were kept. Churches were therefore loci of tremendous supernatural power, arranged both horizontally and vertically in a series of levels and domains that metaphorically stretched from earth to heaven and back again. As Lefebvre notes, monumental buildings like Mission Tumacácori "mask the will to power and the arbitrariness of power beneath signs and surfaces which claim to express collective will and collective thought" (Lefebvre 1991:143).

Supernatural power was much more democratic among the O'odham. There were ritual practitioners—men and women who could diagnose and cure disease, divine the location of enemies, or control the weather—but no priests. "The northern Piman view of reality, very similar to the worldview of other cultures of the American Southwest, conceived of life as an organic whole with no strict separation of the spiritual and the material," observes linguistic anthropologist David Shaul (Shaul n.d.:103). Power was not conceived of in moralistic terms, nor did it flow from supernatural figures like God or the Devil. Instead, it was, in the words of anthropologist Ruth Underhill, "impersonal, a great unknown force pervading the earth. It can be harnessed (to use a modern illustration) like an electric current, and used for anything, good or bad. Like the current, it is dangerous to him who uses it if he is not wise" (Underhill 1938:13–14). The O'odham employed ritual, and ritual practitioners, to maintain and restore balance and well-being—in individuals, in communities, throughout the universe.

In his unpublished analysis of *doctrinas* (religious materials) translated into O'odham by Jesuit and Franciscan missionaries, Shaul argues that the restoration of balance, not redemption from sin, remained central to the O'odham as they confronted Catholic ritual. In a sense, the O'odham language acculturated Christian concepts, not vice versa. For example, doctrinas prepared in Nevome, the dialect of the Pima Bajo in south-central Sonora, and Altar Piman, the dialect of O'odham living along the Río Altar in northwestern Sonora, express the concept of "sin" as "not good deeds" or "ruined deeds" that produce "sadness," not guilt. "Blessedness," the opposite of "sin," is translated as "good-hearted" or "to feel good about oneself" (Shaul n.d.:123–34). According to Shaul, "'Sin' results from the momentary upsetting of one's balance; balance was presumably restored by ritual mechanics (saying the rosary, confessing, attending mass, etc.)" (Shaul n.d.:134). The eschatological struggle between good and evil—fundamental to Christian theology—was not part of the O'odham worldview and did not become so despite more than a century of missionary evangelism.

In all probability, then, the O'odham took what they wanted from their new church just as they did from the missionaries themselves. The images of the saints became sources of power with their own "way." Rituals like the rosary became new forms of oratory and song to maintain or restore well-being. Meanwhile, established rituals and ceremonies continued to be carried out, even if they had to be conducted outside the spaces controlled by missionaries.

Whatever their interpretation of San José de Tumacácori, the O'odham of the mission had less than a generation to enjoy it. Hispanic settlers were crowding in around them, carving up and acquiring legal title to more and more of the Upper Santa Cruz Valley. As financial support for the missions, presidios, and Apache peace program withered after Mexico won its independence from Spain, the Western and Chiricahua Apaches intensified their raids on O'odham as well as Mexican settlements and herds. By the mid-nineteenth century, Tumacácori would no longer be an O'odham community, and the Tumacácori land grant would no longer belong to O'odham hijos del pueblo. The mission dream was dying, and the ascendancy of private property was at hand.

4

Hispanic Settlement and the
Final Displacement of the O'odham

The transformation of the Upper Santa Cruz Valley from a social space where community and landscape were inseparable into an increasingly fragmented space of capitalist production culminated in the early twentieth century, when a fraudulent land grant held by speculators settled uneasily on the ashes of the mission dream. But the seeds of that transformation were planted much earlier, a decade before Kino began his evangelization of the Pimería Alta. Spanish settlers of the late seventeenth century never envisioned the speculative frenzy of the Baca Float or Rio Rico, but they did establish individual rather than communal claims to stretches of the Santa Cruz Valley. Those claims would gradually become more formalized, initiating the process of alienation that divorced land and water from any communal forms of ownership, obligations, or control. Rather than being an extension of community—a bundle of resources held in trust for generations of *hijos del pueblo*—the former mission lands became, first, a means of production for private gain, and then, in the words of geographer David Harvey, "a form of fictitious capital" (Harvey 1999:347) bought and sold for the future profits that could be wrung from it. The surreal yet seemingly inexorable metamorphosis from mission to pseudo-Spanish subdivision was underway.

cattle frontiers

The first to arrive was José Romo de Vivar, a prominent settler in the Bacanuchi Valley who served as the *teniente alcalde mayor* (lieutenant alcalde) mayor of Sonora. After silver was discovered in the mountains near Bacanuchi in 1678, Romo de Vivar established the ranch of San Lázaro at the bend of the Santa Cruz River. He also ran stock around Cananea and on the southern slopes of the Huachuca Mountains in the

San Rafael Valley (Kessell 1970; Officer 1987). Gold and silver may have lured him northward but Andalusian longhorns were his instruments of occupation on the virgin grasslands of the eastern Pimería Alta.

Romo de Vivar was not unique in that respect. Ranching and mining developed symbiotically in Sonora just as they did in Parral and other mining districts of northern New Spain (West 1949). Mine owners needed hide sacks to haul ore out of their shafts and tallow to light their tunnels. They also required meat, milk, cheese, and wool to feed and clothe their miners. Mines provided the largest market for the thousands of head of sheep, cattle, horses, and mules that thrived on Sonoran ranges. As early as the 1660s, cattle and mules were so abundant in the province they "hardly had a price" (quoted in West 1993:59). By 1685, the ranching frontier had reached as far north as the headwaters of the Río Sonora and Río Moctezuma, with six ranches in the Bacanuchi Valley and four in the Teuricache Valley. After glutting Sonoran markets, ranchers often had to drive thousands of head across the Sierra Madre Occidental to sell in the mines of Nueva Vizcaya, where raids by Tobosos and other Indians from the Bolsón de Mapimí had decimated local herds (West 1993).

In his magisterial *North American Cattle-Ranching Frontiers*, geographer Terry Jordan (1993) argues that Spaniards brought two very distinct stock raising traditions with them from the Iberian peninsula. The first and most extensive developed on the western Meseta, or interior plateau, where sheep outnumbered cattle by ratios of 10:1 to 25:1. There the powerful royal *meseta*, dominated by sheep raisers, controlled a system of driveways and common pastures that allowed huge herds of sheep to move from summer to winter pastures each year. Cattle raising, in contrast, was more localized and more confined. Calves were castrated to make them more docile and cattle were usually herded on foot by old men or boys. Rock-walled pastures segregated cattle from sheep, sharply curtailing their movement. Extremadura and Castile were not the cradles of the range cattle industry, as they are often depicted to be.

Instead, free-ranging longhorns and the mounted *vaqueros* (cowboys) who pursued them flourished in coastal salt marshes rather than on windswept plains. The largest and most important was Las Marismas south of Seville, where the Guadalquivir River and its tributaries formed an enormous delta of shifting channels that flooded twice a year. In late spring, after winter floodwaters began to recede, the famous Iberian longhorns drifted into the Andalusian marshlands to graze its bunch-grasses. Often uncastrated and rarely controlled, the longhorns remained there until fall, when mounted vaqueros employed *garrochas* (lances) to round up the semiferal beasts and drive them to higher ground before winter floods surged again. "Here, truly, was found the embryonic cattle frontier of Latin America," Jordan (1993:35) contends.

Immigrants from Andalusia, Extremadura, and Castile implanted both traditions as they colonized the many environments of Mexico. When Spaniards began moving up the north-central corridor of the Mesa del Norte, the huge central plateau between the Sierra Madre Occidental and Sierra Madre Oriental, wealthy sixteenth-century pioneers like Francisco de Ibarra ran herds of more than 100,000 cattle. But over time, the Meseta tradition prevailed. Sheep proliferated on degraded ranges, and the range cattle industry receded. In some areas of Nuevo León, around outposts like Monterrey, Camargo, and Laredo, sheep outnumbered cattle by 20:1. Cattle did not dominate the ranges of the north-central corridor —Chihuahua, Coahuila, Nuevo León, Nuevo México—until the cattle boom of the late nineteenth century (Jordan 1993).

The Pacific Coast corridor, in comparison, provided a series of environments better suited to the Andalusian tradition. As Nuño de Guzmán slashed his way through the densely settled lowlands of Nayarit and Sinaloa, slaving forays and Old World diseases decimated Indian societies. Depopulation cleared the way for cattle, which thrived much better than sheep in the lowland thorn forests. Cáhita-speaking Indians north of Culiacán halted Spanish expansion for half a century, but when the push northward resumed in the 1580s, both Spanish frontiersmen and missionaries from the Society of Jesus established herds of cattle wherever they settled. In San Felipe y Santiago, the most important community on the advancing northwestern frontier, pioneer Jesuit Andrés Pérez de Ribas noted that its Spanish inhabitants "are sustained by many cattle ranches, as well as cultivated fields, from which the surrounding mining camps get supplies, for which they pay the residents of the villa in silver" (Pérez de Ribas 1999 [1645]:193). The great military leader of the expansion— Captain Diego Martínez de Hurdaide—even employed cattle as instruments of conquest. When rebel Tehueco Indians from the Fuerte River took refuge among the Tepahue Indians living along a tributary of the Mayo River, Martínez de Hurdaide drove a herd of four hundred cattle into battle with him to feed his forces (Pérez de Ribas 1999 [1645]:239).

If longhorns were the quintessential frontier animals, able to fend for themselves for much of the year, sheep required a greater level of domesticity. The Jesuits introduced these *ganado menor* among their mission neophytes. "To correct their barbarousness, which made them indifferent toward covering themselves, the priests brought sheep to Sinaloa so that the Indians could weave mantas of wool with which to clothe themselves," Pérez de Ribas wrote of the Yaquis, whom he missionized in 1617. "Once they are made to wear clothing they get to like it so much that some become obsessed with it. Indeed, in order to obtain clothing, or more precisely, to be elegantly dressed, they sometimes leave their homes and women and travel fifty leagues or more to [find] work outside the province" (Pérez de Ribas 1999:375).

Historian Cynthia Radding (1997) argues that as the competition for Indian labor intensified in colonial Sonora, Indians exacted payments of cloth from their priests in return for remaining in the missions. Locally produced cloth came from only three sources—cotton, wool, and, less commonly, the fibers of agave. Sheep raising was obviously critical to meet the growing regional demand.

Nonetheless, available figures demonstrate that sheep never overwhelmed cattle as they did east of the Sierra Madre Occidental. At the mission of San Pedro de Aconchi on the Sonora River, for example, there were 1,681 head of sheep and 1,475 cattle in 1749, a nearly equal ratio (Radding 1997:77). By 1778, Sonoran missions possessed more cattle than sheep (15,101 cattle vs. 11,669 sheep, with 1,213 pairs of oxen) (Radding 1997:92–93). Mission inventories for 1794 reveal that sheep once again outnumbered cattle (2,721 cattle, 357 pairs of oxen, 4,021 sheep), but never by the 10:1 or 20:1 ratios found in Nuevo León (Radding 1997).

The missions of the Santa Cruz Valley ran both *ganado mayor* and *ganado menor*. Kino seems to have introduced more cattle than sheep. By 1701, there were three hundred head of cattle at San Luis de Bacoancos near where Rancho Buenavista would later be established and one thousand head at Mission San Xavier. During the second half of the eighteenth century, both Guevavi and Tumacácori possessed more sheep than cattle. By the end of the colonial period, however, the number of cattle rose sharply at both Tumacácori and Bac (5,000 and 8,797 in 1814, respectively). In 1804, the presidial community of Tucson also ran more cattle (4,000) than sheep (2,600). These figures mirror a similar ratio farther south at the presidio of Pitic (modern Hermosillo) (5,000 cattle and 3,422 sheep in 1804). And since cattle were worth five pesos and sheep only one peso, cattle were far more important to the regional economy (Radding 1997:218).

Early settlers and the open Range

Regardless of the mix of cattle and sheep, stock raising in the Santa Cruz Valley remained a dangerous frontier enterprise whose transaction costs rose or fell depending upon relationships with surrounding Native Americans. The massacre at Mototicachi in 1688 sparked an O'odham rebellion that drove early ranchers like Romo de Vivar from the Santa Cruz. Three decades later, Spanish frontiersmen once again settled the great bend of the river they called the San Luis Valley. Perhaps the first were Diego Romero and his four sons, Nicolás, Cristóbal, José, and Ignacio, who founded the Santa Bárbara and Buenavista ranches. Members of the Grijalva, Figueroa, Bohórquez, Tapia, Gallego, Núñez, Fernández, Amésquita, Samaniego, Rivera, Villela, Barba, Ortega, Durán, and Covarrubias families soon followed (Garate 2003).

These early pioneers were jacks-of-all-trades, running stock, raising wheat and corn, prospecting the surrounding mountains. Gold and particularly silver mining provided much of Sonora's wealth, but the daily realities of most settlers' lives revolved around crops and cattle, not ore. With the exception of the strange silver strike at Arizonac in 1736, mining operations in the Pimería Alta were small, dangerous, intermittent endeavors—a handful of silver mines in the Arivaca area, a gold mine near Guevavi, a mine or two in the Santa Ritas (Garate 2003; Officer 1987, 1991). None of these mines lasted long or produced much ore. The Romeros and their neighbors lived on the edge of the Apachería, their lives and modest fortunes constantly threatened by Apache raids. The mountains of the far horizon may have promised riches beyond compare, but the dangers usually overshadowed the dreams.

Nevertheless, a frontier elite began to emerge with connections to capital and political influence beyond the region. One such enterprising individual was Juan Bautista de Anza the Elder. Anza was Basque, one of the many *vizcainos* drawn to northern New Spain. Born in Hernani, Spain, in 1693, he sailed for Mexico in 1712 when he was nineteen years old. By 1718, he had reached Sonora, where he owned and operated a store and silver mine in the mining *real* of Aguaje south of modern Hermosillo. Characteristically, the other two mine owners in Aguaje were Basques as well. Two years later, Anza and four Basque companions founded the *real de minas* of Tetuachi in the upper Sonora River drainage south of the mission of Arizpe. They dedicated it to Nuestra Señora de Aránzazu, a manifestation of the Virgin Mary who appeared to a Basque goatherd in 1447. Anza was a young and ambitious entrepreneur, but his success was due in part to a close-knit network of Basque merchants and miners that extended from Mexico City to the mining camps of Sonora and Nueva Vizcaya (Garate 1995, 2003).

Extremadurans, Castillians, or Andalusians may not have found the Sonoran landscape surpassingly strange. To Basques like Anza, however, the heat and relentless aridity must have been oppressive, at least at first. They had been born and raised in cool, green mountain country, not the scorched, thorn-ridden terrain from which they now wrested a living. Yet these Basque pioneers put down some of the deepest roots in the region. They may even have bequeathed the state of Arizona its name—Arizonac, "the good oak"—after the camp in the oak woodlands southwest of modern Nogales where the slabs and chunks of silver were discovered in 1736 (Garate 1995, 2003).

Their rise to prominence was rapid but hard fought. The vizcainos won their first major political battle in 1726. For years, they had protested the corruption of Gregorio Alvarez Tuñón y Quirós, captain of Fronteras presidio, the only military garrison on the Sonoran frontier. For years, Tuñón y Quirós had thwarted their parries and continued to use presidial soldiers as his own private labor force (Polzer and Sheridan 1997; Garate 2003). But when Brigadier Pedro de Rivera Villalón arrived on his inspection of the northern presidios, Tuñón y Quirós could not bribe or dissemble his way out of a final reckoning. Rivera removed him and replaced him with Anza (Naylor and Polzer 1988).

In the decades that followed, Basques like Anza, Bernardo de Urrea, Antonio de Vildósola, and, most illustrious of all, Juan Bautista de Anza the Younger, dominated the frontier military. They commanded the presidios of Fronteras, Altar, Pitic, and Tubac (Polzer and Sheridan 1997). They married into one another's families and supported one another in political squabbles and military campaigns. And even though they pursued their military duties with vigor and competence, they invested heavily in ranching and mining as well. The Pimería Alta was in many respects a Basque political and economic frontier.

Again, Anza the Elder served as the prototype. Because the San Luis Valley was filling up with settlers, many of them Basque, Anza pushed deeper into the Pimería Alta, founding four ranches north of the modern international border. Manuel José de Sosa and his wife Nicolasa Gómez de Silva operated Rancho Guevavi near the mission of the same name. Opata Indian Juan Núñez and his mulatta wife, María Rosa Samaniego, ran Rancho San Mateo at the confluence of the Santa Cruz and Sonoita Creek, near the O'odham community of Toacuquita, later the mission visita of Calabasas. Juan Manuel Bais and his wife, María Josefa de Luque, administered Rancho Sópori along Sópori Wash. The historical record is mute about who took care of Rancho Sicurisuta near modern Peña Blanca Lake (Garate 1995, 2003).[1]

Bound by his duties at Fronteras, Anza never resided at any of these ranches. Instead, he entrusted them to family friends and employees like Sosa and de Luque, who epitomized the tenacity of these early pioneers. María Josefa remained on the Sópori for the rest of her life, surviving the death of her first husband in 1747 and the Pima rebellion in 1751. As late as 1775, the year Anza the Younger led his colonizing expedition to San Francisco Bay, she served as *madrina* (godmother) at a baptism at Mission Tumacácori. Her daughter, María del Carmen del Bais, married Juan Nicolás de Sosa. They gave birth to Manuel Vicente de Sosa, who acted as *padrino* with his grandmother at the baptism in 1775 (Garate 2003).

The ever-expanding ties of marriage and *compadrazgo,* sanctified by the sacraments of Catholicism at Mission Tumacácori, were the bonds that wove pioneer families together along the Santa Cruz. If you have ever visited the rural communities of Sonora, you can smell the mesquite smoke rising from their fires and see their simple, flat-roofed adobe homes and their mesquite corrals. You can also follow the calendar of their year—sowing wheat in November, corn and beans in March and July, celebrating the saint's days, the hard, good life of planting and weaning broken all too often by the murder of a neighbor, the theft of a horse herd. These were the people who became the first Hispanic settlers of Arizona—vecinos, padrinos, madrinas, employers, allies, and occasionally enemies of the O'odham.

Some of these early frontiersmen may have obtained *títulos de merced*—legal grants of land—from the Spanish Crown, which claimed all land in the Indies. If so, those titles have not yet surfaced. More likely, they simply occupied the open range, coming to agreements with their neighbors about where their ranch ended and their neighbors' began (West 1993). Because ranges were not fenced, all the ranchers in an area would periodically join together to round up cattle and horses, brand calves and foals, and cull animals they wanted to slaughter or sell. During periods of relative peace with the Apaches, cattle roamed freely, the extent of their range determined by the availability of water. Herds of goats and sheep, in contrast, foraged under the watchful eyes of *sabaneros* (herdsmen) to keep them from falling prey to coyotes, wolves, mountain lions, black bears, and grizzlies.[2] But as Apache raids intensified, even cattle and horses had to be corralled each night to prevent them from being stolen. The open range spasmodically contracted as hostilities escalated.

water and the common Good

During most of the colonial period, insuring access to water was more important than establishing fixed boundaries to grazing land. Water determined where and when you could plant, and where your livestock could forage. Hispanic stock raisers undoubtedly dug out springs and excavated shallow wells in the floodplains of rivers and arroyos, such as the famous La Canoa north of Tubac. But they did not yet possess the technology to construct the artificial water sources that would have allowed them to distribute their herds evenly across the landscape. The centrifugal windmill was not invented until 1854 and not adopted by Arizona ranchers until the 1870s. During the eighteenth and most of the nineteenth century, animals as well as crops relied on the Santa Cruz and its tributaries.

Spain was much better prepared than other European colonial powers to confront scarce water resources. Much of the Iberian peninsula was semiarid. Irrigation was an ecological imperative. Each successive wave of invaders, from Romans to Moors, contributed its own hydraulic technologies and social organizations of technology to the agrarian landscape. As the Spanish kingdom emerged from the crucible of the Reconquista, its legal system drew from Visigothic, Islamic, and especially Roman traditions to balance the rights of powerful interest groups with those of individuals and communities.

That system was first codified in 1275 under the direction of King Alphonso X. Called Las Siete partidas, that visionary endeavor served as the model for subsequent codifications in the New World, particularly the monumental Recopilación de leyes de reynos de las Indias, published in 1681 (Meyer 1984). A common thread running through these and other examples of Spanish jurisprudence was the importance of community and the social contextuality of property. Private property was acknowledged and protected, but it was also bounded by obligations and restrictions designed to protect the well-being of the larger community within which private property was embedded.

Nowhere is that embeddedness clearer than in Spanish water law. According to the Siete partidas, everyone could use flowing surface water for certain purposes—drinking, bathing, fishing, navigation, and transport. Irrigation and industrial uses of water, in contrast, had to be carefully regulated "because it would not be wise that the benefit of all men be hindered by the interest of some individuals" (Partida 3, Título 28, Ley 8, quoted in Meyer 1984:118). Moreover, land grants in both Spain and the Americas did not necessarily entitle landowners to water. Unlike English common law, Spanish jurisprudence did not recognize riparian rights. The owner of land along a river could use river water for domestic purposes and for watering livestock. Without an additional bundle of rights, however, the landowner could not divert the river onto his or her fields (Meyer 1984).

In other words, land and water were not always conjoined. Spanish law recognized different classifications of land, some with explicit or implied water rights, others without (Meyer 1984). There were at least three types of farmland. *Tierras de pan sembrar* were dryland fields. *Tierras de pan coger*, usually called *tierras de temporal* in northern New Spain, referred to fields dependent upon runoff from seasonal rains. In Sonoran agricultural communities today, *temporales* are usually located along normally dry arroyos. When floodwaters surge down them, farmers channel the temporary flow onto their fields (Sheridan 1988b). *Tierras de pan llevar*, in comparison, were irrigable and conveyed irrigation rights. Land classified as *labores* also included water rights (Meyer 1984).

Grants of grazing land, whether they were *sitios de ganado mayor* (ca. 4,338 acres) or *sitios de ganado menor* (ca. 1,928 acres), did not transmit irrigation rights unless specified. When they did, they usually designated only a small portion of the grant as labores that could be irrigated. Surface water, scarce in Spain and even scarcer on the northern frontier of New Spain, had to be carefully allocated to insure that private access did not dry up the fragile web of acequias (canals) upon which communities depended.

Subsurface water, in contrast, was a private resource shorn of most communal obligations. Springs, water holes, or wells that originated on a grant belonged to the landowner, who could draw as much of the water as he or she wanted as long as it was not used maliciously to harm a neighbor. Rainfall may have been common property but French scientist Pierre Perrault did not demonstrate the causal relationship between precipitation and springs until 1674. Even then, according to historian Michael Meyer, "the discovery never quite caught up to Spanish jurisprudence" (Meyer 1984:120). Medieval anachronisms—that surface flow and subsurface aquifers were unrelated, that great underground rivers fed springs and wells—continued to distort water policy in both the United States and Mexico well into the twentieth century.[3]

The Bourbon Reforms and the Privatization of Property

We have already seen that Mission Tumacácori and the presidio of Tubac joined together to manage the surface flow of the Santa Cruz for irrigation. We also know that mission Indians, presidial soldiers, and civilian settlers ran their livestock together, at least when Anza the Younger was captain at Tubac in the 1760s and 1770s. The threat of Apache raids made the survival of community essential to the survival of individuals. Frontier conditions prevented the privatization of the landscape for most of the colonial period.

We may never know how many cattle and sheep Hispanic frontiersmen grazed along the Santa Cruz. The chronicles of the time simply did not record the details—numbers, rotation, seasonality—that would allow us to venture some educated guesses about the ecological impact of these early herds. All we can do is speculate about where they ranged. Spanish longhorns were notoriously hardy, able to go several days without water in the summer and longer in the winter. During times of peace, the *corrientes* must have spread up the Santa Cruz and its tributaries into the foothills of the Santa Ritas, San Cayetanos, Tumacacoris, Atascosas, and Pajaritos. During times of danger, however, settlers must have tried to keep them close to the relative security of mission and presidio. The bottomlands of the Santa Cruz, Sonoita Creek, Sópori Wash, Josephine Canyon, Peck Canyon, and Portrero Creek must have endured relatively heavy and sustained grazing pressure beginning in the 1720s. Grazing in the uplands, in comparison, must have been sporadic, periods of expansion punctuated by long periods of contraction when few animals survived predation or Apache raids. Southern Arizona never seems to have supported the vast herds of feral cattle reported for southeastern Texas during the colonial period (Jackson 1986).

Nor do we know much about where and how the pioneers marketed their livestock. Were the cattle slaughtered for hides or driven to mining centers? Were the sheep sheared for local consumption or regional demand? Tubac absorbed some of these animals. And there were the pulses of demand created by the discovery of silver at Arizonac in 1736 and the gold rush at Cieneguilla in the 1770s. But all we have are fragmentary snapshots. Contested frontiers rarely yield the quantitative data necessary to do anything more than sketch economic or environmental history in broad strokes.

What we do see, however, is the expansion of cattle ranching toward the end of the colonial period. Presumably this represented a response to expanding markets. The growing militarization of Sonora provided one outlet, because soldiers needed to be fed. At the same time, the success of the Apache peace policy reduced raiding and lowered the transaction costs of livestock production, with the Apache peace camps providing an additional market for beef as well. In the Santa Cruz Valley, both missions and private ranchers increased their herds and dreamed of pushing the cattle frontier eastward onto the grasslands of the San Pedro and San Bernardino Valleys.

The late colonial period also was an era when the cumulative effects of the Bourbon reforms succeeded in reshaping the legal, philosophical, and administrative landscape of Sonora. With few exceptions such as Pedro de Perea's colony of Nueva Andalucia, missionaries from the Society of Jesus spearheaded the conquest of Sonora in the 1600s.[4] Skirting the dry coastal plains of the Sonoran Desert, the Jesuits followed river valleys northward, establishing missions in Lower Pima, Eudeve, and Opata communities. They never were able to exclude Spanish settlers from those valleys, but missions established by the Jesuits in the seventeenth century enabled some Indian communities to maintain control of their communal land bases into the nineteenth and even twentieth centuries. Their resilience—and the slow development of regional markets—prevented the rise of huge landed estates in Sonora and the Pimería Alta (Sheridan 1988b; Radding 1997).

After the Jesuits were expelled, however, Bourbon reformers like José de Gálvez weakened the economic and political influence of the Franciscans while expanding the professional military. Enterprising frontier families—the Anzas, Urreas, Vildósolas, Elías Gonzálezes, and others—used military careers to consolidate their positions as leaders of regional elites. Meanwhile, the non-Indian population was increasing, generating greater demand for land as well as Indian labor (Sheridan 1992). Customary use rights to the floodplain and open range gave way to private property rights as the missionaries lost power and the Indian communities lost ground.

A variety of legal instruments formalized these rights, growing ever more supple as land became more of a commodity and less an extension of community. The *merced*—or royal land grant—remained the foundation, reflecting the primacy of the Spanish Crown as the fundamental land-holding entity in the Americas. As the great Spanish legal scholar Juan de Solórzano Pereira wrote in his *Política Indiana*, "Except for the lands, meadows, pastures, woodlands and waters that by particular concession and grant have been made . . . all the rest of this land, and especially that which is yet to be plowed and cultivated, is and should be of the Royal Crown and Dominion" (quoted in Meyer 1984:118).[5]

Nonetheless, there were other instruments as well. One was the *composición*, which legalized customary use rights to land. Another was the *denuncia* (statement of claim) and subsequent public auction of lands considered either *realengos* (public domain held in the name of the king) or *baldíos* (vacant lands). Radding (1997) notes that non-Indian settlers resorted to both the composición and denuncia with ever-increasing frequency in the eighteenth and early nineteenth centuries. Vecinos employed composiciones to obtain title to farmland along the floodplains. They utilized denuncias to secure *sitios de ganado mayor* or *ganado menor* on *agostadero* (non-arable grazing lands) in the foothills and surrounding mountains (Radding 1997).

Accelerating this trend toward privatization was the decentralization of authority to distribute land. At first, the Spanish Crown limited that authority in New Spain to the Council of the Indies, the viceroy, and the *audiencia de México*. By the late eighteenth century, however, governors, intendants, and even presidial commanders could issue grants (Radding 1997). This greatly facilitated the process of land transfer. It also increased the power of regional officials and regional elites.

Land Grants in the Santa Cruz Watershed

In the Santa Cruz Valley, Spanish officials authorized only three grants before Mexican independence: to Toribio Otero north of Tubac in 1789; to the O'odham of Mission Tumacácori in 1807; and to Agustín Ortiz of Tucson in 1812, who received two sitios de ganado mayor in Arivaca.[6] The sons of Agustín Ortiz—Tomás and Ignacio—petitioned for another grant in September 1820, but it was not approved until December 1821, several months after the end of Spanish rule. This was San Ignacio de Canoa—four sitios de ganado mayor (4 square leagues; about 17,354 acres) along the Santa Cruz River north of Tubac. Ignacio Elías González, commander of Tubac presidio, surveyed the grant himself (Willey 1979).[7] Elías González was Tomás Ortiz's father-in-law. In 1827, he and Nepomuceno Félix received their own grant of San Juan de las Boquillas y Nogales along the San Pedro River.[8]

San Ignacio de Canoa was clearly intended to be a stock raising operation. The starting point of the survey was the famous "paraje de la Canoa," where Spanish travelers had stopped to water for more than a century. But wayfarers did not quench their thirst from a flowing stream. According to Elías González, the Santa Cruz Valley between Tubac and Mission San Xavier "contains a wide plain, through the middle of which runs the river of this military post [Tubac], although without water, because of its many sandy places which interrupt its flow at a distance of half a league from the post" (quoted in Willey 1979:154). La Canoa was the only location along this dry stretch where water could be obtained from shallow wells. This was the place where Juan Bautista de Anza and 239 other people bedded down on October 23, 1775, their first night out of Tubac en route to California. "Here during most of the year water is found, although it is not running, but by a little digging in the sand enough can be had for whatever is required," Anza noted in his diary (Bolton 1930, 1:6). Later owners of San Ignacio de Canoa developed artesian wells, irrigated wheat fields, and even created a five-acre artificial lake, but the Ortiz brothers did not have the technology to turn Canoa into an irrigated oasis (Willey 1979; Hadley 2000). They wanted it for livestock, not crops.

Before Tomás and Ignacio Ortiz could take possession, however, they had to outbid Fray Juan Vañó of Mission San Xavier. Canoa had originally been appraised at thirty pesos a sitio because it had no flowing water. Backed by Tucson vecinos, who probably wanted San Xavier's huge herd to move south, Vañó escalated the bidding as high as fifty-two and one-half pesos. The Ortiz brothers dropped out, then changed their minds and offered sixty-two and one-half pesos per sitio. That was more than Vañó was willing to pay (Kessell 1976).

Clearer than anything else, the Canoa bidding war revealed that land had finally become a commodity in the Santa Cruz Valley. During the relative peace of the early nineteenth century, both missions and settlers were running out of room as they expanded their herds. Moreover, members of the regional elite, particularly the Elías González family, decided that the grasslands of southern Arizona were a good place to invest capital from their ranching and mining operations in the Sonora River watershed. Customary use rights withered as competition for rangeland increased. As a result, more and more of southern Arizona was carved into private estates with formal surveys and fixed boundaries.

This process of privatization soon encroached upon the mission lands of Tumacácori. In the spring of 1821, while the war for independence was still raging to the south, León Herreros filed a denuncia to "the place called Sonoita, the very ancient pueblo of the Indians, abandoned because of the incursions of the Apache Indians." A resident of Tubac like the Ortiz brothers, Herreros requested "two sitios of lands," which he promised to stock "with cattle and horses" because he had no lands on which to maintain his *bienes de campo* (livestock).[9]

Once again, Ignacio Elías González directed the survey. One of the members of the survey party was Manuel de León, who had measured the Tumacácori grant fourteen years earlier. Herreros wanted the center of the grant to be "the same walls of the aforementioned Sonoita."[10] These may have been the ruins of the church Father Francisco Pauer built in the 1750s. Kino had established Los Santos Reyes de Sonoita as a visita of Guevavi in the late 1600s. Captain Coro and more than five hundred other Sobaipuris from the San Pedro Valley withdrew there after a dramatic battle with Jocomes, Sumas, Mansos, and Apaches in 1698 (Sheridan n.d.). By 1821, however, Sonoita had been abandoned for nearly fifty years, the black hole into which the Sobaipuri frontier collapsed.[11] Located in a pass between the Santa Rita and Patagonia mountains, Sonoita was where the descendants of the avengers of I'itoi took desperate refuge until they either fled or died.[12]

The surveying party under Elías González began its work in the heat of late June 1821. They marked off sixty-three cord lengths to the northeast, ending just upstream from a spring (*ojo de agua*) at the foot of a small hill. Then they returned to the center—the ruins of visita—and continued down the canyon until they had measured off "more or less two sitios." Because of the "cragginess" and "roughness" of the bordering mountains, however, the surveyors only extended the boundaries of the grant twenty-five cord lengths on each side of the canyon. The canyon twisted and turned so much that the surveyors often could only measure partial cord lengths. You can sense Elías González' fatigue and frustration in the pages of his report.[13]

The next day, the surveyors completed their work. Starting from the center, they paced off 312 cord lengths down canyon to the south, ending at a spot along the *camino real* to Tubac called the "first ford" (*primer vado*). To the right, facing west, they measured twenty-five cord lengths and erected a pile of stones as a boundary marker on a small hill above a little valley. To the left, they did the same, ending at the first of two small hills known as Los Cuates (The Twins). "Rancho de Calabazas," which belonged to Mission Tumacácori, lay about two leagues to the southwest. North of the grant was no-man's-land "through which the enemies [the Apaches] enter and leave to commit their robberies and hostilities." Because of all the contortions of the terrain, Elías González and his crew were only able to survey one and three-fourth sitios. Herreros registered the tract "for the raising of cattle and horses and the cultivation of *tierras de pan llevar*."[14]

Treasury officials in Arizpe appraised the Sonoita grant at sixty pesos per sitio because it had "flowing water and some *aveones* [*sic*; perhaps *peonías*] of tierra de pan llevar."[15] Unlike Canoa, Sonoita included lands that could be irrigated, so it implicitly conveyed water rights as well. During the requisite thirty days of public notice, no one contested Herreros' denuncia or the survey, and no one offered more than the appraised 105 pesos. Herreros took possession of the grant, although he was not issued formal title until May 15, 1825. Fittingly, that was *el día de San Isidro*, the feast day of Saint Isidore of Madrid, the patron saint of farmers.

Tumacácori's missionary, Fray Juan Bautista Estelric, apparently did not concern himself with Herrero's occupation of the old visita. Perhaps he was too busy trying to collect the twelve thousand pesos owed the mission by Ignacio Pérez, who had purchased four thousand head of cattle from Tumacácori to stock his new San Bernardino grant. Or perhaps his ever-more scandalous involvement with the young woman who attended him diverted his attention. Less than a year after Herreros' denuncia of Sonoita was approved, however, his cattle were breaking into the fields of O'odham farmers near the junction of Sonoita Creek and the Santa Cruz. Fray Ramón Liberós, Estelric's more vigorous successor, protested. He pointed out that the Tumacácori grant included rangelands owned by the Jesuits as well as the fundo legal along the floodplain and the estancia at Calabazas (Kessell 1976).

Herreros and Liberós resolved their differences by agreeing to a boundary at Loma de las Cruces, perhaps the first of the two hills called Los Cuates where Elías González had erected a cross at the end of his survey.[16] Herreros could still run cattle down the canyon of Sonoita Creek, but O'odham from Calabazas were the only ones who could farm its lower stretches. Four years later, Herreros sold the Sonoita grant itself to Mission Tumacácori (Kessell 1976).

But that sale was never recorded in Arizpe, a fatal oversight in an increasingly legalistic environment. Soon afterward, in December 1827, the federal congress signed a law expelling Spaniards from Mexico. Officials of the short-lived state of Occidente (Sonora and Sinloa) removed Liberós and most other Spanish Franciscans the following spring. In 1831, Herreros, old and illiterate, sold Sonoita a second time to Joaquín Elías for two hundred fanegas of wheat (Kessell 1976). Elías may have been the brother of Rafael, the owner of the San Rafael del Valle land grant, and Ignacio and Eulalia, owners of the Babocómari grant.[17] The O'odham families farming Sonoita Creek were no match for the powerful Elías clan. With the departure of Liberós, they had lost their last vigorous champion in a world that valued paper titles more than living communities.

The Demise of Mission Tumacácori

You can feel the noose tightening around mission lands. By the end of the 1820s, the Elías González family owned much of the upper San Pedro watershed and its tributary, the Babocómari. Along the Santa Cruz itself, Francisco José de Juvera of Arizpe denounced the Romeros' abandoned ranch of Buenavista just south of Tumacácori's boundaries. He died before the grant was confirmed, but his widow, Josefa Morales, received title to four sitios in 1831 (Officer 1987). Seven years later, Joaquín Astiazarán received the largest Mexican land grant of them all—El Sópori—31^7/$_8$ sitios (137,583 acres) running east of the Santa Cruz from Tubac to Mission San Xavier (Wagoner 1975). Astiazarán never occupied the grant, but the landscape of the Santa Cruz watershed was now a sea of private claims surrounding Mission Tumacácori.

In November 1832, Fray Rafael Díaz reported that there were nineteen adult males at the mission, suggesting a total population of perhaps eighty to one hundred people.[18] For the next decade, they eked out a living as drought withered their crops, Apaches stole their livestock, and settlers in Tubac appropriated more and more of their dwindling resources. Before he left, Fray Liberós appointed O'odham Ramón Pamplona as mission administrator. Pamplona did a good job managing Tumacácori's affairs, but after he resigned, a series of settlers—Tomás Ortiz, Buenaventura López, José Sosa—took over. Tensions escalated, particularly with Sosa, whom the O'odham accused of abuse and embezzlement. In 1830, the mission possessed about eight hundred sheep and four hundred cattle, most of them feral because the Apaches prevented mission cowboys from rounding them up. By 1834, one hundred of those sheep bore Sosa's brand. Meanwhile, Ignacio Ortiz leased two of Tumacácori's four wheat fields, and Esteban Velos held the wool-weaving concession (Kessell 1976). Slowly but surely, the mission was being picked apart.

Two decades later, there was no more meat on its bones. In May 1841, Francisco González applied for Los Nogales de Elías—7^1/$_2$ sitios and 2 *caballerías* (32,763 acres) of oak grassland southwest of Tumacácori.[19] Ignacio Pamplona, Tumacácori's O'odham governor, accompanied the survey crew to identify the landmarks of the mission's estancia. González asked Pamplona if he could borrow Tumacácori's title to "learn the boundaries" (quoted in Kessell 1976:296). The O'odham of Tumacácori never got the title back.

No one knows if it was collusion or happenstance, but two years later, the Tubac *juzgado de paz* (justice of the peace) filed a report on Mission Tumacácori that set the stage for its final alienation. President Antonio López de Santa Anna was toying with the idea of inviting the Jesuits back into northern Mexico. Sonoran authorities therefore wanted to know if any of the missions possessed "ancient Jesuit *fincas* [properties], houses known as community houses, cultivated fields known by the name of mission fields, the state in which they are found, the value of the rents they produce, their investment value, as well as whether some of these fincas have also been sold and with what authority." The Tubac justice of the peace responded negatively. He informed Joaquín Quiroga, the sub-prefect of San Ignacio, that "in this mission or pueblo of Tumacácori, no fincas of the Jesuits or houses called community houses have been known, only the houses of the convento in which the missionaries of said pueblo used to live, whose structures had been situated there in 1821 along with its chapel."[20]

The justice of the peace went on to say that most of the buildings "had fallen to the ground and those that remain threatened [to become] ruins" except for the church. There was one mission field to the south and another across the river about half a league away. "Both are found to be unfenced and abandoned since 1828, full of mesquite and other shrubs, because of a shortage of water in the river. There is only enough water for some few Indians to irrigate their meager sowings."[21]

The litany of desolation went on. Of rents or houses or irrigated fields there were none. The ranch and irrigated fields (*labores*) of Calabasas, along with the mission and estancia of Guevavi and the *sitio* of Sonoita, "are cast away, without buildings or goods, without a single cow except for the few wild ones that have fled to the mountains."[22] Santa Anna's chimerical Jesuits were not going to have much to come back to in the Santa Cruz Valley.

Instead, *caudillo* (military strongman) Manuel María Gándara snatched Tumacácori out from under the O'odham. Gándara was the most powerful man in Sonora in the mid-nineteenth century, seesawing in and out of power as he fought José de Urrea and then Ignacio Pesqueira for control of the state. An opportunist allied with centralist forces in Mexico City, Gándara often joined forces with Yaquis, Mayos, and Opatas fighting to retain control over their communal lands. That led his opponents to accuse him of inciting a "war of the castes." But Gándara was no friend of the O'odham. After the so-called Papago War broke out in the western Pimería Alta, Gándara organized an expeditionary force that cornered the Tohono O'od-ham in a canyon at the foot of Baboquivari Peak, I'itoi's sanctuary, on January 14, 1841. He and his men killed more than forty O'odham and recovered over one thousand head of livestock (Officer 1987).[23] Gándara's commitment to the colonial pact depended upon whether he needed Indians on his side or out of the way.

In Tumacácori, he clearly wanted them gone. On April 16, 17, and 18, 1844, the treasury of the Department of Sonora advertised a public auction in Guaymas, Sonora's most important seaport more than two hundred miles away from the mission. On the block were "the arable lands and lands for the raising of cattle and horses of the four leagues of the fundo legal of the deserted pueblo of Tumacácori and of the two sitios of the estancia of the same [Tumacácori] at the points of Guevavi, Portrero, Cerro de San Cayetano, and Calabazas, whose areas, borders, boundary markers, and *colindantes* (adjacent areas) are delineated in the corresponding official survey carried out in the year 1807 by the commissioned land surveyor, Don Manuel de Leon." The auction took place at noon on April 18 after the requisite three days of public notice. "In loud and clear voice," the auctioneer, Florentín Baldizin, repeated the lengthy legal description of the property. Then he said, "Going once! Going twice! Going three times! That it be declared! That it be declared! That it be declared! How good! How good! How good that it goes to Señor Don Francisco Alejandro de Aguilar!"[24]

Aguilar, a prominent Guaymas merchant, was the sole bidder. He also was Gándara's brother-in-law. Acting as Gándara's agent, Aguilar bought the mission and its lands—shortened throughout the rest of the title to "the four leagues of the fundo legal of the deserted pueblo of Tumacácori and the two sitios of its estancia of Calabazas, and other adjoining points" —for five hundred pesos.[25] Tumacácori was declared to be "deserted" despite the fact that the parish priest from San Ignacio continued to perform both baptisms and marriages at the mission between 1844 and 1848 (Kessell 1976). But no O'odham were present in Guaymas to contest Aguilar's claim. Even though they did not know it yet, the beleaguered little community at Tumacácori had finally been severed from the land that had sustained them long before Kino had ridden into their valley.

Aguilar orchestrated the land grab under the provisions of an 1837 law and 1842 decree that allowed abandoned mission lands to be sold at auction to benefit Mexico's depleted public treasuries as long as their value did not exceed five hundred pesos.[26] They were part of a series of laws passed after Mexican independence between 1828 and 1842 that represented the culmination of the Bourbon reforms. Their foundation was Decree 89, which allowed vecinos to hold office in Indian communities and only recognized landed property with legal title. Decree 89 and the decrees that followed put a torch to the colonial pact. First, they subordinated the limited political autonomy of Indian communities to Mexican municipal authorities. Then they eviscerated Indian control over their communal land bases. These decrees enabled regional elites to denounce Indian lands as "vacant" and purchase them at auction (Radding 1997). Tumacácori was no anomaly. The land grab just seemed more blatant because it took place so far away.

It also seemed to be part of a pattern of deliberate expansion by one faction of what historian Stuart Voss (1982) calls Sonora's "urban notables." Gándara and his family owned the haciendas of Bamori and Topahue near Ures on the lower Sonora River. He married the daughter of Victor Aguilar, a prominent hacendado at San Miguel de Horcasitas, the old colonial capital of the *provincias internas* (northern New Spain). If you look at a map of Sonora, you see that Ures and Horcasitas, on the lower San Miguel River, are almost parallel to one another, forming the wings of a "V" that come together at Hermosillo, which was developing into Sonora's most important commercial center. Ures, Horcasitas, and Hermosillo were the cities that served Sonora's most dynamic agricultural region, a region where hacendados like the Gándaras and Aguilars had already wrested the rich bottomlands of the Sonora and San Miguel rivers away from the Lower Pimas.

Gándara acquired Tumacácori through Francisco A. Aguilar, Victor Aguilar's son, who had established himself as a merchant in Guaymas, Sonora's gateway to the world. An even wealthier and more prominent Guaymas merchant was Manuel Iñigo Ruiz, also from Horcasitas. Iñigo was Gándara's biggest financial backer throughout his civil wars with Urrea and Pesqueira. Gándara therefore represented the political and economic interests of an axis of merchants and landowners that ran from Ures and Horcasitas to Hermosillo, and from Hermosillo to Guaymas. Through their control over Sonora's most important port, and Gándara's intermittent control over the state government in Ures, the axis monopolized much of Sonora's trade for three decades (Voss 1982).[27]

Another member of this network was Joaquín Astiazarán. A Spanish immigrant, Astiazarán married the daughter of Iñigo, who received the hacienda of La Labor between Horcasitas and Hermosillo as part of her inheritance (Voss 1982). There Astiazarán served "the best of wines" and lived in a red brick house surrounded by gardens laid out "in the English style," according to an English visitor (Ward 1829 2:446). In 1837, just as Gándara was rising to power, Astiazarán acquired the immense Sópori land grant. The Guaymas-Horcasitas-Ures elite apparently saw the Santa Cruz Valley as an arena for growth, a good place to invest some of their capital in livestock and land despite the danger from Apaches.

Their relationships with the Arizpe-based Elías Gonzálezes were more problematic. The Elías González family had staked their future and their fortunes on the northern frontier, fighting Apaches for control over the mineral wealth and rich grasslands of northeastern Sonora and southeastern Arizona. By the 1840s, three of the brothers—Simón, José María, and Ignacio—were third-generation military commanders, keenly aware that frontier conditions had deteriorated dramatically since Mexican independence. They therefore favored a federalist rather than a centralist national government, convinced that they were better prepared to confront Sonora's problems than politicians and bureaucrats in Mexico City. Their longstanding alliance with the powerful Almada family of Alamos and their federalist sympathies occasionally aligned them against Gándara and his allies (Voss 1982; Officer 1987).

Those rivalries never had a chance to express themselves in southern Arizona, however. Bankruptcy and civil war kept Mexico from taking effective action against the Apaches, who penetrated deeper and deeper into Sonora and Chihuahua. By the outbreak of the war with the United States in 1846, all the Arizona land grants except "deserted" Tumacácori had been abandoned because of Apache hostilities (Officer 1987).

Two years later, in October 1848, Lieutenant Cave Johnson Couts, an officer with Major Lawrence Graham's dragoons, rode down the Santa Cruz Valley. "The churches in this valley are remarkable," he wrote. "At Tumacacori is a very large and fine church standing in the midst of a few common conical Indian huts, made of bushes, thatched with grass, huts of most common and primitive kind. . . . This church is now taken care of by the Indians, Pimas, most of whom are off attending a jubilee, or fair, on the other side of the mountain."[28] Couts went on to say, "No Priest has been in attendance for many years, though all its images, pictures, figures &c remain unmolested, and in good keeping. No Mexicans live there at all" (Dobyns 1961:58–59).

In other words, a decade after the Ortiz family had abandoned Arivaca and Canoa, and the Elías Gonzalezes their land grants in the San Pedro Valley, a small community of O'odham remained at Tumacácori. There they continued to cultivate their crops and care for the church and its santos even though the land now belonged to Gándara. Ironically, the presence of a large Apache Manso community at Tubac enabled them and the vecinos at Tubac to cling to the Santa Cruz floodplain (Officer 1987). But their days were numbered as well. A census taken early in 1848 revealed that Tubac's population had declined to 249, most of them Apache Mansos. Then, on December 9, 1848, Apaches attacked Tubac and Tumacácori, killing nine at the presidio. The Tubaqueños decided to abandon their community and move north to the relative security of San Xavier and Tucson (Officer 1987).

The few O'odham at Tumacácori had no choice but to join them. They carefully removed the santos from their church and packed up the vestments and other sacred items, carrying them to safety at San Xavier, intending to return as soon as Apache hostilities subsided.[29] For a century and a half, O'odham at Tumacácori had resisted or selectively adopted what the Jesuits and Franciscans offered them, gradually evolving their own interpretation of Catholic rituals and beliefs. They had absorbed the Sobaipuris, fought the Apaches, secured and lost legal title to their lands. But soon another people and another government with no appreciation for communal traditions would hold sway along the Santa Cruz. The mission dream flickered for a little while longer in exile at San Xavier, but Tumacácori would never again be the center of a communal space that held land and water in trust for future generations. The mission church would become an icon of a vanished era, divorced from the people who built and worshiped in it. The landscape itself would become the object of litigation and speculation, commodified in ways the Sonoran notables could never have envisioned. Gándara had betrayed the O'odham at Tumacácori. The government of the United States eventually declared that betrayal illegal but gave the land to speculators instead.

PART II

Landscapes of Fraud

5

Early Anglo Speculation and
the Tumacácori Land Grant

When the last O'odham families left Mission Tumacácori in December 1848, most of the Santa Cruz Valley was a ghost landscape of abandoned ranches and deserted settlements. The O'odham had retreated to the riparian oasis of Bac. Hispanic Arizona had taken refuge behind the presidial walls of Tucson. Western Apaches haunted the surrounding mountain ranges, descending on moonlit nights to pick over the bones.

But the biggest change hovered beyond the eastern horizon like a line of thunderstorms massing over the mountains. For the last three years, the mother country had fought a losing battle against Manifest Destiny and the westward expansion of the United States. The Treaty of Guadalupe-Hidalgo ceded California, New Mexico, Texas, and Arizona north of the Gila River to the United States in 1848. The ratification of the Gadsden Purchase six years later added southern Arizona and the Mesilla Valley of New Mexico. Even though Arizona would remain a contested frontier for three more decades, it now belonged to a restless young entrepreneurial giant, not a bankrupt, demographically stagnant backwater wracked by civil war.

Speculation—in canals, railroads, mines, and land—was the adrenaline that propelled the United States across the North American continent. Arizona was too arid to attract the land rushes that drew thousands of pioneers to the midwestern heartland. In mining circles from San Francisco to New York, however, legends of Jesuit gold and Arizonac silver shimmered like the blue lights Mexican prospectors believed emanated from buried treasure. The lure of precious metals, not cheap land, enticed the first speculators to Arizona. Land grants like Tumacácori and Arivaca were secondary considerations—pawns in the chess game of competing mining claims and hyperbolic promotion. Meanwhile, submerged beneath the legal wrangling, O'odham ties to Tumacácori would be forgotten as speculators scrambled to raise the capital they needed to finance their ventures on an isolated and dangerous frontier.

The California Gold Rush

Southern Arizona might have remained a part of Mexico if James Marshall had not seen flecks of yellow at the bottom of the American River while supervising the construction of Sutter's mill in northern California. When the flecks assayed as gold, Californians, Sonorans, and Oregonians flocked to the "diggings." By 1849, the California Gold Rush was sucking "argonauts" from Maine to Chile into its maw (Billington 1956). That year, at least twenty thousand traveled the so-called Southern Route, a network of trails converging on the Colorado River at Yuma Crossing (Etter 1998). The two most popular trails intersected the Santa Cruz River at the presidial communities of Santa Cruz or Tucson. North of the Tucson Basin, the gold seekers followed the dry riverbed to the Pima villages along the Gila. Hispanic Arizona was no longer a forsaken finger of Sonora but a way station to the promised land along the Pacific Coast.

Since that promised land now belonged to the United States, the U.S. government negotiated with Mexico to buy the Southern Route as well. Those negotiations culminated in the Gadsden Purchase, the smallest of five plans presented to Mexican president Antonio López de Santa Anna. Northern interests thwarted Southern designs to build a transcontinental railroad along the thirty-second parallel. Nonetheless, the California Gold Rush set in motion two profound transformations. First, it effectively spanned the continent. In a world hungry for specie, gold provided a powerful incentive for thousands of argonauts to leave their homes in the East and brave the Great American Desert. The United States was now a transcontinental, if deeply divided, nation.

Second, the discovery of gold in California in 1848—and in Australia in 1851—triggered a revolution in global finance. As Western Europe and the eastern United States made the transition from mercantile to industrial capitalism, the need for capital led to rapid expansion of systems of credit, generating paper money such as bank notes. Money in a capitalist system had to function both as a medium of circulation and as a measure of value—a fundamental contradiction according to Marx. During the nineteenth century, industrializing nations struggled to resolve this contradiction in order to avoid the devastating panics that followed speculative periods of expansion. One tool was the gold standard, whereby banks, at times regulated by a central national bank, had to maintain a certain ratio of gold to paper currency.

England, the leading industrial nation during the nineteenth century, adopted the gold standard in 1816 after the successful conclusion of the Napoleonic wars (Cochran 1971). Because of the dramatic drop in taxes during the postwar period, an estimated forty to fifty million pounds of British capital became available for investment each year (Myers 1970). Millions of those pounds found their way to the United States, where they financed canal and railroad companies and a host of other ventures. With the centralized Bank of England guaranteeing the soundness of British currency, the British became the biggest creditors of U.S. banks and London the money market center of the world (Myers 1970; Cochran 1971).

Until the amount of gold in circulation increased, however, other nations like the United States hesitated to follow suit. As geographer David Harvey (1999:306) points out, "The simplest way to regulate the quality of money in society is to tie it to some universally accepted money commodity like gold. The disadvantage is that the value of social labor is tied to the condition of concrete labor in gold production." In other words, the adoption of the gold standard limits the world's supply of money to the global production of gold. Because gold was relatively scarce in the first half of the nineteenth century, voraciously entrepreneurial nations like the United States expanded the amount of money in circulation by relying on irredeemable paper currency or wedding themselves to a bimetallic standard of silver and gold. Different currencies of wildly different solvencies may have slowed the circulation of capital in a capital-hungry world, but the universal acceptance of the gold standard would have paralyzed it.

But then California and Australia injected huge new quantities of gold into the world's financial markets. The amount of gold mined in the United States alone rose from $889,000 in 1847 to $50 million in 1850, hovering annually between $40 to 50 million for the next several decades (Cochran 1971). Germany adopted the gold standard in 1871. The United

States effectively did the same in 1879 when it declared Civil War green-backs redeemable in specie, even though official adoption did not come until 1900. During the late nineteenth century, the strongest and richest nations in the world created an international monetary standard that greased both the imperialist expansion of Western Europe and the global penetration of capital beyond imperial boundaries. The ramifications of the Gold Rush rippled on long after the last of the forty-niners had crossed jungle, desert, or plain.

Those transformations may have been little more than glimmers in the imaginations of the argonauts. Nevertheless, most agreed with news-paper editor John L. O'Sullivan, who proclaimed that it was "our national destiny to overspread and to possess the whole of the continent which Providence has given us for the development of the great experiment of liberty and federated self-government entrusted to us."[1] As they trudged down the Santa Cruz, the gold seekers were as convinced of their superi-ority over Mexicans as Spaniards had been of theirs over the O'odham.

What those early travelers observed confirmed their racial and cul-tural stereotypes. To most of them, the Santa Cruz Valley was a landscape of natural abundance but cultural desolation—one haunted by mute ar-chitectural reminders of the past. H. M. T. Powell, who sketched Mission Tumacácori in 1849, mused that "the monks had every accommodation to make life comfortable, as they usually contrive to do." Tubac, on the other hand, was "a mere pile of tumble-down adobe houses. The church has no roof. . . . It was not worth the trouble of sketching" (Powell 1931:142).

Boundary commissioner John Russell Bartlett was even less compli-mentary when he ascended the Santa Cruz in July 1852. "The houses of Tucson are all of adobe, and the majority are in a state of ruin," he wrote. "No attention seems to be given to repair; but as soon as a dwelling becomes uninhabitable, it is deserted, the miserable tenants creeping into some other hovel where they may eke out their existence" (Bartlett 1854 2:296). Proceeding upstream, Bartlett described the community of San Xavier del Bac as "truly a miserable place, consisting of from eighty to one hundred huts, or wigwams, made of mud or straw, the sole occupants of which are Pimo Indians, though generally called Papagos. In the midst of these hovels stands the largest and most beautiful church in the State of Sonora" (Bartlett 1854 2:298).

When he reached Tubac, Bartlett could scarcely summon the energy to take up his pen at all. "In a book of travels in a strange country, one is expected to describe every town he visits; but as for this God-forsaken place, when I have said that it contains a few dilapidated buildings, and an old church, with a miserable population, I have said about all" (Bartlett 1854 2:304). He did not even bother to visit Mission Tumacácori, although he noted, "Its beautiful and picturesque church showed finely among the thick grove of trees by which it is inclosed" (Bartlett 1854 2:308). Out of such impressions sprang the myth of a romantic mission past contrasted with a squalid and shiftless present.

Bartlett went on to generalize about Anglo-Saxon superiority in words that sound eerily similar to Frederick Jackson Turner's frontier thesis half a century later:

What a marked difference there is in Spanish and English colonization! Here the zealous Missionary preceded all others, planting the cross along with the banner of his country. Then commenced the work of baptizing; and as soon as a sufficient number of converts had been made, a fertile valley was chosen, and a church erected with buildings to accommodate some hundreds. Next came the colonists, whose main efforts were to support the Mission and its priests. The Anglo-Saxon pioneer entered the wilderness with his axe, his plough, and his rifle; and after he had erected his own dwelling, the mill and blacksmith's shop rose up. Lands were brought into cultivation, the mechanical arts flourished; and when the colony became large enough and rich enough to support a pastor, a church was built. For the results of the two modes of colonization, compare Texas, New Mexico, California, Sonora, and Chihuahua, before the three first became annexed to the United States, and the States of Ohio, Indiana, Illinois, and Michigan. The latter had attained more wealth, more population and importance, and had done quite as much towards promoting Christianity in the first ten years after their settlement, as the former States had in two centuries. (Bartlett 1854 2:299–300)

Land speculation and westward expansion

Both Bartlett and Turner left out an essential figure on the nineteenth-century frontier. Before the first farmers broke the sod or the first lumbermen felled the trees, huge grids of the West belonged to speculators who created imaginary "financescapes" of town sites and credit networks. As one nineteenth-century French political scientist noted, "The striking and peculiar characteristic of American society is, that it is not so much a democracy as a huge commercial company for the discovery, cultivation, and capitalization of its enormous territory" (Boutmy 1891:127–28). The image of the "Anglo-Saxon pioneer" entering "the wilderness with his axe, his plough, and his rifle" masked the enormous imprint of British and U.S. capital (Bartlett 1854 2:299–300).

During the 1800s, that capital gnawed at every corner of the North American continent like a ravenous but unpredictable beast. It moved in bursts, or "business cycles," periods of manic speculation followed by panics, bankruptcies, and depressions.[2] In the process, the scramble to invest the profits of the China trade, the India trade, or later, manufacturing, transformed what historian William Cronon (1991) calls the "first nature" of natural ecosystems into a "second nature" of commodity production, transportation networks, and capital flows.

Indians, who had been shaping their own "second nature" for millennia, were exterminated or pushed westward—a brutal North American variant of what Marx termed "primitive accumulation." In some cases, the extermination was direct. In other cases, Old World epidemic diseases decimated Indian populations long before the pioneers arrived (Denevan 1992). Depopulation and "Anglo-Saxon" Indian removal programs transfigured North America into a "wilderness" of natural wealth—the pine forests of Michigan and Wisconsin, the fertile soils of Illinois and Iowa, the grasslands of the Great Plains. The land policies of the federal government then converted that wilderness into free or nearly free land, stimulating a series of rushes unparalleled in their exuberance and greed. In 1800, the minimum coast of federal land was set at $2 per acre. In 1820, the price was lowered to $1.25 per acre. Sales were by auction, which often had raucous and occasionally violent atmospheres. Contrary to Turner's unilineal evolutionary progression from Indian to fur trader to rancher to farmer to manufacturer, the westward expansion of the United States was more like a roller-coaster ride of booms and busts fueled by the seizure of Indian lands, the exploitation of labor, the pulses of paper credit, and the manipulation of land laws designed for very different ends.

From the crucible of the Revolution to the reclamation movement of the early twentieth century, the public lands were a political battleground between speculators and agrarian visionaries. Visionaries dreamed of a republic of Jeffersonian yeoman farmers cultivating their own lands and creating orderly communities on the advancing frontier. Even before the Founding Fathers defined American democracy, however, land speculation burned at the core of the American soul. Enormous grants from the British Crown gave individuals and companies title to vast tracts of land along the Eastern seaboard during the 1600s. By the mid-1700s, even larger grants drew speculators west of the Allegheny Mountains. One of the most ardent was George Washington. Washington dabbled in the Ohio Company, which received a grant of 500,000 acres south of the Ohio River. He also secretly hired an old friend, Captain William Crawford, to find and preempt other choice lands on the western frontier (Sakolski 1932).[3]

After the United States won its independence from England, land speculation fanned beyond the boundaries of Anglo-American settlement like prairie wildfire. There were three great booms followed by three devastating crashes before the Civil War: 1818–19, 1835–37, and 1850–57 (Gates 1996). "Everyone was imbued with a reckless spirit of speculation," wrote Levi Beardsley, a New Yorker caught up in the 1830s boom. "The mania, for such it undoubtedly was, did not confine itself to one particular class, but extended to all. Even the reverend clergy doffed their sacerdotals, and eagerly entered into competition with mammon's votaries, for the acquisition of this world's goods, and tested their sagacity against the shrewdness and more practiced skill of the professed sharper" (Beardsley 1852:252).

The mania was stoked by what historian Frederick Merk (1969:ix) called "the greatest real estate transaction in modern history." Between independence and the Gadsden Purchase, the United States swelled to more than three times the size of the original thirteen colonies. It occupied the Northwest Territories. It bought the Louisiana Purchase from France and Florida from Spain. It annexed Texas, seized California and the

Southwest from Mexico, and negotiated with Britain for the Oregon Territory. Each of these acquisitions gave the United States enormous amounts of land. The federal government then granted four-fifths of that land to states, veterans, canal and railroad companies, and individuals. The mammoth transfer did not end until the Taylor Grazing Act effectively closed the public domain in 1934.

The siren song of public lands was so seductive because there were few other opportunities for profit. "Until the modern corporation came to be the dominant factor in American economic life, the principal opportunity for investment was in real estate," the historian Paul Wallace Gates observed (Gates 1996:7). Gates (1996) revealed the magnitude of land speculation in a seminal essay titled "The Role of the Land Speculator in Western Development." During the boom of 1835–37, for example, speculators acquired twenty-nine million (81 percent) of the thirty-six million acres of public domain sold during those three years. Although much of the land was purchased for agricultural purposes, speculators were far more interested in town sites because they brought much higher prices. The result was a fantastical urban landscape before there were city dwellers to populate it. In the words of William Cronon, "Fictive lots on fictive streets in fictive towns became the basis for thousands of transactions whose only justification was a dubious idea expressed on an overly optimistic map" (Cronon 1991:32).

United States land booms could not have occurred without easy credit. After President Andrew Jackson vetoed the renewal of the charter of the Second Bank of the United States in 1832, the number of state banks doubled and the paper value of bank notes in circulation tripled, particularly in the West and South (Myers 1970). Western banks and eastern capitalists devised numerous ways to purchase the lands themselves or through proxies. Moneylenders representing them also haunted the auctions of public lands in Illinois, Wisconsin, and Missouri, advancing credit to squatters at usurious interest rates. If the squatters could not make their payments, the banks took over their lands and their improvements (Gates 1996).

The absence of a centralized banking system with centralized monetary control exacerbated a fundamental contradiction of capitalism noted above—that money had to function both as a medium of exchange and as a measure of value. Credit systems, such as the state bank notes of the 1830s, speed up the circulation of commodities such as real estate. Unless they are guaranteed by the state or some universally accepted standard of value like gold, however, the capacity of credit monies "to represent 'real' commodity values is perpetually suspect," according to David Harvey (1999: 249). In the unregulated atmosphere of the 1830s, credit expanded rapidly to lubricate land sales, but the bank notes flowing into the federal treasury grew ever more "suspect," particularly to Andrew Jackson himself.

Jackson, who had driven the Five Civilized Tribes of the Southeast into exile in Oklahoma Territory, worried that speculators were swindling his beloved frontiersmen. With more populist outrage than financial sense, he issued his famous Species Circular of 1836 to "repress alleged frauds, and to withhold any countenance or facilities in the power of the Government from the monopoly of the public lands in the hands of speculators and capitalists." Thenceforth, public lands could only be purchased with gold or silver, which were in short supply on the western frontier. Within months, the scaffolding of paper debt came tumbling down. Western banks quickly exhausted their species reserves and many bank notes could not be redeemed. The Bank of England refused credit on U.S. imports. Since the English were the biggest creditors of U.S. banks and the largest market for agricultural commodities like cotton, banks defaulted and the prices of farm products plummeted. The result was the Panic of 1837 and one of the worst depressions in U.S. history. Speculative frenzy followed deregulation. Then the real estate market collapsed —a pattern that has characterized land booms and busts from the 1830s to the 1980s.

The southern Arizona Mining Frontier

Southern Arizona missed the 1830s frenzy because it was still part of Sonora. Another land rush erupted between 1847 and 1855, however, one triggered by congressional passage of four land acts granting veterans more than sixty million acres. Few veterans settled the bounty lands, most of which were in the upper Mississippi and Missouri River Valleys. Instead, most sold their land warrants to eastern brokers, who shipped them to agents in land office towns on the western frontier. A common frontier transaction was the time entry loan, whereby the agent sold the warrant to a buyer on one year's credit, often at very high interest rates. If the buyer repaid the loan, he received title. If not, the agent retained the land (Oberly 1990).[4]

There were no bounty lands in Arizona. Nonetheless, the speculative flurry of the times brought the first trickle of capital to the Arizona frontier. By then, business organizations in the United States had grown more sophisticated. During the early years of the republic, both government and the general populace viewed corporations with suspicion, equating them with monopolies. The initial industrialization of textile production in New England depended upon mercantile capital accumulated in the China trade, not the sale of stock. In other words, you had to have money from commerce—or real estate to mortgage—in order to invest in manufacturing (Myers 1970).

As the U.S. economy developed, however, corporations gradually replaced proprietorships and partnerships, particularly for bigger and riskier ventures. This institutional evolution did not make the economy any less speculative, but it did provide greater opportunities for investors and greater capital for entrepreneurs. It also spread the risks of investment among the many rather than the few.

Not surprisingly, the only industry that attracted significant capital on the Arizona frontier was mining for precious metals. Silver and gold were high in value and low in volume—the only type of resources that could hope to justify the huge transaction costs of Indian depredations and long-distance transportation by mule back or freight wagon. But as mining companies proliferated, some purchased ranches and land grants as well. A linkage between mining and ranching was being established, one that led to the development of some of the largest ranches in southern Arizona, such as the Empire and the San Rafael (Stewart 1974; Sonnichsen 1974; Hadley and Sheridan 1995).

One of the first corporate ventures was the Sonora Exploring and Mining Company and its subsidiary, the Santa Rita Mining Company. Its principal founder, Samuel Peter Heintzelman, came to Arizona in November 1850 to erect a military post at the junction of the Gila and Colorado Rivers. Like many military officers of the time, Heintzelman supplemented his pay by investing in various business enterprises. He bought beachfront property in San Diego, acquired a ranch and grocery business in the Yuma area, and became a partner in the Colorado Ferry Company, the major ferry at Yuma Crossing (North 1980). But his most ambitious endeavor was the mining company, which he organized with Charles DeBrille Poston and Thomas and William Wrightson in March 1856.

Based in Cincinnati, the partners elected Heintzelman president and dispatched Poston to supervise operations in the "Gadsden Purchase lands." When he reached Tucson, Poston met an old companion, German mining engineer Herman Ehrenberg, and together they set up the company's headquarters in the deserted presidio of Tubac. On December 26, 1856, they also purchased the land grant of Arivaca from Tomás and Ignacio Ortiz. Title included mines and mineral rights as well as seventeen thousand acres of land. Along with two other German mining engineers, Frederick Brunckow and Charles Schuchard, Poston and Ehrenberg discovered silver at Salero in the Santa Rita Mountains on January 1, 1857, and in the Cerro Colorado Mountains a month later. Brunckow named the Cerro Colorado discovery the Heintzelman Mine (North 1980).

Back in Cincinnati, Heintzelman tried to drum up investors, using the Wrightsons' *Railroad Record* to promote the company. One early advertisement proclaimed it "the most important Mining Company on this Continent." The ad went on to say that it was located along the line of the proposed Southern Pacific Railroad in the best area for the future capital of the Territory of Arizona.[5] Unfortunately, Heintzelman was at the worst place in the worst time to be looking for money. In August 1857, the Sonora Exploring and Mining Company incorporated under the laws of Ohio as a joint-stock company with twenty thousand shares valued at one hundred dollars apiece. Twelve days later, the Ohio Life Insurance and Trust Company in Cincinnati failed, triggering the nationwide Panic of 1857. Bloated by speculation in railroad securities, banks failed, species payments were suspended, and money markets contracted violently (Myers 1970). Heintzelman and his associates were searching for venture capital as the boom went bust.

Nonetheless, the partners struggled to keep the company afloat. Poston himself was an inveterate booster, making exaggerated claims that the other officers of the corporation repeated as they tried to woo investors. In September 1857, he bragged that "the Heintzelman mine is probably richest in the world-known." Heintzelman was growing increasingly skeptical of his flamboyant partner. But when Poston wrote, "A space in the H. mine 150 ft. long 25 deep and 3 wide will yield two million and a quarter dollars," Heintzelman excitedly concluded, "The Heintzelman mine is in 'bonanza'" (quoted in North 1980:38). From his headquarters at Tubac, which Poston christened the "Athens of Arizona," the "Commandant and Managing Agent" of the Sonora Exploring and Mining Company painted a picture of utopia on the Arizona frontier—a place where there was "no law but love, and no occupation but labor. No government, no taxes, no public debt, no politics. It was a community in a perfect state of nature."

Unfortunately, the law of love soon unraveled and the earth did not yield the returns necessary to keep pace with the pressing need for capital. Poston and the German engineers located as many as eighty mines but never developed any of them into paying propositions. Labor problems also intensified as tension between German or Anglo managers and their largely Mexican work forces erupted into violence (Sheridan 1986). In desperation, Heintzelman turned to Samuel Colt, the inventor of the revolver who pioneered the production line and interchangeable parts at the largest private armory in the world in Hartford, Connecticut. Colt, whom Heintzelman referred to as the "Pistol man," offered ten thousand dollars cash and ten thousand dollars worth of arms in return for one hundred thousand dollars worth of stock. The company accepted Colt's offer in December 1857. In April 1859, stockholders reorganized the company and elected Colt president. Colt quickly forced Heintzelman out and seized control.

But even Colt, whose firm made a fortune selling firearms during the Civil War, could not make the venture pay. Another financial crisis rocked the U.S. economy in 1860 as European investors sold many of their U.S. securities and drained specie out of the country because of the approaching conflict. Once war broke out, federal troops abandoned southern Arizona and Apache hostilities escalated. The Sonora Exploring and Mining Company suspended operations completely in August 1861 after Mexican workers killed Poston's brother and forced Poston to take refuge at Fort Yuma (North 1980). When travel writer J. Ross Browne visited Poston's "Athens of Arizona" in 1864, he wrote, "On reaching the old pueblo of Tubac we found that we were the only inhabitants. There was not a living soul to be seen as we approached. . . . All around were adobe houses, with roofs fallen and the walls crumbling to ruin." (Browne 1974:147).

Despite its failures, however, the Sonora Exploring and Mining Company and Sylvester Mowry's Patagonia Mine put southern Arizona on the international financial map. Mowry also conjured an Arizona that never was in order to sell stock. Addressing the American Geographical and Statistical Society in New York in 1859, Mowry claimed that Spanish Arizona consisted "of more than forty towns and villages" that "teemed with an agricultural and mining population" (Mowry 1859). Such evocations of Hispanic prosperity promised an even more abundant future. There was more than a tinge of racism to the underlying assumption: If Spaniards could flourish in the Santa Cruz Valley, there was no limit to what Yankee ingenuity could accomplish.

Gándara's Hacienda at Calabasas

The Civil War and the final struggle of the Apaches kept that ingenuity at bay for almost two more decades. During the early territorial period, the Tumacácori land grant remained in the hands of Manuel María Gándara. On December 9, 1852, Gándara even drew up a contract at his hacienda of Topahue to provide five thousand sheep, one thousand goats, one hundred cows with calves, one hundred brood mares, ten yokes of oxen, six pack mules, and ten saddle horses to stock his hacienda of Calabasas. The firm of Payeken, Hundhausen and Company agreed to develop and manage the hacienda in return for a 50 percent interest in the estate. Two signatories of the contract—Federico Hulsemann and another German, perhaps Hundhausen—took up residence there, repairing the mission visita and turning it into a fortified ranch house. They even erected a woolen factory, or at least a handloom, to weave blankets and serapes.[6] When Andrew B. Gray and his party passed through Calabasas in April 1853 while surveying a southern railroad route, the party's artist, Charles Schuchard, sketched the hacienda. An engraving based on his drawing in Gray's report shows a peaceful pastoralist scene in which sheep and longhorn cattle graze the floodplain below the reconverted church and a new Sonoran row-style building (Fontana 1971).

That engraving left out what came next. While Gray and his men camped nearby, this idyllic scene shattered into a mounted battle between more than one hundred Western Apaches and a force of presidial soldiers and Apache Mansos from Tucson. The presidiales and their Apache allies prevailed, lancing Western Apaches in the back as they fled up Sonoita Creek. Pioneer Peter Brady recorded the carnage and its trophies in macabre detail. A three-foot-long string of dried apples turned out to be Apache ears with shell, copper, and button earrings dangling. The "sadly altered" face of Romero, a Mexican captive who served as interpreter for the raiding party, glared down from a spike outside the mess hall. "Gray could not refrain from a joke," Brady noted wryly. "He said he supposed they had hung up the head near the mess room door as a kind of sign, 'hash within'" (Gray and Brady 1963:212).

Despite this victory, however, Apaches continued to whittle away at Gándara's flocks. The Germans and their Mexican, O'odham, and Apache Manso retinue clung to the hacienda, which one German observer described as "a citadel with walls about twenty feet high, unbroken except by a solitary doorway, provided with very heavy doors."[7] But when Mexican troops at Tucson departed for Imuris in March 1856, Hulsemann decided to drive the hacienda's stock to safety in Sonora as well. There Gándara apparently doublecrossed his German partners. José Elías, the prefect of the San Ignacio District and a Gándara partisan, seized the animals. Hulsemann was never able to recover them, losing an estimated fifty thousand dollars. The partnership dissolved, and Gándara never again ran stock on the Tumacácori grant (Fontana 1971).

A decade later, the aging caudillo made one last attempt to consolidate his hold. In 1864, Gándara petitioned to have the grant surveyed in order to secure congressional confirmation under the provisions of the Treaty of Guadalupe Hidalgo. The surveyor general of Arizona ignored his request (Mattison 1967). A year later, the French invaded Sonora with Gándara's support. In one of the ironies of history, his nemesis, Governor Ignacio Pesqueira, took refuge at Calabasas, driving a large herd of livestock across the border to pasture on his enemy's land (Fontana 1971; Acuña 1974).

Figure 3. Calabasa [Calabasas], Santa Cruz Valley, Sonora. Engraving based on an original drawing by Charles Shuchard, 1853. (Gray and Brady 1963; courtesy of the Arizona Historical Society/Tucson, no. 60208)

C. P. Sykes and the Calabasas Land and Mining Company

But Calabasas proved to be a bitter exile. An outbreak of malaria followed by dysentery devastated soldiers at nearby Fort Mason. Pesqueira himself fell ill with "enteritis" and could barely move for several months. His wife, Ramona, died (Acuña 1974). The general and his retinue remained at Calabasas until republican forces drove the French out of Sonora in September 1866. After Pesqueira returned to Sonora, Sabino Otero continued to operate a large cattle ranch from Tubac, but the rest of the valley filled up with Anglo-American and European, not Mexican, claims.

First came the squatters. A "Township Map of the Santa Rita Including the Aztec and Tyndall Mining Districts," published in Richard Hinton's 1878 *Handbook of Arizona*, reveals a string of farms or ranches between the "Old Mission of Tumacacari" [*sic*] and the border. The mission itself was "enclosed in the King farm," with its farmhouse about a quarter mile from the church on the east side of the Santa Cruz (Hinton 1878:190).[8] Below Joseph King's spread were ranches occupied by Captain Smith, who fought off Cochise at the Hacienda del Santa Rita in 1861; George Allison, who came to Calabasas to make bricks in the late 1870s; Pete Kitchen, who raised pigs along the Portrero; and other lesser-known figures such as the Reynolds and the Benedicts.

But the biggest influx came from mining companies, which burrowed into mountain ranges across southern Arizona. According to Hinton (1878:127), "Up to October 1st, 1876, 975 mines were recorded in Pima County, and this number is rapidly increasing." He published a table listing 136 of these mines, the only ones to which he could attach names. The Santa Rita Mountains cradled two of the most active districts—the Tyndall and Aztec—north and east of Tumacácori.

The Tumacácori land grant itself soon sprouted a hallucinogenic mushroom of a promotion along the Santa Cruz. The primary dreamspinner was Colonel C. P. Sykes, a New Yorker who had hoped to become a Universalist minister in his youth. After his stepfather persuaded him to quit school and run the family farm, however, the consuming entrepreneurial spirit of the time enflamed his soul and drove him across the North American continent. He rode the land boom of the 1850s to Wisconsin, founding the *La Cross Democrat* in 1858 just after the boom collapsed. Two years later, "being a bold and adventurous business man," he sold his newspaper and "started for the wilds of Colorado," according to a biographical sketch in the *Pacific Coast Annual Mining Review*. "He soon accumulated an ample fortune, owning large interests in some of the best gold mining property in Colorado," the sketch continued. "He was the first to perceive the necessity for placing the mining interests of Colorado before Eastern capitalists, going to New York himself, where he organized a number of first-class mining companies."[9]

Sykes lost most of his Colorado fortune after the Civil War. Returning to New York, he formed a partnership to publish another newspaper, but mining soon drew him west again. By 1875, he was in San Francisco, the center of western capital. There he cast about for investments as the U.S. economy struggled to pull itself out of the first major depression of the industrial age triggered by the failure of Jay Cooke's financial empire and the ensuing Panic of 1873 (Martin 1980). After hearing about the fabled mineral wealth of southern Arizona, he organized the San Xavier Mining and Smelting Company, securing title to the San Xavier Lode south of Mission San Xavier del Bac. In 1878, he also purchased the Tumacácori grant from Gándara, who died shortly after the sale (Mattison 1967).[10]

Gándara had to wait more than three decades to make money from Tumacácori. Sykes, in contrast, wasted little time in developing the grant. He quickly sold a three-sixteenths interest to John Curry, an ex-judge of the California Supreme Court, for nine thousand dollars. The new partners then convinced other prominent San Francisco businessmen including Senator John P. Jones to form the Calabasas Land and Mining Company. Curry was elected president. Sykes became managing director.[11] The Tumacácori grant's transition from a landscape of community to a landscape of speculation was complete.

The early years of Sykes's venture were a good time to be searching for capital. The Compromise of 1877, which threw the presidential election to Republican Rutherford B. Hayes, calmed North-South tensions by dismantling Reconstruction and abandoning blacks to Klan terror and Jim Crow. The resulting political stability ushered in a period of unprecedented economic growth that lasted, with one major interruption, from 1877 until 1893. New technological innovations in electricity and coal-powered steam engines stoked this growth, while new industries like steel built its industrial infrastructure. But every enterprise depended upon the revolutionary expansion of the railroads, which turned the United States from what historian Allan Nevins called an "invertebrate" to a vertebrate nation after the Civil War (quoted in Martin 1980). In 1860, there were only 30,000 miles of railroad in the nation. By 1890, that number had soared to 170,000 miles, with an average 8,000 miles added each year during the boom decade of the 1880s. Because of such rapid expansion, "American society now occupied the most tightly integrated large landmass in the world," economic historian Albro Martin (1980:96) observed.

During this heady era, the Calabasas Land and Mining Company did everything it could to live up to its name. The company took over five of the six mining locations of Sykes's San Xavier Mining and Smelting Company. The new enterprise also laid out a townsite on "old Don Gaudera's [*sic*] ranch" of Calabasas. Sykes clearly wanted Calabasas to eclipse Tucson as the gateway to northern Mexico, and he used his contacts in the press to advance his vision. "Tucson does a trade with Sonora of at least $6,000,000 per annum. It is seventy-five miles from the northern line of Mexico," wrote "Explorer," a columnist for the *New York Daily Graphic*. "Calabasas is but ten miles therefrom. When the large warehouse of which report speaks as to be constructed is opened here it is hardly probable that 'the greasers' will drive their two-wheeled carts or their pack mules sixty-five extra miles."[12]

Setting a precedent for future promotions, Sykes's company used the Santa Cruz Valley's mission past to sell itself. The same issue of the *New York Daily Graphic* featured six lithographs titled "Views on the Property of the Calabasas Land and Mining Company, Pima County, Arizona." A portrait of Sykes, bearded and judicious, is flanked by a brooding "Mount Wrightson, From Calabasa, Santa Cruz Valley" on the left and the "Ruins of Mission Tumacacori, Destroyed by Apache Indians" on the right.[13] Below Sykes is an "Ear of Corn Grown on Calabasas Rancho in 1876 without Irrigation."[14] To the left of the corn is the "Plan of The Hotel and Plaza at Calabasas as It Will Appear when Completed." To the right is "San Xavier del Bac."[15] At the bottom is a "Map of the San Xavier Mines, 1878" divided into the six "locations" owned by Sykes. Sykes, the Yankee entrepreneur, presides over and unites the romantic past with the industrious future—a future of agricultural abundance, luxurious amenities, and mineral wealth apportioned into the precise rectangles of mining claims. "Views on the Property of the Calabasas Land and Mining Company" was a representation of space bursting with speculative exuberance.

Key to Sykes's schemes was the construction of a railroad through the Santa Cruz Valley linking Mexico and the United States. His first venture was the Arizona Southern Railroad Company, which was incorporated on August 16, 1880, five months after the Southern Pacific Railroad reached Tucson. The incorporators included Arizona entrepreneurs like Sykes, ex-territorial governor Anson P. K. Safford, and Tucson businessman C. H. Lord, as well as investors from Boston with ties to Southern Pacific's rival, the Atchison, Topeka, and Santa Fe. The Santa Fe itself bought one thousand shares of stock in the Arizona Southern for ten thousand dollars (Myrick 1975).

Sykes emphasized the importance of a rail line by portraying Calabasas as the center of a transportation network linking southern Arizona and northern Mexico. He also geared his promotions to various audiences, with Calabasas growing ever more grandiose the further away from Arizona prospective investors were. According to a sardonic article in the *Tombstone Epitaph*, three prospectuses were circulating by 1882— one in Arizona, another in the United States, a third in Europe. "This European prospectus was a grand affair," the *Epitaph* jeered. "It was filled with magnificent drawings representing the raging Santa Cruz at high tide, with steam boats and heavy vessels at the docks unloading while yonder in the distance could be seen the smoke of a dozen furnaces with lively locomotives hauling [ore?] to the numerous mills."[16]

Where Sykes conjured up the image of a navigable Santa Cruz remains to be determined. According to journalist Sybil Ellinwood, the illustrations were adapted from those circulated in Boston and New York newspapers by Sylvester Mowry almost three decades earlier. "With them the ambitious Sylvester Mowry had tried to promote Eastern capital for mining ventures by picturing a line of steamers puffing up the Colorado River to Yuma, thence up the Gila to Maricopa, and finally up the Santa Cruz, invisible for much of its course, to within twenty miles of the Mowry mine," Ellinwood (1964:35) wrote. But Mowry himself made no mention of steamboats on the Santa Cruz in his major published work, *Arizona and*

Figure 4. Views on the property of the Calabasas Land and Mining Company, Arizona. (*New York Daily Graphic*, Oct. 18, 1878; courtesy of the Arizona Historical Society/Tucson, no. 2783)

Sonora: The Geography, History, and Resources of the Silver Region of North America (1864). On the contrary, he correctly stated, "Like most streams, the Santa Cruz is intermittent, sinking and rising at irregular intervals" (Mowry 1864:25). Whatever the origins of Calabasas as bustling river port, Arizonans scoffed. Stung by the sarcasm, Sykes offered a reward for any poster portraying steamers on the river (Ellinwood 1964). No one replied. Nonetheless, Sykes continued to use the mythical waters of the Santa Cruz to woo investors across the ocean.

But even a Danube in the desert could not make the Arizona Southern a reality. Sykes managed to convince Congress to grant his railroad a right-of-way through the Papago Indian Reservation around San Xavier, but the city of Tucson turned down his request for financial support. More damaging was the construction of the Santa Fe's New Mexico and Arizona Railroad, which built eighty-eight miles of line between Benson and Nogales in 1881–82. The road ran south along the San Pedro River, servicing the booming mining district of Tombstone. Then, at Fairbank, it veered west and followed Babocómari Creek until it crossed a divide into the Sonoita Valley. Cattlemen moving onto the finest grasslands in Arizona suddenly had rail access to markets across the United States, and cattle proliferated like flies.

To reach the Mexican border, the New Mexico and Arizona snaked down Sonoita Creek to Calabasas. Sykes lobbied hard for the railroad to build its international depot there, but the New Mexico and Arizona chose the infant border community of Nogales instead. On October 25, 1882, a crowd cheered and poured champagne on the engineers as a locomotive of the New Mexico and Arizona, draped in red, white, and blue, steamed south to face a locomotive of the Santa Fe's Sonora Railway, sporting Mexico's national colors of red, white, and green. The silver spike driven into a mahogany crosstie to commemorate the occasion drove a stake through the heart of Sykes's visionary community as well (Myrick 1975).

But Sykes was more than a decade away from giving up. That evening, he hosted a banquet for seventy-five guests who attended the Nogales ceremony at his new Santa Rita Hotel. By then, Calabasas had grown into a community of about 150 people with 5 stores, 2 dancehalls, 2 Chinese gambling dens, an opium den, and 16 saloons. The Santa Rita was easily the most elegant structure in town. With its two stories of solid brick surrounded by a white picket fence, the Santa Rita looked like a Yankee vision of prosperity and decorum. Sykes made sure the interior was elegant as well, furnishing it with three carloads of furniture from Boston and staffing it with proper Bostonian women (Myrick 1975). During its brief heyday (1882–93), famous visitors like General Nelson Miles and prominent settlers like Sabino Otero slept under its roof and ate in its famous dining room. One guest pronounced the hotel "the best between San Francisco and Denver" (Ellinwood 1964:37).

The Calabasas, Tucson, and North Western Railroad Company and the Arizona Cattle and Improvement Company

Even though the New Mexico and Arizona brought patrons to his hotel, however, Sykes still wanted a railroad of his own. In 1885, backed by New York capital, he organized the Calabasas, Tucson, and North Western Railroad Company. John Rice, a former member of Congress from Maine, was president. Sykes was vice-president. The treasurer was Thomas James, former postmaster general of the United States and president of Lincoln Bank in New York. General C. C. Dodge, "Late of Phelps, Dodge and Co.," served on its board. With such distinguished names on its masthead, the Calabasas, Tucson, and North Western planned to extend a rail line down the Santa Cruz to Tucson, Florence, and Phoenix. It also projected two feeder lines: one to Arivaca and the mining boomtown of Quijotoa to the west, another to the coal fields of Deer Creek along the San Pedro River and the mining district of Globe to the northeast.[17]

Sykes was initially more successful in capitalizing his second railroad venture. He asked the Pima County Board of Supervisors to issue two hundred thousand dollars worth of bonds to construct the line to Tucson and the northern border of the county. The supervisors liked the proposal and scheduled a special election on May 23, 1885. The bond issue passed by an overwhelming majority of 939 to 87 (Myrick 1975).

The Calabasas, Tucson, and North Western also proposed to pay for itself by issuing first mortgage, 6 percent thirty-year bonds guaranteed by a second corporation, the Arizona Cattle and Improvement Company. The directorships were largely interlocking, with Sykes serving as vice-president and general manager and James as treasurer for both companies. The president of the Arizona Cattle and Improvement Company was the Honorable William Windom, ex-secretary of the U.S. Treasury, with Rice serving on its board. In return for 49 percent of the capital stock of the railroad, Sykes received 99,940 of the cattle company's 100,000 shares of capital stock. According to the "Prospectus of the Calabasas, Tucson and North Western Railroad Company and the Arizona Cattle and Improvement Company," cattle were the currency that would bankroll the rails.

The first order of business was to sink deep wells along the route and then pump the water through a pipeline "sunk in the road-bed, for the use of stock in desert places."[18] In italics, the prospectus proclaimed, *The right of way of the railroad, with a pipe line to carry water for cattle, will practically control the grazing land along* the line of the road, for many miles upon each side for many years to come, as the lands are not yet surveyed."[19] During the late nineteenth century, controlling water meant control over the open ranges of the West.

What followed was an elaborate bovine house of cards. In order to construct the line, the Calabasas, Tucson, and North Western signed a contract with an unspecified "English Syndicate." For the first fifty-five miles of construction between Calabasas and Tucson, the English syndicate would supply 370 head of cattle for each mile of construction. In return, it would be paid "all the railroad first mortgage bonds on that division, which will be issued at the rate of $30,000 per mile."[20] Upon completion of this first stage, the Arizona Cattle and Improvement Company would have a herd of 20,350 head.

The prospectus then marched through a series of Alice-in-Wonderland-like calculations to show how rapidly the herd would increase, how quickly the railroad would be paid for, and how handsomely the investors would be rewarded. During the first year, 4,400 three-year-old steers would be sold at $30 per head, generating $132,000 in revenue. Second-year revenues would be the same, but by the third year, 4,400 cows would be sold as well, raising revenue to $220,000. When the entire 350-mile line was built, the cattle company's herd would have swelled to a staggering 129,500 head, "with annual sales of 56,000 head, equal to $1,400,000." Interest on the entire line's bonded debt, in contrast, would only be $530,000. Deducting another $100,000 for estimated ranching expenses, the company would have $770,000 to distribute as a 30 percent annual dividend to stockholders in the cattle company.

And that was a conservative estimate that did not take into account revenues from cargo hauled by the railroad itself. *"There are at least one thousand mining claims within ten miles on each side of the proposed railroad,"* the prospectus trumpeted.[21] There were also the Deer Creek coalfields, which would produce 51,333,000 tons of coal. Finally, there was southern Arizona's great agricultural fertility, where "it is not an uncommon occurrence that sixty bushels of wheat per acres is [sic] harvested."[22] Judicious and understated after such astonishing numbers, the prospectus concluded, "With this safe financial outlook the companies have no hesitancy in declaring that the public has never had a better prospect presented for a safe and profitable investment."[23]

The public was less than impressed. On October 16, 1885, the Pima County Board of Supervisors approved of Sykes's plans and stipulated that the first county bonds would be issued if work on the railroad began within three months and was finished within a year. But Sykes was unable to raise much capital in New York because of a national depression that began in 1882 and culminated in the so-called Panic of 1884, when one major New York brokerage firm and two New York banks failed (Myers 1970). During this period, business failures rose from 6,738 in 1883 to almost 10,000 in both 1884 and 1885 as production declined by one-fourth. Unemployment climbed to 15 percent and labor unrest intensified, especially in 1886, when a series of strikes and their brutal repression swept the country. As a result, the Calabasas, Tucson, and North Western did not lay a single rail. A year later, after the venture failed to meet any of its deadlines, 109 individuals petitioned the board to grant a six-month extension. The supervisors refused, "the company not even having made a good showing at commencement" (Myrick 1975:258).

Sykes tried to revive his railroad once last time. In January 1891, he circulated petitions to convince the Pima County Board of Supervisors to once again issue two hundred thousand dollars in bonds. He also promised to build a one-hundred-thousand-dollar hotel and sanatorium if the Tucson City Council gave him the old Military Plaza. In an article in the *Tucson Citizen* on February 5, 1891, prominent citizens generally supported Sykes's schemes but recommended that no county funds be expended until the railroad was completed. "If the parties mean business and will do as they say in a specified time I am heartily in favor of the propositions," merchant Samuel Drachman commented. But then he bluntly added, "I want to see the contract drawn up in such a shape that not a dollar of money or fit land will be given till the work is satisfactory [sic] performed."

Once again, it was the same sad story. The supervisors approved the bonds as long as the first stretch of rail was constructed by March 1, 1892. March 1 came and went, Sykes requested another extension, and New York investors continued to ignore the Tucson, Calabasas, and North Western. Then the Panic of 1893 plunged the nation into a much deeper depression than the one a decade before. The 1880s witnessed the construction of more railroads than any other decade in U.S. history. The 1890s saw many of those lines end up in receivership. By 1895, companies controlling 40 thousand miles and representing $2.5 billion in fixed capital that could not be transferred to other industries had failed.

Railroads were already consolidating before the Panic of 1893, with main lines buying up feeder lines to become self-sustaining systems. In 1892, thirty-three railroads capitalized at more than one hundred million dollars apiece controlled 70 percent of the tracks and even more of the traffic in the United States. After the Panic of 1893, investment bankers like J. P. Morgan swallowed up the weaker roads and established the shape of the railroad industry for the next fifty years. The proliferation of railroads encouraged overbuilding and ruinous competition. Morgan and his fellow bankers reorganized the U.S. system into six or seven "communities of interest," in which big companies bought one another's stock (Chandler 1980; Martin 1980; G. Moore 1980). Those big companies were the largest business enterprises on the globe.

A speculator like Sykes was hopelessly out of his league in such an environment. In 1903, two years after he died on another fruitless search for capital in New York, the Calabasas, Tucson, and North Western bonds were destroyed in the presence of the Pima County Board of Supervisors and the county clerk. Two other companies—the Twin Buttes Railroad and the Tucson and Nogales Railroad Company, a Southern Pacific subsidiary—connected Tucson with Calabasas, Nogales, and Mexico in 1910 (Myrick 1975). That was the year that Sykes's widow, who had remained in the Santa Rita Hotel, died. By then, Calabasas was little more than a ghost town slowly being reclaimed by mesquite.

The Legal Death of the Tumacácori Land Grant

While Sykes was trying, and failing, to turn Calabasas into the gateway to Mexico, the Tumacácori land grant died as well. When Sykes and Curry purchased the grant from Gándara on July 24, 1877, the surveyor general of a state or territory had the power to investigate the validity of any land grant in his jurisdiction (Bradfute 1975). In the Arizona and New Mexico territories, claimants had to present titles from Mexican archives along with supporting documentation. The surveyor general examined the documents, took affidavits from witnesses, and made a recommendation to the secretary of the interior. If the secretary declared that the claim was valid, his report was sent to Congress for final confirmation or rejection (Mattison 1967; Bradfute 1975).

Sykes and Curry initiated this process on December 15, 1879, when they sent a petition and packet of documents to John Wasson, surveyor general of Arizona. The packet included Spanish transcriptions and English translations of the original Tumacácori grant, its sale to Francisco Aguilar, and Gándara's sale to Sykes and Curry. Wasson took the testimony of Theodora Varela de Troil and Pete Kitchen, who both attested that Gándara had indeed occupied the grant in the 1850s. R. C. Hopkins, "familiar with the Spanish language and well acquainted with the character of Spanish handwriting," swore that the documents were, "in his opinion, unquestionably genuine, written and signed at the time of their respective dates."[24]

Wasson recapitulated the paper trail and discoursed on the legal history of missions, presidios, and pueblos in his "Opinion and recommendation." *"The missions had no ownership of the lands which they occupied with their Indians and stock*," he pronounced (italics in original). He went on to note that "the boundaries of the mission possessions were only conventional, and that they were constantly reduced as lands embraced therein were from time to time, granted by the government to private individuals until the establishments were finally extinguished by decree of secularization."[25] Wasson did recognize that Spanish law granted pueblos a *fundo legal* of four square leagues, but added, "a much less quantity than four square leagues was included within the measurements actually made as shown by the field-notes of the survey made in 1807." Moreover, "the said measurements of the 'estancia' or stock farm, embrace a much less quantity than the two *sitios* called for in the title papers, and the addition thereto, asked for by the Indians and granted to them, was limited by boundaries, and hence the quantity cannot be known without an actual survey."[26]

Wasson also stated that the mission of Tumacácori "and the Indian pueblos pertaining thereto" were abandoned at the same time that "Spanish troops" abandoned the presidio of Tubac. Therefore, the sale of Tumacácori to Aguilar on April 18, 1844, was valid under the law passed by the Mexican Congress in 1842. Wasson recommended that Sykes and Curry's claim be confirmed. The secretary of the interior forwarded Wasson's recommendation to Congress on May 24, 1880, but Congress took no definitive action.[27] For the next two decades, the grant wound its way through a maze of claim and counterclaim that led all the way to the U.S. Supreme Court. At no time in this process were the O'odham ever a party to the legal wrangling.

Sykes was little more than a bystander himself. In 1881, the Calabasas Land and Mining Company, incorporated in California, exchanged stock with the Santa Rita Mining Company of Colorado. Santa Rita ended up with the Tumacacori grant minus the Calabasas townsite and the Arizona Southern Railway Company's right-of-way. Nine years later, in 1890, a purchasing committee representing former stockholders of Santa Rita bought the company's holdings, including the Tumacácori grant, at a foreclosure sale. The stockholders formed an association and appointed William Faxon of Boston as trustee to manage the Santa Rita properties until they could be sold at a decent price. Faxon granted the Santa Rita Land and Cattle Company a seven-year lease on the grant beginning on April 28, 1892.[28]

Meanwhile, several other claimants surfaced. One was George Hill Howard, who asserted title to the "lands of Guebavi." Howard contended that before Francisco Aguilar formally conveyed Tumacácori to Manuel María Gándara in 1869, Gándara sold one square league of the grant to Claude Jones on July 6, 1864. Jones transferred the deed to Isaac

Domingo Marks and Edson Adams in 1865. In 1878, Isaac Marks sold his share to Joshua Marks, who sold out to Edward Head that same year. Three years later, Head transferred his half share to Adams as well. Adams then conveyed the entire property to Howard in 1883.[29]

A more intriguing claim arose from Dolores Astiazarán and thirteen other members of the Aguilar-Gándara extended family.[30] Astiazarán, who had married into the clan claiming the enormous Sópori grant, was one of seven children of Dolores Aguilar and Manuel María Gándara. The rest of the plaintiffs were her siblings or cousins. Their suit, first brought against the Santa Rita Mining Company in the district court of Arizona in 1887, argued that Dolores and the others were the heirs and grantees of Francisco Alejandro Aguilar, Dolores's uncle. The suit does not mention either Gándara's sale of Guevavi to Claude Jones in 1864 or Aguilar's sale of Tumacácori to Gándara in 1869.[31] The district court ruled in favor of Santa Rita, a decision upheld by the Supreme Court of the Arizona Territory. Astiazarán and her fellow plaintiffs appealed to the U.S. Supreme Court in 1893. The Supreme Court dodged the issue by declaring that since Congress had not yet acted on Wasson's report of 1880, the grant could not be challenged (Mattison 1967).

By then, at least four corporations and 120 homesteaders and squatters had established claims to portions of the Tumacácori grant. On October 1, 1888, a group of them led by George Atkinson petitioned the U.S. General Land Office to investigate the grant and restore any lands to the public domain that were found to be "unlawfully held in reservation."[32] Commissioner Stockslager examined the grant, concluded that Wasson's approval was "improper," and ruled that "there is not and has never been any lawful, valid or actual reservation of lands for the Tumacacori and Calabasas claim."[33] Suddenly, all claims to the grant were in jeopardy.

The Santa Rita Mining Company appealed, and Secretary of the Interior W. H. Schurz reversed Stockslager's decision in 1893.[34] But Schurz's ruling did not confirm Santa Rita's title to the grant. On the contrary, it merely stated that the reservation of the grant from the public domain had been legal under the provisions of the Gadsden Purchase pending a decision by Congress. "As before said, the policy of our law was to treat all these Mexican grants as conferring only inchoate or equitable rights, needing confirmation to ripen into a legal title, which could be accorded by Congress alone," Schurz wrote.[35] He went on to note that although the law creating the U.S. Court of Private Land Claims in 1891 repealed congressional authority and transferred it to the new tribunal, that transfer in no way abrogated the original reservation.

The three parties claiming Tumacácori then turned to the Court of Private Land Claims, which was created for the sole purpose of determining the legality of Spanish and Mexican land grants (Bradfute 1975). Faxon and his fellow plaintiffs brought suit against the individuals and corporations already ensconced on the grant, including C. P. Sykes, George Atkinson, the Sonoita and Santa Cruz Land and Water Company, the Salero Land and Cattle Company, and the New Mexico and Arizona Railroad Company.[36] Howard and the Astiazarán-Gándara-Aguilar-Oceguera extended family also submitted their petitions. Rather than hearing the cases individually, however, the court consolidated the three suits. In the end, the fate of the grant hung on the one claim the three petitions had in common—that Francisco Alejandro Aguilar's purchase of the grant in 1844 had been legal and valid under Mexican law.

In 1895, the Court of Private Land Claims most emphatically decided that it was not. Wading through Mexican statutes passed during a particularly chaotic period in Mexico's history, the justices determined that Ignacio López, treasurer general of the state of Sonora, had no authority to auction off public lands. Title to such lands could only be conferred by the national treasury.[37] Associate Justice William W. Murray filed a concurring opinion, noting that the grant was never duly recorded as a *toma de razón* in the "proper book" as required by the Treaty of Mesilla in 1853 (Gadsden Purchase).[38] Finally, the court pronounced:

IT IS THEREFORE ORDERED, ADJUDGED, AND DECREED [capitals in original] That the claim to the property known as and included in what is called the Calabasas, Tumacacori and Guebabi grant or private land claim, and being situated in the county of Pima, Territory of Arizona, under a grant alleged to have been derived from the Republic of Mexico, executed by Ygnacio Lopez, Treasurer General of the Department of Sonora in favor of Francisco Alejandro Aguilar, and dated the 19th day of April, 1844 be and the same is rejected and said petitions are dismissed.[39]

The three parties appealed their consolidated case to the U.S. Supreme Court. In a decision titled *Faxon v. United States*, the Supreme Court upheld the Court of Private Land Claims in 1898. After reviewing the Mexican legislation cited in support of the case, Chief Justice Melville W. Fuller, who delivered the opinion of the court, concluded, "While these various laws are rather confusing in their number and minuteness, nothing is clearer than that the power to make sales and grants was vested in the treasury department of the nation, and governed by strict rules and regulations, none of which contemplated that any single officer could make the sales."[40] Fuller also agreed with the lower court that "the missionaries and Indians only acquired a usufruct or occupancy at the will of the sovereign" under the 1807 Tumacácori grant. After the decree of April 16, 1834, secularized the missions, the lands themselves were no longer "temporalities" of the "church or its ecclesiastics." "And, as many years before the sale in question, the lands of this pueblo and mission were abandoned," Fuller went on to say, "it would seem that they thus became a part of the public domain of the nation, and that as such the only laws applicable to their disposal were the laws of the nation in relation to its vacant public lands, to which the proceedings in this instance do not purport to have conformed, or to have been made under them."[41] It was the end of the line for George Hill Howard, the former Santa Rita bondholders, and the fading Aguilar-Gándara Sonoran elite.

The O'odham, who had defended their church and their stretch of the river years after the other Mexican land grants in Arizona had been deserted, were not even ghosts haunting the pages of court testimony. The official records of the grant's history agreed, without any evidence, that the "land had been abandoned about the year 1820."[42] Almost three decades of occupation—more than a generation of tilling the soil and fighting Apaches—were obliterated by Gándara's subterfuge.

And yet, buried in archives like those of the Diocese of Tucson are other records—records that the O'odham not only inhabited but tried to reclaim their lands. In the 1850s, when Gándara was trying to turn Calabasas into a sheep ranch, nineteen O'odham from Tumacácori convinced the O'odham governor of San Xavier del Bac to press their case. The governor petitioned Prefect José Elías to retrieve their titles from Gándara. Elías, a *gandarista* (partisan of Gándara), paid no attention to their plea. Even though they continued to care for their santos and church ornaments separate from those of San Xavier, their legitimate claim to the Tumacácori grant vanished from the legal record (Kessell 1976).

Nonetheless, memories of an O'odham Tumacácori lingered on. In 1931, Franciscan missionary Bonaventure Oblasser published the reminiscences of Carnación, a blind and ancient O'odham woman living at San Xavier. According to her:

> Tumacacori belongs to us, too. It happened this way. The Apaches drove our kinfolks from that mission. These wild people were going to burn the statue of St. Cajetano. The flames had already commenced to consume the image, when a shower extinguished the fire. Their statue and many others were brought here by the women, who carried them in their Kiahats (burden baskets). The statue of Maria Santisima, however, was brought tied on a horse. I missed seeing the cavalcade arrive at the old mission, but I did hear the ringing of the mission bells as they reached this place. One of the statues, the one of the Blessed Virgin with child, was taken to Tucson. (Oblasser 1931:98)

6

Fictitious Capital and
Fictitious Landscapes

Sarah Black and her husband, John, were teachers who came to Arizona in 1882. Sarah taught for two years in the mining town of Oro Blanco and then moved to Tubac, where she offered classes for a year in a hotel room until the town built a schoolhouse for her. Most of her neighbors were Mexicans, and the only big rancher in the area was Sabino Otero, who employed about twenty vaqueros. Sarah recalled "lots of little Indian scares" in those early days, times when the townspeople would take refuge in Otero's store. "It had a dirt roof. We huddled in there and told Indian stories—they were enough to scare anyone to death." But she did not remember anyone getting killed. "They wanted these men to go to Tucson, then they wanted to take the women in but they wouldn't go, they were not built that way, so we all stayed here," the pioneer teacher said. "No, I never worried much about the Indians."[1]

United States marshals, not Apaches, drove Sarah from her home. Sarah's husband built a two-room house on 240 acres of land south of Tubac. Many homesteaders followed, particularly after the U.S. Supreme Court invalidated the Tumacácori grant in 1898. Like their neighbors, the Blacks ran some cattle and raised chile, tomatoes, and watermelons in the rich alluvial soil. In 1914, however, the Supreme Court confirmed Baca Float No. 3, an enormous square of land straddling the Santa Cruz River. The heirs of the Baca family—speculators, not family members—demanded that all settlers along the Santa Cruz abandon their ranches. Congress passed a relief bill permitting the evicted homesteaders to select in lieu lands elsewhere in Arizona. Many accepted the government's offer and settled near Buckeye.

Others, like Sarah Black, refused. Federal marshals evicted the recalcitrants. "My land looked like an auction yard. They put everything out-doors, the furniture and dishes and everything," the ninety-two-year-old pioneer recalled. "It was the most brutal thing that ever happened. I don't know as I cared so much, but it was pretty hard for the people who were too old to begin again."[2]

For the second time in less than two decades, the highest court in the United States issued a decision that destroyed an agrarian community along the Santa Cruz River. A real grant had been obliterated. A fictitious grant squatted in its place. Once again, people making a living from the land—people with names like Aguayo, Gastelum, Tanori, and Sinohui—had been uprooted and dispossessed.

Land, Law, and Custom in the Southwest

The chain of events that led to Sarah Black's eviction began in 1845, when the United States declared war on Mexico. The war was an exercise in territorial arrogance on both sides. Mexico, bankrupt and in political chaos after its struggle for independence, fought to preserve the northern boundaries Spain had bequeathed it under the Adams-Onís Treaty of 1819. Those boundaries, which drew a firm line between northern New Spain and the Louisiana Purchase in return for Spanish Florida, jogged from real rivers to abstract longitudes and latitudes across a huge, three-tiered swath of western North America. The region contained all the present U.S. states of Texas, New Mexico, Arizona, Utah, Nevada, and California and parts of Kansas, Colorado, and Wyoming (Weber 1982; Meinig 1993). But Mexican settlement itself was limited to a few scattered enclaves tucked into a landscape that mocked imperial dreams. Outside those enclaves, Comanches, Kiowas, Apaches, Navajos, Utes, Paiutes, Pueblo peoples, Pais, River Yumans, O'odham, and a host of California groups held sway. They had their own boundaries and their own dreams.

The United States, in contrast, was attempting to swallow the continent whole. The British had driven the French from Canada and the Midwest during the French and Indian War (1756–63). The United States eliminated the French presence in North America altogether when it doubled its national territory by purchasing Louisiana from Napoleon in 1803. But even though the War of 1812 ended U.S. designs on Canada, the aggressive new nation pushed westward, subjugating Indian nations east of the Mississippi and force-marching them to Indian territory in Oklahoma. Meanwhile, Anglo colonists seized Texas. By the 1840s, enflamed by the quasi religious ideology of Manifest Destiny, the United States parried and thrust to the Pacific Coast. Diplomacy thwarted British interests in Oregon. Military force wrenched the Southwest from Mexico. Millions of acres of land lay waiting to be digested by speculators and settlers convinced of their superiority over barbaric Indians and backward Mexicans.

The Treaty of Guadalupe Hidalgo, which ceded the Southwest to the United States in 1848, was supposed to keep the conquerors from running roughshod over the conquered. Articles 8 and 9 guaranteed the property rights of Mexicans regardless of whether or not they resided in the ceded territory or chose to be citizens of the United States. And Mexican property was substantial; lands claimed under Spanish and Mexican grants encompassed about thirty-eight million acres in the Territory of New Mexico (New Mexico, Arizona, and southern Colorado) alone. New Mexico possessed the lion's share—about nineteen million acres—with grants covering about a quarter of its surface, mostly in the north. Southern Colorado contained another seven million acres. Claims in Arizona totaled twelve million acres, mostly in the Santa Cruz and San Pedro watersheds. The exception was the Peralta-Reavis claim, a colossal fraud that jutted like a battering ram from the Salt River Valley to Silver City (Bradfute 1975; Walker and Bufkin 1979). Once Surveyor General Royal Johnson exposed the intricate deception, grants in Arizona shrank to 850,000 acres (Wagoner 1975).[3]

Despite Article 8's solemn assurance that "property of every kind . . . shall be inviolably respected," however, Guadalupe Hidalgo was flawed from the very beginning. Article 10 of the original treaty stated, "All grants of land made by the Mexican Government . . . shall be respected as valid, to the same extent that the same grants would be valid, if the said territories had remained within the limits of Mexico" (Griswold del Castillo 1990:180). That provision followed the legal precedent set by Chief Justice John Marshall in *U.S. v. Percheman* (1833), which ruled that Article 8 of the Adams-Onís Treaty confirmed Spanish land grants in Florida. But the U.S. Senate struck the article, and it never appeared in the final treaty. United States authorities then operated according to the principle that most Spanish and Mexican land grants were "imperfect," that is, that their owners had not yet perfected title to those lands under Mexican law. By assuming sovereignty over the ceded territory, the United States assumed the right to determine the confirmation process as well. Such an interpretation placed the burden of proof on the conquered, not the conquerors. Land grant owners became claimants who had to hire lawyers, provide titles, and put together cases that often dragged on for decades (Ebright 1994).

The result was a dispossession of monumental proportions. Of the 248 grants brought before the U.S. Court of Private Land Claims, the court confirmed a mere 88. Those confirmed grants represented approximately 2 million of the 38 million acres claimed (Bradfute 1975). Family patrimonies dissolved. Community land bases disappeared. Speculators with political connections triumphed over people who actually worked the land (Bradfute 1975, Griswold del Castillo 1990, Ebright 1994).

Even when U.S. authorities proceeded honestly and with good intentions, they usually failed to comprehend the differences between the Spanish and Anglo-American legal systems. Local custom determined the adjudication of disputes over land and water in New Mexico more often than formal Spanish law (Ebright 1994). Land grant law was not codified in any detail until after Mexican independence, when the Colonization Law of 1824 and the Regulations of 1828 were passed. Even then, the challenges of life on a dangerous frontier made the survival of your neighbors vital to your own survival as well. The logic of the market had not yet alienated land from the communities that depended upon its soil, grasses, timber, fuelwood, and water.

The United States, in contrast, had already divorced itself from communal use rights and the communal ownership of land recognized by English common law. Peasant corporate communities once dominated much of rural Europe, including the British Isles (Bloch 1966; Netting 1981; Vassberg 1984; Sheridan 1988b). But as the European capitalist world system developed and diversified, land increasingly became a private commodity rather than a communal resource. During the eighteenth and early nineteenth centuries, the so-called Enclosure Laws privatized most British commons (Thompson 1963).

In colonial New England, common property barely took root. English settlers justified their seizure of Indian lands by contrasting their "improvement" of lands with Indian hunting and gathering (Cronon 1983). "As for the Natives in New England," John Winthrop observed, "they inclose noe Land, neither have any settled habytation, nor any tame Cattle to improve the Land by, and soe have noe other but a Natural Right to those Countries" (quoted in Cronon 1983:56). Enclosure and agricultural intensification, in comparison, created a superior, civil right of ownership. At best, Indians could only claim their cornfields. As minister John Cotton proclaimed, "In a vacant soyle, hee that taketh possession of it, and bestoweth culture and husbandry upon it, his Right it is" (quoted in Cronon 1983:56–57).

After the Mexican war, then, two very different legal systems collided on a very uneven playing field. One recognized customary rights and common property, and gave precedence to people who actually worked the land. "Although written evidence of title was not without importance under the Spanish and Mexican legal systems," Malcolm Ebright observed, "for Hispanos, possession was indeed nine-tenths of the law." Ebright goes on to say, "Most Hispanos never conceived of the possibility that the common laws of their community grants were in jeopardy because under their laws and customs, the common lands could never be sold" (Ebright 1994:38).

To Anglo-American lawyers, judges, and surveyors general, in comparison, common property was an anachronism and written title reigned supreme. The men who controlled the legal process either dismissed or did not understand the intricate web of laws, customs, and social relationships that attached communities to their land. And since many of those power brokers were unscrupulous land speculators, legal subterfuge subverted the land grant confirmation process at every stage. One tactic the speculators employed to pick apart community grants was to buy out the *poblador principal*, or principal settler, who in some cases was the only name listed on the grant's title. Another was the partition suit. A lawyer representing the grantees often received a portion of the grant in return for his legal services. Once the New Mexico territorial legislature passed a partition statute in 1876, the lawyer, now a grantee himself, could demand the division of the grant. If such a division reduced its value, the grant had to be sold in its entirety (Ebright 1994). More than 80 percent of the confirmed grants ended up in Anglo-American hands

(Lamar 2000). The result was a lawyers' banquet that made beggars of thousands of Hispano grantees.

The Santa Fe Ring and Baca Float No. 3

One such banquet was Baca Float No. 3. The saga of Baca Float No. 3 began on the plains of northeastern New Mexico during the last days of the Spanish empire. After Juan Bautista de Anza forged alliances with Comanches, Utes, Navajos, and Jicarilla Apaches in the 1780s, New Mexican stock raisers moved onto the vast grasslands beyond the Sangre de Cristo Mountains. Some were wealthy sheep and cattlemen who manipulated their ties with officials in Guadalajara or Durango to secure enormous private grants. Others were small ranchers and farmers who petitioned the Spanish and Mexican governments for community grants. Baca Float No. 3 was a lawyer's answer to the collision of these two competing visions of the landscape on a huge, arrow-shaped block of terrain projecting into the Southern Plains.

The first to lay claim was Luis María Cabeza de Baca, a prominent sheepman along the Río Grande. In 1821, Baca and his seventeen sons and sons-in-law received title to the grant of Las Vegas Grande, which stretched for more than half a million acres east of the Pecos River. During the 1820s, the Baca family drove their herds of sheep onto this ocean of grass, part of that brief spasm of expansion that propelled ranchers like the Elías Gonzálezes onto the virgin grasslands of southeastern Arizona. But the alliances that allowed them to advance unraveled after Mexican independence. The Bacas occupied the grant for no more than a decade before Comanche raiding forced them to retreat to their hacienda of Peña Blanca on the Río Grande. Apparently the only improvement they made on Las Vegas Grande was a "little hovel at the foot of a cliff" called Loma Montosa, where a "swarthy ranchero" offered Josiah Gregg "a treat of goat's milk" in 1831 (Gregg 1954:76–77; Ebright 1994; Officer 1987).

A few years after the Bacas abandoned their grant, however, *vecinos* from San Miguel del Vado petitioned for a community grant with similar but not identical boundaries. Reflecting a change of policy, New Mexican officials granted their petition in 1835. During the eighteenth century, privileged individuals snared most grants. But as Pueblo Indian populations declined because of disease and displacement, the government awarded more community grants to encourage agricultural production and to plant more Hispanic settlers on a dangerous frontier (Ebright 1994). The Las Vegas community grant was part of that trend, a trend that became increasingly desperate as Mexico sought to reinforce its northern borders against the Anglo-American onslaught (Weber 1982).

By 1845, the year Mexico and the United States went to war, 297 families were cultivating fields and running stock on the Las Vegas grant (Ebright 1994). They lived in a string of little communities along the Gallinas River, but the settlements, at least at first, were known collectively as Nuestra Señora de los Dolores de Las Vegas. By 1860, twenty-two hundred people inhabited the town of Las Vegas itself.

The Baca heirs protested the community grant, but their objections fell on deaf ears during the tumultuous 1840s. Following Guadalupe Hidalgo, however, they renewed their claims. In 1860, the U.S. Congress recognized both grants as legal but allowed the heirs of the community grant to remain on the land. To compensate the Bacas, Congress authorized them to select "an equal quantity of vacant land, not mineral, in the Territory of New Mexico, to be located by them in square bodies not exceeding five in number."[4] Two of the chosen "floats" were in Arizona: Baca Float No. 5, northwest of Prescott, and Baca Float No. 3 in the heart of the Santa Cruz Valley.

John S. Watts, the attorney representing the Baca heirs, selected Baca Float No. 3 on June 17, 1863. Originally from Indiana, Watts descended on New Mexico for the same reasons Stephen Benton Elkins, Thomas Benton Catron, and other members of the so-called Santa Fe Ring did—because land grant litigation had turned the territory into a golden cash cow for lawyers and their political allies. Watts represented Ramón Vigil in his successful attempt to win confirmation of a fraudulent grant along the Río Grande where Los Alamos is today (Ebright 1994). He also served as associate justice and later chief justice on the New Mexico Territorial Supreme Court. In the late 1850s, while seated on the court, Watts informed a congressional committee that he was representing forty-three land-grant cases as well (Lamar 2000). The New Mexico legal system apparently did not worry much about conflict of interest during those avaricious days.

Watts's interests in Baca Float No. 3 went beyond legal fees, however. On May 1, 1864, less than a month after the commissioner of the General Land Office approved the selection, a long list of Baca heirs sold their interests in Baca Floats Nos. 2, 3, and 4 to Watts for three thousand dollars.[5] Each of those three floats—No. 2 on the Canadian River north of modern Tucumcari, New Mexico, No. 3 in the Santa Cruz Valley, and No. 4 in the San Luis Valley of southern Colorado—contained 99,289.39 acres. They totaled 297,868.17 acres, more than 465 square miles. In other words, Watts paid the Baca heirs one cent an acre for three-fifths of their patrimony. On May 30, 1871, he purchased Baca Float No. 5 northwest of Prescott for sixty-eight hundred dollars.[6] Manuel María Gándara would have tipped his hat in admiration at those transactions.

According to Watts's application to the surveyor general of New Mexico, Baca Float No. 3 was "entirely vacant unclaimed by anyone, and is not mineral, to my knowledge."[7] Watts was either incomprehensibly ignorant of the Santa Cruz Valley or breathtakingly brazen in his greed. The original 1863 location of Baca Float No. 3 encompassed most of the Tumacácori and portions of the Calabasas and Sonoita grants. It also included the communities of Tubac, Tumacácori, and Calabasas. Hispanic settlers from Sonora had raised families and fought Apaches for almost two centuries along the river, and Spanish, Mexican, and Anglo miners had searched for silver throughout the western foothills of the Santa Rita Mountains. The original location of Baca Float No. 3 was neither "vacant land" nor "not mineral" (Mattison 1967; Wagoner 1975). Watts was playing a high-stakes game of land grant poker, gambling that the surveyor general of New Mexico would not realize what a choice piece of real estate Watts was trying to grab.

The gamble, if it was a gamble, paid off. Surveyor General John Clark certified and approved Watts's application the same day he submitted it. Commissioner of the General Land Office J. M. Edmunds bounced it right back, stating, "Your approval of the location under consideration is found to have ignored the imperative condition that the land selected at the base of Solero [sic] mountain . . . is vacant land and not mineral." On April 2, 1864, Clark replied, "there is no evidence in the office of the surveyor general of New Mexico" that Baca Float No. 3 "contains any mineral, or that it is occupied." Then he gave himself some wiggle room by adding:

There have been no public surveys made in the neighborhood of said tract, and there is no record of or concerning the land in question in the surveyor general's office, nor—as I believe—in the office of the register or receiver of the land office of New Mexico. As I am personally unacquainted with that region of country, I cannot certify that the land in question is "vacant and not mineral" or otherwise. Those facts can only be determined by actual examination and survey.[8]

Whether Clark had any ties to Watts or the Santa Fe Ring remains to be determined. At least three of the other eight surveyors general of New Mexico were "blatant land speculators," so Clark may not have been as ignorant as he claimed (Ebright 1994:41). Regardless of Clark's motives, however, Watts was not working alone. Buried in the hundreds of pages of titles, indentures, quitclaims, and testimony that ascend from the District Court of Arizona to the Supreme Court of the United States is a remarkable document no published account of Baca Float No. 3 even mentions. On March 2, 1863, more than three months before Watts requested the first location of Baca Float No. 3 and more than a year before the Baca heirs formally sold the property to him, Watts declared that he was "the owner of one of the unlocated floats containing about one hundred thousand acres of land granted to the heirs of Luis Maria Baca." He also claimed "full power and authority to make the location for said heirs under said act, and cause to be made a title in fee of the same after such proper location and survey."[9]

After establishing those two claims, Watts stated the following:

Now, therefore, be it further known that I, John S. Watts, have this day sold to William Wrightson, of the city of Cincinnati, State of Ohio, the said unlocated tract with all of its privileges, for and in consideration of the sum of one hundred and ten thousand dollars, the receipt whereof is hereby acknowledged, and I hereby bind myself, my heirs, executors or administrators, to make a full and complete title in fee simple of said land to said William Wrightson, his assigns or legal representatives, whenever thereunto required. And I, the said John S. Watts, hereby authorize and empower the said W. Wrightson to make the location under the said act in as full and ample manner as the said heirs could do the same.[10]

A speculator in railroads and mines, Wrightson was one of the founders of the Sonora Exploring and Mining Company. He also was president of the Santa Rita Mining Company, a subsidiary formed in 1858 to "occupy and develop the Silver Mines in the Santa Rita Mountains" (quoted in North 1980:39). None of the mines yielded enough ore to pay expenses, but Wrightson hung on even after the Sonora Exploring and Mining Company collapsed around him. Watts had the Baca heirs in his pocket. Wrightson knew where the most likely silver prospects were. Together the two men hatched the scheme that eventually evicted Sarah Black from her home during the First World War.

Watts and Wrightson filed the sale of the float in the District of Columbia, not in Tucson or Santa Fe. From 1861 to 1863, Watts served as New Mexico's elected delegate to Congress, where he secured passage of the Organic Act establishing Arizona as a separate territory (Wagoner 1970). His strongest supporters were Ohio members of the House of Representatives like James M. Ashley and John A. Gurley, whose support was not coincidental. Cincinnati investors ran the Sonora Exploring and Mining Company and the Santa Rita Mining Company, which were incorporated in Ohio. During the debate over splitting Arizona from New Mexico, Watts hoisted a piece of silver ore from the Heintzelman mine to press home his claim that Arizona was a land of fabulous mineral wealth (Lamar 2000; Sacks 1964). The Cincinnati entrepreneurs and the Santa Fe Ring embraced one another in Washington and set their sights on the western foothills of the Santa Rita Mountains.

On April 9, 1864, the commissioner of the General Land Office approved Watts's selection and ordered it to be surveyed. Wrightson and mining engineer Gilbert Hopkins rode into the Santa Ritas with their surveyor's chains. Wrightson had survived Apache attacks, labor unrest, and the removal of federal troops during the Civil War. But his luck ran out in February 1865, when Apaches ambushed him and Hopkins in a thicket five hundred yards away from Fort Buchanan (Pumpelly 1920). Instead of a fortune in silver, Wrightson got a bloody death and his name on the Santa Ritas' highest peak.

Before he died, however, Wrightson discovered a major error in the original location of the float. On April 30, 1866, Watts petitioned the commissioner of the General Land Office to authorize the surveyor general to move Baca Float No. 3 north and east. "The existence of war in that part of the Territory of Arizona and the hostility of the Indians prevented a personal examination of the locality prior to the location," Watts stated. He argued that a "mistake" in the "initial point of location" had been made, one that "would result in leaving out most of the land designed or intended to be included in said location."[11] Watts requested that the amended location begin at a spot three miles southwest of "the building known as the Hacienda de Santa Rita," the headquarters of Wrightson's mining operations. Watts added, "this land which will be embraced in this change of the initial point is of the same character of unsurveyed vacant public land as that which would have been set apart by the location as first solicited."[12]

The amended location of Baca Float No. 3 was certainly more "vacant" than the first. It did not contain Tubac, Tumacácori, or Calabasas, and it did not straddle the Santa Cruz River or overlap the Tumacácori, Calabasas, or Sonoita grants. What it did do, however, was take in the Salero mine and what soon became the Aztec and Tyndall mining districts, the most active centers of mining in the Santa Cruz Valley (Hinton 1878). By relocating Baca Float No. 3, Wrightson and Watts hoped to gain control over a much greater portion of the Santa Rita Mountains and their mineralized foothills. If Wrightson had not been killed, and Watts had not selected the wrong initial location, they or their heirs might have ridden the Santa Cruz's silver boom of the 1870s and 1880s.

Details about this stillborn partnership remain murky. Did Wrightson ever pay Watts such an enormous sum for the grant? If so, where did he get the money? A more likely possibility is that no money exchanged hands, that Watts, Wrightson, and their silent partners intended to keep the sale quiet until the float was surveyed and confirmed. There were, after all, legal niceties that had to be observed. Whatever the arrangements, Wrightson's death severed the deal, because no partners or heirs ever stepped forward to claim his share of the enormous square of land.

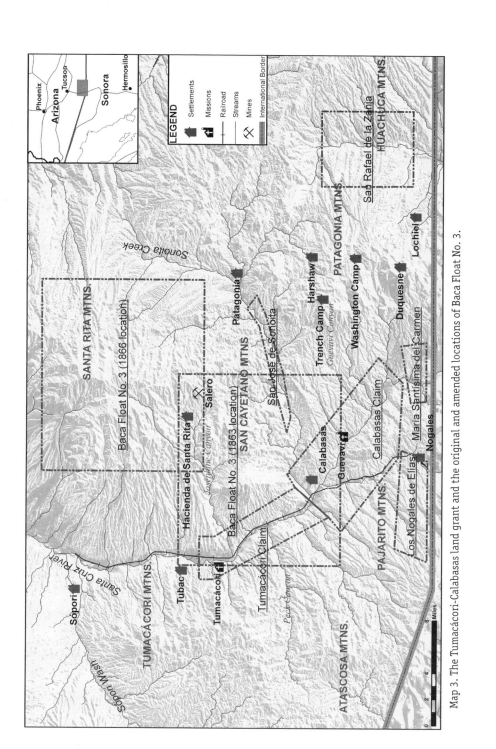

Map 3. The Tumacácori-Calabasas land grant and the original and amended locations of Baca Float No. 3.

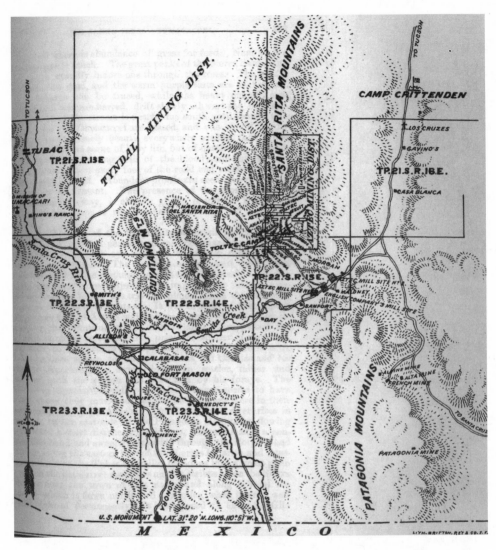

Figure 5. Plan of the Aztec Mining District, Pima County, Arizona. (Lithograph by Britton, Rey and Company in Hinton 1878; courtesy of the Arizona Historical Society/Tucson)

Watts, deeply involved in railroad as well as land speculation by the mid-1860s, had to pursue the scheme on his own.

The result was confusion and legal limbo along the Santa Cruz. After considering Watts's request for an amended location, the commissioner of the Land Office directed the surveyor general of Arizona to authorize the change. But no official survey of the amended location was ever carried out. Instead, both claimants and the Land Office treated "the metes and bounds described" in Watt's request of April 30, 1866, for the amended location "as the proper description of metes and bounds of the Baca Float No. 3."[13] The handful of southern Arizonans aware of the float assumed so too. "I first heard of Baca Float No. 3 sometime in the '70's when I was in the Surveyor General's office; that was in 1870," seventy-year-old George Roskruge, who surveyed the amended location for Colonel David Bouldin in 1887, stated. "From that time up to the year 1899 the Baca Float No. 3 was always supposed to lie in the Santa Rita mountains, covering the Santa Rita mountains. I never heard it located anywhere but in that district."[14]

For the next thirty-three years, "Judge" Watts and the heirs and claimants who followed him fought for confirmation of the amended location. They tried on several occasions to have the float surveyed and located, but the authorities always demurred. The Sonora Mining and Exploration Company, "which purported to hold the title to the amended location of Baca Float No. 3," sent John Magee to "take charge and look after that title and have it surveyed" in late December 1874. But when Magee described the grant to Surveyor General John Wasson, Wasson "point blank refused to survey it on the ground that it was known to be mineral for one hundred years showed mineral on its surface from one end to the other."[15]

Several years later, J. H. Watts, son of Judge Watts and attorney for his heirs, petitioned Commissioner of the Land Office J. A. Williams to relocate the float to the amended location. He did so on the grounds that the first location had been disapproved because no evidence had been presented that it was nonmineral. Williams replied that no such disapproval had been issued, but that the 1860 act authorizing the floats had placed a three-year limit on their selection. Because Watts's 1866 request for relocation exceeded that limit, "this office cannot authorize a re-location of Baca Float No. 3 without special legislation of Congress to that effect."[16] According to historian Ray Mattison, Charles Poston, who also claimed an interest in the float, made the same request the same year.[17]

But as bureaucrats kept passing the buck, titles to Baca Float No. 3 kept proliferating. On January 6, 1870, Judge Watts sold the amended location to Christopher Eldredge Hawley of Pennsylvania. After Watts himself died intestate in 1876, however, his widow and heirs conveyed two-thirds of their shares to D. W. Bouldin. Bouldin turned around and sold "one third of one-third" to fellow Texans John Ireland and Wilbur H. King on February 21, 1885.[18]

Meanwhile, New Yorker John Robinson claimed that on January 13, 1870, Hawley had given James Eldredge power of attorney authorizing *him* to sell the property.[19] Eldredge did so, conveying it to Robinson on May 5, 1884.[20] On February 13, 1885, Robinson asked the commissioner of the General Land Office to relocate the float to a third location because both the original and amended locations were mineral. Acting Commissioner L. Harrison recommended that Robinson's request be granted, but Secretary of the Interior L. Q. C. Lamar quickly squashed it for the same reason that Commissioner Williams had denied relocation to Watts's son.[21]

Stymied by the Department of the Interior, Robinson and others appealed to Congress itself—the final arbiter of land grants prior to the creation of the Court of Private Land Claims in 1891. James Eldredge continued to advise Robinson—an intriguing connection back to Hawley, particularly if Christopher Eldredge Hawley and Eldredge were related. In a remarkably cynical letter, Eldredge urged Robinson to approach Congress. "You know the '*step*' and capacity of the present American Statesman [*sic*] and the road to reach them," Eldredge sneered. "Charly E. [Eldredge] wants me to go to Washington to help. To enable me to be of any service over there, I should have to get drunk on d——d mean whiskey and remain drunk all the time I was there to enable me to tolerate the mixing up with such a d——d vulgar set of loafers as is now running the Govt."[22] Robinson apparently did so, and bills permitting the relocation were introduced into both the Forty-seventh and Forty-eighth Congresses. But the Senate Committee of Private Land Claims opposed relocation and the bills died (Mattison 1967).

Nevertheless, Robinson continued to play ping-pong with his claim throughout the early 1890s. Before his request for relocation was denied, Robinson and D. W. Bouldin entered into an agreement to sell the relocated float and split the proceeds.[23] Seven years later, on March 17, 1892, C. P. Pushaw, who claimed to have an option for thirty-five thousand dollars on Robinson's share, agreed to convey the north half of the float to Powhattan and James Bouldin, sons of D. W. Bouldin, in return for the deed to the southern half. Apparently Pushaw never exercised that option, because on November 12, 1892, Robinson and the Bouldins filed an indenture exchanging half interests in the float, with Robinson receiving the southern portion.[24] Two weeks later, Robinson transferred his half to John W. Cameron of Washington, D.C., in return for 10 percent of the proceeds. Then Cameron and Mrs. A. T. Belknap (September 22, 1893), Ireland and King (February 7, 1894), and Powhattan W. Bouldin and James Bouldin (February 7, 1894) all sold their shares in the south half to Alex Mathews, who apparently was trying to buy up all claims no matter how spurious. On April 30, 1896, Robinson even sold the north half of the float to S. A. M. Syme of Washington, D.C., for five dollars.[25]

The chain of claims started by Robinson eventually ended up in the hands of Arizona Copper Estate, a corporation organized in Arizona with an office in New York City. S. A. M. Syme and N. L. Boyce transferred the claim to James Simmons. James Simmons sold it to the American Exploration Company for a schedule of payments totaling $125,000. Apparently the company couldn't make the payments, so Mathews and Syme issued a quitclaim to Arizona Copper Estate in return for a mortgage on the property.[26]

Another corporation—the Santa Cruz Development Company—purchased the remaining shares of the Watts heirs. By then, Watts's children had scattered far and wide from Santa Fe. Watts himself died in Bloomington, Indiana. His widow lived out her remaining years in Berkeley, California. J. H. Watts moved to Missouri and then Kansas. His brother, J. Howe Watts, bounced from Arizona to Honduras to Mexico, where he was "in the mining business." He settled in San Pedro, California, whereas a sister—Mrs. Fanny Bancroft—resided in San Francisco.[27] Between 1899 and 1913, James and Katherine Vroom of Denver, Colorado and New York City bought out Watts's children and sold their claims to the Santa Cruz Development Company.[28]

On the eve of the First World War, then, four different parties—Arizona Copper Estate, the Santa Cruz Development Company, the Bouldin family, and two West Virginia lawyers, Cornelius Watts and Dabney Davis, who originally represented Syme and Mathews—claimed portions of the huge square. Beneath the formal language of quitclaims and indentures, you sense capital flows and family undercurrents, accumulating debts and predatory speculators. The "tangled web," as Mattison (1967) described the controversy over the Baca land grants, stretched from Santa Fe to the Santa Cruz Valley, from Dallas, Texas, to New York City and Washington, D.C. Speculators had created a fictitious landscape of competing claims that hovered like vultures over the miners, homesteaders, and ranchers struggling to make a living from the actual land itself.

Joseph Wise and the Lost Baca Heir

A final chain of claims attempted to bind Calabasas and the Hacienda de Santa Rita back to the plains of north-central New Mexico. Unlike other speculators, Joseph Wise had long and visceral ties to the Upper Santa Cruz Valley. Born in Waynesburg, Pennsylvania in 1867, he first settled at Santa Rita in 1884, when he was seventeen. His father, Morgan, a former Pennsylvania congressman, had been there since 1879, squatting in that crumbling outpost of Spanish dreams. "The Hacienda de Santa Rita consisted of some ruined buildings," Wise testified in 1914. "There were some buildings that were fit for habitation when I started living there; they needed repairing. I lived in some of the old buildings." Wise remained there until 1888. He met David W. Bouldin and George Roskruge, and even though he did not accompany Roskruge on his survey, he came across some of Roskruge's monuments while riding "over the country a great deal."[29]

His father, Morgan, in fact, wrote the commissioner of the General Land Office protesting Roskruge's survey in 1887. Morgan Wise pointed out to the commissioner that he and his son had a patented mining claim within the float along with "15 or 20 others." He also declared that David Bouldin had told him he intended "to let a contract and fence" the float despite the fact that the float was mineral. According to Wise, Bouldin did not want the government to survey the float. Commissioner William A. J.

Spar recommended that Wise bring the matter to the attention of the U.S. attorney general.[30]

Son Joseph pursued and enlarged his father's dream. Wise was a cowboy—"that was my vocation; that was my business"—who dreamed of being a cattleman. "I occupied portions of the land on Baca Float, as I understood it, prior to 1907, when I purchased the interest from Mr. Wilbur King," Wise stated. He purchased John Ireland's share from his widow on April 8, 1907, and King's share from King himself several weeks later.[31] Those two transactions supposedly gave Wise one-ninth of Bouldin's original purchase from Watts's heirs, even though John H. Watts later argued that the transaction with Bouldin had never been a deed of sale but a "contract" or "agreement" with Bouldin to quiet the float's title.[32]

Wise also owned several patents for mines and mill sites on both the original and amended locations, and homesteaded 160 acres near Calabasas, fencing the quarter section in 1889 and proving up on it in 1908. By then, he had established his headquarters at Calabasas, where he had lived since 1888. His wife, Lucia, claimed another forty acres there. Lucia was the daughter of C. P. and Mary Sykes. The two of them lived in the Santa Rita Hotel—Sykes's vision of New England prosperity on the Arizona frontier—until Wise built an elegant home of their own in 1910.[33]

Together the taciturn cowboy and the heiress of a failed visionary methodically set out to capture as much of the Baca float as they could. Once in possession of Ireland and King's shares, Wise began fencing off up to twenty-five thousand acres of the float. According to neighbor George Atkinson, "Wise has got one pasture on the Baca Float of about a thousand acres, known as the 'Garden' pasture. His biggest pasture is 'Sinquitona.' Probably he has got 4,000 acres in it and a small pasture of 1,000 absolutely. He is in absolute control of that because he has got it fenced. He also uses a lot of other grazing land; he has got cattle running on them."[34] Wise was living on the cusp, a product of the open range fighting to fence off as much of that range as he could.

He also had the mesquite-stump stubbornness of a pioneer who believed that possession was nine-tenths of the law, as the following interchange between him and Mr. Kingan, counsel for plaintiffs Watts and Davis, suggests:

Q: Prior to 1907 the first fences that you built outside of your 160 acres you built them upon what you believed was the public domain, isn't that a fact?

A: Why, I didn't, but I built them and I took them down because the government brought a suit against me and compelled me to take them down but I believed I had a right to fence them as long as there was a grant there.

Q: You yourself believed it was the public domain at that time, did you not?

A: No sir, I did not.

Q: That your only object in acquiring the King and Ireland title so called was to give you a color of title to fence up that float?

A: It is not.

Q: Isn't that a fact?

A: It is not.[35]

You can sense the anger of the forty-eight-year-old rancher mounting as the lawyer probed. But Wise dug much further into the past than King and Ireland to advance a second claim upon the float. Piecing together a convoluted genealogy, he argued that he possessed the share of a nineteenth Baca heir—Antonio Baca—who died before his father, Luis María Baca, but left a widow and children. The architect of Baca Float No. 3—Judge Watts—never knew about this dead son, or confused him with another heir, José Antonio Baca. According to Wise, Watts could not have conveyed Antonio's share to Christopher Hawley in 1870 because he never possessed it in the first place.[36]

Wise employed a grandson of Luis María Baca named Marcos C. de Baca to track down the heirs of the mysterious nineteenth son. A letter to Wise from Baca and Jesse Wise, Joseph's brother, spelled out the terms of the deal. "Witnesseth said Marcos de la Baca hereby agrees to secure from various heirs of Luis Maria Baca a deed or deeds for their interests in certain premises in Santa Cruz County, Arizona, said premises are now occupied by Joseph E. Wise et al. as a cattle ranch, said Marcos de Baca is to receive for said services thirty-five ($35) Dollars for each heirs' name in said Estate."[37] Baca, an attorney in New Mexico, was Wise's headhunter, scouring old court records and exploiting family connections to provide Wise with another boot hold on the float.

Most of Baca's headhunting took place in New Mexico. On August 20, 1913, he secured quitclaim deeds from the widow and children of José Baca, Antonio Baca's grandson. A day later, he got others from the widow and children of Ignacio Baca, another son of Antonio. On August 25, Marcos C. de Baca sold the deeds to Jesse and Joseph Wise "for and in consideration of the sum of One Dollar and other valuable consideration," which is what Baca paid the Baca heirs for their purported shares in the float.[38]

The genesis of Wise's claim arose at least six years earlier. On March 13, 1907, Wise paid Teodora and Manuel Baca of Cananea, Sonora, ten dollars for their title to the Baca Float. As a cattleman, Wise had extensive dealings in Sonora, eventually purchasing El Rancho Arizona south of the border. He also invested heavily in Nogales, where he moved his family in 1916 and served as mayor from 1933 to 1935. That 1907 quitclaim deed did not state Teodora and Manuel Baca's relationship to Antonio Baca, if there was one. But somehow Wise ferreted out Bacas in Cananea and concocted his most elaborate claim to the land he had been trying to monopolize since the late 1880s.[39]

The Department of the Interior vs. the Baca Float

While all these claims and counterclaims were bouncing from one assignee to another, the Department of the Interior was growing increasingly skeptical about the validity of the float itself. After the U.S. Supreme Court nullified the Tumacácori land grant, the General Land Office opened the former grant lands to homestead entries. At first, the Baca assignees paid little attention because they were still fighting over the amended location, which did not include any of those lands. In 1899, they even requested another survey of the amended float.

The General Land Office forwarded the request to Secretary of the Interior E. A. Hitchcock on May 6, and Hitchcock rendered his decision on July 25. After reviewing the history of Baca Float No. 3, he posed three questions that had to be answered: (1) Whether the original selection of

June 17, 1863, or the amended selection of April 30, 1866, was binding on the applicants. (2) Whether the "character of the land selected," that is, whether or not it was vacant and nonmineral, was to be determined at the date of selection or the date of approval of the claim's survey. And (3) "By whom and in what manner is the character of the land to be ascertained and determined?"[40]

Regarding the first question, Hitchcock supported the decisions of his predecessors, ruling that the "so-called amended location . . . was in reality, except as to the very small area common to both, an application to make a new selection." Because the three-year time limit had expired by 1866, Hitchcock declared, "The Department is therefore of the opinion that the grant claimants are bound by the selection of June 17, 1863."[41] Regarding the third question, Hitchcock contended that despite the creation of the Court of Private Land Claims in 1891, the Surveyor General of Arizona still possessed the authority to survey and locate the Baca floats. Regarding the second question—the one that cut right to the heart of the legality of the float itself—Hitchcock instructed the surveyor general to investigate the matter and hear the testimony of anyone claiming an interest in the float "adverse to the grant claimants" regarding whether it was non-mineral and vacant on June 17, 1863.[42]

The adverse claimants lost no time in being heard. On October 23, 1899, attorneys for twenty-three petitioners, including George Atkinson and the Wises, notified the surveyor general that they had occupied lands selected by the float for many years. There they had "at great expense, erected valuable and permanent improvements thereon; and, at great cost to themselves, they have reclaimed their said land, so occupied by them by bringing water thereto and irrigated the same therewith." All had filed entries and proven up on their land once the General Land Office had opened the Tumacácori and Calabasas grants to homestead entries. They also declared that portions of the float were "generally and notoriously known to be" mineral, that "well-known mines" were situated there, and that "large numbers of men have been engaged in such work continuously since a time prior to 1860." In conclusion, they argued that Baca Float No. 3 was "void" because the land was neither vacant nor nonmineral on June 17, 1863, when the original location was selected.

Secretary Hitchcock denied most of the petition except the question as to whether the original location of the float was vacant and non-mineral.[43] The same attorneys therefore presented a Brief of Contestants on January 25, 1900, appending the testimony or affidavits of long-time Arizona settlers Charles D. Poston, George Atkinson, Peter R. Brady, Fritz Contzen, Peter Kitchen, Teodora de Troil, Sabino Otero, and Joseph King. All those Arizona pioneers reiterated that portions of Baca Float No. 3 were being farmed, ranched, and mined in the early 1860s. They told about Manuel María Gándara's attempts to establish his hacienda at Calabasas. They talked about mining in the Santa Ritas during the 1850s and early 1860s.

Some noted the presence of even earlier mining activity. "Throughout these mountains [surrounding the Santa Cruz Valley] are many shafts, tunnels, and dumps, some of them showing great age," testified cattleman Sabino Otero, one of the heirs to the oldest Spanish land grant in Arizona. "At Tumacacori there is a large slag dump, deposited there many years before my recollection, and in which large mesquite trees are growing, and have been since my earliest recollection," Otero continued. "I was informed by my uncle and also my father that ores were brought principally from the Salero mountain and the Huebavi and from surrounding camps to Tumacacori and were treated there. The Guevavi or Huevavi mines were situated about 3 miles North of the old Huevavi mission on a range of mountains between the Potrero Creek and the old mission, and just South of old Fort Mason."[44]

Most of the pioneers had never heard of Judge Watts or Baca Float No. 3. "If Baca Float No. 3 had been located on the ground in 1863, where it is now claimed to be located, I, in common with all my neighbors, would certainly have known it," Otero declared. "I remember that in the year before Wrightson was killed, a survey was made, and that my father at that time protested against them including his property in their survey; but the survey as then made, and as I then understood it was to the North and East of the San Cayetano Mountains."[45] In other words, the survey was of the amended, not the original, location.

Charles Poston, in contrast, testified that he knew Judge Watts when Watts was a delegate to Congress. According to Poston, "said Watts was well acquainted with the character of the lands included within Baca Float No. 3, and its mineral character."[46] Poston was general manager of the Sonora Exploring and Mining Company, and may have been privy to the secret deal between Watts and Wrightson. To the rest of the pioneers, however, the Baca Float was a fiction that had nothing to do with the people who had lived and died along the Santa Cruz River for the last forty years.

On June 30, 1900, the Department of the Interior ruled that even though the U.S. Supreme Court had nullified the Tumacácori and Calabasas grants, they and the San José de Sonoita grant were "in a state of reservation" when the original location of the float was selected in 1863. Consequently, any lands that the surveyor general found to be occupied or homesteaded on the former grants had to be excluded from the government survey. James Vroom, acting on behalf of himself and John Watts as claimants to the float, took issue with that decision on September 4, but his petition was denied.[47]

Barnes and Martin and John B. Wright, the attorneys for the adverse claimants, filed a scathing response to Vroom's petition. Painting a romantic picture of Gándara's hacienda at Calabasas, and citing Poston and J. Ross Browne about mining activity on the float, they characterized Watts's attempt to locate the float "as a fraud upon the Government, as well as a fraud upon the 150 or more miners whom Poston and Brown [sic] say were at the time mining within the boundaries of this land, taking out ores and known to be there by Judge Watts." "The attempt to sustain Baca Float No. 3 has been turned down by the Department time after time," they thundered. "It has been hawked through lawyers' offices from San Francisco to Washington, by persons who offered contingent fees of one-half of whatever might be recovered, for some thirty years last past. We thought we had the hydra killed, but now there comes another who wants to be heard. How many more there may be we cannot tell, but it seems that now is the opportune time to finish this claim with a *quietus* from which it shall never recover."[48]

The Department of the Interior delivered no such *coup de grace*. Instead, it awarded the contract to survey Baca Float No. 3 to Philip Contzen, U.S. deputy surveyor of Tucson, in 1905. Surveyor General Frank Ingalls then notified interested parties that hearings would be held at Nogales, Calabasas, and Tubac. Land that was vacant and nonmineral on June 17, 1863, would be included in the survey. "All lands that may be ascertained by me to have been occupied, or known to have been mineral at the date of the location" were to be excluded, Ingalls asserted.[49] In response, George Atkinson called a meeting of "all the claimants to the agricultural lands within the boundaries," whom he stated were "all bona fide settlers." He submitted a list of sixty-four names to Ingalls, forty-seven of whom were Hispanic.[50]

Contzen began his survey in early fall, 1905. By late October, he had progressed enough for Ingalls to launch his investigation. Ingalls traveled from Phoenix to Nogales and then proceeded northward, interviewing settlers and mining experts. In the process, he visited the ruins of Gándara's hacienda, Mission Tumacácori, and the Hacienda de Santa Rita at Salero. Riding horseback around Salero Hill, he photographed many patios and arrastras, "some of which are in a fair state of preservation. Others are barely distinguishable." "The country surrounding Salero Hill is conspicuously mineralized," Ingalls reported, "and a person not conversant with the surface character of a mineral belt cannot fail to observe the existence of precious minerals, for its presence is apparent everywhere."[51]

All the settlers and mining men who testified concurred, including William P. Blake, professor of geology and mining at the University of Arizona. Blake first came to Arizona in 1853 as a mineralogist and geologist assigned to R. S. Williamson's survey of a rail route from the Mississippi Valley to the Pacific Coast. Six years later, while serving as editor of *Mining Magazine and Journal of Geology*, he wrote an article titled "Silver and Copper Mining in Arizona." His primary informant was Charles Poston, although he also utilized the reports of numerous other observers. Blake characterized southern Arizona as "the northwestern extension of the great silver region of Mexico." "The most celebrated modern localities are Arivaca, Sopori, the Arizona mountains, the Santa Rita Range, the Cerro Colorado, the entire vicinity of Tubac," he noted. "Titles were acquired to many veins of silver ores in the Santa Rita mountains, among which were the old mines of Salero and Ojero." Blake's article also enumerated the mines worked by the Sonora Exploring and Mining Company and the Santa Rita Mining Company. "Some of these mines were worked long ago and large amounts of silver taken out," Blake concluded (Blake 1859:3).[52]

Two other witnesses—Thomas Gardner of Patagonia, who visited the

Salero Mine in 1857, and William McCoy, who worked as superintendent of the Santa Rita Mining Company between 1858 and 1860—testified that the Tyndall Mining District in the Santa Ritas was known as the "Wrightson Mining District" as early as 1858.[53] Joseph King, whose ranch was "about 800 yards east of the old Tumacacori Church or Mission," even worked on Wrightson's survey of Baca Float No. 3 until a heavy storm interrupted it on New Year's Day, 1865.[54] Through these witnesses, along with excerpts from the published work of J. Ross Browne, Raphael Pumpelly, Hiram C. Hodge, and Richard J. Hinton, Ingalls clearly established both the existence and notoriety of mining on the float prior to the original location in 1863.

Then, in an eloquent and emotional passage, Ingalls declared:

I am satisfied in my own mind that the passing of title to the Grant's heirs of any of the lands included in this survey, and particularly those lands in the N.E. corner thereof, surrounding Salero Hill, which I instructed Deputy Contzen to segregate by instructions dated June 17th, 1905, would be a great injustice, not only to those who are developing this country and extracting valuable mineral therefrom at the present time as grantors or heirs of former occupants, but an injustice to those who have passed within the Great Beyond, who sacrificed their lives at the hands of the blood-thirsty Apaches in the development thereof, long before the Baca heirs dared attempt the perpetration of this fraud on these hardy pioneers and blazers of the western trail. Perhaps, like coyotes in the night, they sneaked into this country after an Apache raid, or before a prospective one, and found the inhabitants had fled temporarily, and they then proclaimed the country vacant, unoccupied and non mineral.[55]

Finally, Ingalls attempted to cut off the last head of the hydra by taking aim at the originator of the "fraud," Judge Watts himself. Turning Watts's own florid prose against him, he quoting a speech Watts gave before the second session of the Thirty-seventh Congress (1861–62). "Mr. Speaker, it is the general impression that this distant Territory is a God-forsaken portion of the world, of no interest to anybody, and that nobody need take any interest in," Watts teased, holding up a specimen of Arizona silver. "Now, I wish to satisfy the House that this is a mistake; that although every acre of ground that is within the limits of Arizona will not produce seventy-five or eighty bushels of corn, it will produce seventy-five or eighty or one hundred dollars worth of the precious metals, including gold." Watts then had the clerk of the House read a letter from the director of the Philadelphia Mint stating that ore from the Heintzelman Mine had assayed at $1,660 a ton. "From my intimate knowledge of that section of the country, the Territory of Arizona alone will furnish to the circulating medium of the country $50,000,000 per annum in the articles that I have exhibited to you," Watts concluded. "An Italian sunset never threw its gentle rays over more lovely valleys or Heaven-kissing hills, valleys harmonious with the music of a thousand sparkling rills, mountains shining with untold millions of mineral wealth, wooing the hand of capital and labor to possess and use it."[56]

Even though Watts did not mention "Heaven-kissing" Salero Hill in his paean, Ingalls argued that the judge was "intimately conversant with its mineral-bearing veins." Why else would he include the area around Salero Hill in both his original and amended locations? In Ingall's opinion, Watts was biding his time until federal troops subdued the Apaches so Watts "and his followers" could "return to reap their reward, by extracting the valuable ore from these mines." Ingalls recommended that the "selection be rejected in its entirety" because it violated the provisions of the congressional act of 1860 that restricted the Baca floats to vacant, nonmineral land.[57]

The commissioner of the General Land Office affirmed Ingall's recommendation on May 13, 1907. The Baca heirs appealed, and on June 2, 1908, First Assistant Secretary Pierce of the Department of the Interior issued his decision on behalf of the secretary. Pierce reviewed the history of "this remarkable litigation," which involved "title to a tract of land more than twice the area of this District of Columbia, vast mineral wealth and the rights of a multitude of settlers."[58] He dismissed the appellants' contention that title passed to the Baca heirs when the original selection was made and approved by the surveyor general of Arizona in 1863 or when the surveyor general ordered a survey in 1864. "During all these years, the land selected on June 17, 1863, has been retained on maps and records as part of the public lands," Pierce declared. "The grantees have never been in possession and have never paid a cent of taxes upon it as private property, but, on the contrary, until recent years have treated it as a piece of land unwisely selected but happily not so far appropriated by them in settlement of their claim as to prevent, if the Government would permit, a new selection."[59]

Pierce also stated that lands included within the Tumacácori, Calabasas, and Sonoita grants had been reserved at the time of the original location and would be excluded from the float. He then ordered the surveyor general of Arizona to notify the appellants of his decision and to allow them sixty days after notification to request another hearing to present evidence rebutting the claims of Atkinson and other settlers. If no such motion for review were filed within that period, "the entire selection" would be "finally rejected."[60]

Ingalls sent the notice out on August 13, 1908. On September 21, he informed the commissioner that no motion for review had been filed by September 12, which, according to departmental policy, was the expiration date.[61] By then, those fighting Baca Float No. 3 may have thought that the "hydra-headed monster" had finally been slain.[62]

The Baca Float and the Courts

In less than a decade, however, the monster rose triumphant and devoured all the adverse claims. After the Department of the Interior issued its decision in 1908, the General Land Office opened the float to homestead entries. By then, the major claimants were John Watts and James Vroom, who traced their claims back to the widow and children of Judge Watts, and Cornelius C. Watts (apparently no relation) and Dabney C. T. Davis, whose claim descended from Watts's sale to Hawley in 1870. The three parties petitioned the U.S. District Court of Arizona to enjoin the Secretary of the Interior and the commissioner of the General Land Office from permitting further entries.[63]

According to the reminiscences of Arizona pioneer Alexander Davidson, Watts and Davis were West Virginia lawyers commissioned by "Sims and Mathews," another law firm in Virginia. Davidson's brother had been a Union surgeon during the Civil War who had cared for a wounded Confederate prisoner named Colonel Sam Sims. The two men became close friends.

Davidson was in his nineties when Mrs. George S. Kitt interviewed him in the early 1930s, so his memory for names may have been faulty. "Sam Sims" was probably S. A. M. Syme of Washington, D.C. and Alexandria, Virginia, whereas Mathews was undoubtedly Alexander Mathews, who resided in West Virginia.

Sometime in the 1890s, Davidson's brother asked him to look after Syme and Mathews's interests in the float. Before the U.S. Supreme Court invalidated the Tumacácori land grant in 1898, Davidson advised Syme and Mathews to "lay low and let the settlers and the Calabasas and Tumacacori people fight it out because, if these grants were genuine their claim antedated that of the Baca Float and would stand, whereas, if they were not genuine the settlers were fighting Sims and Mathews battle for them." After the court threw out the Tumacácori grant, Davidson told Syme and Mathews to press their claims and have the float surveyed. According to Davidson, they paid five thousand dollars to "Senator Edmunds, the great International lawyer," to examine their case. He concluded their title was valid because the surveyor general of New Mexico had approved it.[64]

By then, according to Davidson, Syme and Mathews were "broke." Syme "was a great promoter and speculator and made much money just after the War," Davidson recalled. "But later because of unstable loans in an endeavor to aid the Southern people, the firm failed." Syme and Mathews hired Watts and Davis to represent them in return for a 30 percent interest in the grant. Syme and Mathews also employed "Senator Baily"—probably former Senator Joseph W. Bailey of the firm Bailey, Nichols and Bailey of Dallas, Texas—to quiet that part of the title claimed by Judge Watts's heirs. But when Bailey found out Watts's claim on the float was good, he "flopped over and went in with Watts to secure part of the property." Again, Davidson's memory was cloudy. "Judge Watts" was long dead by then, so Bailey must have entered into an agreement with son John Watts and James W. Vroom. According to Davidson, "The question was finally settled by a compromise whereby Watts and Baily were given the north half of the grant for the consideration of $25,000."[65] At some point in the process, Watts and Davis must have secured the rest of Syme and Mathews's claim to the southern half of the float, because their names disappear from the legal record.

The U.S. District Court of Arizona granted John Watts, Vroom, and Watts and Davis the injunction to prevent further entries on the float. "Judge Rouse was employed to gather evidence in Arizona," Davidson recalled. "But Judge Rouse had just lost his son Charlie, which was a great blow, and nine tenths of the time he was 'indisposed?' so I had to hustle around and do most of the work myself."[66] The settlers appealed the injunction to the Ninth Circuit Court of Appeals, but it affirmed the lower court. Secretary of the Interior Franklin K. Lane and Clay Tallman, commissioner of the General Land Office, then stepped in on behalf of the settlers and appealed the decision to the U.S. Supreme Court.

The case was called *Lane v. Watts*. The Supreme Court heard it in the late spring of 1914. On June 22, it affirmed the decisions of the two lower courts. Contrary to the arguments of the Department of the Interior that the land could not be withdrawn from the public domain until a survey of the float had been completed, the Supreme Court ruled that title to Baca Float No. 3 "passed out of the United States and vested in said heirs on April 9, 1864" when the commissioner of the Land Office approved the location. All subsequent claims and withdrawals were therefore invalid. *Lane v. Watts* had nothing to say about the overwhelming evidence that the float was neither vacant nor nonmineral when the float was selected.

The day after the court's decision, Watts and Davis filed suit in the U.S. District Court of Arizona to quiet the title. Defendants included both the Wises and the Bouldins, who claimed most of the north half of the float. On December 14, the court ruled that Watts and Davis held title to "an undivided eighteen nineteenths of the south half" of the float whereas three Bouldins—Jennie, David, and Helen Lee—together held eighteen nineteenths of the north half. Joseph and Margaret Wise each possessed "an undivided one thirty-eighth of the whole of said tract."[67]

Four different suits appealed the decision to the Ninth Circuit Court of Appeals. The suits were consolidated, and on January 8, 1917, the appeals court issued its opinion. *Lane v. Watts* had already determined that title to Baca Float No. 3 had passed to the Baca heirs in 1864; subsequent commissioners of the General Land Office had no power to revoke it or change its boundaries. In other words, the amended location, which the speculators had pursued for almost half a century, was not and never had been valid.

The appeals court then turned its attention to the Wises' claim that they held title to the share of Antonio Baca, the elusive nineteenth son. The District Court of Arizona had affirmed that title. The appeals court reversed it. "We assume that Luis María Baca had a son named Antonio Baca, who died before his father," the opinion stated.[68] But after reviewing the original Baca grant in New Mexico, the appeals court concluded that Antonio Baca was not one of the claimants. "Neither Antonio Baca nor any of his heirs ever having made any claim to any land granted by the Mexican government, they had no claim to waive, and manifestly waived none," the appeals court stated. As a result, "Joseph E Wise and Margaret W. Wise acquired no interest in the land in controversy through the heirs of Antonio Baca, who had no interest therein to convey."[69]

Homesteaders: The Second Dispossession

The second dispossession of the Santa Cruz Valley soon ground forward. Once the decision was announced, the Bouldins and Watts and Davis filed suits to evict settlers living on Baca float lands. By then, there were 18 patented entries encompassing 2,352 acres and 41 pending entries covering 5,527 acres on the float (Mattison 1967). Watts and Davis named seventy-five defendants living on the south half of the grant.[70] At least fifty-two of those names were Hispanic. The Bouldins and Weldon M. Bailey, son of ex-Senator Joseph W. Bailey, enumerated 161, of whom 101 had Hispanic surnames.[71] Most of these people were immigrants from Sonora, including Opata and Yaqui Indians who had fled the genocidal policies of the Mexican government under President Porfirio Díaz (Gastellum 1995).

Louis Gastellum, who was four years old when federal marshals forced his family from their land in 1919, wrote a memoir of life along the Santa Cruz in the early 1900s. Gastellum's Basque ancestors migrated from Spain to Alamos in the early 1700s. A century later, they were raising cattle in the Altar Valley, where his great-grandfather was born in 1828 in the former mission community of Tubutama. His father, Santiago, moved from Tubutama to Tubac in 1898. Santiago was no stranger to the Santa Cruz Valley. For at least a century, close ties of trade and kinship had linked families along the Río Altar in northwestern Sonora to families in Tucson and Tubac (Sheridan 1986).

Santiago Gastellum went to work as a cowboy for Luis Acuña, another Sonoran pioneer from the former capital of Ures. In 1886, Acuña home-steaded 120 acres of floodplain land just south of Tubac. By 1895, he had brought 100 acres under cultivation and had sunk a well, fenced his property, and built a corral, stable, chicken coop, and two-room adobe house. Santiago soon became part of the family when he married Santos, Acuña's seventeen-year-old daughter, in 1903 (Gastellum 1995). For the next decade and a half, Santiago worked as a foreman for both Acuña and Sabino Otero while he built up his own herd. At that time, Otero's cattle ranged across an immense arc that stretched from the Santa Cruz Valley to the Baboquivari and Santa Rosa Districts of what is now the Tohono O'odham Nation. Because of his hard work, Santiago and his family pros-pered, and more Gastellums moved from Tubutama to Tubac. After Acuña died in 1911 and his wife in 1915, Santos and her sister inherited the homestead and all its improvements and animals. The Gastellums were now property owners, cattle ranchers, and farmers, their livelihoods gov-erned by the rhythms of the range and their floodplain fields.

Many of the names mentioned in the eviction petitions were their neighbors and friends. Rosa Lim was the midwife who delivered Luis and his six brothers and sisters. One of his aunts married Ramón Andrade whereas another wed Eduardo Sierras. Sarah Black taught two genera-tions of Acuña and Gastellum children, and the Casanega, Madril, Lowe, Gomez, and Valdez children were their schoolmates. The Trujillo, Gomez, and Lowe families raised many of the fine horses that raced one another at every major fiesta, and Frank Burruel, Lola Villa, and Francisco Cota provided the music for dances held on the patio outside the Alday home (Gastellum 1995).

Their way of life was as ancient as Spaniards in the Sonoran Desert. Their fields sprouted Old World green in the winter—wheat, barley, oats, lentils, fava beans—and New World green—corn, beans, squash, and chile—when frosts were no longer a danger. On the bajadas descending from the Santa Rita and Tumacácori mountains they grazed livestock domesticated in the Near East and gathered agaves, cactus fruit, and wild greens just like the O'odham who preceded them. By the early 1900s, they were driving their cattle to railheads and shipping them to feed lots and slaughter houses in the Midwest, but theirs was still a semisubsistence economy involving as much barter and sharing as cash. Life on the ranchos along the Santa Cruz was little different from life in Tubutama, Ures, or the other riverine towns of Sonora where they had been born.

The settlers of the Upper Santa Cruz Valley did not give up that life without a fight. Responding to the Bouldins's suit against them in the U.S. District Court of Arizona, those on the north half of the grant listed the legal boundaries of their properties, which they had been in "open, notorious, continuous, peaceable" possession for twenty years or more. When they or their predecessors occupied those tracts, they were "in a wild and uncultivated condition, covered with brush and trees, rough, and not capable of being cultivated." Then, in dry, legal language that barely hinted at a generation or more of sowing and reaping, of calving, castrating, and branding, of flood, drought, childbirth, and death, they went on to say that they "have cleared and leveled the land, built fences to enclose their said several tracts, constructed ditches to conduct water onto the land, and made many and valuable improvements thereon, and in good faith greatly enhanced the value of said land and premises in a large sum, to wit, more than Two Hundred Thousand Dollars ($200,000.00)."[72]

Once again, the settlers and their lawyers pointed out the cynicism and opportunism of the speculators. From 1866 until 1905, the plaintiffs made no claim to the original 1863 location of Baca Float No. 3. Instead, they "repeatedly denied that they had any interest in said land, and claimed and insisted that they were the owners of the lands included within the amended location of 1866."[73] During those four decades, the plaintiffs were "fully aware" that the settlers were occupying and improving lands on the original location. "With reckless indifference to the effect upon these defendants and cross-complainants and all other persons willing to assume the risk, hazard and danger to life consequent upon contributing to the building up of the undeveloped lands of Arizona," the plaintiffs encouraged the settlers to "avoid" the amended 1866 location and claim lands on the original location.[74] In telling words, the settlers argued that "the asserted claim of the plaintiffs has never been maintained by them honestly or in good faith, as a true or citizenlike ownership of the said lands, but has been exploited by them as a matter without risk or expense to themselves, of speculation, for the joint benefit of themselves and real estate operators and others."[75] According to the defendants, Judge Watts and his heirs had "abandoned" the original location and had no claim upon it now.

Their arguments fell on deaf ears. *Lane v. Watts* had given the Bouldins and Watts and Davis the legal foundation they needed to quiet all claims. George Atkinson, who had come to Calabasas to build Colonel C. P. Sykes's Santa Rita Hotel, offered $250,000 for the grant. The speculators demanded $400,000. He then asked Congress to offer some relief to those about to lose their lands. "As for myself, it does not matter so much," Atkinson stated. "Although I spent $40,000 in one jolt to fight this case, I still have enough to support me to the end of my days. I still have my cattle" (quoted in Wagoner 1975:206). Atkinson proposed that the government pay the speculators and allow the farmers and ranchers who had homesteaded the land to remain where they were (Wagoner 1975).

The government declined. Instead, the Sixty-seventh Congress passed "An Act for the Relief of Settlers" after the Sixty-sixth Congress had turned it down. President Warren Harding signed it into law on July 5, 1921. Individuals who had received patents to their land prior to December 13, 1917, were entitled to select en lieu lands elsewhere in Arizona. The lieu lands could not surpass twice the amount of land they lost along the Santa Cruz. Some settlers accepted the offer and selected lands near Buckeye along the Gila River. Others, like Sarah Black and the Gastellum family, refused and had to be removed by federal marshals. Livestock had to be moved. Property had to be stored. Family homesteads had to be surrendered to people who bought and sold paper in Dallas, New York City, or Washington, D.C. "The eviction occurred at a most inopportune time, as my mother had just given birth to my younger brother, Manuel," Luis Gastellum remembered. "Complications developed and my mother underwent surgery, which confined her to bed for several weeks" (Gastellum 1995:7).

The Gastellums were fortunate. They owned land at Reventon, about five miles north of Tubac. The children had to commute three hours instead of five minutes to school each day, but their roots along the Santa Cruz were not completely ripped away. Other Mexican families either left the valley or moved onto small plots of land that could not support them. "Consequently, they became migrants and followed the harvesting seasons to the Salt River Valley and to California," Gastellum recalled. "As a result, many of the children had to leave school for two to four months each year" (Gastellum 1995:12).

The O'odham dispossessed by Gándara's land grab represented a culture that had inhabited the Sonoran Desert, including the Santa Cruz Valley, for a millennium or more. The Gastellums and their neighbors were part of an agropastoralist way of life that had flourished in the river valleys of Sonora since the 1600s. But the strokes of pens in distant places made them squatters—or ghosts—on lands they had cleared and plowed and seeded season after season, generation after generation. Two distinct land-based societies had been dismantled between Tubac and Guevavi. The triumph of speculators in the Upper Santa Cruz Valley was now utter and complete.

The Bottom of the Bottle

Now that the speculators had won, they had to figure out what to do with the 99,289.39-acre rectangle federal courts had dumped in their laps. They spent the first decade swatting down the last of the suits against them and trying to sell off their windfall. No single architect with any grand design emerged from the legal and financial maneuvering.

Then time and the Great Depression caught up with the victors. There was no bonanza in the foothills of the Santa Ritas, no commercial entrepôt to be conjured up now that Ambos Nogales straddled the international border. The geography of capitalism in southern Arizona had not yet evolved to a point where there was another way to make a profit off land except for the extractive industries of mining, ranching, or agriculture. Neither the Bouldins nor Watts and Davis wanted to go into the cattle business. The float remained a speculator's fantasy, not a cash cow.

But even fantasies require capital to sustain them. Beginning in 1929, wealthy "dudes" from back east began to turn the float into a playground of the rich. Their leader was Talbot T. "Tol" Pendleton, a former All-American football player from Princeton. Like Eastern scions before and since, Pendleton went into the Texas oil business after graduation and the First World War. As he absorbed Texas culture, however, Pendleton must have realized that the ultimate symbol of western aristocracy was a showcase ranch, not an oil derrick. Taking advantage of plunging land prices, Pendleton and his partner, F. M. Dougherty, bought out the Bouldins and Watts and Davis. By 1932, they were ready to form Baca Float Ranch.

For the next three decades, Pendleton lived the life of the gentleman rancher. He imported Santa Gertrudis cattle from the King Ranch in Texas. He raised racehorses. Whenever he got strapped for cash, he sold off portions of the float to wealthy friends. Retired executives from General Motors donned cowboy boots and drained martinis with Hollywood stars like Stewart Granger and John Wayne. From his ranch headquarters on Santa Gertrudis Lane, Pendleton became the center of a social whirl that reeled from La Caverna bar in Nogales, Sonora, to the Arizona Inn and Mountain Oyster Club in Tucson. Drinking was the primary form of recreation, the cattle business a backdrop to the endless parties. Baca Float No. 3 had become a stage where wealthy heiresses and remittance men starred in their own bourbon-fueled fantasies of western life.

A Handful of Homesteaders Return

Before Pendleton strode onto the scene, however, the Bouldin family and Watts and Davis spent more than a decade trying to make the float pay. Watts and Davis refused to sell back any homesteads on the south half of the float.[1] The Bouldins, in comparison, informed John Henry Campbell, their chief attorney in Tucson, that they were willing to sell any land except the Burruel and Black homesteads. The price they asked was fifty dollars an acre for first-class land and fifteen dollars an acre for second-class land. Settlers on the north half of the float held several meetings in Tubac with their attorneys, Duffy and Purdum of Nogales, to consider the Bouldins' offer. After their final meeting, Duffy informed Campbell's firm "that nearly all the Mexicans have decided that they will not go any further in regard to a settlement. They seem to have come to the conclusion that their 'best bet' is to leave the land by ejectment and then appeal to the United States Government for assistance."[2]

Nonetheless, twenty homesteaders did offer to pay fifty dollars per acre for cultivated land, twenty-five dollars per acre for lands that could be cleared and cultivated, and ten dollars per acre for grazing lands. The Bouldins and Weldon Bailey, the Washington, D.C., lawyer who represented them in return for one-fourth of the north half, accepted the offers of only five: Thomas Casanega, Manuel King, Charles Karns, Ramón Burruel, and Rómulo Alegría. They rejected others like Louis Lim and William Rosenberg, offering to lease them the land instead for fifty dollars per year. Two elderly settlers—Guadalupe de Vásquez and Evaristo Gómez—made special pleas through Sarah Black to remain on their land because their sons were serving in the military during the First World War. Campbell replied that they would be allowed to do so if they agreed to "sign a memorandum lease acknowledging that they are holding under our clients and pay a trifling rental."[3]

Henry Ohm was one of the homesteaders dispossessed by the court's decision. According to his final proof, Ohm, a Louisiana native, settled along the Santa Cruz in 1893. He filed his entry six years later. He and his wife and three children cleared the floodplain of mesquite and expanded their fields from fifty to one hundred acres. They also built a home, threw up a hay shed, installed a steam pumping plant, hammered together chicken houses and other outbuildings, and strung a barbed wire fence around their property. Ohm was fifty-two years old when he proved up his claim in 1908.

Ten years later, he was hiring the Nogales Engineering Company to survey his homestead and corresponding with Campbell to buy back his land. The Bouldins turned him down. On July 15, 1918, Ohm sent them $250 in rent. That payment allowed him to remain on his land no later than November 1 in order to harvest his crops.[4] Two and a half decades of hard work evaporated like light rain under the Arizona sun.

Tumacácori Mission National Monument

Another of the dispossessed was Carmen Mendez. Mendez moved his young family to Mission Tumacácori in 1884 when he was thirty-six years old. Fashioning bricks from local mud, or scavenging them from the mission's convento, he built a small adobe home for his eighteen-year-old wife, Catarina, and their baby, Ramón. A stone's throw to the north, the ruins of the mission church slowly crumbled into desert soil.

Mendez was a citizen of Mexico when he arrived, but the international border meant little to anyone in the region except lawyers and politicians then. While Catarina gave birth to a baby every two years, Mendez cleared thirty acres of land, sunk a well, dug irrigation ditches, and planted crops except for two or three years of "drouth."[5] In 1896, he filed a Declaration of Intention to become a citizen of the United States. In 1899, he applied for a homestead of 160 acres after the U.S. Supreme Court wiped the Tumacácori land grant off the map. Nine years later, Mendez submitted his final proof. He and four witnesses testified to the improvements he had made and to his continuous occupation of the land.[6]

That same year, Mendez deeded ten acres of his homestead to the United States. Those ten acres embraced the heart of Mission Tumacácori, which was being gutted by treasure hunters and defaced by vandals who scrawled their names on its walls and knocked off pieces of interior frescos for souvenirs. The Arizona Pioneers' Historical Society appealed to the newly created Forest Service to save the site. The Forest Service conducted a survey and Secretary of Agriculture James Wilson attested to its historical importance. On September 15, 1908, under the provisions of the fledgling American Antiquities Act, President Theodore Roosevelt proclaimed Mission Tumacácori a national monument.

Then the ratification of Baca Float No. 3 erased both Mendez's homestead and the monument. Mendez lost his land and had to move on like most of the other homesteaders, but James Bouldin and his wife deeded ten acres of Mission Tumacácori back to the United States in 1917. After control passed from the Forest Service to the newly created National Park Service, Frank Pinkley, the superintendent of Casa Grande National Monument, wrested four hundred dollars from the government to begin stabilizing the church. That stabilization proceeded in fits and starts, cement patchwork here, adobe patchwork there. Tumacácori National Monument was a slowly emerging vision, not a master plan.

The Silo Land and Cattle Company and the Ghost of John S. Robinson

The biggest challenge the Bouldins faced was the Silo Land and Cattle Company, a paper corporation assembled in El Paso, Texas, in 1918. The company appeared to be the brainchild of Selim Franklin, the Tucson attorney who always seemed to come out on the losing end of the fight over the float. Franklin had represented the Wises in their quixotic quest to promote a lost Baca heir. In the early 1890s, however, he had briefly worked for James S. Bouldin, trying to peddle the Greaterville placers to investors in England and New York.[7] Franklin also served as attorney for John S. Robinson, who swapped paper transactions with the Bouldins around the same time.[8]

The notice of incorporation for the Silo Land and Cattle Company appeared in the El Paso papers on March 1, 1918. It listed El Paso residents

C. L. Galloway, Robert L. Holliday, and A. H. Culwell as president, vice-president, and secretary-treasurer. According to the articles of incorporation, Silo's purpose was to "buy, own, sell and convey real estate and minerals in the State of Arizona, and to engage in mining, agriculture, and stock raising in said State of Arizona." The company planned to issue five thousand shares of capital stock at one dollar a share.[9]

Several days before, however, Silo held the first meeting of its board of directors. The three-man board appointed Franklin as resident agent of the corporation in Pima County and Otto Herold of Nogales as resident agent in Santa Cruz County. Then Galloway, Culwell, and Holliday tendered their resignations and were replaced by A. M. Franklin as president, Henrietta Franklin as vice-president, and H. E. Heighton as secretary-treasurer.

At its second meeting on March 22, the new board reported that all five thousand shares had been subscribed. It also noted that "heirs and persons interested in the estate of John C. Robinson, deceased, who claimed ownership" in Baca Float No. 3 were willing to convey one-half of the north half of the float for twenty-five hundred dollars. The money was to be paid to Franklin, Silo's attorney. A condition of the sale was that Silo, at its own expense, would bring suit to quiet title to the entire north half of the float. Silo's board voted to do so.[10] That same day, four heirs of Robinson—Mary Whitney Robinson, Julia Robinson Collier, Caroline P. Hall, and Anne Gertrude Robinson—signed the agreement.[11]

Silo filed suit against Bailey and the Bouldins in April. Another corporation—the Robinson Land and Cattle Company—did the same against Watts and Davis. Bailey and the Bouldins immediately sued back. They also launched a countersuit against Robinson's heirs. The two cases were transferred from Santa Cruz County to Pima County in December. On January 8, 1919, Judge G. W. Shute of Pima County Superior Court set fire to Franklin's paper company by decreeing that Silo did not have "any right, title, interest or claim whatsoever" in the north half of the float. He also found in favor of Bailey and the Bouldins regarding their cross-complaint. They were "the owners in fee simple of the whole of the said North half of said tract of land known as Baca Float No 3 and are entitled to the possession thereof," Shute declared.[12]

Judge W. H. Sawtelle of the U.S. District Court of Arizona in Tucson rendered a similar judgment in the countersuit against Robinson's heirs.[13] The Robinson Land and Cattle Company met the same fate in its suit against Watts and Davis.[14] The ghost of General John S. Robinson—and all the other speculators who had gambled on the float for half a century—haunted Arizona courtrooms no longer.

The Baca Float Mining and Cattle Company and the Mineral Segregation

The Bouldins never intended to develop the float themselves. Ever since patriarch David W. Bouldin purchased the north half of the float from Judge Watts's widow and children in 1884, he and his sons, James and Powhattan, had swapped shares and titles with a string of other speculators. Meanwhile, the float—original or amended—hovered in legal limbo above the dry southern Arizona landscape. "I can easily testify that the major part of my Father's time was given directly to the interests of Baca matters," Powhattan recalled, "also that he put *many thousands of dollars* into this." Powhattan accompanied his father on trips to "Arizona, New Mexico, California and other places hunting up records and papers pertaining to the Baca business." Of his father's "supposed friends," he remembered Charles Pushaw as a "sharp crook," James Eldredge as "a sharp shrewd schemer," and A. M. Syme as "about the same thing. Syme all through pretended he was working for my Father's interests or rather ours."[15]

After their title was confirmed, the Bouldins unpacked the float's resources like a box of Christmas toys and tried to rent or sell them off one by one. They leased their grazing lands to Russell Durrell of Van Horn, Texas, from 1917 to 1919 during a Texas drought. The price was seventy-five hundred dollars for nine months a year.[16] During the summer of 1919, they negotiated with Henry Boice of the Boice-Gates-Johnson Cattle Company of Los Angeles, California, to do the same. The price had risen to eight thousand dollars a year, and Bouldin indicated that he would be willing to offer a five-year lease at "$9,500 per annum, with the privilege of cancellation after one year in case of sale of the property."[17]

The Bouldins also trafficked in mining claims. They collected royalties from Leonard Tobin, who was operating the Eureka or Virginia Lee group of mines, from John Reid, who was working the Trudie group, and from the Santa Cruz Syndicate, which was extracting ore from the Royal Blue Mine. On January 14, 1918, however, James E. Bouldin took a $750,000 option on the World's Fair Mine in the Harshaw Mining District of the Patagonia Mountains.[18] When royalties from the float could not cover Bouldin's option on the World's Fair, he and Bailey sold an option on eight thousand acres in the northeastern corner of the float to Walter G. Clark of New York City for one million dollars in July 1918. Clark also purchased an option on two thousand contiguous acres for a townsite to service his mines.

This was the origin of the so-called Mineral Segregation, the only part of the float the Bouldins eventually retained. It very quickly took on a life of its own, and led to a series of court battles as well. In a handwritten letter from Salero Camp, Leonard Tobin complained bitterly to Judge Campbell that Clark and his associates had taken possession of all the mines on the north half of the float. "It was my work of showing them over the property and my report that had largely to do in selling their Baca Float. For your own information [I] will say that I have never been so disappointed in my life at the way I have been treated by Mr. Bouldin," Tobin groused as he prepared to enlist in the American Mining Engineers during the First World War.[19]

Clark must have dropped his option because he disappears from Campbell's correspondence. On February 5, 1919, the Bouldins granted another option "to purchase the greater part of the north half of that certain tract of land known as Baca Float No. 3" to A. R. Grund of St. Louis, Missouri. Three days later, Grund agreed to transfer his option to the Baca Floats Mine Company, which had just been organized by Tucson mining entrepreneur John Mets with a capital stock of three million dollars.[20] A. R. Conner and S. L. Kingan, the law partners of Judge Campbell, filed the articles of incorporation of the Baca Float Mines Company on March 4. Campbell was appointed legal agent. On March 10, the first meeting of the new company's board of directors elected its officers, with Conner as president and Mets as treasurer. The officers of the company resigned immediately after voting to accept Grund's transfer of his option to the north half of the float. The board then elected Grund president in one of those legal shuffles so common in the float's speculative history.[21]

That particular shuffle lasted less than two months. The purchase price of the option was $1.5 million, with all royalty payments from mining leases to be credited toward the sum. On May 3, Grund notified the Bouldins that the Baca Float Mines Company could not meet its first payment and surrendered the option. The Bouldins' first major chance to cash in on the float fell through in the legal blink of an eye.[22]

The Bailey Interlude

The Bouldins then turned to someone closer at hand. During the summer of 1919, Weldon Bailey threatened to file a partition suit to divide the north half of the float. Bailey, who controlled 25 percent of the north half, wanted to buy enough additional land from the Bouldins "to make a large enough ranch to justify the hope that I could make something out of it." "You declined to consider that proposition, giving as your reason that I would not be willing to pay you what the land was worth," he wrote James E. Bouldin. Bailey therefore proposed to buy out the Bouldins or have the Bouldins buy him out.[23]

Two days later, James Bouldin scrawled a handwritten note to Judge Campbell from the Colonial Hotel in Springfield, Missouri. "Weldon is always looking for the best of it," Bouldin complained. "Life is too short to worry along and hold joint interest with him. He would always keep me tied up. I have been more than fair with him, but he is cold as a clam." He authorized Campbell to file the partition suit.[24]

The squabbling partners evidently changed their minds, because on January 6, 1920, the Bouldins sold their three-fourths share of the north half to Bailey. The only exceptions were the ten acres for Mission Tumacácori, four parcels of farmland homesteaders Manuel King (110 acres), William Lowe (105 acres), Charles Karns (95 acres), and Thomas Casanega (100 acres) had purchased, and eighty-five acres that had been sold to the law firm of Duffy and Purdum of Nogales. The Bouldins did retain the mineral rights, however, as well as the right to occupy the Shultz House near the old Salero Mine.[25] Dreams of a big strike in the Santa Ritas still lingered.

Not everyone shared that dream. G. H. Brevillier, a New York attorney representing the Alto Mines Company in a suit against Bailey and the Bouldins in 1917, was one such skeptic. "Since I looked over the Baca

Float from the rear platform of a train to and from Nogales in February 1916, I have had very little confidence in it as a commercial proposition," he sneered. "The grant never appealed to me as a mineral proposition. It has been thoroughly prospected for over half a century without any real mine being found on it."[26] Nonetheless, speculators continued to dive into the Float's murky waters. In March 1920, Judge Campbell unsuccessfully negotiated with Bailey and the Bouldins to buy the mineral rights to the entire north half. Two years later, A. R. Grund returned with a new corporation, the Baca Float Mining and Cattle Company, to resurrect the proposition once again.

This time, he had Bailey as a partner. On February 7, 1922, Bailey and the Bouldins came to a detailed agreement about the float. Bailey gave the Bouldins a number of small properties, including the "Ohm place," the "Arballo place," and the "Alegria place." He also transferred the rest of the north half of the grant—forty-five thousand acres of grazing land east of the Santa Cruz, the "Townsite of Tubac," the "Gomez place," the "Mabis Place," and others—to the Baca Float Mining and Cattle Company.[27] Names that evoked a generation of family toil—calloused hands shelling corn, cutting firewood, shoeing horses—bobbed through the legal documents like dead fish while paper companies incorporated in Delaware or Dallas darted about trying to feed.

The partners formalized the convoluted swap on May 5, 1922. The Bouldins transferred their portion of the float and its mineral rights to the new company. That same day, Weldon Bailey and the company signed a promissory note for $640,000 due in six months and payable to James E. Bouldin and Joseph W. Bailey at the American Exchange National Bank in Dallas.[28] Bouldin apparently kept an interest in the company and was elected treasurer. Despite the postwar depression gripping the United States, the Bouldins and Baileys kept trying to make their legal crapshoot pay off. But the Baca Float Mining and Cattle Company turned belly-up as well. When it failed to pay off its note, Joseph Bailey and his bank took legal action. On November 8, 1924, the Santa Cruz County Superior Court issued a writ of execution ordering the county sheriff to sell off the north half of the float at public auction. American Exchange National Bank was the highest bidder at $250,000. After Bailey and the bank paid off delinquent taxes, Harold Brown, the sheriff of Santa Cruz County, issued them a sheriff's deed.[29] The press identified Joseph Bailey as owner of the float.

A former U.S. senator from Texas, Bailey first waded into the speculative free-for-all as a lawyer for S. A. M. Syme and Alexander Mathews (see Chapter 6). After he figured out that their claims to the float were weak, he deftly hopped over to the Bouldins.[30] Now he owned most of the north half of the float.

But it was his son, Weldon, who decided to play rancher. Earlier in 1924, Weldon had applied for a loan of $25,000 from the Federal Land Bank in Berkeley, California. He sought to mortgage 478 acres of farmland along the Santa Cruz. Because he listed Judge Campbell as one of his debtors, the bank contacted Campbell to ask if Bailey was "a real farmer" and was not applying for the loan just to sell the property.[31] "Weldon Bailey apparently has no very great liking for the practice of law and his father gave or sold to him his share of the fee in this case," Campbell replied. "He has taken a great interest in this land and seems to like to live upon it rather than to practice law."[32] A graduate of the Virginia Military Institute and the University of Virginia Law School, Bailey defaulted on his mortgage two years later.[33] Nonetheless, he spent the rest of his life in Tubac, dying in southern Arizona in 1948.

The Bouldins, in comparison, retained only a few parcels of farmland along the Santa Cruz. One of those was on the south half of the float and belonged to Jennie Bouldin, the widow of the patriarch. Her son, James, spent the summer of 1924 sparring with Watts and Davis over a small piece of adjacent grazing land. In a letter to Campbell, he grumbled about their penny-pinching and said that Davis "acts like a pawn broker instead of a man wanting to give any one a square deal."[34]

Watts and Davis, the Sorrells, and the Drought of the Early 1920s

Cornelius Watts and Dabney Davis were trying to sell off their share of the float as well. On February 18, 1920, they conveyed most of the south half to J. R. and Roy Sorrells of Santa Cruz County. The sale involved three large tracts totaling 45,916 acres. The transaction excluded much of the floodplain of the Santa Cruz River along with water and ditch rights necessary for irrigation. Watts and Davis also retained one-half interest in the mineral rights, including oil and gas.[35]

Unlike Weldon Bailey, the Sorrells were pioneer ranchers in Santa Cruz County. They had fought Apaches and cattle baron Colin Cameron in the San Rafael Valley, and they knew the cattle business as homestead ranchers, not speculators.[36] During the First World War, the price of beef rose as rail rates dropped and the importation of frozen beef from Argentina ceased. Moreover, drought in west Texas forced many Texas cattlemen like Russell Durrell to ship their animals to Arizona. Such competition made Arizona stockmen eager to expand their ranges at a time when many had the capital to do so.

But the early 1920s were not kind to the cattle business. Once the war ended, demand plummeted as international trade resumed. The result was a national agricultural depression that hit Arizona farmers and ranchers hard (Sheridan 1995). Drought withered Arizona as well, decreasing fodder production by 40 to 55 percent. Lack of feed led to a dramatic increase in cattle mortality, from an average of sixty-one per one thousand during the preceding decade to one hundred per one thousand in 1920. Some ranchers survived by driving their cattle onto Sonoran ranges (Wagoner 1952). Others lost their herds as banks foreclosed on them.

One of those ranchers in the Santa Cruz Valley was David John Cumming, who ran cattle in the foothills of the Atascosa Mountains.[37] The valley was open range, like most of the rest of Arizona. The U.S. Forest Service was just beginning to carve national forests into grazing allotments assigned to individual ranchers. The Taylor Grazing Act, which did the same on the rest of the public domain, was more than a decade away. Cattle not only foraged freely but shared the range with bands of wild horses and thousands of wild burros as well.[38]

That meant that the range was overgrazed during the best of seasons. Dry seasons meant disaster, especially when they followed one another, as they did in the early twenties. The drought started in the summer of 1922. Clouds floated across the summer sky but rarely piled into the great black thunderheads that produced the monsoon rains. "Instead of lush grass nearly two feet high, as was usually the case," John Cumming's son,

Douglas, recalled, "the ranges had only acquired a scrawny growth of grass that was seldom over six inches high."[39]

That winter, many older cows and cows nursing calves died. The ranchers waited for the early spring rains to save them. The rains never arrived. "During May, cattle began dying by the hundreds," Douglas Cumming wrote in his unpublished autobiography. "Near springs that had not yet gone dry, the stench of dead cattle was almost unbearable. Occasionally we would come upon a cow, down and too weak to ever get up again. Dad would dismount and mercifully shoot her. Orphaned calves wandered about bawling for their dead mothers."[40]

Like many other small ranchers, John Cumming had borrowed money from a local bank in Nogales. When their notes came due in the fall of 1923, the bank sent roundup crews to gather up the surviving cattle of those who could not pay. Those crews scoured the Atascosas and drove what remained of Cumming's herd carrying his 9L brand to stockyards along the railroad. Only Cumming's superior knowledge of the mountains kept him in the ranching business. He hid his four best horses in a remote canyon called Pine Gulch. His wife also owned about twenty heifers under her Rocking H brand that had been too young to calve when the drought hit. "When the year of 1923 was over, the Cumming Ranch consisted of four illegitimate horses and twenty of Mother's cows," Douglas Cumming noted.[41]

The Sorrells must have gotten caught in the same trap, dreams of expansion shriveling as cattle prices dropped and ranges dried up. When the Sorrells could not pay their mortgage, Watts and Davis took them to court. On January 15, 1922, the Santa Cruz County Superior Court issued a writ of execution foreclosing on Roy and Hazel Sorrells and Ozella Sorrells, widow and administratrix of the estate of John R. Sorrells. The Sorrells owed Watts and Davis $148,401 plus $8,095 interest at 7 percent annum and attorney fees of $34. Watts and Davis purchased the three tracts at public auction from the sheriff of Santa Cruz County a year later, on January 22, 1923. They paid $171,839.[42]

Baca Float Ranch

Those setbacks left the Bouldins and Watts and Davis searching for other buyers at a time when the cattle business was reeling. Not much happened for the rest of the decade. Then, in 1929, two Texas oilmen—Talbot T. Pendleton and Francis M. Dougherty—brought the first era of Baca Float speculation to a close.

Not much information is available about Dougherty, who sold out to his partner in the 1930s. Pendleton, in contrast, must have cut quite a dashing figure in the Santa Cruz Valley. His father was Nathaniel S. Pendleton of Virginia, a graduate of West Point and former member of the U.S. War Department. Tol Pendleton himself sounded like Frank Merryweather, All-American boy. While attending Princeton, he starred in football, baseball, and track. He was a member of Princeton's national champion football team in 1911 and captain of the team the following year, winning Walter Camp All-America honors at halfback.

What Pendleton really wanted to do was play major league baseball. Despite several major league offers, however, Pendleton had to turn them down. Professional baseball was a blue-collar sport then, full of tobacco-chewing country boys and tough kids from the slums. Ivy leaguers like Pendleton were not supposed to associate with ruffians like George Herman Ruth, the delinquent son of a Baltimore saloonkeeper, or Tyrus Raymond Cobb, so foul tempered he once jumped into the stands to beat up a heckler. "The ball players of that era were not regarded by everybody as socially acceptable," notes baseball historian Shirley Povich. "The stuffier hotels scorned their patronage. Baseball athletes rated only one cut above the plug-uglies of the professional prize ring; the chaw of tobacco was their badge and the corner saloon the hangout of so many" (Povich 1988:60). "Family persuasion" steered Pendleton away from his childhood dream.

Instead, he followed a more respectable path to adventure, serving as a fighter pilot in France in the Seventeenth Night Pursuit Squadron of the Army Air Corps during the First World War. After the war, Pendleton joined Roeser and Pendleton, an independent oil company in booming Fort Worth, Texas. By the end of the 1920s, Pendleton decided to sink part of his fortune into the Baca Float. The reason he decided to invest in land, according to Tucson newspaper reporter Bernice Cosulich, was "due to the uncertainties of the future" (Cosulich 1942:41). The location he chose depended upon an old school chum, Weldon Bailey. "Tol came to the area because he and my father went to high school together in West Virginia and when times got tough with the Depression, Tol bought up a lot of land," Sarah Bailey, Weldon's daughter, recalled. "Tol, my father, and Dougherty remained great friends all those years."[43]

Pendleton and Dougherty began buying up pieces of Baca Float No. 3. in the spring of 1929, just months before the Great Crash. They purchased the north half from the American Exchange National Bank for $125,000 on June 1. The mortgage was payable in ten promissory notes of $12,500 each over a ten-year period. A month later, Dougherty and Pendleton acquired the south half of the float from Watts and Davis for $140,000, also payable in ten promissory notes over the same period. For the first time since Judge Watts, Baca Float No. 3—most of it anyway—belonged to a single interest.

Watts and Davis sold their entire interests in the south half of the float. The sale included all water and water rights, the only exceptions being railroad and highway rights-of-way and about two thousand acres claimed by the San José de Sonoita Grant.[44] The north half, in contrast, was more complicated. Transportation rights-of-way and Tumacácori National Monument remained outside the deal. But the biggest exception was the Mineral Segregation, which the American Exchange National Bank reserved for itself. Located in the northeast corner of the float, the Mineral Segregation consisted of "all mines and minerals of whatsoever nature lying in or under" about 8,656 acres. For the next decade, the Mineral Segregation bounced back and forth between the First National Bank of Dallas, the new name of the American Exchange National Bank, and the Bouldins. In 1946, Jennie N. Bouldin, James's widow, leased the Mineral Segregation to J. W. Grotty, who later assigned it to the Salero Metals Corporation (Glannon 1949).

Once they had secured the surface rights to most of the float, Dougherty and Pendleton spent the next two years putting the remaining pieces together, mostly tracts of farmland along the Santa Cruz. They bought several parcels from Bailey and the Bouldins. They also grabbed some sheriff's sales during the early days of the Great Depression, including Manuel King's homestead. These were hard times for the returned homesteaders. In a desperate effort to wring more water from the Santa Cruz, farmers near Tubac and Tumacácori waged war on cottonwoods, "ringing," that is, cutting the bark around the giant trees' circumferences, to strangle the flow of nutrients and kill them. After they died and dried out, the giant skeletons, as large as thirty-five feet around, were set aflame. Meanwhile, increased groundwater pumping lowered water tables and sucked the life from other riparian vegetation. By the eve of the Second World War, the floodplain had been largely denuded, and only fifteen farming families survived in the Tubac-Tumacácori area (Logan 2002).

To prove they were good citizens, Dougherty and Pendleton conveyed a small parcel to the Calabasas School District. Otherwise, they used their capital in a cash-starved time to assemble the largest ranch in Santa Cruz County.[45] By 1932, Pendleton, Dougherty, and their wives were ready to create Baca Float Ranch to protect their other assets. According to assessor's records, the new corporation controlled 95,025 acres by 1934. The float was almost whole, at least for a time.[46]

More wealthy Easterners Arrive

Pendleton plunged into the cattle business, stocking Baca Float Ranch with Santa Gertrudis cattle from the King Ranch in Texas. He also bred racehorses and built a stud barn for his stallions. When someone asked how much the racehorses cost, he replied, "Well, I guess it was about $2.00 an oat."[47]

To pay the mortgage on the ranch and maintain his extravagant lifestyle, Pendleton sold off pieces of the float to rich friends. The first to buy was E. T. Strong, the retired president of General Motors. He and his wife, Grace, purchased the King homestead and adjoining parcels on the north half of the float in the spring of 1935.[48] Hal Prince, who had moved from La Osa Ranch in the Altar Valley to operate a dude ranch for Pendleton in 1933, designed the Strong's home (Brownell 1986).[49] The Strongs ran a dude ranch and then a working cattle ranch—the Upper S Bar S—until Strong died in 1948 (Glannon 1949).

A year later, Pendleton and Baca Float Ranch sold three tracts just south of Mission Tumacácori to another retired GM executive, Harry J. Mallery. Mallery had been comptroller and then vice-president of the Buick Division of GM. He and his wife, Virginia, paid twenty-five thousand dollars for the land and stocked it with registered Herefords (Cosulich 1942).[50] They named it Rancho de Pavón (Peacock Ranch) (Brownell 1986). Mallery died in the Pioneer Hotel fire in Tucson in 1970 (Accomazzo 1985).

In late December of the same year, Joanna Fay Shankle purchased another parcel on the north half of the float.[51] Shankle also bought land north of Tubac from Thomas D. Casanega, who moved there after being booted off the float. An accomplished aviatrix, Shankle regularly commuted in her own plane between Boston and the Santa Cruz Valley after building an airstrip north of Chavez Siding. She therefore named her ranch Pajaritos Migradores (Migratory Birds) (Brownell 1986). During the late 1930s, Shankle established a profitable cotton farm on her land and even served as vice-president of Baca Float Ranch (Cosulich 1942).

The newcomer Pendleton was most intimately associated with was Hubert Merryweather. Merryweather was a tall, handsome man from Ohio who moved to Arizona in 1935. After attending the University of Arizona, he bought into Baca Float Ranch itself, serving as vice-president before he enlisted in the army and served for four years in the South Pacific during the Second World War. "Everybody in the valley used to know Hubert Merryweather because he was an absolute screwball," Charles Day, who eventually bought Merryweather's San Cayetano Ranch, recalled. "He was a hell of an attractive guy. Old Tol Pendleton was not very smart and he let Hubert get something like 49 percent of the Baca Float Ranch. He and Tol fought over this thing for many, many years."[52]

Some of these Easterners did not need to make money off their land and used their ranches as winter homes. Others started dude ranches, which flourished in Arizona during the 1920s and 1930s. Unlike most other businesses, dude ranches were Depression-proof and often quite luxurious. They catered to a wealthy Eastern clientele who, in the words of *Progressive Arizona* in September 1925, escaped to Arizona to "meet nature in her ruggedness and still live a 'white-man's life.'" (Sheridan 1995:242).

One of the first to do so on the Baca Float was Doris Oesting (later Doris Oesting Hannah). Pendleton sold her one hundred acres and his first ranch headquarters. Sarah Bailey, who played with Pendleton's daughter, Anne, when she was a young girl, remembered the rambling structure. "Tol had built the house with a big kitchen including a summer dining room and a winter dining room. His daughter had her own area and there was a grand living room, a pool and the entire compound was enclosed by adobe walls."[53] In 1936, Mrs. Rockwell Kent rented the compound and remodeled the dining room. To build a new fireplace, she used bricks from Colonel C. P. Sykes's hotel in Calabasas, which had been bulldozed so cotton could be planted on the old Calabasas townsite.[54] Oesting turned the compound and surrounding property into the famous Rancho Santa Cruz (Brownell 1986).

A good example of the noblesse oblige that existed among these Easterners was a permit granted by Pendleton to Oesting "permitting the said Doris Oesting, her employees, friends, and guests to ride upon and over the lands of said Baca Float Ranch, Inc., and to hold picnics, camp thereon." Pendleton granted a similar permit to William Allen's Kenyon Ranch, a dude outfit west of Tubac that was not even on the Baca Float. E. T. and Grace Strong received even greater access—"the perpetual right to enter upon all uncultivated and unimproved range lands and all roads and trails with all portions of Baca Float No. 3, owned by grantor, and of walking, riding, driving and camping theron." (Glannon 1949). Pendleton and his friends never allowed the cattle business to interfere with their socializing.

William Otto Fraesdorf Jr., who sold ranches in the Santa Cruz Valley after the Second World War, knew many of these wealthy Easterners. During an interview in 1987, Betty Lane of the Tubac Historical Society asked why they moved there. "Well, they would start vacationing, and then guest ranching was quite popular and quite the 'in' thing to do," Fraesdorf replied. "So they would become involved in a guest ranch like the Rex Ranch, or the Kenyon, or the Circle Z or any one of them, and it sort of puffed them up. Made them feel good. Made them feel bigger in some way, (chuckles) and then they would consider buying. Some of them didn't live here year round, but they would always winter here and then summer back east someplace."[55]

The only exception to this trend was the sale of the Salero Ranch in the northeast corner of the float. On November 22, 1938, Baca Float Ranch sold its biggest parcel yet—26,602 acres centered around Salero Mountain—to Roy and Helen Adams.[56] According to Charles Day, "Old Roy

Adams was another character they say in those days. He was a cowboy from way back. He was married to the same gal three times, I think."[57]

Adams's hold on the Salero Ranch was apparently even looser than his hold on his wife. Less than a year after he bought it, he sold the ranch to W. D. Parker and F. Lee Fisher. They assumed Adams's mortgage from the Valley National Bank with an unpaid balance of forty-three thousand dollars.[58] On February 15, 1940, Fisher and his wife sold their share of the ranch to Parker, who became sole owner.[59] "Dink" Parker was one of four brothers who moved with their parents from Ozona, Texas, to Hachita, New Mexico in 1910. The Parker family brought a herd of five hundred horses with them, including both Morgan and quarter horse brood mares and stallions. Opie "Oak" Parker bought a ranch along the San Pedro River. Claude "Bud" Parker became one of the most famous cattle buyers in southern Arizona. "Bud Parker was dealing in cattle by the millions," Charles Day recalled. "He was very much respected. He would go down to Mexico and buy a thousand head of cattle and never put down a dime, and bring them back, and they'd take his word for it."[60] Unlike the Easterners who lived on "Millionaires' Row" along Santa Gertrudis Lane, the Parkers were cattlemen born and bred.

showcase Ranching on the santa cruz

But cattlemen born and bred were rare along the Santa Cruz in those days. "Today coon hunts, station wagons, thoroughbreds, lovely homes, and private airplanes are part of the valley's life," reporter Cosulich rhapsodized in 1942. "Retired captains of industry, eastern socialites, and young play boys and girls of inherited wealth dominate a region in which still live the descendants of Spanish conquistadores and American pioneers" (Cosulich 1942:14). Guest ranches such as Rancho Santa Cruz, Kenyon Ranch, and Rex Hammaker's Rex Ranch near Amado Siding attracted many wealthy patrons, some of whom, as William Fraesdorf pointed out, got a taste of the West and bought their own places.

Even more impressive were the showcase cattle ranches up and down the valley. The largest was Canoa Ranch, headquartered on a Spanish land grant north of Tubac called San Ignacio de Canoa. Canoa had been a watering spot in the Santa Cruz Valley for millennia. Even though the Santa Cruz did not flow above ground there, the water table was so shallow that travelers could slake their thirsts by digging shallow wells in the riverbed. On October 23, 1775, Juan Bautista de Anza's expedition to San Francisco stopped there its first night out of Tubac. The name of the grant itself—*canoa*—came from the hollowed-out log some enterprising pilgrim had placed there to water horses (Willey 1979; Sheridan 2000; Hadley 2000).

The man who developed Canoa into the largest ranch in southern Arizona was Levi Manning, the former mayor of Tucson, who closed the town's gambling dens and all-night saloons in the early 1900s (Sonnichsen 1982). Manning purchased the entire grant of 17,203 acres in 1912. Four years later, he sold the north half to the Intercontinental Rubber Company, which tried to raise guayule, a rubber substitute, during the First World War. That land became the nucleus of Green Valley, southern Arizona's premier retirement community, in the 1960s (Hadley 2000).

Manning expanded Canoa to one hundred thousand acres by picking up ranch land adjacent to the south half of the grant. But it was his son, Howell Manning Sr., who transformed Canoa into the crown jewel of the Santa Cruz Valley. He was one of the first Arizonans to raise Arabian horses with his famous stallions El Jafil and Saraband. He also crossed Arab stallions with Standardbred mares to supply his ranch with working cow horses. At its height in the 1940s, Canoa sprawled across about five hundred thousand acres of private, federal, and state trust lands from the Santa Cruz to the Altar Valley west of Arivaca. Manning employed forty to forty-five ranch hands at various camps, including ten to twelve families who lived at his ranch headquarters (Willey 1979; Hadley 2000). That headquarters was a small town, with blacksmith and welding shops, small adobe houses for the married cowboys and their families, a school for their children, and a Sonoran row-style bunkhouse for unmarried ranch hands. There were also corrals, barns, concrete pit silos to store ensilage, and the longest feeding trough in the United States. It stretched for a third of a mile and could feed fifteen hundred head at a time (Hadley 2000).

Manning's most gracious creation, however, was his own artificial oasis. In addition to irrigating twelve hundred acres of pasture, he dug a five-acre lake filled by a canal fed by pump-powered wells. Stocked with catfish and shaded by cottonwoods, it attracted frogs and migratory waterfowl, etching itself with dappled hues into the memories of Santa Cruz Valley residents. Manning commuted back and forth between Canoa and the Manning House in Tucson in his own private railcar along the Tucson and Nogales Railroad line. Canoa Ranch headquarters was so impressive that Samuel Goldwyn filmed *The Westerner*, starring Gary Cooper, there in 1939 (Hadley 2000).

The Bottom of the Bottle

Manning was a legendary host, entertaining guests at Canoa as well as at his mansion in Snob Hollow in Tucson. He and Tol Pendleton were close friends who used to go to baseball games together. Pendleton's Baca Float Ranch may not have been as large as Canoa, but the social scene was even more intense. "He had a great many friends and a lot of them visited from back East, including his Princeton cronies," Sarah Bailey recalled. "There was a stream of them visiting all the time."[61] When Tubac historian Elizabeth Brownell asked longtime Pendleton employee Lena Salcido Gómez whether the stories about the parties were true, Gómez replied, "Oh yes. Today in one house, next day in another house, next day another party, all through the week. And they would start all over again. Lots of drinking."[62]

The drinking was the reason many people referred to the Santa Cruz Valley as Santa Booze Valley. Santa Gertrudis Lane, where Pendleton had his ranch headquarters, was known as Santa Booze Lane. One of Pendleton's guests even immortalized the parties with their constant flow of liquor in a novelette whose English translation is the *Bottom of the Bottle*. That guest was George Simenon, the famous Belgian crime novelist, who lived in southern Arizona from August 1947 until October 1950 (Keller 2002).

Simenon was as colorful as his hosts. A compulsive philanderer who once told director Federico Fellini that he had slept with ten thousand women, Simenon was just as prodigious when it came to words. He published 196 novels and 21 volumes of memoirs under his own name, including his celebrated Inspector Maigret series, along with hundreds of novels and stories under various pseudonyms. When he moved from Tucson to Tumacácori in 1948, he rented two dwellings from Hubert Merryweather. One was a former schoolhouse, where Simenon's wife Régine, their son Marc, and Simenon's longtime cook and mistress, Henriette Liberge, settled. The other was Pendleton's reconverted stud barn, about a mile away across Josephine Canyon. There Simenon and his secretary and current mistress, Denyse Ouimet, set up house (Keller 2002). Tigy, as Simenon's wife was called, put up with her husband's affairs, and the odd little domestic group apparently met with bemused tolerance among Simenon's hosts.

Most of them were not exactly prudes themselves. Merryweather was so charming he could beguile "his bankers into finding ways to open his trust accounts," according to Jack Greenway, the owner of the Arizona Inn. "Simenon and Hubert were fellow philanderers," Greenway added wryly (Keller 2002). Tall, handsome, and wildly impractical, Merryweather epitomized Santa Gertrudis society. "He was a very bright and personable person, had a delightful wife—a darling he divorced," William Fraesdorf remembered, "but he couldn't make any money on that vast ranch. Why, I don't know, but he couldn't, and Tol kind of kept it together."[63] One of his money-losing propositions was the Tumacácori general store, which he stocked with S. S. Pierce gourmet delicacies. To his surprise and delight, Simenon encountered "more than 20 kinds of cognac, 30 brands of whiskey, never mind French, Italian, and California wines, liqueurs, spices, who knows what all" within its rustic walls. Merryweather ventured into politics around the same time Simenon was observing the antics of him and his friends. He served as state senator from Nogales from 1948 until 1954, capping his career as president of the Arizona Senate. "He could have been governor, if the guy hadn't been so crazy," Charles Day said. "He was really an attractive guy."[64]

Merryweather himself did not become a character in Simenon's novelette. But his wife Ann—small, petite, and dark haired, the "darling he divorced"—may have served as a model for two of the women in the book. Simenon also incorporated Merryweather's house and butler into the story. The butler's name was Watkins Jackson, which Simenon barely transmuted to "Jenkins." "He was a big, old, dark boy," Charles Day stated. "He was a character."[65]

The butler Jenkins is a steady, smiling, almost demonic force in the *Bottom of the Bottle*. The main character, Patrick Martin Ashbridge, a lawyer from a lower-middle-class background married to an heiress, prides himself on being able to leave the bar before he passes out or gets too drunk to drive home. But when his brother, a convicted murderer who escapes from prison, arrives unexpectedly, P. M., as everyone calls him, feels himself slipping out of control. The atmosphere becomes even more claustrophobic when the Santa Cruz floods, stranding the socialites and the convict on the east bank of the river. Losing track of his drinks, P. M. worries, "Manhattans and martinis, that was traditional. And that Jenkins, in his starched white uniform, leave [*sic*] you no respite, loving to play barman" (Simenon 1954:178).

Simenon relentlessly chronicled the drinking, which Ann Keller points out is as much a character in the *Bottom of the Bottle* as the Santa Cruz River (Keller 2002). People float from one home to another, drinking day and night, as the floodwaters surge past their doors. "It's awfully well organized," P. M. remarks at the beginning of the novelette. "Everything seems accidental, your gestures are the most casual in the world, and, in the long run, it allows you to drink without seeming to. It's like a secret order, with signs understood by the initiated throughout the country and probably in every country in the world" (Simenon 1954:135).

And so from the 1930s through the 1950s, Pendleton, Merryweather, and the others along Santa Gertrudis Lane played poker and raised purebred cattle, alcohol lubricating their insular little society. Guests came and went, people died and ranches changed hands, but the new owners were usually wealthy as well. Working ranchers like John Cumming had to supplement their incomes with other jobs. Cumming became a lion hunter and hunting guide. On one deer-hunting trip into his beloved Atascosas, he slipped from a ledge and fell forty-five feet, breaking his hip and both legs and suffering serious internal injuries. It took a rescue party twenty hours to haul him out, and the fall crippled him.

Pendleton and Merryweather, in comparison, glided through life, the Santa Cruz Valley their playground. Near the end of the *Bottom of the Bottle*, P. M. searches for his brother, who is trying to cross the border into Mexico. He runs into Cady, another member of the Santa Gertrudis crowd.

But Cady is different. Unlike old Pemberton, who "maintained that a gentleman must only breed cattle and horses," Cady raised cotton and potatoes and employed two to three hundred workers during harvest season. "He had Mexicans and Negroes brought over in trucks. He brought whole families, for the women were as useful as the men. He parked them in shacks he'd built on the edge of the fields," P. M. observed. Cady "didn't give a damn about being a gentleman" (Simenon 1954:229). The migrant camps were "a little like the leprous part, the shameful part of the valley" (Simenon 1954:229).

Pendleton, who probably served as the model for "old Pemberton," may have drilled for oil in Texas. E. T. Strong may have battled unions in Detroit. But the Santa Cruz Valley was their refuge, an aristocracy of wealth insulated from the forces reshaping the West during the mid-twentieth century. The space they produced was a leisurely façade—a private, monied version of an Old West movie set—that masked where the money came from. Pendleton and his friends could afford to play with or drink away their fictitious capital while the land itself waited for the transformations of Arizona's postwar boom.

8

Rio Rico and the Great Arizona Land Rush

On December 21, 1951, a drunken truck driver swerved across the Old Nogales Highway and slammed into a truck driven by Howell Manning Jr., who ran his father's half-million-acre Canoa Ranch. Manning died at the scene. His widow, Deezie Manning Catron, remembers hearing the phone ring at her father-in-law's house, where she was waiting for the return of her husband to have dinner. Howell Sr. slumped, dropped the receiver, and walked out to the corral. The showcase ranch with its Arabian horses and purebred Herefords turned to ashes as the old man struggled to grasp the death of his son.

Two years later, Manning sold much of his deeded land to liquor wholesaler Kemper Marley, who was later implicated in the bombing murder of reporter Don Bolles. With the sale went most of the federal and state trust land grazing leases as well. The greatest ranch in southern Arizona shrank from five hundred thousand to twenty thousand acres (Hadley 2000).

It was the end of an era in the upper Santa Cruz River Valley. Manning held onto the southern half of the San Ignacio de la Canoa land grant. Tol Pendleton still ran Baca Float Ranch. But the high times were winding down as age, alcohol, and the changing economy of Arizona took their toll. When George Simenon left southern Arizona in 1950, the landscape of the upper Santa Cruz still conjured romantic visions of Spanish missions and the old West. By the 1960s, those visions were being chewed up and spit out by the transformation of the American West triggered by the Second World War (Nash 1985). Arizona was one of the fastest growing states in the country. Military bases and defense plants attracted thousands of newcomers during the war. Business-friendly tax laws and right-to-work legislation lured even more businesses during the postwar boom (Sheridan 1995).

Then Del Webb, who had made fortunes off federal contracts since the

New Deal, found yet another way to make money in Arizona. Webb looked at the demographics of postwar America and built Sun City west of Phoenix, a self-contained community for "active seniors" who wanted to thaw out and play golf in the Arizona sun. Sun City quickly became the model for other retirement communities across the state, including Green Valley south of Tucson. Soon the showcase ranches were surrounded by a curious mixture of the old extractive Arizona—dark pecan orchards along the Santa Cruz and great open pit copper mines in the eastern foothills of the Sierrita Mountains—and the new Arizona of red-tiled roofs and jaunty retirees (Sheridan 1995).

In the process, land values seemed to rise as fast as the velocity of traffic on I-19, the new freeway that sliced the valley in half and sped travelers between Tucson and the international border at Ambos Nogales. Once again, speculators descended on the Santa Cruz Valley. This time, they were not searching for silver or gentlemen's spreads. Instead, they wanted grids on the bare ground they could sell to sun-starved buyers from Chicago or the East Coast. The geography of capital was making the transition from rural to exurban with a rapidity that bordered on the surreal.

The Postwar Housing Boom and Suburban Sprawl

Developers are often portrayed as the root of environmental evil in the modern West. Battles in the Southwest have been particularly incendiary, with two of the most radical environmentalist organizations—Earth First! and the Center for Biological Diversity—originating there. "Arizona is the native haunt of the scorpion, the solpugid, the sidewinder, the tarantula, the vampire bat, the conenose kissing bug, the vinegarroon, the centipede, and three species of poisonous lizard: namely, the Gila monster, the land speculator and the real estate broker," Edward Abbey growled (Abbey 1977:147). He went on to say that metropolitan Phoenix, with a population of 1,355,000 in 1976, had "swollen up worse than a poisoned pup" (Abbey 1977:148).

Those figures seem quaint by comparison to the more than three million people living in the Salt River Valley today. Down south, Pima County's visionary Sonoran Desert Conservation Plan tries to control metropolitan Tucson's growth by tying it to the endangered wings of the cactus ferruginous pygmy owl. Meanwhile, bulldozers chew up thirteen acres of desert a day in eastern Pima County alone.

Half a century ago, in contrast, a home-hungry nation hailed developers as industrial pioneers. In 1940, only 41 percent of nonfarm Americans owned their own homes. That was the same rate of homeownership Herbert Hoover decried when he launched a national crusade to modernize the construction industry in 1921. Henry Ford had democratized automobile ownership through the techniques of mass production. Hoover wanted the "backward" and "inefficient" building trades to do the same. "To own one's home is a physical expression of individualism, of enterprise, of independence, and of freedom of spirit," the buttoned-down engineer turned secretary of commerce rhapsodized. "This aspiration penetrates the heart of our national well-being. It makes for happier married life, it makes for better children, it makes for confidence and security, it makes for courage to meet the battle of life, it makes for better citizenship. There can be no fear for democracy or self-government or for liberty or freedom from home owners no matter how humble they may be" (quoted in Rome 2001:24).

Hoover wanted homebuilding Henry Fords to step forward, and resisted any attempt at federal intervention, even after he became president. But the Great Depression torpedoed both his political career and his dream of expanded homeownership. Housing starts plummeted while home foreclosures soared. By 1932, even *Fortune* magazine concluded, "Housing is the one field where private enterprise and individual initiative have failed" (quoted in Rome 2001:26).

Ironically, Franklin Roosevelt's New Deal laid the foundation for the resurrection of Hoover's dream after the Second World War. In 1934, Roosevelt ramrodded the National Housing Act through Congress. Until then, homebuyers had to cough up 50 percent down payments and pay off their mortgages in five to ten years. The National Housing Act allowed the new Federal Housing Administration (FHA) to back twenty-year mortgages for up to 80 percent of a home's cost. Twenty percent of broke was still broke during the depression years, but low down payments and long-term mortgages revolutionized home financing during the postwar boom (Rome 2001).

By insuring mortgages, the FHA rode the Keynesian wave of rising federal manipulation of economic affairs. British economist John Maynard Keynes and his disciples contended that consumer spending drove modern industrial economies. National governments should encourage spending, particularly for durable goods like cars, houses, and appliances. To accomplish that goal, they had to increase the flow of capital and spread it more evenly across their populations.

One way to do so was to expand and democratize the available money supply by making saving, investing, and lending more secure. The Federal Deposit Insurance Corporation (1933) guaranteed bank deposits and protected savers against bank failures. By guaranteeing long-term mortgages with low down payments, the FHA enlarged the pool of prospective homebuyers and made loaning money to them more attractive to savings and loans. For the first time in U.S. history, the federal government put its immense resources and growing revenue-generating ability behind home buyers, the housing industry, and the financial institutions upon which both producers and consumers depended. That strategy paid off with a vengeance when the GIs came home from war.

At first, the returning soldiers faced a severe housing shortage. Some of them had to live in tents, streetcars, or even the fuselages of scrapped bombers. To stimulate both construction and home ownership, Democratic and Republican administrations alike passed legislation such as the GI Bill, which eliminated down payments for veterans and granted them thirty-year, low-interest mortgages. Such measures boosted demand, and also made it easier for builders to borrow the money they needed to construct subdivisions, not just single homes (Rome 2001).

The march to the suburbs was on. Builders like William Levitt in New York—or John F. Long in metropolitan Phoenix—developed "planned communities" on the fringes of urban centers where land was cheaper. In these Levittowns or Maryvales, nonunion workers assembled homes with almost the same standardization as Detroit manufactured cars. By 1956, 60 percent of Americans owned their own homes. By 1959, big builders using mass production techniques had cornered 64 percent of the housing market. Hoover's dream was becoming a reality through FHA and Veteran Housing Administration (VHA) loans (Rome 2001).

Along with tract homes came built-in appliances and a skyrocketing dependence upon the automobile. Historian Adam Rome (2001) reveals how giant appliance manufacturers helped create the postwar consumer culture by convincing developers to add refrigerators, stoves, washing machines, and water heaters to their dwellings. Journalist Godfrey Hodgson called it the "suburban-industrial complex" as defense industries converted to the production of consumer goods with the same ideological fervor with which they had churned out wartime supplies (quoted in Rome 2001:43).

But if FHA and VHA loans fueled the housing boom, the interstate highway program of the 1950s propelled the exodus from the "inner" cities. Urban America was being reconfigured as white ethnics moved to the suburbs and the construction of suburban shopping centers bled downtowns. Those left behind never had access to the credit needed to revitalize older neighborhoods, which often decayed (Duany, Plater-Zyberk, and Speck 2000). In the West, small cities like Albuquerque, Phoenix, and Tucson largely bypassed urbanization altogether and developed as massive suburbs with puny mass transit systems and mobile populations that often seemed to be just passing through (Luckingham 1989; Abbott 1993; Sheridan 1995).

Cold war fears and military contracts kept defense plants in the Southwest. Cheap labor, low taxes, and aggressive promotion attracted new companies as well, primarily in the electronics and aeronautics industries. Once air-conditioning vanquished desert heat, at least inside offices and homes, thousands of servicemen who had trained in Arizona during the war returned to buy tract homes with VHA loans. The result was a suburban geography of mass-produced neighborhoods with mass-produced homes filled with mass-produced appliances, including air-conditioners. The only way to reach those neighborhoods, of course, was by mass-produced automobiles with built-in ACs. Both personal and business spaces were being produced that defied regional constraints like climate.

Green Valley and the End of Santa Booze Lane

But young veterans wanting to start families were not the only ones flocking to Arizona suburbs. In 1962, Del Webb appeared on the cover of *Time* magazine. *Time* did not bestow the honor because Webb was co-owner of the New York Yankees during their postwar glory years. Nor did he achieve that recognition for building mobster Bugsy Siegel's Flamingo Hotel in Las Vegas. Del Webb made *Time* because he mass-marketed a new kind of community on the Arizona landscape—one designed for retirees who wanted to play golf rather than shovel snow (Sheridan 1995).

Webb's Sun City northwest of Phoenix was a particularly brilliant feat of entrepreneurship. Postwar prosperity freed a growing segment of America's elderly from the need to live with their children. Advances in health care allowed them to live longer after they reached retirement age. Many of these middle-class retirees were not ready for the rocking chair. Instead, they wanted to golf, swim, play tennis, and socialize with people their own age. They had survived a depression and won a world war, and now they wanted to have fun. Webb recognized a latent market for planned retirement communities and turned it into an aggressively active one. Youngtown (1954) might have been the first age-segregated "geriatric ghetto," but Sun City was the biggest and best promoted. There would be many more.

The most spectacular in southern Arizona was Green Valley, which took root on the northern half of the San Ignacio de la Canoa land grant. Located along I-19 about thirty-five minutes away from Tucson and its medical facilities, Green Valley was an exurban rather than a suburban retirement community like Sun City. Its vistas—at least to the east—were breathtaking: desert bajadas rising to the majestic peaks of the Santa Rita Mountains. Developers provided not only tract homes with Spanish colonial accents but golf courses, shopping centers, and recreational facilities as well. Marketed across the country, Green Valley defined a new lifestyle in the Santa Cruz Valley. Beaming retirees piloted their golf carts across billboards, newspaper ads, and television commercials across the country. Not since the establishment of Tubac presidio had a group of outsiders colonized the valley so quickly.

The result was a highly visible demographic revolution. In 1940, 4.7 percent of Arizona's population was 65 or over. By 1980, the proportion had more than doubled to 11.3 percent. The numbers rose even more impressively, from 24,000 on the eve of the Second World War to 308,000 forty years later. Almost 30,000 elderly people migrated to Arizona from 1955 to 1960. That figure climbed to 50,000 between 1965 and 1970, and to almost 94,000 a decade later. Those figures did not include the thousands of seasonal "snowbirds" who wintered in the state. Not all newcomers to Arizona were elderly, but from November through April, it often seemed that way (Sargent 1988).

What Tol Pendleton or Hubert Merryweather thought about the newcomers never made the clip files of local archives. By the 1960s, both men were long past their primes. Merryweather spent the last years of his life engaged in a bitter family squabble. In 1969, he sued his brother and sister, along with two corporations and three other individuals, for two million dollars. Merryweather contended that he had temporarily transferred his shares in Baca Float Ranch to his siblings in order to pay off other loans from the parties named in the lawsuit. When he defaulted on one of those loans, his brother and sister sold the Baca Float shares to a Florida-based land development company called Gulf American Corporation for $4.5 million. Merryweather claimed that the price was $2 million more than the cost of his loans, and he was entitled to the difference. The suit was still dragging on when he died in a Dallas hospital in 1976. He was fifty-eight years old.[1]

Tol Pendleton's final years were more graceful. In 1967, he sold what was left of his share of the Float—55,000 acres—to Gulf American for $3.5 million. He and his wife, Dicky, moved to Tucson, where he died on June 4, 1973. By then, the prize-winning Santa Gertrudis cattle, the endless parties, the legendary poker games that occasionally featured John Wayne were gone.[2] The Upper Santa Cruz Valley no longer was a playground of the rich. Retirees and real estate speculators were reconfiguring its spaces as patrician visions gave way to more plebian marketing schemes.

Gulf American and the Great Arizona Land Rush

When Pendleton sold the Baca Float to Gulf American in July 1967, the transaction was part of the greatest land boom in Arizona history. Land and canal companies lured thousands of would-be farmers to the Salt River Valley in the 1890s. The cotton boom during the First World War attracted thousands more. But those booms were agricultural, not urban. They restricted themselves to the Salt and Gila River Valleys, where huge irrigation projects transformed creosote flats into the rectangular geometries of agribusiness. None of them compared to the methamphetamine frenzy of the postwar boom (Sheridan 1995).

Land tenure numbers tell part of the story. Indian reservations and the federal government controlled almost 71 percent of the state. State Trust Lands encompassed another 13.2 percent. That left only about 16 percent in private hands. As Phoenix and Tucson sprawled outward, devouring the desert and regurgitating it as low-density subdivisions, ranches and homesteads within commuting distance became prime real estate. Some of the residents of those subdivisions could also afford a summer home in the high country. Phoenix streamed up I-17 and the Beeline Highway and turned Payson, Prescott, Flagstaff, and the White Mountains into recreational colonies. Tucson's mountain destinations included Mount Lemon and Mount Graham. During the 1950s and 1960s, suburban developments multiplied like jackrabbits while exurban growth leapfrogged up and over the Mogollon Rim (Sheridan 1995).

It was a wide-open game. Some of the projects like Robert McCulloch's Lake Havasu City and Fountain Hills were legitimate but exhibited a truly grotesque disregard for their desert settings. Others were little more than paper fictions that failed to provide basic services like roads, water, or electricity. Before a car bomb blew off his legs and right arm in 1976, Don Bolles of the *Arizona Republic* calculated that swindlers had peddled more than six million lots and raked in one billion dollars in fraudulent real estate deals during the postwar boom. "Things were literally out of control," Bruce Babbitt, Arizona's attorney general when Bolles was murdered, recalled. "The public had gone to sleep, the press was on the sidelines, law enforcement was demoralized, frustrated. There was an air of indifference in Arizona, sort of a sense that anything goes. I was always reminded of Woody Guthrie's statement that, you know, it's somehow okay to steal as long as you use a fountain pen instead of a gun" (quoted in Sheridan 1995:336).

Enter Gulf American Corporation. Unlike the more than three-dozen fronts set up by Ned Warren, the godfather of Arizona land fraud, Gulf American was a behemoth, not a fly-by-night scam. Founded in 1957, it was the largest land company in Florida, the epicenter of real estate development in the United States since the early 1900s. According to a front-page story by Kenneth J. Slocum in the *Wall Street Journal*, Gulf

American made more than $22 million in profits from $144 million in sales during fiscal year 1965–66 alone. It accounted for one-fourth of all the land business in Florida, even though it had more than 200 competitors. "It owns some 300,000 acres of Florida land (and another 100,000 elsewhere), ferries potential buyers in a dozen big aircraft, throws 12,000 cocktail parties a year for potential customers across the nation and employs 5,000 people," Slocum reported.[3]

Gulf American got to be so big so quickly by aggressively marketing its developments throughout the United States and abroad. Rather than waiting for buyers to come to them, the corporation flew people from all fifty states and sixty countries across the world to its Florida properties. Airplanes were key to its success. "Since much of the Gulf American land, some 300,000 acres, is sloshy swampland, walking on it can be a dampening experience," Albert Winnikoff noted in his book the *Land Game.* "Therefore, prospective Gulf American buyers are flown over the property at a height of 1,500 feet. From the air, it looks green, lush, beautiful. But below the verdant beauty is the Big Cypress Swamp."[4]

Even in Florida, where developers and politicians were as cozy as hibernating copperheads, Gulf American's sales tactics created a scandal. Responsible for 25 percent of Florida's land sales, Gulf American received 64 percent of all complaints. After several years of top-secret, undercover investigations, regulators from Florida's State Installment Land Sales Board accused Gulf American of widespread violations. One common tactic of Gulf American salesmen was to provide prospective customers with glossy promotions but no property reports, a legal requirement in Florida. A color-studded brochure for Remuda Ranch Grants southeast of Naples offered membership in a hunt club, saddle club, and charter boat marina in return for purchasing lots at $1,250 an acre. The elusive property report, in contrast, noted that the subdivision had never been platted or surveyed, and that 80 percent of it was under water.[5]

An even more insidious abuse was lot switching. In the early 1960s, Gulf American sold specific parcels in its Golden Gates Estates near Naples, Florida, to about one thousand customers. In 1963, it reassigned the same lot numbers to different plots on company maps.[6] Similar switching occurred in the company's Cape Coral Estates. In one case alone, according to the Land Sales Board's show-cause order, Gulf American "did unlawfully breach 1,300 installment land sales contracts . . . by assigning the identical unit numbers to parcels of land" as distant as seven miles from the original lots.[7] Leonard Rosen, chairman of Gulf American, justified the switching in Golden Gates Estates by stating that the company had discovered "muck" under the land and assigned the customers better lots. But Gulf American did not get around to sending buyers a "Here's good news we know you'll welcome" notice about the switching until two to three years after the original sales.[8]

Gulf American also failed to notify the Florida Land Sales Board about the switches, selling lots that had never been filed as well. Unfortunately, the regulators, who hid in car trunks and tape-recorded sales pitches, reported to a five-member sales board that included one Gulf American vice-president and two other members who did business with the company. Although the board had the power to suspend Gulf American sales in Florida, it never seemed to be able to reach a decision. "It was seldom anything you could put your finger on," one official noted, "but in the time these three were on the board the Gulf American hearing never seemed to get anywhere. Somebody always was sick or tired or had to catch an airplane."[9]

Meanwhile, Gulf American dodged or denied the accusations while strutting across the pages of the *New York Times* in a sixteen-page advertisement that boasted of the land it owned (573,760 acres), the number of people it employed (7,070), and its prominence as the fourth-largest publicly traded company in Florida.[10] This was, after all, a corporation with annual sales of $140 million. It had more 150,000 active customer contracts.[11] "When in Doubt, Promote!" seemed to be Gulf American's motto.

In 1967, however, the state's new Republican governor, Claude Kirk, promised, "The era of 'Let the buyer beware' is over. Let the unscrupulous seller beware."[12] After the Florida legislature passed a tougher land sales law, Kirk appointed a new seven-member Land Sales Board. The board took office on August 1 and quickly ordered Gulf American to show cause why its registration certificate to sell land in Florida should not be revoked or suspended. After the Florida Land Board announced its show-cause order, the American Stock Exchange suspended the trading of company stock.[13]

While Gulf American's troubles in Florida were piling up like thunder-heads off the Gulf of Mexico, the company brought its swampland swagger to southern Arizona. In November 1966, Leonard Rosen kicked things off by announcing that Gulf American would spend up to $150 million to develop Rio Rico over a fifteen- to twenty-year period. Promotions like the one released by Samuel R. Kaufman, Gulf American's broker in Tucson, envisioned the construction of four "core cities" surrounded by suburbs and recreation areas on the semiarid mesas of the Baca Float. After the *Wall Street Journal* articles appeared the following summer, Rosen met with Arizona governor Jack Williams and assured him that Gulf American was legitimate and that Arizona as well as the corporation would profit from Rio Rico. Williams told Rosen the firm would be welcome as long as it followed Arizona rules and regulations.[14] When the Associated Press reported on the completion of the sale of the Baca Float, it noted that the "ranch was started in 1863 by Arizona pioneer Luis Maria Baca."[15] The wire service had apparently never heard of Judge Watts, who would have appreciated Gulf American's tactics.

Soon afterward, Gulf American won approval for its first zoning change from the Santa Cruz County Planning and Zoning Commission. In question were eighty-nine hundred acres, where the core city of Rio Rico was to be developed. Rancher Cabot Sedgwick voiced the only objection, fearing that the rezoning would destroy the land's natural beauty. Ironically, Josephine Bailey, the widow of Baca Float promoter Weldon Bailey, chaired the zoning commission at the time.[16]

Several weeks later, in September 1967, the Santa Cruz County Board of Supervisors approved the Planning and Zoning Commission's recommendation. Supervisor F. J. Baffert extracted the donation of two school sites covering thirty acres from Gulf American. The corporation also pledged performance bonds of twenty-five thousand dollars per mile to pave and drain Rio Rico streets.[17] The following month, Gulf American broke ground for its Very Important Traveler reception center and awarded other contracts to build an access road and a bridge across the Santa Cruz River. Ronald Sandler, Gulf American's administrative director of Rio Rico, dismissed the allegations in Florida, pointing out that no formal charges

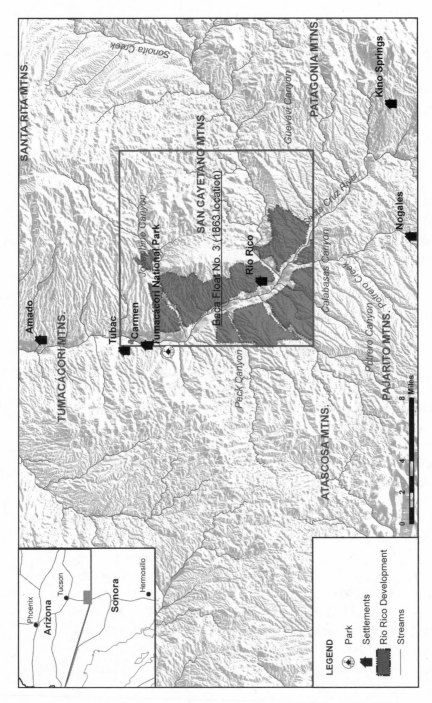

Map 4. Rio Rico and the modern Upper Santa Cruz River Valley.

had been leveled. It's the "penalty of leadership," he said. "Doesn't Avis take pot shots at Hertz because it (Hertz) is No. 1?"[18]

Later, Sandler elaborated on what the rezoned area—the first of Rio Rico's four "core cities"—would include. It was as grandiose as any of Gulf American's Florida promotions: a one-hundred-room hotel with a trading post, restaurant, and swimming pool; two recreation centers; trap shooting ranges with kennels for hunting dogs; riding stables; a rodeo arena. It sounded like a country club for Virginia gentry with a western twist. Some of the Easterners along Santa Gertrudis Lane would have felt right at home.[19]

The same newspaper article quoted Arizona real estate commissioner J. Fred Talley, who stated that subdivision plans had to be approved by the Santa Cruz County Board of Supervisors before Gulf American could file for a state permit to sell land. A few days later, Talley, doing his best imitation of a watchdog, intoned that even though Gulf American's application was under consideration, the Arizona Real Estate Board would be "in no hurry" to act on it because of the Florida allegations.[20]

Gulf American won a small victory in Florida when it refused to let the State Land Board hold a public investigation of the company. That allowed it to block Arizona's access to the investigation's records. Governor Williams called for the company to come clean so that it would "be accepted as a welcome member of the family of companies operating in Arizona." Williams went on to say, "Arizona's progress has been due in no small part to the fine body of developers now operating in the state."[21] Don Bolles must have chuckled.

Then, early in November 1967, Gulf American abruptly pleaded guilty to five charges of fraudulent or misleading practices. The Florida Land Sales Board suspended its sales in Florida for thirty days and appointed five outside businessmen to monitor the company for a 150-day probation period. It also imposed a $5,000 fine and ordered the corporation to issue refunds to buyers with legitimate complaints. Kirk and the Sales Board were doing their best to force Gulf American to reform.[22]

Santa Cruz County paid no attention. Less than a week later, the Board of Supervisors unanimously approved subdivision plans for 1,499 lots at Rio Rico "lying above the floodplain." This was a revision of Gulf American's original proposal, which wanted to develop the floodplain as well. Gulf American had no problem with underwater lots, but the supervisors decided that floodplain development would have to wait until the company built flood control dams on Sonoita Creek and won approval from the Army Corps of Engineers.[23]

The next month, Governor Williams announced that he planned to meet with Florida Governor Kirk when he flew to a conference of Republican governors in Palm Beach. Williams's office stated that Kirk would share "all the pertinent information" about Gulf American and send him weekly reports from the five-man team of monitors.[24]

On December 21, the corporation filed its first application with Arizona Real Estate Commissioner Talley.[25] "We're going to be very cautious on it," Talley responded. "This is a tremendous filing, the first of 55,000 acres." He mentioned the three planned subdivisions Gulf American hoped to build: Rio Rico Ranchettes, Rio Rico Estates, and Rio Rico itself. Talley went on to note that any decision by him had to wait until Gulf American applied for a corporate realty brokerage license and obtained title insurance and Arizona Health Department approval of sewage disposal and water supply plans.[26] Arizona state officials were being coy in their public statements. Meanwhile, procedures of approval sailed through the Santa Cruz County courthouse.

Back in Florida, the legal twists and turns continued, as murky as a channel through a cypress swamp. On January 20, the corporation resumed land sales at the end of the thirty-day suspension. Gulf American released a statement that its "sales and service personnel will return to work with fresh incentive and under improved techniques of direction and supervision." It also claimed that the company was "in a strong financial position. This is important not only to our shareholders and employees but also to our more than 150,000 customers in the U.S. and overseas."[27] Rio Rico was still awaiting approval to sell land in Arizona, but sales resumed in all other states where Gulf American operated except New Jersey, which suspended sales indefinitely.[28]

Florida and Gulf American Square Off

The Florida Land Sales Board was not about to go easy on the company, however. After the suspension ended, Carl Bertoch, the board's director, threatened to prohibit Gulf American "from ever resuming sales in this state" if the company refused to allow the monitors to do their jobs for the rest of the 150-day probationary period.[29] At its January meeting, the board turned down Gulf American's petition to register and open eight new sales areas in its Florida developments and rejected the company's financial advertising, arguing that it was misleading to list only assets and not liabilities. The board also ordered Bertoch to request funds for additional investigations of Gulf American from the Florida legislature. According to a report released at the meeting, the five-member monitoring committee was "almost completely frustrated." The board contended that Gulf American's refusal to let monitors examine company records violated an agreement made by Rosen and Bernard Herzfeld, vice-chairman of Gulf American, in a Tampa motel room the previous November before the company pleaded guilty to fraudulent and misleading sales.[30]

Gulf American returned the volley by reiterating its claim that Florida had wrung the guilty plea out of them under the threat of economic sanction. "Furthermore," company secretary Joseph E. Maddelone added, the board's actions demonstrated that certain members were "trying their utmost, for competitive or other reasons, to do damage to Gulf American." Chairman Rosen even called for the Florida legislature to "investigate the Florida Land Sales Board, particularly the possibility of a conspiracy between a major Gulf competitor and certain board staff members." "We would welcome a legislative investigation of the Florida Land Sales Board," Bertoch replied, "particularly if it goes back to the time Mr. Rosen was on it" from 1963 to 1965.[31]

Gulf American's moral outrage assumed comic-opera proportions soon afterward, when it filed a lawsuit in Tampa seeking sixteen million dollars in damages. The suit named not only Carl Bertoch and Governor Kirk's press secretary and executive assistant but *Wall Street Journal* reporter Kenneth Slocum and the *Journal*'s publisher, Dow Jones and Company, as well. Gulf American claimed that Slocum's articles were based on confidential reports that never should have been released.[32]

Beneath the braggadocio, however, Gulf American's troubles were deepening. In February 1968, disgruntled customers filed three lawsuits totaling $4.14 million against Gulf American. The largest, brought jointly by two Massachusetts corporations, alleged that the company misled them about the properties they purchased and never provided them with property reports. A couple from Detroit filed another suit, which alleged that salesmen promised the couple their lot was two and one-half blocks from the ocean. It turned out to be more than nine miles away from the Gulf of Mexico. Chicago entertainer Robert Bennett had the opposite problem. A Gulf American representative from Golden Gate Estates drove him and his family through an area of beautiful mansions and told them their land was nearby. Bennett, who also never received a property report, soon found out his five acres were under water.[33]

From Gulf American to GAC

At Gulf American's annual meeting in December 1967, Rosen assured shareholders that the corporation was in "the best financial condition ever" with earnings of more than three million dollars on more than thirty-four million dollars in sales for its first fiscal quarter ending on November 30.[34] Those confident words masked growing desperation. The following month, Rosen told a chamber of commerce audience that the brothers were considering offers to buy Gulf American from "two fine firms." He declined to mention their names. Instead, he launched into a virulent attack on the Land Sales Board, calling its members "bums." "We thought they wanted a pound of flesh," he ranted. "They didn't want the pound of flesh, they wanted our blood."[35]

Rosen lashed out like a cornered animal because he was. In April, Gulf American released its first half-year sales and earnings figures. Net income had plummeted from $7,384,000, or 77 cents a share, to $2,026,000, or 21 cents a share. Sales had nosedived from $63, 977,000 to $44,742,000.[36] In July, Rosen announced that he was resigning as chairman and chief executive of Gulf American "in order to devote a greater portion of my energies to educational and philanthropic activities in which I have long been interested." The corporation's board replaced the budding humanitarian with Herzfeld. Rosen continued to serve as a director and his brother Julius remained president of the company.[37]

Despite changes at the top, however, Gulf American's financial fortunes kept tumbling. The day after Herzfeld was elected chairman, the corporation released its nine-month statement. Earnings stood at $2.9

million, or 30 cents a share, declining from $11.5 million, or $1.20 a share, a year earlier. Sales dropped from $95.9 million to $67.5 million during the same period. The 75 percent freefall prompted Herzfeld to declare that he would do everything he could "towards cementing our relationship with the Florida Land Sales Board through complete cooperation with its members and staff."[38]

The next day, July 18, the *Wall Street Journal* reported that GAC, formerly General Acceptance Corporation, had decided to buy Gulf American in exchange for about two hundred million dollars of GAC stock. GAC was a diversified holding company with interests in everything from manufacturing and retailing to insurance and financing. Based in Allentown, Pennsylvania, the company specialized in taking over "troubled corporations."[39] Gulf American was its first major venture into land development, however. The purchase of Gulf American would give it not only 372,276 acres and 25 percent of the land sales business in Florida, but also 65,680 acres in Arizona, 51,000 acres in New Mexico, 5,680 acres in Utah, and 95,102 acres in British Honduras (Belize). Unlike Gulf American, GAC's earnings and revenues were rising, from $7 million net on revenues of $114.8 million in 1966, to $9 million on $124 million in 1967.[40]

When Gulf American's fiscal year ended on August 31, 1968, the numbers demonstrated what a toll its battle with the Land Sales Board had taken. The corporation posted a net loss of $1.6 million, an enormous drop from the $16.8 million in earnings for fiscal year 1967.[41] Gulf American had gone *mano a mano* with Governor Kirk and the board. It had bullied, blustered, and blackmailed, but Kirk and the board had not blinked. The Rosens and their associates had raked millions from their Florida developments during the decade they controlled the company. But their fraudulent ways finally caught up with their corporation, if not with them. GAC was a salvage operation, trying to wrest Gulf American's enormous land holdings from the ruins of its reputation.

Shareholders in both companies voted to approve the mergers in February 1969. The merger took place on February 24.[42] Gulf American, which once claimed to be the world's largest land company, became GAC Properties, a subsidiary of GAC.[43] The new company commanded GAC salesmen, many of whom had worked for Gulf American, never to use the Gulf American name (Pew 1971).

While the merger of GAC and Gulf American was being finalized, the Arizona Real Estate Department approved the sale of lots at Rio Rico. Governor Williams issued a statement saying, "Governor Kirk advised me that everything was now cleared up in connection with the company's troubles in Florida."[44]

His assurances were premature. GAC may have bought out Gulf American but the sales tactics were the same: fly in customers from across the country and ply them with drinks and the hard sell. On May 19, the first official selling day, potential Rio Ricans from Michigan and Nebraska landed in Tucson. Then, in the words of reporter Ken Burton, "A flock of Yankees happily followed the black asphalt road (and some turquoise signs) yesterday in a 1969 version of the Great Land Rush." The road was the Nogales Highway, because I-19 had not been completed yet. Billboards urged drivers to visit Rio Rico and be a "VIT," or Very Important Traveler. Radio ads swelled with full orchestra and female chorus. Salesmen on the bus boasted, "All the ranchettes in Unit 4 are gone already. There may be a few left." They also drew their captive audience's attention to "what's left of the old town . . . that's where Cortez traded with the Indians."[45] Their history may have been garbled, but they wanted to give their raw land some Spanish colonial mystique.

Once the bus got to Rio Rico headquarters, sales tactics intensified. Customers received a four-color brochure that promised to make them "tingle with the excitement of Rio Rico." Property manager Herb Lipsky rhapsodized about the "dynamics" of the development. "We can feel it every day when we see the bulldozers, the tractors and the engineers walking across the land." "Nary a one was visible" from the faux Spanish colonial headquarters overlooking Rio Rico, according to Burton, but details never slowed the salesmen down. Did Will Rogers Jr., whose face was on the cover of the brochure, endorse the project or own land there? "Let's face it, Will Rogers is a brand name," Vice-President Ronald Nitzberg replied. What was the price range of the lots? No answer. How soon could a buyer begin building or move into a new home? "Well, that depends," another executive answered. Salesmen worked the crowd by announcing, "Ladies and gentlemen, how about a nice, warm Arizona welcome for Mr.

And Mrs. XYZ of Nebraska, who just picked up Lot No. . . . ."[46] GAC wanted to create an atmosphere of carefree conviviality with an undertone of fear: If you don't buy, you're missing the opportunity of a lifetime.

GAC also hoped to jump on another new bandwagon along the border —the so-called twin cities or border industrialization program. Authorized by the U.S. and Mexican governments after the *bracero* (guest worker) program was terminated, the twin cities scheme permitted U.S. firms to build plants on both sides of the U.S.-Mexico line. Parts manufactured in the United States could be exported duty-free to Mexico, where workers assembled them for thirty-five cents an hour in 1969. Firms only had to pay a value-added tax to import them back to the United States. Mario Yrun, vice-president of GAC Properties of Arizona, stated that the company was "very definitely interested" in promoting the concept and intended to construct two industrial parks on the north and south ends of Rio Rico.[47] This was the beginning of the *maquila*, or border factory, phenomenon, which would attract millions of Mexicans to border cities from Tijuana to Matamoros over the next three decades.

Rio Rico began building homes east of I-19 in the foothills of the San Cayetano Mountains during the summer of 1969. By the end of the year, S. Hayward Wills, the chairman and president of GAC, gloated that the new subsidiary would post earnings of $23 to $25 million on more than $150 million in sales.[48] A year later, the $5-million Rio Rico Inn opened with 160 units. Thirty-one homes had been constructed, nine of them occupied. Yrun announced that GAC expected to build an additional 175 homes in 1971, and that the industrial park on the south end of Rio Rico was negotiating with several businesses to locate there. Yrun predicted that Rio Rico's growth would be "phenomenal" if it followed the trajectory of GAC's Cape Coral development in Florida, which had attracted 15,000 people, two 18-hole PGA golf courses, and more than 250 businesses.[49]

GAC and the Empire Ranch

Rio Rico soon had a twin brother. During the fall of 1969, GAC bought the historic Empire Ranch in the rolling grasslands north of Sonoita from the Boice family for about three million dollars. That sale, along with the purchase of the Olander Hammond Ranch to the south, gave GAC more than thirty-five thousand deeded acres of some of the best grassland in Arizona.[50]

From the very beginning, however, GAC's plans for the Empire Ranch encountered much stronger opposition than Rio Rico. One reason was scope. Proposing to chop the magnificent Sonoita Valley into one-acre pieces, GAC envisioned a city of 180,000 people spreading across a grass sea. Its Empire-Sonoita Regional Plan encompassed 60,000 acres, 25,000 of which GAC did not own. GAC's own ecologists warned that only 13,000 acres could support such high-density housing. Developing the entire area would reduce grass cover and soil moisture and lead to severe erosion.[51]

An even greater concern was water. Cienega Creek flowed north into Pantano Wash, which drained into the Rillito and Santa Cruz Rivers. GAC was therefore threatening to suck an enormous amount of water from one of Tucson's most important watersheds. More than 150 people showed up at the Pima County Planning and Zoning Commission's public hearing on June 30 to protest the plan. GAC contended that initial tests revealed there was enough water to support a city, but admitted that the final water report would not be completed "for several years." In the face of such opposition, the commission postponed a decision until the plan's impact upon the ecology and water reserves of the area could be determined.[52]

In July, University of Arizona professor Robert Cauthorn from the College of Business and Public Administration hammered the water issue home to Tucson audiences. He argued that a development of only eighteen thousand people "could easily clobber the Tucson ground water supply." Citing a study by University of Arizona range scientist Philip Ogden, Cauthorn said that bulldozing the natural vegetation to build homes would carry more silt into the Pantano and Rillito Rivers and clog the recharge of Tucson's aquifers. He also drew attention to the burdens a growing population would place upon law enforcement and other Pima County services.[53] Soon afterward, the Planning and Zoning Commission called a special meeting and voted to take no further action until GAC provided a series of reports on everything from water to a title search to determine just how much property GAC owned within the regional plan.[54]

Aesthetics also mobilized people throughout Pima and Santa Cruz counties. The Sonoita Valley undulated majestically between the towering Santa Rita Mountains to the west and the Whetstone and Mustang Mountains to east. Oaks grew on its ridges, but the valley floor rippled with unbroken expanses of grass, tawny during the dry seasons, bright green after the summer rains. In July, seventy-eight residents from Sonoita, Elgin, and Patagonia presented the Planning and Zoning Commission with a petition expressing the agony of everyone fighting to preserve landscapes they loved: "To destroy our environment, to deprive wildlife of their natural habitats, to pollute our air, to congest our area, to increase our taxes and to bring the crime and lawlessness that an influx of 180,000 persons represents is the summation of our violent objection."[55] That November, Stewart Udall, former secretary of the interior during the Kennedy and Johnson administrations, joined the Citizens' Council for Empire Ranch.[56]

GAC fought back on a number of different fronts. First, it trotted out its hydrological hired guns. Two firms—Gerahty and Miller of New York and Layne Western Company of Kansas City—stated that there were two layers of water underlying the region. "It is estimated there is as much as 365 billion gallons of water stored in the upper aquifer within the basin," Frank Deluca of Gerahty and Miller announced. "This amount alone could supply a population of 180,000 people for 33 years without additional water." The upper level, however, would be reserved for farms within the area. GAC would only pump the lower aquifer, about eight hundred feet below the surface, which was equal to or greater than the upper one, according to Carl Muzan of Layne Western. The hydrologists also claimed that recharge in the region averaged a staggering six million gallons per day. In other words, there was plenty of water for everybody, a developers' mantra as old as speculation in the arid West.[57]

Then Harry Montgomery, the newly elected president of the Arizona Pioneers' Historical Society, announced that GAC had promised to donate the Empire Ranch headquarters to the Society. Montgomery said the Society wanted to turn the headquarters into a living ranch museum in cooperation with the Arizona Cattle Growers Association—an ironic concept, since GAC's plan would have destroyed some of the best ranch land in Arizona.[58]

Finally, an editorial in the *Arizona Daily Star* expressed the sentiments of the development community, arguing that GAC had "gone far beyond what anyone might normally have expected in taking into account environmental factors, relationship with neighboring properties and future growth." The editorial contended that GAC's Empire Ranch development should not be limited to the fifty-three hundred acres recommended by the Planning and Zoning Commission. "GAC is not and cannot be expected to be a landholding company, or a land bank. It must move land to sustain itself and realize a profit."[59]

GAC probably would have gotten away with its proposal if the Empire Ranch had been in Santa Cruz County, like Rio Rico was. But Tucson's nascent environmental community kept up the pressure on the Pima County Board of Supervisors. Environmental concerns skyrocketed after Anaconda Copper Company announced that it planned to develop an open-pit copper mine on the east side of the Helvetia Mountains. The prospect of both a copper mine and a city materializing along one of Tucson's most important watersheds scared more than just tree huggers and desert rats.

In December, after deferring a vote once, the Pima County Board of Supervisors adopted the Planning and Zoning Commission's recommendations. GAC would have to "substantially develop" fifty-three hundred acres before any additional rezoning would be considered. When asked to define "substantial," Thomas Jay, chairman of the Board of Supervisors, replied, "They would have to show the people they're not only buying lots. There would have to be churches, banks, schools and other services for the people." Angry at the restrictions, GAC replied that it would have to study "possible alternatives." When reporters asked GAC attorney James Webb if pulling out of the project was one of those alternatives, he answered, "This is one in a range of possibilities. We will have to replan the area to see if we can make any money."[60]

Trouble on the Baca Float

At the same time he was hedging about the Empire Ranch, however, Webb tried to quell rumors that the corporation would run out on Rio Rico as well. "GAC wishes to make it clear that today's decision will in no way affect other Arizona projects," Webb said. "The company will continue to fulfill its commitments there."[61] But all was not well on the Baca Float.

During the summer of 1970, GAC petitioned the Arizona Department of Property Valuations to decrease the valuation of Rio Rico from $26.8 million to $182,075. Deputy Director Don Beach replied that the request amounted to a tacit admission that Gulf American was selling lots for about four thousand dollars more than they were worth. The ubiquitous Webb huffed that Beach had referred to GAC as Gulf American, and that "property valuations throughout the state have been and should continue to be modified by the fact the developer has yet to make major expenditures in improving property." Beach fired back that GAC had already sold seventeen thousand lots at Rio Rico, charging customers for streets, bridges, and other improvements that might not be constructed for another decade. "They are telling us that while the lots are selling for an average of $5,000, they will not be worth that much for another 10 years," Beach observed. "They claim the lots are now worth only about $400."[62]

Beach overestimated GAC's valuations. GAC lawyers contended, in fact, that Rio Rico lots should be valued at $185 an acre for tax purposes. That meant that the true value of the lots was 4 percent of their selling price—a healthy profit margin even by Gulf American standards. GAC claimed that the five thousand dollars covered twenty-five hundred dollars in selling expenses and the costs of future improvements. When the Arizona Board of Property Tax Appeals turned down GAC's petition in July, GAC filed suit in Santa Cruz County Superior Court. But then the company turned around and asked for a change of venue because the Santa Cruz County assessor had valued the lots at $1,666 apiece. GAC attorneys argued that the lots should be valued according to their current, not considered, use. Because much of its Baca Float land could not be developed until the current grazing lease expired at the end of 1971, GAC wanted to pay taxes on range, not real estate. Rent-a-cow operations were an increasingly common tax dodge in Arizona.[63]

GAC pursued the reduction of its property taxes so aggressively because Rio Rico was operating at a huge deficit. Addressing his board of directors at the Rio Rico Inn on January 28, 1971, GAC chairman and president S. Hayward Wills said that the corporation had spent $50.3 million on Rio Rico. To date, however, the company had only reaped $9.8 million in principal and $4.5 million in interest, leaving a cash deficit of $36 million. How could GAC be called "money grabbers"? Wills wanted to know. Critics argued that GAC was proceeding too slowly, with only seventy-eight housing starts in its first twenty months of operation. But Coral Gables started only twenty units in its first twenty months, and now housing units exceeded five thousand. "Land development is a cash deficit operation," Wills noted, assuring his board that GAC had the financial resources to absorb the negative cash flow. What it could not do, however, was "build roads or lay pipe in areas where there will be no houses for ten years."[64] Wills apparently did not feel he needed to justify GAC's practice of making current lot buyers pay for those future services, not to mention huge sales fees.

In 1971, Thomas W. Pew Jr., the editor of the *Troy Daily News* of Troy, Ohio, decided to investigate out-of-state development companies selling land in Ohio. Pew published a vivid account of his visit to Rio Rico in the *Saturday Review* (Pew 1971). Heading south from Tucson on I-19, Pew drove by a red, white, and blue billboard with a sketch of Teddy Roosevelt proclaiming: "'LAND IS THE BASIS OF WEALTH': INVEST IN RIO RICO." When he reached the Rio Rico sales office, salesmen immediately double- and triple-teamed him, signing him up as a VIT (Very Important Traveler) and singing the praises of the Arizona climate. Then one led him down a corridor lined with cubicles. Isolating Pew, the salesman launched into a rapid-fire sales pitch, whipping out maps, contracts, and charts. When Pew pulled out a notebook to write down what the salesman was saying, the salesman stopped and asked, "Are you going to take all of this down in writing?" "Oh, no, sir, not all of it," Pew answered, "but when I get home my wife will ask me all sorts of questions, and if I don't make some notes I won't be able to tell her what happened at Rio Rico and we won't be able to decide whether or not we can buy land here" (Pew 1971:49).

The salesman did not like the notebook but continued the hard sell anyway. Lots in Rio Rico were an investment. You did not have to build right away. "What you do is buy a piece of land and then jockey for position with it. Say if you buy a piece of property for $8,000 and it goes up to $16,000 in three years you can exchange it for a piece of property of equal value. But 97 percent of our land is already sold; so there's not much to work with," the salesman warned. "When we get the Empire Ranch opened up to housing we'll be trading between here and there too. The only problem we have, Mr. Pew, is that we just don't have enough land to sell. Our brokers all over the United States are crying for more land to sell. But we just don't have any left. We're an investment company, you see, we want to sell you stock—I mean land—because it's a good investment. We're on the New York Stock Exchange, remember" (Pew 1971:49).

It sounded like a pyramid scheme to Pew. After he extracted himself from the salesman's clutches without signing an option, he examined a contract in his car. It included none of the promises the salesman made—no free membership in the country club until 1978, no pledge that utilities would all be installed by 1978, no waiver of property taxes. What it did contain was a clause stating that "Seller" could assign another site to "Buyer" if "engineering problems," "Act or Acts of God," or "any other unforeseen development problems" made the lot "unsuitable for the purpose for which it is sold and unfeasible for land development" (Pew 1971:49). In other words, GAC reserved the right to lot-switch, just like Gulf American.

Pew then did some digging. J. Mercer Johnson, special counsel for the State of Arizona, told him GAC contracts only guaranteed roads and water, not electricity or other utilities. Pew interviewed a Michigan couple who had bought their lot sight unseen. When they arrived at Rio Rico to visit their land, a salesman "drove us up to the top of a hill and pointed out over the desert and said, 'There, your lot is out there somewhere.'" The couple also was appalled to learn how inflated the price of their lot was. "People like us pay for sales promotion to bring in more people to buy more land," the Michigan woman said. "And while they used our money, we would be getting billed for taxes every year on this property we couldn't use or sell" (Pew 1971:50). Tucson realtor William Franklin drove that point home to Pew when he said, "You can buy a choice one-acre lot in the Catalina Foothills of Tucson, where I live, for $7,500 right now. That price includes paved streets, power, and water. At Rio Rico you pay $4,000 or $5,000 right now and it may well be ten years before the utilities are brought in. And the cost of the utilities will probably up the purchase price" (Pew 1971:50).[65]

Finally, Pew talked with several former GAC salesmen themselves, all of whom had worked for Gulf American. "Gulf American may have a new parent company but the old sales team is still using the old ways of selling the land," one said. Another claimed that its success in Florida made the sales team "drunk with power." "At first we sold Cape Coral in Florida as a legitimate community, and today it is a community," he confided. "Then we sold Golden Gate with roads, then River Ranch with nothing, and finally Remuda Ranch under water. Everything worked. One of the bosses said one time that 'eventually we'll reach the point where we'll just mail contracts and the people will send them in and we'll tell them where we'll put them'" (Pew 1971:51).

Gulf American Revisited

GAC's legal problems and bad publicity escalated in the fall of 1971. In late September, California's attorney general and real estate commissioner asked a California Superior Court judge to ban GAC from selling land at Rio Rico in California without notifying the state and obtaining a subdivision prospectus. The judge ordered GAC to appear at a hearing on October 8 to answer charges that its promotional tactics were misleading.[66] In early October, the Federal Trade Commission announced that it would probe GAC sales practices in Rhode Island, where the Rhode Island Consumers Council was already holding hearings concerning the company. Witnesses testified that GAC changed dates on sales contracts, misrepresented details in sales pitches, and forged names on contracts. "We have had one of the largest groups of people for consumer hearings in recent times here," the head of the Consumers Council told reporters. "Utility hearings have been cemeteries by comparison."[67]

The Rhode Island Consumers Council brought its complaints to the Department of Business Regulation, which held another hearing. The most damning indictment came from John Assalone Jr., a former GAC salesman. Assalone accused GAC Properties of misrepresenting the value of its lots and the completion dates of developments. He also alleged that the company changed the terms of contracts without the knowledge of its customers. GAC refused to rebut any of the charges. "We don't feel there is anything to be gained by the individuals or the state of Rhode Island were these hearings to continue," a GAC lawyer replied. Instead, the corporation agreed to a six-point plan that ordered it to refund the money of Rhode Island residents to whom it made misrepresentations and to make no future sales unless a licensed broker supervised the transactions and stipulated that customers understood final purchase agreements prior to signing them.[68] A month later, the Rhode Island Department of Business Regulation ordered GAC to stop sales of land in Florida until all customer complaints had been addressed. "There have been roughly 100 complaints filed since the hearings ended last month, and the only ones GAC has settled are those involving Massachusetts residents," Donald Medici, a field investigator for the department, said.[69]

By the end of 1971, even the *Arizona Daily Star* was beginning to question GAC's sales tactics. A series of five articles beginning on December 26 investigated "Land Development in Arizona: Empty Promises?" One of the conclusions of the investigation was how little control Arizona exercised over developers. Unlike California, whose Real Estate Commission enforced tough laws governing development, Arizona divided its authority among the counties and several state agencies. Counties had to approve subdivision plans and zoning changes but had no authority over water or power. Prior to the passage of the Arizona Groundwater Management Act in 1980, no state agency ensured that developers provided an adequate water supply. Nor did the state require developers to supply power, either. California, in contrast, demanded that developers install roads, water, sewers, and electricity, or make "adequate financial provision" to do so, before selling lots. Customers buying Arizona lots signed contracts that allowed developers to delay supplying "front-end" costs for up to twelve years.[70]

California also insisted that lots be appraised. If the sales price was considerably higher than the appraisal, the development would not be approved. At Rio Rico, in contrast, GAC tried to convince the Arizona State Property Tax Appeals Board that lots selling for $5,000 were only worth $185. When *Arizona Daily Star* reporters questioned Commissioner Talley about these practices, he defended the developers and questioned the need for statewide regulations. He agreed that buyers should be informed about the parcels they were buying but went on to say, "There are those who would go beyond providing information to a process that might be called 'coddling' people. This process has already covered our young people."[71]

Rio Rico definitely did not coddle its customers. Roads and utilities did not have to be delivered for twelve years. Salesmen promised that lots would appreciate in value at 20 percent a year even though an investment prospectus provided to bond investors, not buyers, stated, "The prices at which (GAC) Properties sells land under installment contracts do not reflect the current market prices for cash purchases of comparable developed or undeveloped land. There is no significant resale market for installment land contracts."[72] Salesmen also lied about the amount of taxes that would have to be paid on lots, and failed to inform customers about "betterment fees" of $904 to $1,700 to hook up water and electricity, and an additional $500 to install septic tanks.[73] Buyer Beware reigned supreme.

In February 1972, the Council of Better Business Bureaus issued a warning about investing in land sold by GAC Properties.[74] Frank Steffens, the new president of GAC Properties, called the report "essentially a fair one," but complained that it failed to point out that GAC had fired more than two-thirds of the 430 salesmen accused of misrepresentation.[75] A few days later, GAC announced losses of $65.4 million for 1971, the first time the parent company had failed to show a profit in its history.[76]

Later that spring, disgruntled Rio Rico property owners filed a class action lawsuit against GAC for one hundred million dollars, arguing that fraudulent GAC sales tactics violated numerous federal laws. Most of the accusations concerned claims about the value and investment potential of Rio Rico land. There was no likelihood that resale values "would ever increase to a value equal to the investment price within the foreseeable future," the lawsuit contended. Rio Rico was a bad investment because "undeveloped land was selling for substantially less in the vicinity." Dire warnings by salesmen that Rio Rico was running out of lots were false because "a high percentage of investors defaulted on their contracts, creating a constant flow of salable land." "There was, and is, no open market for land at Rio Rico. The only market for land at Rio Rico is an artificial market created by high-pressure sales tactics and fraudulent practices." The suit even alleged that sales booths were bugged so that salesmen could hear what customers were saying to one another and tailor their pitches accordingly.[77]

Five Rio Rico homeowners filed another suit in the summer of 1972 for $550 million. Their suit asserted that the townhouses they purchased lacked promised amenities and were already falling apart.[78] GAC countered with a full-page ad in southern Arizona papers. "Rico Rico has more behind it than golden canyons and cactus flowers," the ad trumpeted. "Rio Rico has GAC." The ad touted GAC's Florida developments and stated, "Rio Rico is designed to grow carefully." Noting that only 15 percent of Arizona was private land, the ad answered its own question, "Does it make good business sense to consider Rio Rico?" by arguing, "people, industry pour into Arizona. And land becomes more and more desirable. Particularly in well-planned communities like Rio Rico."[79]

The day after the ad appeared, reporter Steve Auslander, who covered southern Arizona land development for the *Arizona Daily Star*, drew attention to an article in the *Arizona Review*, a University of Arizona journal focusing on business and economic development. The article surveyed seven major developments in southern Arizona and discovered that the resale value of lots ranged from 58 to 88 percent of their original prices. Rio Rico had one of the lowest resale values, 63 percent. GAC spokesman Jimmy Dudley hemmed and hawed that the article was "strictly one man's opinion" and finally blustered, "When he says the resale value is 63 per cent, I think if you check nationally that is a pretty high figure."[80]

But no amount of bluster could halt GAC's downhill slide in southern Arizona. In November 1972, the Department of Housing and Urban Development (HUD) held a two-day hearing in Phoenix on Arizona land fraud. GAC Properties was one of six developers accused of deceptive sales practices by angry consumers. Two others were the Great Southwest Land and Cattle Company and the Queen Creek Land and Cattle Corporation, fronts created by Ned Warren (Sheridan 1995). Representative Morris Udall demanded that developers post surety bonds to ensure they kept their promises. He also called for a ban on interstate land sales. "The rape of our unique desert environment must be stopped," Udall concluded. Ron Asta, who chaired a Pima County Board of Supervisors briefly committed to controlling growth in the 1970s, pointed out that remote subdivisions not only chewed up the desert but imposed heavy burdens on county taxpayers as well. Tax revenues generated by those subdivisions never covered the costs of county services provided to them.[81] That fiscal drain became one of the underlying reasons Pima County launched its ambitious Sonoran Desert Conservation Plan to control urban sprawl and exurban leapfrogging almost three decades later.

As pressure to curb land fraud rose, and company stock fell from twenty-five dollars a share in 1972 to three dollars a share in June 1973, GAC decided to cut its losses. "Getting out of the land-sales business is part of a new company concept," Jimmy Dudley told the press. "We are liquidating other property in Florida, the Bahamas, and some in Arizona." One such property was the Empire Ranch. GAC had done nothing to develop its grandiose satellite city of 180,000 residents except drill two wells.[82] Anamax Mining Corporation purchased the 35,000-acre ranch in December for $12,868,000.[83]

GAC did not plan to sell Rio Rico. Nonetheless, the federal noose was tightening around GAC just as the state of Florida had slowly strangled Gulf American five years earlier. As a result of its hearings on deceptive sales practices a year earlier, HUD changed its regulations on December 1, 1973. HUD's Office of Interstate Land Sales Registration now required full disclosure of a developer's financial condition. Soon afterward, HUD demanded that GAC Properties change its property reports within fifteen days or show cause why such changes were not necessary. GAC proxy statements to stockholders listed debts, negative cash flows, and the necessity to sell off GAC subsidiaries to improve the corporation's financial health. GAC property reports included no such information. Unless GAC complied, HUD would force the corporation to suspend all land sales throughout the nation, including Arizona.[84]

GAC spokesman Jimmy Dudley tried to put an optimistic spin on the notice by claiming that the sale of two GAC subsidiaries would generate $130 million to pay interest on debts coming due at the end of the year. "I think HUD is actually backing the sale, which will ensure that GAC is financially stable at the end of the year," Dudley proclaimed. "I think the whole thing will clear up after the stockholders' meeting."[85] George Bernstein of HUD's Office of Interstate Land Sales Registration quickly took issue with Dudley. "The sale [of the two subsidiaries] will give them sufficient funds to pay off some of their obligations—the ones due immediately—but it will not allow them to pay off their long-term debts," Bernstein noted. "The company will still report a negative cash flow."[86]

Even though stockholders approved the sale of the subsidiaries, federal regulators continued to close in. In March 1974, the Federal Trade Commission (FTC) forced GAC to agree to refund the money of some lot buyers at Rio Rico and nine Florida developments. The FTC also stipulated that future sales contracts had to contain a ten-day escape clause for buyers. Moreover, the first page of every contact had to state in dark letters bigger than newsprint, "The future value of this land, like all undeveloped real estate, is uncertain."[87] That summer, the settlement of the class action suit filed in 1972 required GAC to issue partial refunds to many lot buyers and to install improvements for others at Rio Rico, where 22,000 lots had been sold and 600 people were living. The settlement applied to 43,940 buyers at the Arizona subdivision and two developments in Florida.[88] By the end of 1975, GAC had paid $500,000 in cash and $17.5 million in credit to former customers.[89]

During the same period, the Arizona attorney general's Strike Force on Organized Crime began investigating Real Estate Commissioner J. Fred Talley. James Cornwall, the former president of Great Southwest Land and Cattle Company, testified that Warren funneled bribes from six land developers to Talley. Talley also was accused of issuing real estate licenses to felons. Talley denied any wrongdoing but admitted that he did try to rehabilitate exconvicts.[90] At a legislative subcommittee hearing chaired by Arizona Senate Majority Leader Sandra Day O'Connor in July, Representative John Wettaw (R-Flagstaff) told Talley that people in the state were "appalled at some of the people who are given licenses . . . it is obvious there are Mafia connections here one way or the other."[91]

The next month, the Arizona Real Estate Commission ordered Talley to appear before them. During the two-day hearing, Talley admitted that one land developer had given him a six-hundred-dollar watch and another had floated him a seven-thousand-dollar loan. These were not bribes, according to Talley, but the commission voted to suspend him for ninety days without pay. A week later, Talley resigned to spare his family "deep anguish." He still claimed he had done nothing wrong, but stated, "I am the center figure around whom the vast potential for disruption and unhappiness revolves. My personal vindication is not as important as my service to the commission, Gov. (Jack) Williams, to the Legislature, etc." Talley died following heart surgery that November.[92]

A year later, HUD ordered GAC Properties to stop selling lots on installment at Rio Rico and a Florida development. Even though the parent company had sold its consumer credit and insurance subsidiaries, along with Empire Ranch, its financial subsidiary, GAC Properties Credit, faced a $35.5-million debt payment due on November 15, 1975. The financial subsidiary scrambled to negotiate an extension and failed. Even though debtors holding 62 percent of GAC's maturing bonds agreed to exchange them for cash and 12 percent bonds payable in 1980, GAC failed to get the 80 percent necessary. That meant that the trustee for an additional $43.5 million in debentures payable in 1977 had the right to collect on those bonds immediately.[93]

GAC Properties Credit filed for bankruptcy on December 12.[94] GAC Properties followed suit the next day.[95] The receiver, David L. Hughes of Miami, stated that he doubted the bankrupt company would be able to meet the terms of the class action lawsuit against it. That meant that many lot owners might never receive the roads, water, or electricity GAC had promised to install.[96]

In an editorial, the *Arizona Daily Star* proclaimed, "The failure of GAC, the largest land developer in the nation, signals at least a temporary end to one of the most pervasive land hustles in American history."[97] The editorial was only referring to GAC, Gulf American, and the real estate scams of the postwar boom. It made no mention of Manuel María Gándara's theft of the Tumacácori land grant in 1844 or the triumph of Baca Float No. 3 in 1914. The thread that linked Gándara, Judge Watts, Colonel Sykes, the Bouldins, Watts and Davis, and Tol Pendleton to the Florida corporations lay buried in archives, hidden from view. Yet the sordid truth was this: Land fraud had been central to the production and destruction of space in the Upper Santa Cruz Valley for at least 130 years. Rio Rico was simply a stage in the process. People who wanted to farm or ranch or build a retirement home lost out to speculators manipulating paper titles. With few exceptions, legal systems and government entities from the state of Sonora to the U.S. Supreme Court validated the speculators and dispossessed the settlers until the modest reforms of the 1970s imposed a few curbs. Even then, the heirs of the O'odham and the homesteaders never returned.

9

Buried Landscapes

If you search the web for "Rio Rico, Arizona," most of the hits are real estate promotions that toss in a little garbled history the way teenagers add fruit punch to Everclear. Take, for example, the web page of the Nogales-Santa Cruz Chamber of Commerce. "Long before Geronimo and Will Rogers walked these trails, Rio Rico was home to a pre-historic race known as 'The Forgotton [*sic*] Ones,'" the web page informs us. "When mastodons and swamps disappeared, sometime between the birth of Christ and 400 AD, they gave up their caves for primitive dwellings. An 18-acre village constructed by the Forgotton [*sic*] Ones was rediscovered in 1954. Fortunately the village was partially rebuilt by the Upper Pima Indians, providing the first link to modern history."[1]

On a muggy day in late July 2004, I turn off Interstate 19 onto the Tumacácori exit and head east down Santa Gertrudis Lane. Storms are building on the southern horizon in Mexico, but the lane is a dark arbor of huge mesquites that almost block out the sky. On either side an impenetrable *bosque* (forest) of mesquite, acacia, and hackberry closes in around me. I can imagine a PR hack conjuring "The Forgotton Ones" stalking mastodons bogged down in a muddy swamp nearby. But the bosque primeval thrives on treated wastewater from Nogales. Ironically, the riparian vegetation along this stretch of the Santa Cruz was probably never as lush as it is now, at least not since the end of the last ice age, when mammoths did indeed roam the region.

Shifting the Southwest Center's aging Toyota into four-wheel drive, I roll through muddy puddles and the Santa Cruz River. Gated lanes lead through the trees to ranch houses and fields where fat horses graze. Did Simenon cast his cold compulsive eye on the drunken antics of socialites behind those walls half a century ago?

But when I leave the floodplain, the ghosts of Tol Pendleton and Hubert Merryweather fade as I turn onto paved Pendleton Road. Tales of

Santa Booze Lane seem almost as fantastical as "The Forgotton Ones" stalking mastodons at the time of Christ. Heading south, I enter another space from a more recent time: the old Rio Rico, the legacy of Gulf American and GAC. On a whim, I climb up a ridge of the San Cayetano Mountains along Ruta Camaron (Shrimp Route). There are several homes in the distance below San Cayetano Peak, but Ruta Camaron leads nowhere, its pavement eroding into high desert. Hundreds of miles of such roads snake up the western slopes of the San Cayetanos and along both sides of Josephine Canyon to the north. Perhaps a couple from Michigan or Nebraska bought a lot up here in the late 1960s. Did they ever visit it? Are their four decades of unpaid back taxes piling up in the Santa Cruz County Treasurer's Office?

On my way down, I skirt rock slides and shrubby mesquite and intersect Pendleton again on Calle Pulpo (Octopus Road). Another hack must have sat down with a Spanish dictionary when these imaginary subdivisions were being platted, searching for themes that captured a whiff of Old Mexico and the Sea of Cortez.

The new Rio Rico, in contrast, is booming. I drive past the Rio Rico Fire District and the Rio Rico Fitness Center to the Rio Rico Country Club along the lower stretches of Sonoita Creek. Then I take Avenida Coatimundi to the Rio Rico Community Center and The Villages at Rio Rico, a series of high-density neighborhoods. I follow Rio Rico Drive into the southern foothills of the San Cayetanos, past pseudo-Mediterranean villas with tennis courts and more modest brick or block homes on smaller lots.

The new Rio Rico rises at the juncture of Sonoita Creek and the Santa Cruz, where mission herds from the *visita* of Calabasas once grazed. This is where Colonel C. P. Sykes wanted to build his gateway to Mexico, and this is where Manuel María Gándara established his hacienda after he stole the Tumacácori land grant from the O'odham. If there were any justice in history, Calabasas would be part of the Tumacácori District of the Tohono O'odham Nation. Instead of Rio Rico Resort with its par seventy-two Trent Jones Sr. golf course snaking up the Sonoita floodplain, there might be a glittering casino luring snowbirds and Sonorans with slot machines and nostalgia acts.

But even though the O'odham held onto their grant until 1848, at least five years after the Sonoran elite had abandoned grants eventually confirmed by the U.S. government, there is no Tumacácori District of the Tohono O'odham Nation.[2] The O'odham did not speak the language of lawyers, and no lawyers spoke for them in the late nineteenth or early twentieth centuries, when the fates of the Tumacácori land grant and Baca Float No. 3 were being determined. They became the "Forgotton Ones." Baca Float No. 3 and Rio Rico squatted on their lands.

Avatar and Modern Rio Rico

For two decades following GAC's bankruptcy in 1975, Rio Rico remained a phantom development. The Rio Rico Resort continued to do business, but the scars of the roads up the San Cayetanos bore stark witness to Gulf American and GAC's big dreams and hollow promises. After a one-hundred-dred-million-dollar lawsuit was settled in 1974, U.S. District judge James A. Walsh ordered GAC to make sure every lot the company sold had roads and utilities. He also demanded that GAC exchange lots in Rio Rico's core at Calabasas for thousands of lots to the north where development was as likely as rain in May.[3] A bankruptcy court in Miami authorized GAC to do so, and the owners of 1,120 lots northeast of Tubac were given the chance to trade for lots in developed areas or areas that were to have utilities by 1979.[4] By 1979, GAC was even promising to build new homes in its core of seven hundred acres, where three hundreds homes had already been constructed and seven hundred to eight hundred residents lived.[5]

But even after GAC metamorphosed into Avatar Holdings, the current owner of Rio Rico Properties, attrition characterized the project in the 1980s and early 1990s. A group of Scottsdale investors led by John Ratliff purchased sixteen thousand acres of Rio Rico at a bankruptcy auction. The Ratliff group then contracted with Phoenix-based First United Realty to sell forty-acre parcels in the five-thousand acre Tubac Foothills Ranch east of Tumacácori and the five-thousand acre Sonoita Creek Ranch to the south. The Ratliff group also sold five thousand acres to the Arizona State Parks Department, which incorporated the parcel into its Sonoita Creek Natural Area. Avatar's Rio Rico empire shrank from fifty-five thousand to thirty-six thousand acres in the process.[6]

Then, in the mid-1990s, the corporation brought in developers from California and changed strategies. By 1997, Avatar had largely abandoned the sluggish lot-selling business. Under the leadership of Guy Tobin, president of Rio Rico Properties, the company created The Villages at Rio Rico, where customers could choose from 14 home plans ranging from $80,000 to $150,000. The homes could be situated at thirty-eight different elevations from Sonoita Creek up the San Cayetanos' southern slopes.[7] Within three years, Avatar had built and sold about 250 homes.[8]

Its 255-acre Rio Rico South Industrial Park also neared build out as produce companies and suppliers of *maquiladoras*, the border assembly plants located in Nogales, Sonora, constructed warehouses along I-19. Thereafter, Tobin announced that Rio Rico's commercial development would largely be restricted to restaurants, services, and retail at the interchange of Rio Rico Drive and the freeway. Tobin planned to further concentrate residential growth within a thirty-three-hundred-acre "core" that was "intact and contiguous." "We are hoping to master plan a senior-oriented community around the golf course," Tobin declared.[9] In 2002, Avatar even sold the Rio Rico Resort and Country Club for $5.49 million to American Property Management, one of the largest hotel companies in the United States. "We've been looking for a real hotel operator to come in and invest money to take it to the next level," Tobin noted. "It's not part of our core business."[10] Rio Rico built and sold homes. Its epicenter, and its future, would continue to be located on the old mission *estancia* of Calabasas.

Like Gulf American and GAC, Avatar is headquartered in Florida. According to Reuters Abridged Business Summary, "Its assets consist primarily of real estate in the states of Florida and Arizona." Avatar Holdings is traded on the NASDAQ as AVTR. Gerald Kelfer, its president and CEO, makes $5.58 million a year. Jonathen Fels, president of Avatar Properties, makes $2.44 million.[11]

Unlike Gulf American and GAC, however, Avatar seems to be a success story. For the first three months of 2004, both revenues and expenses were more than 60 percent higher than the same period in 2003. "The increase in revenues is attributable to increased closings at Poinciana and Rio Rico, as well as closing at Bellalago and Cory/Lake Isles," its quarterly report to the Security and Exchange Commission states.[12] Avatar also appears to operate within the limits of the law with a long-term commitment to southern Arizona. In 2003, Rio Rico Properties sold 259 acres of riparian habitat along 4 miles of Sonoita Creek to Arizona State Parks for $1.5 million from the Heritage Fund, whose revenues come from the Arizona Lottery. The corridor extends from the juncture of the Santa Cruz upstream to the Sonoita Creek State Natural Area west of Patagonia Lake.[13]

Because of Avatar's profitability and civic gestures, *Big Builder* magazine named it top home builder in the United States for Most Innovative Product Design for both homes and communities in 2003. The company came in second for Most Admired Builder in the nation.[14] Stories circulate that Avatar employed some of Gulf American and GAC's hard-sell tactics in the 1990s, when it would fly in customers, many of them Koreans from southern California, to sell them lots at inflated prices. But those tactics appear to be a thing of the past, at least for now.

The hard sell may not be necessary any more. By 2004, unincorporated Rio Rico had an estimated population of fourteen to sixteen thousand. Some were retirees, but others worked in the produce warehouses and other NAFTA (North American Free Trade Agreement)-related businesses on both sides of the border. Home buyers included managers of maquiladoras and agents in the rapidly swelling Border Patrol. The community had grown by about 10 percent a year since 1994, and most estimates of future growth in the Nogales area identified Rio Rico as the prime target.[15] Rio Rico had become not just a resort or retirement village but a middle-class bedroom community for Ambos Nogales as well. Even though the boom days of the maquiladora phenomenon seemed to be over—employment in Nogales, Sonora, factories dropped by 35 percent in 2003 as companies found cheaper labor in China and Southeast Asia— NAFTA seemed to be picking up the slack.[16]

Metro Tucson and the I-19 Corridor

Rio Rico's boom is part of a pincer movement along I-19, one that may absorb exurban islands like Green Valley into a suburban corridor that stretches from Marana to the border. Metropolitan Tucson marches southward, gobbling up private and State Trust Lands in the middle Santa Cruz Valley between Tucson and Green Valley. For the last four decades, Tucson's growth has been increasingly land extensive. In 1930, when Tucson's population was 32,506, there were 4,526.7 persons per square mile in the city. Densities rose slowly through the 1960 census, and then began to fall: 3,306.0 in 1970; 3,344.1 in 1980; 2,573.3 in 1990; and 2,490.7 in 2000. In 1990, a staggering 35 percent of land within the incorporated limits of the city of Tucson remained undeveloped (Sheridan 2003).

Meanwhile, the population of metropolitan Tucson kept climbing, exceeding eight hundred thousand by 2003. Because land is generally cheaper on the edges of an urban center, demand and the housing market have provided bigger lots in new subdivisions, not greater urban densities and infilling within existing municipal boundaries. The result is urban sprawl and exurban leapfrogging as almost five thousand acres of desert a year are bulldozed (Sheridan 2003).

A consensus seems to be emerging among city of Tucson and Pima Association of Governments prognosticators that eastern Pima County (the Tohono O'odham Nation controls most of the county to the west) will not reach the limits of its water supply until 1.7 million people have settled there by 2050. In other words, population will double during the next fifty years. As Pima County's Sonoran Desert Conservation Plan goes into effect, much of that growth will be channeled south and southeast of metro Tucson because there are fewer endangered, threatened, or vulnerable species of animals and plants to provoke lawsuits and raise the costs of development.[17]

Tucson's southward sprawl is already nipping at the Tubac-Tumacácori area. Private lands (156,455 acres; 35 percent) and State Trust Lands (212,745 acres; 47 percent) compose 82 percent of the Santa Cruz watershed (449,684 acres)(Pima County 2000:40). State Trust Lands can and are being auctioned off to developers at a rapidly increasing rate.[18] The expansion of Green Valley has already spun off several high-end subdivisions, including Rancho Sahuarita and Quail Creek in the western foothills of the Santa Rita Mountains (Sheridan 2003).

Meanwhile, the formerly agrarian community of Sahuarita is aggressively annexing land and courting developers. Sahuarita incorporated in 1994, when it had a population of 2,159 residents. Since then, its numbers have more than doubled. In 1996, the Pima Association of Governments projected a population of 23,374 in 2050. That projection is probably low. Municipal planners anticipate that Sahuarita Road will become a major corridor of residential development as metro Tucson's population continues to increase. This will intensify development along the I-19 corridor in the Green Valley-Sahuarita areas.

Water will be the only limiting factor. The Upper Santa Cruz River Valley consists of four subbasins—Nogales, Rio Rico, Tubac, and Amado—that form pockets of alluvium from the border to the conjunction of the Santa Cruz and Sópori Wash to the north. Both businesses and homes depend upon the water stored in that alluvium. The Nogales International Wastewater Treatment Plant may be able to process 1.7 million gallons of sewage a day from Ambos Nogales, but no one is going to drink it.

During most of the period covered in this book, upstream water use did not have much impact upon either surface or groundwater flow from Calabasas to Tubac. But as Nogales, Arizona, continues to grow, stacking up along the narrow ravines that feed the Santa Cruz, the aquifer of the Nogales subbasin will strain to meet its needs. According to hydrologists Leonard and Philip Halpenny (1991:1), the Nogales subbasin is divided into four "microbasins"—"a shoestring aquifer of alluvial deposits"—that extend from the border to Guevavi, where Jesuit missionary Eusebio Francisco Kino established his first mission among the O'odham in southern Arizona. Kino did so because the "bedrock boundary" of Guevavi Narrows forces water to the surface, creating a stretch of perennial flow. In 1991, the city of Nogales purchased 490 acres of bottomland with its attendant water rights from Ralph Wingfield at Guevavi Ranch to capture that flow for municipal use (Halpenny and Halpenny 1991).

Now that Rio Rico is drawing more and more water from the Rio Rico subbasin, however, Nogales is blocked to the north. Despite the ability of these aquifers to recharge quickly after heavy rains, droughts and drawdowns during dry times of the year will mean water scarcity, water rationing, and water conflict. The fates of Nogales, Arizona, and Nogales, Sonora, will grow ever more intertwined as both scramble to provide their expanding populations and businesses with the water they require (Ingram, Laney, and Gillilan 1995).

Restructuring and Resistance

It may be decades before such natural limits are reached, and even longer before they are accepted. But growing numbers of people in southern

Arizona are unwilling to wait for nature to bat last. One of the major themes of historian Adam Rome's (2001) *The Bulldozer in the Countryside* is that postwar America's suburban sprawl spawned its own antithesis— an environmental movement composed of people who moved into those subdivisions and wanted the bulldozers to stop at the end of their streets. In southern Arizona, acts of resistance are mounting against the development juggernaut.

The fight against the subdivision of Empire Ranch in the 1970s was one of the first. Another took place at Canoa Ranch, once the headquarters of the Manning family's legendary ranching empire. In 1999, Fairfield Homes, a prominent developer in Green Valley, pushed hard for a high-density rezoning of the southern part of the San Ignacio de la Canoa land grant. To preserve open space and dark skies, a coalition of environmentalists, neighborhood activists, and astronomers from the Smithsonian's Whipple Observatory on Mount Hopkins in the Santa Rita Mountains joined forces to oppose them. Fairfield tried to pack hearings with employees and subcontractors, but many more people turned out to speak against the rezoning. By a 4–1 vote, the Pima County Board of Supervisors denied Fairfield's request. It was the first time in twenty-five years that the board rejected a major rezoning (Hadley 2000; Sheridan 2000).

Many of us who fought that battle felt it ended in a draw, not a victory. A compromise ramrodded by the Pima County administrator allowed Fairfield to build high-density homes and a golf course west of I-19 and to develop commercial properties along an eastern strip of the freeway at the Canoa Road interchange. About forty-eight hundred acres, or 80 percent of Canoa Ranch, in contrast, remained in rural homestead zoning, one house per 4.3 acres. Pima County then purchased that portion of Canoa Ranch, including its abandoned and deteriorating headquarters, in 2001 (Sheridan 2003). Plans call for a county park and possibly a historical museum there. The coalition that opposed the rezoning hoped against hope that a line had been drawn, that the southern urban boundary of metropolitian Tucson had finally been defined.

But Canoa is one small island in a spatial and demographic tsunami. Fairfield Homes wasted little time in bulldozing ridge tops and building homes and a golf course west of I-19 opposite Canoa headquarters. Then, in October 2004, First United Realty of Phoenix paid twenty-two million dollars for the enormous Sópori Ranch southwest of Canoa. The Sópori embraces 12,600 acres of deeded land, more than 2,800 of which are within one-half mile of I-19.[19] Within the next twenty years, an unbroken chain of subdivisions and shopping centers may stretch from the San Xavier District of the Tohono O'odham Nation to the international border.

The Sonoran Desert Conservation Plan (SDCP) will try to arrest that trend. In May 2004, voters approved the sale of $174 million of Open Space bonds to purchase or acquire conservation easements on biologically sensitive lands in Pima County.[20] Pima County may try to acquire the forty-three hundred acres of the Sópori within its boundaries, and perhaps even parts of the ranch in Santa Cruz County as well.[21] In February 2005, the Pima County Board of Supervisors also voted 5–0 to buy 9,574 deeded acres of Rancho Seco, southwest of the Sópori, for $20.6 million.[22] Public efforts such as the SDCP, and private efforts by organizations such as the Nature Conservancy, the Trust for Public Lands, and the Arizona Open Land Trust are providing capital to compete with developers in the real estate market to preserve open space, wildlife habitat, and working ranches.

Tumacácori National Historical Park

Another oasis of open space is Tumacácori National Historical Park. Tumacácori National Monument was originally established in 1908 under the Antiquities Act. Until the 1970s, when six acres of fiesta ground were added, the monument rested on ten acres donated, first by homesteader Carmen Mendez, and then by the Bouldin family after Baca Float No. 3 drove Mendez and other homesteaders off their lands. In 1990, however, Congress approved the acquisition of an additional 22 acres encompassing the mission visita of San Cayetano de Calabasas and 7.76 acres surrounding Mission Los Santos Angeles de Guevavi. It also changed the name to Tumacácori National Historical Park. Both Calabasas and Guevavi remain hidden by mesquite and closed to the public, except during guided tours.

The biggest expansions came in 2004, thanks to the determination of Superintendent Ann Rasor. The year before, Congress authorized $1.49 million to purchase the 90-acre Mission Ranch to the south. Internal

Figure 6. Laura Kermen, famed Tohono O'odham potter, preparing to fire pottery, Mission Tumacácori, Apr. 2, 1972. (Courtesy Dewey Doramus, Tumacácori National Historical Park)

National Park Service funds enabled the park to buy another 220 acres north and east of Mission Tumacácori. These dramatic expansions extend the park to the Santa Cruz River and incorporate portions of the mission orchard, fields, and *acequia madre* (main irrigation canal) into park boundaries. Research is already being conducted to identify and reestablish mission-era fruit trees. In the future, visitors may also have the opportunity to see other heirloom crops like wheat and fava beans in mission fields and perhaps even *churro* sheep and *corriente* cattle grazing the floodplain of the river. A shard of the mission's corporate community —a very small shard of the 1807 Tumacácori land grant—has been preserved.

A View from Calabasas

David Yubeta and I poke through the adobe ruins of Calabasas, which is protected from sun and rain by a metal-roofed ramada surrounded by chain-link fence and concertina wire. David is a native of southern Arizona, a historic preservation specialist at Tumacácori, and one of the leading adobe conservators in the nation. He learned adobe from his grandfather and uncles growing up in South Tucson. His grandfather taught him how to taste dirt to determine whether or not it would make good bricks. He spent hundreds of hours repairing and plastering family homes. For David, Calabasas's adobe walls are not a bureaucratic preservation project, but living, breathing fabrics of the past. Jesuit and Franciscan missionaries celebrated mass inside them. Gándara's employees fortified and took refuge from Apaches within them.

His colleague, Park Historian Don Garate, puts names on the people who passed in and out of these walls. Through Mission 2000, a computerized database of mission records, we know the individuals—O'odham, Yoemem (Yaqui), Basque, Castilian, mestizo, mulatto—who were baptized, married, and buried there. The staff of Tumacácori is doing its best to preserve the mission past and make it come alive for future generations of Arizonans.

Despite their efforts, however, Tumacácori will never be more than a celebration of the past. The living link that keeps Mission San Xavier del Bac from being more than an ambiguous icon of the Spanish conquest has been severed at Mission Tumacácori. The Tohono O'odham of the San Xavier District still worship within San Xavier's walls. Most O'odham who visit Tumacácori come during festivals to sell fry bread or to demonstrate their dances and crafts. Unlike San Xavier, Tumacácori is a museum, not a living parish.

This is not the fault of the National Park Service. Without the protection of dedicated NPS personnel, Tumacácori, Calabasas, and Guevavi would have melted away or been destroyed by vandals. If one institutional hero emerges from these pages, it is the Department of the Interior, which not only preserved Mission Tumacácori but fought against Baca Float No. 3 as well.

Yet even the Department of the Interior is compromised. Manuel María Gándara buried Tumacácori's O'odham community before it was dead. Then Surveyor General John Wasson and the government lawyers, justices, and Indian agents who followed allowed the theft of the Tumacácori land grant to go unchallenged. They never questioned Gándara's assertion that Tumacácori had been abandoned around 1820, more than a generation before the last O'odham fled the Apaches to take refuge at San Xavier.

Why did U.S. government officials buy that story of abandonment? Perhaps it was conscious subterfuge, but that seems unlikely. When the Tohono O'odham were fighting to reclaim their ancestral lands in the early twentieth century, they and their federal stewards apparently never protested the confirmation of Baca Float No. 3. If they did, their protests never reached the court records. The Tumacácori land grant was thrown out and the Baca Float awarded without an official O'odham voice being heard.

More likely, federal officials were guilty of historical ignorance compounded by lazy racism. Did any of them bother to ask the O'odham about their connections to Mission Tumacácori or its land grant? It probably never entered their minds. The O'odham were not living at Tumacácori when they reviewed the claims of Anglo speculators. And what, in their minds, would simple, childlike Indians know of such complex matters anyway? Without the paternalistic guidance of the missionaries, how could they possibly have held onto their mission on such a dangerous frontier?

Unless the O'odham resurrect their claim to the Tumacácori land grant, then, Tumacácori National Historical Park will remain a museum, no matter how vibrant its interpretations of the past may be. The O'odham presence will remain confined to exhibits, festivals, and living history demonstrations. Their landscapes, and the landscapes of the homesteaders who followed them, have been buried, and no real estate promoter or chamber of commerce is going to exhume them. Land fraud and dispossession do not sell.

Restructuring and Re-formation: The Tune Without Cease

As David and I drive away from the ruins of Calabasas, I reflect on the landscape that surrounds us now. For the foreseeable future, the Upper Santa Cruz Valley belongs to the subdivisions crawling up the foothills of the mountains and the warehouses swelling with fruits and vegetables from Mexico below, to the semis rolling along I-19, to the hundreds of undocumented Mexicans and Central Americans who trudge north through the valley each night risking death by heat stroke or exposure to search for work *al otro lado* (the other side; the United States). The historical geography of capitalism in the early twenty-first century is dancing to an international tune as NAFTA floods the border with exports and *maquilas* in Sonora continue to exploit the labor of young women to assemble clothing, electrical equipment, and medical supplies. In a sense, Colonel C. P. Sykes has been vindicated. Restructured as Rio Rico, Calabasas has finally become a gateway to Mexico.

"The inner contradictions of capitalism are expressed through the restless formation and re-formation of geographical landscapes," David Harvey wrote. Geographer Edward Soja argues that Harvey was wielding a blunt theoretical instrument when he made that statement. "Harvey's inaugural reading focuses on the hard logics of the landscape, its knife-edge paths, its points of perpetual struggle, its devastating architectonics, its insistent wholeness. Here, capital is the crude and restless *auteur*," Soja (1989:157) observes. According to Soja, actual landscapes are "more subtly composed and filled with many different historical and geographical subtexts to be identified and interpreted. Capital, above all, is never alone in shaping the historical geography of the landscape and is certainly not the only author or authority" (Soja 1989:158).

In the Upper Santa Cruz Valley, climate and topography have certainly played a role, limiting agriculture to the floodplain and making ranching the only extractive industry that produced enough of a surplus to generate profits—usually very small profits—until the postwar boom. Geology also shaped the production of space by tantalizing miners with traces of silver that never turned into mother lodes. It remains to be seen whether water will be made to flow uphill toward money once the aquifers along the Upper Santa Cruz have been wrung dry.

There are cultural forces configuring the landscape as well. The capital pouring into real estate now confronts constituencies that want to stop developments in their tracks. Those constituencies invoke federal laws that protect endangered species and pressure counties to deny rezonings and demand the preservation of open space in the subdivisions that do get built. These neighborhood activists, environmentalists, hunters, horse people, artists, and scientists are trying their best to convince governments, and their fellow citizens, that development is not the highest and best use of the desert that remains.

Despite the ideologies used to justify them, however, efforts to preserve open space take place within and generate capitalist restructuring of their own. Land continues to be commodified, but now it is no longer simply a factor of production but a web of amenities people are willing to pay for through rising home prices or higher taxes. And as more and more people take advantage of the open spaces, they create new entrepreneurial niches—eco- and heritage tourism, businesses that specialize in selling ATVs to the recreationists who want speed and binoculars and spotting scopes to those who want to bag a Coues whitetail or add another bird to their life list. It goes without saying, and perhaps without conscious moral accounting, that all such forms of recreation, consumptive and "nonconsumptive," depend upon the automobile.

Most of us involved in this restructuring of the real estate market— buyers as well as sellers, regulators as well as regulated—cloak the fundamentally capitalist nature of these exchanges in the scientific language of ecology or the poetry of place. Those of us who do not make our money off the land convince ourselves that our motives are purer than those who do—the "rapacious developer" or the "welfare rancher." Yet we are all implicated to one degree or another. After exploring the limits of Harvey's geography of capitalism, Soja reasserts its explanatory power. "The landscape being described must be seen as a persistently capitalist landscape," Soja reminds us. "The initial mapping, at least, must therefore never lose sight of the hard contours of capitalism's 'inner contradictions' and 'laws of motion' no matter how blurry or softened history and human agency have made them" (Soja 1989:158).

If they had been able to hold onto their lands, the O'odham or the homesteaders may have sold out to developers during the Great Arizona

Land Rush. Or they may have turned their fields into warehouses and shopping centers. We must not let our nostalgia for an agrarian past cloud our understanding of the transformative power of capital regardless of who controls the land. But the O'odham and homesteaders never got the chance to make those choices. We do not have to romanticize them to recognize the injustices they suffered. Meanwhile, the "restless formation and re-formation" of the Upper Santa Cruz Valley goes on.

Notes

AHS   Arizona Historical Society/Tucson
SED   Senate Executive Document
SCCRO   Santa Cruz County Recorders Office
THS   Tubac Historical Society

1 The Production of Space in the Upper Santa Cruz Valley

1. The estimated population of Nogales, Arizona, in July 2002 was 21,280. Profile of Nogales, Arizona http://www.citydata.com/city/Nogales-Arizona. html. Official Mexican census figures reported a figure of 160,000 for Nogales, Sonora, in 2004, but business leaders and government officials placed the actual population between 250,000 and 300,000. Ruben A. Ruiz, María del Carmen Salazar, and Luis Arvayo, "Growth: A Mixed Blessing. The Booming Population of Nogales, Sonora, Creates Stresses that the City's Infrastructure Is Not Equipped to Handle," *El Imparcial* (Hermosillo, Sonora), May 23, 2004.

2. The magnificent baroque retablo at Mission San Pedro y San Pablo de Tubutama in northwestern Sonora contains five oil paintings portraying the life of San José. The unfinished Franciscan mission church at Tumacácori was dedicated to San José, leading some mission scholars to conjecture that the retablo may have originally graced Tumacácori's sanctuary (Officer, Schuetz-Miller, and Fontana 1996).

3. "It is becoming impossible to escape the notion that nature is being murdered by 'anti-nature'—by abstraction, by signs and images, by discourse, as also by labour and its products," Lefebvre writes. "Along with God, nature is dying. 'Humanity' is killing both of them—and perhaps committing suicide into [*sic*] the bargain" (Lefebvre 1991:71).

2 The O'odham World and the Jesuit Intrusion

1. Jeoss, or Jios, derives from *Dios*, the Spanish word for God. As living oral tradition, the O'odham creation story had incorporated some Christian elements by the twentieth century.

2. The most salient phonemic borrowing is the hardening of a system of

glides to produce a new series of stops, which sets Tepiman apart from most other Uto-Aztecan languages but is also found in River Yuman. "In Tepiman, the Proto-Uto-Aztecan (PUA) glides **y and **w, and the PUA labiovelar **kʷ 'hardened,'" they note. "PUA **y became Proto-Tepiman (PT) *d. PUA **w became PT *g. PUA **kʷ became PT *b. This resulted in a distinctive array of 'voiced' stops, *b, *d, *g, in all the Tepiman languages, contrasting with a 'voiceless' series, inherited unchanged from PUA as *p, *t, *k" (Shaul and Hill 1998:379). The PUA word for nose (yaka), for example, became daka in PT, da:k in Tohono O'odham, and daka in Northern Tepehuan, but yahká in Guarijio and yeka in Yaqui. "Comparative linguistic method argues that it is more parsimonious in such a case to assume that the change took place before the breakup of Proto-Tepiman into its present daughter languages rather than to assume that the change arose independently in every single daughter language," Shaul and Hill (1998:379) argue.

3. Shaul and Hill (1998) note the presence of several Zuni loan words in Upper Piman, including siwañ, which means "rain priest" in Zuni and "rain shaman" among the Tohono O'odham, and kihe, which means "ceremonial brother" in Zuni and "brother-in-law" or "sister-in-law" in Tohono O'odham.

4. No mention is made of battles fought along the Salt River. A disastrous flood in 1358 AD may have washed out the irrigation systems of Hohokam communities there and prompted their abandonment a century or more before the invaders arrived (Doelle and Wallace 1990). Recent geoarchaeological research (Waters and Ravesloot 2003), in contrast, finds no evidence of significant landscape change at the end of the Classic along the middle Gila. They make no mention of conditions along the Salt.

5. In his account of the trek, Cabeza de Vaca wrote, "In that land there are small pine trees and the cones of these are like small eggs, but the pine nuts are better than those of Castile, because they have very thin shells." Cleve Hallenbeck, who routed the náufragos through the Southwest, contended that the nuts were from *Pinus edulis*, the pinyon pine common in west Texas and New Mexico. To test an alternative hypothesis that the route swung further south, astronomer Donald Olson and his colleagues at Southwest Texas State University traveled to Coahuila and found pinyons with thin-shelled nuts at the edge of a canyon in Sierra La Gloria southeast of Monclova (Hallenbeck 1940; Olson et al. 1997).

6. Two years earlier, on his fifth expedition with Kino, Manje noted that at San Lázaro, on the bend of the Santa Cruz, "there was an estancia of more than 9,000 cattle belonging to a vecino from the province of Sonora. When the Pima nation rose up against that province, they ran off most of the cattle and killed the rest at this place on Sonora's frontier" (my translation of Burrus 1971:432).

7. In his testimony to Francisco Padilla, Pedro de la Cruz declared that Oacpicagigua told him that when Keller's outburst occurred, "the Father must have been drunk, because he drinks a lot." Keller's defenders mentioned nothing about his drinking and painted a much more temperate portrait of the missionary. When Father Visitor Jacob Sedelmayr reported on his inspections of the Pimería Alta missions early in 1751, however, he included a long passage in German, which he knew only his provincial, Juan Antonio Balthasar, would understand. "The man was drunk and he received me in that state," the German portion of the report states. "He was also drunk that evening and that night. He told jokes about the Superiors and cursed them. This is true. Both I and others have witnessed it at other times. He kept liquor in the house all the time, although this was bad. The priests left him pretty much alone in there" (Matson and Fontana 1996:46).

8. The garrison at Altar was the ancient presidial company of Sinaloa, first established at San Felipe y Santiago in 1585. Detachments slowly moved northward as the Spanish frontier advanced into Sonora and finally the Pimería Alta until the presidio finally came to rest at Altar.

9. The O'odham presidial company of San Rafael de Buenavista, named after the abandoned hacienda of Buenavista in the San Luis Valley it was supposed to garrison, was created in 1783. Initially stationed at San Ignacio, it was transferred to Tubac in 1787.

10. According to Urrea, his force of sixty-three defeated two thousand O'odham during a battle that took place in the dark at 5:30 in the morning. I agree with historian Don Garate, who questions these figures. "One might venture to guess that it appeared to Urrea that there were two thousand warriors attacking him in the dark when, in reality, there probably were not more than a couple of hundred," Garate (n.d.:40) concludes.

11. See "Breve resumen de los desastres," written in 1760, for a community-by-community account of rebel and Apache depredations (Sheridan 1999).

3 The o'odham and the franciscans

1. During his inspection of the northern presidios, the Marqués de Rubí praised Anza for his "activity, valor, devotion, intelligence, and notable disinterest," and described him as a "complete officer." He criticized Anza, however, for incorporating the mules, horses, and cattle of vecinos and the missions into the presidial horse herd. The mules, in particular, inflicted considerable damage to the pastures while the soldiers were pulled away from their duties to act as "herdsmen and servants" (Rubí, Tubac, Dec. 29, 1766). Rubí allowed communal

herding to continue but ordered Anza to make the vecinos and missionaries supply their own cowboys (Rubí, Tubac, Dec. 31, 1766). Both documents are found in Archivo General de Indias (AGI), Guadalajara 511, Seville, Spain.

2. The instructions were issued by the *definitory*, or council, of the new Franciscan custody of San Carlos de Sonora, but Reyes stacked the definitory with supporters of his reforms, which Franciscan leaders of the old missionary *colegios* (colleges) bitterly opposed (Kessell 1976).

3. It was called San Rafael de Buenavista because it was supposed to be garrisoned at the abandoned hacienda of Buenavista, roughly halfway between the presidio of Tucson and the presidio of Terrenate at Las Nutrias just below the present international border (Moorhead 1975).

4. The intendancy system was a Bourbon reform introduced into Spain in 1718. In 1770, one of the first intendancies in New Spain was created when Pedro Corbalan was named governor and intendant of Sonora. The system was extended to the entire viceroyalty in 1786. The intendancy of Durango encompassed Nueva Vizcaya. The intendancy of Arispe incorporated Sinaloa y Sonora. Replacing the office of governor, the intendant enjoyed full civil authority. Military affairs, in contrast, remained in the hands of the commandant general of the Provincias Internas (Barnes, Naylor, and Polzer 1981).

5. As Radding (1997:178) points out, privatization was accompanied by the "decentralization of the power to distribute landed property." According to her, "In practice, the Spanish monarch delegated the power to award land grants to the Council of the Indies, the Audiencia de México, and the viceroy. As the colonial regime matured, provincial governors and magistrates assumed the function of adjudicating land and water rights and of issuing formal title to property. The Bourbon reforms authorized the Crown's intendants to extend land titles and legalize the *composiciones* of land previously occupied without benefit of the royal *merced*. During the final decades of colonial rule in frontier provinces like Sonora, presidial commanders exercised this faculty; and, following the liberal Constitution of Cádiz (passed by the Cortes in 1812 and restored in 1820) town councils began to award land titles." One of García Conde's many titles was "juez privativo de medidas, ventas y composiciones y repartimientos [*sic*] de tierras." Senate Executive Document (SED) 207:3, 46th Cong., 2d. sess., 1886.

6. Juan Legarra was described as a "Papago" in Father Narciso Gutiérrez's 1801 census of Tumacácori. His companions were Felipe Mendoza, José Domingo Arriola, and Javier Ignacio Medina, all Pimas, and Ramón Pamplona, the son of a Papago father and a Yaqui mother (Kessell 1976:207). Kessell credits Father Gutiérrez with coming up with the idea to petition for a formal grant.

7. My translation of SED 207:3. The transcription is fraught with spelling and

grammatical errors. Another transcription of the documents concerning the Tumacácori land grant is the handwritten copy of the petition to John Wasson, United States surveyor general for Arizona, by John Currey and C. P. Sykes. It also contains numerous errors, but in different places. Comparing both helps clarify unclear passages.

8. According to Radding (1997:176), "*Fundo legal* comprised the minimal allotment to Indian pueblos and Spanish as municipal property, conventionally one square league." Meyer (1984) also states that the fundo legal for Indian towns in the north generally consisted of one square league (5,000 × 5,000 varas, or 4,338 acres). But as Kessell (1976:208) points out, "If a pueblo did indeed take for its fundo legal one linear league in each direction, which in the arid north was rare, the area came to four square leagues. More often a pueblo took more in the direction that best served it, three and a half along a river for example, and the remainder on each side. While the total area was far less, the pueblo gained more of a watered river bottom."

9. SED 207:4.

10. SED 207:5. A *sitio de ganado mayor* comprised a square league (5,000 × 5,000 *varas*).

11. The Buenavista ranch, whose headquarters was just south of the present international border along the Santa Cruz River.

12. There were numerous marshy areas along the upper Santa Cruz before groundwater pumping dried most of them up.

13. Kessell (1976:209 n. 72) notes that a Manuel Fernández de la Carrera served as the Franciscans' attorney in Arispe during the 1780s and 1790s.

14. SED 207:8.

15. Testimony of Juan Nepomuceno Apodaca, Dec. 24, 1806, Tubac. SED 207:8–9.

16. The *vara castellana* was the vara of Burgos, adopted as a standard measure in the late sixteenth century by royal decree. It was equivalent to .8359 meter or 32.909 inches. A fifty-vara cord therefore equaled 41.795 meters or 49.862 yards. It must be noted, however, that the value of the vara varied from region to region in Mexico and Latin America (Barnes, Naylor, and Polzer 1981).

17. Primera diligencia de medidores. Miguel de León, José Miguel de Soto Mayor, Jan. 14, 1806, Tumacácori. SED 207:6.

18. Señalamento del centro. Manuel León, San José de Tumacácori, Jan. 14, 1807. SED 207:5.

19. Primera diligencia de medidores. Miguel de León and José Miguel de Soto Mayor, San José de Tumacácori, Jan. 14, 1807. SED 207:6.

20. Segunda diligencia de medidas. Manuel de León, Jan. 14, 1807. SED 207:6.

21. Diligencias de medida para estancia. Manuel de León and José Miguel de Soto Mayor, Jan. 14, 1807. SED 207:7.

22. Segunda diligencia medidas de estancia and auto. Manuel de León, Tubac, Jan. 15, 1807. SED 207:7.

23. Escrito. Ignacio Díaz del Carpio, n.p., n.d. SED 207:9–10.

24. Dictamen. Lic. Tresierra, Arispe, Mar. 31, 1807. SED 207:10.

25. Auto. Alexo García Conde, Arispe, Mar. 31, 1807. The transcription in SED 207:11 is particularly flawed here, so I have based my translation on the handwritten transcription by Currey and Sykes in their petition to Surveyor General Wasson.

26. Ibid.

27. Notificación. Alexo García Conde, Arispe, Mar. 31, 1807. SED 207:11–12.

28. Shaul (n.d.) argues that during the eighteenth century O'odham in the missions of the Pimería Alta moved from incipient diglossia—"a stable bilingualism in which everyone ideally knew both languages but used them in qualitatively different contexts (examples: public vs. at home; formal vs. casual)" (3)— to linguistic compartmentalization. As part of their daily, nonviolent resistance to missionization and Spanish colonization, they carefully separated the O'odham language from Spanish, thereby preventing non-O'odham speakers from understanding other domains of their culture.

29. This is not Devil worship but rituals and songs for curing sicknesses caused by devils living around ranches and mines. It clearly evolved out of the native O'odham tradition of curing disease, but "devils" were supernatural beings incorporated from Christian cosmology (Bahr 1988).

30. It is interesting to note that the O'odham associated "devils" with extractive capitalist activity, that is, ranching and mining.

31. O'odham medicinal theory clearly separates diagnosis and curing. Only shamans can diagnose sicknesses, and their ability to do so depends, in part, upon characteristics of the shamans themselves. Spirits seek out shamans and teach them songs the shamans then sing during the diagnosis (*dúajida*). During the dúajida, they also blow upon the patient to determine the dangerous object that caused the sickness and suck the "strength" of the object out of the patient. The ability of a shaman to do so depends upon his "heart." Ritual curing, in contrast, is instrumental rather than charismatic. According to Bahr et al. (1974: 219), "Briefly, the cures are rationalized as prayers. They do not succeed because of any special potency vested in the curers, but because a spiritual causal agent responds to the curer's actions and rids the patient of his symptoms."

32. For a discussion of the *wi:gida*, and Julian Hayden's (1987) description of the last winter wi:gida held in 1945, see a special issue of the *Journal of the Southwest* titled "The Vigita Ceremony of the Papago" (vol. 29, no. 3, Aug. 1987).

4 Hispanic settlement and the final displacement of the o'odham

1. According to Garate, Sicurisuta is a place name of Basque origin. "*Siku* means 'dry' and can be used to describe a rocky outcropping. Erizut means a 'vertical finger.' The letter *a* means 'the,' and the letter *c* (more properly *k*) pluralizes whatever it follows. Thus, *siku-erizut-a* is possibly the 'upright rocky finger,' which is a perfect description of Thumb Rock above Peña Blanca Lake northwest of Guevavi and present-day Nogales, Arizona" (Garate 2003:266, n. 47).

2. Mexican gray wolves (*Canis lupus baileyi*) favored the Madrean evergreen woodlands of southeastern Arizona and northeastern Sonora, where their preferred prey were Coues white-tailed deer (*Odocoileus virginianus couesi*). According to biologist David Brown, "The Santa Rita, Tumacacori, Atascosa-Pajarito, and Patagonia mountains were all well known as wolf country, as were the Canelo Hills. At least equal numbers inhabited the steeper and rougher, but larger Chiricahua, Huachuca, and Pinaleño mountains" (Brown 1992:22–23).

The *Weekly Arizonian*, Arizona's first English-language newspaper published in Tubac, reported several encounters with grizzlies in the Santa Rita Mountains in the late 1850s (Brown 1985). Geoscientist Paul Martin (personal communication) speculates that grizzlies may have expanded their range southward in response to Spanish livestock in northern Sonora and southern Arizona.

3. Within the *comunidad* of Cucurpe, Sonora, surface flow of the San Miguel River is controlled by local water users' associations called *comunes de agua*. Water pumped from wells, in contrast, is unregulated even though most of the wells are shallow and located along the floodplain, tapping the same aquifers that feed surface flow (Sheridan 1988b, 1996a).

4. In 1640, Pedro de Perea, captain of the presidio of Sinaloa from 1626 to 1630, received concessions from the viceroy to found a new *alcaldía* (district) in central Sonora called Nueva Andalucia. Twenty-five soldiers from the presidio of Sinaloa accompanied him at his own expense. He also paid to bring their families to the new alcaldía. The expedition established its headquarters near Tuape along the San Miguel River in 1641. When the captain of the presidio demanded his soldiers back, Perea recruited twelve new soldiers and their families from New Mexico. He also brought along five Franciscan missionaries, triggering conflict with the Jesuit missionaries already working in Sonora. Perea died in 1644; in 1651, the viceroy sided with the Jesuits and ordered the Franciscans out of Sonora (Almada 1983; Atondo Rodríguez and Ortega Soto 1996).

5. *Política Indiana* Libro VI, Capítulo 12, número 3 (Solórzano Pereira 1930 [1647]).

6. Ortiz, who resided in Tucson at the time, paid 747 pesos and 3 *reales* at the public auction of the grant in Arizpe. But even though there is an entry in the treasury book for that amount, the Ortiz family either never received formal title or lost the title. In 1833, Tomás and Ignacio Ortiz, sons of Agustín, petitioned the alcalde of Tubac to reconfirm their ownership of the two sitios. Three witnesses stated that the Ortiz family had occupied the grant since 1812 and gave vague boundaries for it. Apparently, no survey was conducted, however, and in 1902, the U.S. Supreme Court refused to confirm the grant because its exact location had not been specified (Wagoner 1975).

7. The earliest known *título de merced* to Canoa was issued to the Ortiz brothers in Ures, Sonora, in 1849. The original title, if it ever existed, has not been located. The Ortiz brothers claimed it was destroyed in a fire in Tubac. Willey (1979) argues that the present boundaries of Canoa Ranch are incorrect. He believes that the resurvey conducted by Deputy Surveyor John Harris in 1880 ignored the point from which Elías González started—La Canoa—and failed to locate any of the landmarks Elías González designated as corners of the grant. In his words, Harris's survey "must stand as a monument to incompetent land surveying in Arizona history" (Willey 1979:155).

8. Two cousins—José Ignacio Ramón Elías González and his sister Eulalia— obtained the San Ignacio del Babocómari grant on a tributary of the San Pedro that same year. The following year, another cousin—José Florentino Rafael Elías González—received the San Rafael del Valle grant. The Elías González family or families related by marriage—like the Ortiz and Pérez (owners of the San Bernardino grant)—controlled most of the land grants issued in Arizona (Officer 1987).

9. San José de Sonoita, Arizona Surveyor General's Office Journal of Private Land Claims, University of Arizona Library Film 2174:304.

10. Ibid., 306.

11. In 1762, Spanish authorities ordered all Sobaipuris to abandon the San Pedro in order to reinforce the communities of the Santa Cruz. Some of the O'odham frontiersmen settled at Sonoita, where thirty-four O'odham families, plus two widowers and two widows, resided in 1763 (Kessell 1970). Seven years later, only about twenty-five O'odham remained. Then, in the spring of 1770, Apaches surrounded the visita and massacred nineteen of the inhabitants, including eleven children (Kessell 1976). By 1773, Sonoita was abandoned.

12. Apparently, the Sobaipuris from Sonoita dreamed of returning. Both they and refugees from Guevavi and Soamca maintained distinct identities and lived in separate rancherías when they withdrew to Calabasas (Kessell 1976). But those dreams flickered out in the face of Apache hostilities. Plans to reestablish

the visita never materialized. The deserted pueblo became a funnel through which the Apaches descended upon the Santa Cruz.

13. San José de Sonoita, Journal of Private Land Claims, 306–7.

14. Ibid., 308.

15. Ibid., 309.

16. Ibid., 308.

17. James Officer, who compiled genealogies of the Elías family, notes that even though Joaquín identified himself as his brother Rafael's agent when he petitioned for the San Rafael del Valle grant, "Descendants of Rafael Elías do not include Joaquín among his brothers. The exact relationship remains obscure" (Officer 1987:356 n. 52).

18. Tumacácori had a population of 121 in 1820 (R. Jackson 1994:62).

19. Wagoner (1975) identifies him as Francisco Elías González, married to Balvanera Redondo and father of José Elías, who received title to the grant on January 7, 1843. Officer (1987:374 n. 2) is not so sure, arguing that he could have been Francisco González Forano, the prefect at San Ignacio during the 1850s.

20. Joaquín Quiroga, Cucurpe, [May] 31, 1843. AHES, Carpetón 121, Arizona Historical Society (AHS), Tucson, Ariz.

21. Ibid.

22. Ibid.

23. After their defeat at the hand of Gándara, O'odham fought on for two more years. When Gándara's rival, Tucson-born José de Urrea, took over the governorship in 1841, he ordered Lieutenant Colonel Felipe Flores to mount another campaign against the O'odham rebels. In April and May 1842, Flores's force engaged the O'odham in the Baboquivaris once again, killing six and seizing more livestock. The remaining rebels scattered throughout the Papaguería or fled northward to take refuge with the Akimel O'odham and Maricopas on the Gila River. A strong show of military force and offers of amnesty for the rebels brought the Papago War to an end by the summer of 1843 (Officer 1987).

24. Ignacio López, Título de Venta, Tesorería del Departamento de Sonora, Año de 1844. Senate Executive Document (SED) 207:13–14, 46th Cong., 2d. sess., 1886.

25. Ibid.

26. Ibid.

27. Ures was the state capital of Sonora from 1838 to 1842 and from 1847 to 1879 (Almada 1983).

28. Probably the fiesta de San Francisco in Magdalena, Sonora, held on and around October 4.

29. According to folklorist James Griffith (personal communication), the reclining statue of San Francisco at San Xavier Mission was originally the *santo entierro* (entombed Christ) at Tumacácori.

5 early Anglo speculation and the Tumacácori Land Grant

1. *New York Daily News*, Dec. 27, 1845.

2. There were twenty panics in the United States between 1790 and 1907, about one every six years (Moore 1980).

3. After the British Crown ordered colonial governors to stop granting patents to lands beyond the sources of rivers flowing into the Atlantic, Washington wrote Crawford, "I can never look upon that proclamation in any other light (but this I say between ourselves) than as a temporary expedient to quiet the minds of the Indians. It must fall, of course, in a few years, especially when those Indians consent to our occupying the lands. Any person, therefore who neglects the present opportunity of hunting out good lands, and in some measure marking and distinguishing them for his own, in order to keep others from settling them, will never regain it" (quoted in Sakolski 1932:5–6).

4. Critics contended that speculation in land warrants led to the monopoly of lands and high rates of tenancy. More recent historical and economic analysis suggests that monopoly did not occur, that land remained relatively cheap for the settlers who eventually purchased it, and that tenancy was one rung in an "economic ladder," giving younger farmers the experience they needed to become successful independent farmers later in life (Oberly 1990).

5. *Railroad Record*, April 19, 1857, 107.

6. Affidavits of Fritz Conden, Jan. 1900; Peter Brady, Jan. 1900; Sabino Otero, Nov. 13, 1905; Charles Poston, Jan. 13, 1900. Papers in case of Baca Float No. 5 (and No. 3), National Archives, Pacific Region, Laguna Niguel Office.

7. From an article in the *German Democrat*, republished in translation in the *San Francisco Weekly Chronicle*, Aug. 11, 1855. Quoted in Fontana 1971:79.

8. Joseph King settled "within a few hundred yards of the old Spanish Mission of Tumacacori" in 1865 when he was twenty-eight years old. He had reached the Santa Cruz Valley the year before, performing a survey for a sheep ranch William Wrightson wanted to establish at Salero east of Tumacácori. Affidavit of Joseph King, Pima County, Jan. 24, 1900. Papers in case of Baca Float Nos. 3 and 5, National Archives, Pacific Region, Laguna Niguel Office.

9. C. P. Sykes, *Pacific Coast Annual Mining Review and Stock Ledger*. San Francisco: Francis and Valentine, 1878.

10. On March 9, 1869, Francisco A. Aguilar formally sold the "lands of Tumacácori, Calabazas, and Guevavi" to Miguel Gándara, who represented his father,

for the original sum of $499. Sykes purchased the grant for $12,500 in gold. Translation from the original document by R. C. Hopkins, San Francisco, Nov. 8, 1875. List of papers in case of Baca Float No. 5 (and No. 3), National Archives, Pacific Region, Laguna Niguel Office.

11. C. P. Sykes, *New York Daily Graphic*, Oct. 18, 1878.

12. Ibid.

13. Copied from the lithograph by Britton, Rey, and Co., S.F. (San Francisco) in Hinton 1878, opposite 224; ibid., opposite 194.

14. Copied from a lithograph by Britton and Rey, S.F., in the prospectus of the Calabasas Land and Mining Company. The same prospectus quotes a letter written on April 21, 1877, by A. P. K. Safford, the ex-governor of the Territory of Arizona, who wrote Sykes, "Learning that you are interested in the Calabasas ranch, and about leaving for San Francisco, I desire to present to you an ear of corn that was raised by George Allison on said ranch, without irrigation. I took the ear from a pile of corn where he was harvesting, without any effort to select." Munk Library of Arizoniana, Southwest Museum.

15. Based on the lithograph in J. Ross Browne (1974:143), which shows the log cabin in the right foreground. The rest of the foreground, as well as details of the church, are significantly different from either Browne's illustration or the illustration in Hinton (1878:219).

16. The microfilm copy of the August 12, 1882 edition of the *Tombstone Epitaph* at the AHS in Tucson is poorly filmed and it is difficult to make out words on the left margin of the column in which the article "Calabasas Classics" appeared. The article is misquoted in Ellinwood (1964), who leaves out phrases and sentences.

17. Prospectus of the Calabasas, Tucson, and North Western Railroad Company; and the Arizona Cattle and Improvement Company. New York: Martin B. Brown, Printer and Stationer, 1885. AHS.

18. Ibid., 7.

19. Ibid.

20. Ibid., 8.

21. Ibid., 7.

22. Ibid., 9.

23. Ibid., 12.

24. R. C. Hopkins, Dec. 30, 1879. Senate Executive Document (SED) 207:35, 46th Cong., 2d. sess., 1886.

25. John Wasson, Jan. 7, 1880. SED 207:39.

26. Ibid., 40.

27. Secretary of the Interior Hoke Smith to the Commissioner of the General

Land Office, May 8, 1893. Vol. 12, No. 235. Tumacacori and Calabazas Grant, National Archives, Pacific Region, Laguna Niguel Office.

28. U.S. Court of Private Land Claims, Case nos. 8, 9, and 162 Consolidated, Tumacacori, Calabasas and Huebabi Grant, U.S. Department of Interior, Bureau of Land Management, Phoenix, Arizona (Court of Private Land Claims Consolidated Case). MS 312, Reel 23, Special Collections, University of Arizona Main Library.

29. Amended Petition, *George Hill Howard v. United States*. Court of Private Land Claims Consolidated Case.

30. The petitioners were Dolores Astiazarán, Jesús A. de Oceguera, Francisco Oceguera, Carmen O. de Espíritu, Augustina O. de Robinson, Francisco Gándara, Miguel Gándara, Ana Gándara, Trinidad Aguilar, Fernando Aguilar, Anita Aguilar, Jesús Aguilar, Carmen Aguilar, Victor Aguilar, and Santiago Ainsa, administrator with the will annexed of Frank Ely, deceased. Court of Private Land Claims Consolidated Case.

31. Ibid.

32. Smith to Commissioner, May 8, 1893, 2. Court of Private Land Claims Consolidated Case.

33. Ibid.

34. Mattison is in error when he states that the secretary of the interior "sustained the Commissioner" (Mattison 1967:84).

35. Schurz to Commissioner. Court of Private Land Claims Consolidated Case.

36. Defendants included: "George W. Atkinson, Francisco Q. Acebedo, Francisco S. Acebedo, Gerardo Acebedo, John Doe Arenas, Fidel Aguayo, Lorenzo Aguayo, Leon Aguayo, Jesus Arviso, Charles Altschul, Claudio Acebedo, Inez Andrado, Demetrio Barrios, Charles Beck, J. F. Black, unknown heirs of William Bennett, deceased, James Breen, George Beckwith, Frederick Beckwith, Beckwith Brothers, Fernando Carranza, Pedro Cordova, Thomas D. Casanega, Tomas Cota, Francisco Castillo, W. C. Davis, Edwin Egan, Mateo Estrada, Benito Estrada, Bartolo Figueroa, John W. Fuqua, Fierras Brothers, Timoteo Fierras, Antonio Fierras, W. H. Good, unknown heirs of Henry Guinn, deceased, R. H. James Good, W. Goodman, Charles Gullman, W. J. Glenn, John Doe Henderson, Samuel Hughes, Pauline Jones, R. E. Key, William E. Key, Joseph King, Henry W. Low, Domingo Laguna, John A. Lucas, William Thomas Linnville, Samuel G. Lewis, Thomas Lewis, Juan M. Montano, William Morgan, Theodore Martinez, T. Lillie Mercer, S. B. McCorkle, unknown heirs of S. B. McCorkle, G. R. McCorkle, Francisco Moreno, D. B. McCullough, Joseph Piskorski, James Peters, Antonio Proto, Louis Proto, Proto Brothers, Benjamin H. Page, Zada Fey Reagan, Bernardo Romero, Manuel Ronquillo, Timoteo Ramirez, Eugene K. Sykes, administrator of the estate of George W. Reagan, deceased, Juan Saldate, John Doe Saldate, Ramon Sardina, the Santa

Cruz Valley Water Storage Company, a corporation, Ramon Saavedra, Saavedra Brothers, Eugene K. Sykes, C. P. Sykes, Don A. Sanford, L. J. Sanford, Sonoita and Santa Cruz Land and Water Company, a corporation, Salero Land and Cattle Company, a corporation, Tomas Tapia, F. M. Vernon, Mariano Valdez, Zenobia Villa and Sons, the New Mexico and Arizona Railroad Company, a corporation, Morgan R. Wise, Joseph E. Wise, Solomon B. Wise, William H. Walker, Jose Maria Valdez, Rafael N. Vasquez, Harvey S. Walker, Andrew Roe, Alexander Roe, Abraham Roe, Benjamin Roe, Bernard Roe, Charles Roe, David Roe, Daniel Roe, Edwin Roe, Eugene Roe, Edward Roe, Fred Roe, Frank Roe, George Roe, Henry Roe, Howard Roe, Isaac Roe, Lemuel Roe, James Roe, John Roe, Jacob Roe, Nathan Roe, Philip Roe, Robert Roe, Richard Roe, Samuel Roe, Thomas Roe and William Roe (whose true names are to plaintiffs unknown)." *William Faxon, Junior, Trustee, et al. v. United States of America, George Atkinson, et al.* Court of Private Land Claims Consolidated Case.

37. Decree, U.S. Court of Private Land Claims, Arizona District, 1895. Court of Private Land Claims Consolidated Case.

38. Opinion of Mr. Justice Murray. Court of Private Land Claims Consolidated Case.

39. Decree. Court of Private Land Claims Consolidated Case.

40. *Faxon v. United States*, 171 US 244 (1898).

41. Ibid.

42. Answer, U.S. Court of Private Land Claims. Court of Private Land Claims Consolidated Case.

6 Fictitious Capital and Fictitious Landscapes

1. Story of Pioneer Days of Mrs. Sarah N. Black of Tubac, Arizona. Related on February 14th, 1926. AHS; "Pioneer Teacher in State is Dead," *Arizona Daily Star*, Jan. 15, 1929.

2. Ibid.

3. The U.S. attorney for the Court of Private Land Claims estimated that claims presented in that court alone totaled 34,053,340 acres of the 77,868,640 acres in New Mexico. According to Bradfute (1975:5 n. 9), however, "The figure must be reduced by about 19,000,000 acres, as it included about 12,000,000 acres for the Peralta claim, located mainly in Arizona, and over 7,000,000 acres for the Conejos, Las Animas, and Corpus Cristi claims in Colorado." The Peralta claim, of course, was a fraud; the eighteen other claims in Arizona amounted to 850,050 acres (Walker and Bufkin 1979). Those figures did not include grants confirmed by Congress prior to the creation of the court in 1891, such as the Sangre de Cristo (1 million acres) or Maxwell (1.7 million acres) grants in New Mexico.

4. *An Act to confirm certain private land claims in the Territory of New Mexico.* *U.S. Statutes at Large*, 36th Cong., 1st sess., chap. 167, 12 Stat. 71—71.

5. Consolidated Case 2719, U.S. Circuit Court of Appeals for the Ninth Circuit, Jan. 8, 1917, 9–12 (Consolidated Case 2719). John Henry Campbell Papers, Ms 131, Box 5, Series 13, ff. 64–65, AHS.

6. Ibid., 13–15.

7. John S. Watts to Surveyor General John A. Clark, Santa Fe, June 17, 1863. Consolidated Case 2719, 3–4.

8. *Lane v. Watts*, 234 US 525 (1914).

9. John S. Watts, Mar. 2, 1863. Consolidated Case 2719, 20–21.

10. Ibid.

11. S. Watts to Honorable J. M. Edmunds, Commissioner of Land Office. Consolidated Case 2719, 4.

12. Ibid., 5.

13. Ibid.

14. Testimony of George Roskruge, witness of defendant Joseph E. Wise, in *Cornelius C. Watts and Dabney C. T. Davis, Jr. vs. Santa Cruz Development Company, James E. Bouldin, Jennie N. Bouldin, Joseph E. Wise, Lucy J. Wise, Margaret W. Wise, Jesse H. Wise, David W. Bouldin, Helen Lee Bouldin, M. I. Carpenter, Patrick C. Ireland, Ireland Graves, Anna R. Wilcox, Eldredge I. Hurt, and W. G. Rifenburg* (*Watts and Davis v. Santa Cruz Development Company et al.*), U.S. District Court for the District of Arizona, Mar. 26, 1915, Campbell Papers, Ms. 131, Box 5, Series 13, ff. 62–65, AHS. Roskruge was surveyor for Pima County for many years.

15. Testimony of John S. Magee. *Watts and Davis v. Santa Cruz Development Company et al.*, 66. Please note that there are multiple numberings on these copies.

16. John H. Watts to Commissioner of the General Land Office, Santa Fe, Aug. 15, 1877; Commissioner J. A. Williams to Watts, Washington, D.C., Sept. 20, 1877. *Watts and Davis v. Santa Cruz Development Company et al.*, 60–63.

17. According to Mattison (1967:87 n. 55), Poston claimed to be an assignee of the Baca heirs. D. B. Gracy's Abstract of Title makes no mention of Poston's claim.

18. Deed and Power of Attorney, John Watts et al. to David W. Bouldin, Sept. 30, 1884. Abstract of Title to Forty-nine thousand, six hundred forty-four and 695/1000 acres of land more or less, being the North half of what is known as the Baca Float No. Three and situated in the County of Santa Cruz in the State of Arizona, D. B. Gracy, Attorney-at-Law, Austin, Texas. Campbell Papers, Ms. 1167, f. 5, AHS.

19. In D. B. Gracy's Abstract of Title there is indeed such a power of attorney conferred on "James Eldredge of the City of Paris, in the Empire of France."

20. Gracy Abstract of Title.

21. *Watts and Davis vs. Santa Cruz Development Company et al.*, 65–77.

22. James Eldredge to General John C. Robinson, Astor House, New York, Wednesday, 188. Santa Cruz County Court Records, Ms. 185, AHS. Unfortunately the copy of this letter left out the last digit of the year the letter was written. The Eldredge family clearly had a significant interest in Robinson's machinations over the Baca float. And since Hawley's middle name was Eldredge, James and Charly Eldredge may have been his uncles or cousins if Eldredge was his mother's maiden name. My thanks to Philip Halpenny for bringing this letter to my attention.

23. John C. Robinson by James Eldredge, Atty. to D. W. Bouldin, Agreement filed in the City of Washington, District of Columbia, June 8, 1885. Gracy Abstract of Title. Eldredge, now practicing in New York, is Robinson's attorney.

24. *Watts and Davis v. Santa Cruz Development Company et al.*, 129–31.

25. Ibid., 118–65. Gracy Abstract of Title.

26. Gracy Abstract of Title.

27. Testimony of J. H. Watts. *Watts and Davis v. Santa Cruz Development Company et al.*, 107–8.

28. Gracy Abstract of Title.

29. Testimony of Joseph E. Wise. *Watts and Davis v. Santa Cruz Development Company et al.*, 180–87.

30. Commissioner of the General Land Office Wm. A. J. Spar to Morgan R. Wise, Washington, Nov. 8, 1887. Department of the Interior, Bureau of Land Management, Baca Float No. 3, Arizona State Library, Archives and Public Records, Phoenix, Ariz.

31. Mrs. A. M. Ireland to Joseph E. Wise, April 8, 1907; Wilbur King to Wise, April 24, 1907. Gracy Abstract of Title.

32. Testimony of John Watts, *Watt and Davis v. Santa Cruz Development Company et al.*, 102–8.

33. Wise Papers, 1879–1922, Ms. 879, AHS.

34. Testimony of George Atkinson, *Watts and Davis v. Santa Cruz Development Company et al.*, 51–52.

35. Testimony of Joseph E. Wise. *Watts and Davis v. Santa Cruz Development Company et al.*, 186–87

36. Brief of Joseph E. Wise, As to the 1/19 Interest of the Son Antonio Baca. *Watts and Davis v. Santa Cruz Development Company et al.*

37. Jesse Wise and Marcos Baca to Joe Wise, July 21, 1915. Wise Papers, Ms. 879, AHS.

38. Juana L. Baca et al. to Marcos C. de Baca, Aug. 20, 1913, County of Sandoval, New Mexico. Teofila Baca et al. to Marcos C. de Baca, Aug. 20, 1913, County of Santa Fe, New Mexico. Martina H. Baca et al. to Marcos C. de Baca, Aug. 21, 1913, County of Sandoval, New Mexico. Marcos C. de Baca to Jos. E. Wise et al., Aug. 25, 11913, County of Sandoval, New Mexico. Gracy Abstract of Title.

39. Teodora Baca and Manuel Baca to J. E. Wise, Mar. 13, 1907, County of Cochise, Arizona. Gracy Abstract of Title. Wise Papers, Ms. 879, AHS.

40. Secretary of the Interior E. A. Hitchcock to the Commissioner of the General Land Office, Washington, July 25, 1899, 6–7. U.S. Dept. of Interior, Baca Float No. 3.

41. Ibid., 7–6.

42. Ibid., 10–11.

43. Secretary of the Interior E. A. Hitchcock to Commissioner of the General Land Office, Washington, Dec. 11, 1899. U.S. Dept. of Interior, Baca Float No. 3.

44. Sabino Otero, Jan. 25, 1900. U.S. Dept. of Interior, Baca Float No. 3.

45. Ibid.

46. Affidavit of Charles D. Poston, Jan. 13, 1900. U.S. Dept. of Interior, Baca Float No. 3.

47. Secretary of the Interior E. A. Hitchcock to the Commissioner of the General Land Office, Washington, D.C., Mar. 5, 1901. U.S. Dept. of Interior, Baca Float No. 3.

48. Barnes and Martin, Attorneys for E. Key et al., and John B. Wright to the Secretary of the Interior, Jan. 29, 1901. U.S. Dept. of Interior, Baca Float No. 3. The date does not appear on the printed version, but in a handwritten note on the cover, so it may not be accurate.

49. Surveyor General Frank Ingalls, Phoenix, Sept. 27, 1905. Copies of Ingalls's letter were sent to J. W. Maxwell, Kingan and Wright, J. M. Jameson, Barnes and Martin, Alex F. Matthews, Geo. W. Atkinson, James W. Vroom, W. H. King, W. L. Campbell, T. D. Casanega, Antonio Marena, Will H. Walker, Isabel N. Mercer, Edwin Fagon, Francisco Q. Aceveda [sic], Joe Wise, J. N. Curtis, Mark Lully, and William P. Blake, on October 2. U.S. Dept. of Interior, Baca Float No. 3.

50. G. W. Atkinson to Frank S. Ingles [sic], Surveyor General of Arizona, Calabasas, Dec. 17, 1905. U.S. Dept. of Interior, Baca Float No. 3.

51. U.S. Surveyor General Frank Ingalls to the Commissioner of the General Land Office, Phoenix, Nov. 5, 1906, 4. U.S. Dept. of Interior, Baca Float No. 3.

52. Affidavit of William P. Blake. U.S. Dept. of Interior, Baca Float No. 3.

53. Affidavits of Thomas Gardner and William W. McCoy. U.S. Dept. of Interior, Baca Float No. 3.

54. Affidavit of Joseph King. U.S. Dept. of Interior, Baca Float No. 3.

55. Ingalls to Commissioner, Nov. 5, 1906. U.S. Dept. of Interior, Baca Float No. 3, 5–6.

56. Ibid., 21–22.

57. Ibid., 23–24.

58. First Assistant Secretary Pierce to the Commissioner of the General Land Office, Department of the Interior, Washington, June 2, 1908, Decisions Relating to the Public Lands. U.S. Dept. of Interior, Baca Float No. 3, 456–57.

59. Ibid., 469.

60. Ibid., 471.

61. Surveyor General to Commissioner of the General Land Office, Sept. 21, 1908. U.S. Dept. of Interior, Baca Float No. 3. Note that Sept. 12 was not sixty days after notification.

62. Statement and Brief Before the Honorable Frank S. Ingalls, Kingan and Wright, Attorneys for the Mine Owners and Settlers, n.d. U.S. Dept. of Interior, Baca Float No. 3.

63. *Lane v. Watts*, 234 US 525 (1914).

64. Reminiscences of Alexander J. Davidson As told to Mrs. George F. Kitt 1930–36. Ms. 208, AHS.

65. Ibid.

66. Ibid.

67. *Watts and Davis v. Santa Cruz Development Company et al.*

68. Consolidated Case No. 2719. Jan. 8, 1917, 26. Campbell Papers, Ms. 121, folder 64, AHS.

69. Ibid., 33.

70. *Cornelius C. Watts, et al., vs. George W. Atkinson, et al.* Writ of Possession and Action in Ejectment. District Court of the United States in and for the District of Arizona. Campbell File, Ms. 1167, folder 8, AHS.

71. Complaint of James E. Bouldin et al., v. Benedito Castro et al., Complaint at Law, No. 106, U.S. District Court of Arizona, Campbell Papers, Ms. 1167, folder 8.

72. *James E. Bouldin et al., Plaintiffs, v. Joseph V. de Aguayo et al., Defendants.* Amended and Supplemental Answer and Cross-Complaint. U.S. District Court of Arizona, n.d., 4–5. See also *James E. Bouldin et al., v. Josefa V. de Aguayo et al.*, At Law, No. 96, Amended and Supplemental Answer, U.S. District Court of Arizona, Campbell Papers, Ms. 1167, folder 8, AHS.

73. *Bouldin et al. v. Aguayo et al.*

74. Ibid.

75. Ibid.

7 The Bottom of the Bottle

1. Campbell Papers, Ms. 1167, ff. 1, 7, AHS.

2. Frank Duffy to A. J. Connor, May 25, 1918. Campbell Papers, Ms. 1167, f. 2, AHS.

3. William Henry Campbell to Honorable W. A. O'Connor, Judge, Superior Court, Nogales, Arizona, Oct. 5, 1918. Campbell Papers, Ms. 1167, f. 1, AHS.

4. Campbell Papers, Ms. 1167, ff. 1, 2, 7, AHS.

5. Carmen Mendez, Homestead Proof—Testimony of Claimant, Mendez Homestead File, Tumacácori National Historical Park.

6. Ibid.

7. The Greaterville placers were on the amended location in the northern Santa Rita Mountains.

8. *Silo Land and Cattle Company v. James Bouldin, et al.*, Pima County Superior Court Case no. 6649, 1918. Pima County Collection, Papers, 1864–1985, Box 62, f. 768, AHS.

9. Ibid., f. 769.

10. Ibid.

11. Ibid., f. 768.

12. *Silo Land and Cattle Company v. James E. Bouldin, Jennie N. Bouldin, his wife, Helen Lee Bouldin, David W. Bouldin, and Weldon M. Bailey*, Judgement Case 729. Blacksill Collection, box 1, AHS. Another copy is located in Campbell Papers, Ms. 1167, f. 8, AHS.

13. Judgement of W. H. Sawtelle, May 26, 1919, Case No. E-67, *James Bouldin et al. v. Marie Whitney Robinson, Julia Collier, Clinton E. Collier, Caroline P. Hall and Robert A. Hall*, U.S. District Court, District of Arizona. Blacksill Collection, AHS.

14. *Robinson Land and Cattle Company v. Watts and Davis*, Santa Cruz County Superior Court, Nov. 27, 1918. *Silo Land and Cattle v. Bouldin et al.*, Pima County Collection, box 62, f. 768.

15. Powhattan Bouldin to Weldon M. Bailey, Jan. 31, 1915. Campbell Papers, box 1, f. 3, AHS.

16. Lease Agreement between James E. Bouldin, individually, and as agent for Jennie N. Bouldin, Helen Lee Bouldin and Weldon M. Bailey, parties of the first part, and Russell Durrell, party of the second part. Campbell Papers, Ms. 1167, f. 13, AHS.

17. J. H. Campell to Henry G. Boice, July 26, 1919, Campbell Papers, Ms. 1167, f. 13.

18. Agreement between Frank Powers and Josephine Powers of Santa Cruz County, Arizona, parties of the first part, with James E. Bouldin of Dallas, Texas, party of the second part, Jan. 14, 1918. Campbell Papers, Ms. 1167, f. 10, AHS.

19. Leonard Tobin to Judge J. H. Campbell, Aug. 27, 1918. Campbell Papers, AHS.

20. Agreement between A. R. Grund and John Mets, Feb. 8, 1919. Campbell Papers, Ms. 131, Box 5, Series 13, f. 61, AHS.

21. Minutes of First Meeting of Board of Directors of Baca Float Mines Company, Mar. 10, 1919. Campbell Papers, Ms. 131, Box 5, Series 13, f. 61, AHS.

22. Campbell Papers, Ms. 131, f. 61, AHS.

23. Weldon Bailey to James E. Bouldin, July 21, 1919, Campbell Papers, Ms. 1167, f. 3, AHS.

24. James E. Bouldin to Judge J. H. Campbell, July 23, 1919, Campbell Papers, Ms. 1167, f. 4, AHS.

25. James Bouldin et al. to Weldon M. Bailey, Jan. 1, 1920. Deeds, Real Estate Book 12, 91, Santa Cruz County Recorders Office (SCCRO), Nogales, Ariz.

26. G. H. Brevillier to Hon. John H. Campbell, Dec. 24, 1917. Campbell Papers, Ms. 1167, f. 2, AHS.

27. Agreement by and between Weldon Bailey, James E. Bouldin, Jennie N. Bouldin, David W. Bouldin and Helen L. Bouldin, Feb. 7, 1922. Campbell Papers, Ms. 1167, f. 10, AHS.

28. James E. Bouldin, et al. to Baca Float Land and Cattle Company, May 9, 1922, Warranty Deed, Deeds, Real Estate Book 12, 503. Baca Float Land and Cattle Company and Weldon Bailey to Joseph W. Bailey Jr., May 9, 1922, Deed of Trust, 499, SCCRO.

29. Harold H. Brown, Sheriff of Santa Cruz County, and the American Exchange National Bank, Sheriff's Deed, Jan. 28, 1926. Deeds, Real Estate Book 15, 506–8, SCCRO.

30. Reminiscences of Alexander J. Davidson As told to Mrs. George F. Kitt 1930–36. Ms. 208, AHS.

31. Sims Ely, Treasurer, Federal Land Bank of Berkeley, to John H. Campbell, May 27, 1924. Campbell Papers, Ms. 1167, f. 2, AHS.

32. John H. Campbell to Sims Ely, May 31, 1924. Campbell Papers, Ms. 1167, f. 1, AHS.

33. H. J. Brown, Sheriff of Santa Cruz County, and the Federal Land Bank, Sheriff's Deed, Dec. 1, 1926. Deeds Real Estate Book 16:272, SCCRO.

34. James E. Bouldin to Judge John H. Campbell, Aug. 20, 1924. Campbell Papers, Ms. 1167, f. 4, AHS.

35. Watts and Davis, Trustees, to J. R. and Roy Sorrells, Feb. 18, 1920. Deeds Real Estate Book 12:119, SCCRO.

36. Novelist J. P. S. Brown wrote a fictionalized account of the Sorrells family in his Arizona Saga trilogy, published by Bantam Books.

37. "Sunrise to Sunset: From Texas to the Santa Cruz Valley," Recollections of Inez Cumming. Ms. on file at the Tubac Historical Society. Cumming also owned a farm along the Santa Cruz on the south half of the float. When the float was confirmed, he and his new bride, Inez, a schoolteacher from Texas, had to build a new home up Peck Canyon, which was called Pollack Canyon at the time because of a Polish farmer who had settled there.

38. Autobiography of Douglas Cumming. Ms. on file at the Tubac Historical Society.

39. Ibid.

40. Ibid.

41. Ibid., 7.

42. Sheriff of Santa Cruz County to C. C. Watts and D. C. T. Davis, Aug. 9, 1923. Book 16, 231, SCCRO.

43. Sarah Bailey, quoted in "The Pendleton Home: Renovation of Historic Building," by Regina Ford, *Green Valley News and Sun*, June 5, 2002. Bailey stated that her father and Pendleton went to high school in West Virginia, but Virginia seems a more likely location. Weldon Bailey's father was a former U.S. senator with a law firm in Washington, D.C. Pendelton's father came from Virginia.

44. D. Davis Jr., C. T. Davis and C. C. Watts, Trustees, to F. M. Dougherty and T. T. Pendleton, July 1, 1929. Deeds Real Estate Book 17:130, SCCRO.

45. Various deeds recorded in Deeds Real Estate Books 17 and 19, SCCRO.

46. Dougherty and Pendleton to Baca Float Ranch. Deeds Real Estate Book 19:416, SCCRO.

47. Interview with Nancy Stevens, n.d. Tubac Historical Society.

48. Baca Float Ranch and T. T. Pendleton to E. T. and Grace Strong, Mar. 27, 1935. Deeds Real Estate Book 20:52, SCCRO.

49. *Nogales International*, Feb. 1, 1933.

50. Baca Float Ranch and T. T. Pendleton to Harry J. and Virginia S. Mallery, June 17, 1936. Deeds Real Estate Book 20:303, SCCRO.

51. Baca Float Ranch and T. T. Pendleton to Joanna Fay Shankle. Deeds Real Estate Book 20:411, SCCRO.

52. Interview with Charles Corson Day, Sept. 25, 1987. Tubac Historical Society (THS).

53. Sarah Bailey, quoted in "The Pendleton Home."

54. Program, St. Andrew's Episcopal Church Tardeada, Rancho Santa Cruz, April 8, 1989. THS.

55. Interview with William Otto Fraesdorf Jr., Nov. 3, 1987, THS.

56. Baca Float Ranch to Roy and Helen Adams. Deeds Real Estate Book, SCCRO.

57. Charles Day interview. THS.

58. Roy and Helen Adams to W. D. Parker and F. Lee Fischer, Sept. 16, 1939. Deeds Real Estate Book 23:607, SCCRO.

59. F. Lee and Catherine Fischer to Wirt D. Parker, Feb. 15, 1940. Deeds Real Estate Book 25:31, SCCRO.

60. Charles Day interview, 15. THS.

61. Sarah Black, quoted in Regina Ford, "Pendleton Parties Brought the Rich and Famous," *Green Valley News and Sun*, June 7, 2002.

62. Interview with Lena Gómez, April 17, 1982. THS.

63. William Fraesdorf interview, 13.

64. Charles Day interview, 9.

65. Ibid., 17.

8 Rio Rico and the Great Arizona Land Rush

1. "Brother, Sister Named in Rancher's Complaint," *Arizona Daily Star*, July 12, 1969, B1. *Arizona Daily Star*, Nov. 3, 1976.

2. *Arizona Daily Star*, June 5, 1973; Regina Ford, "The Pendleton Home: Renovation of Historic Building," *Green Valley News and Sun*, June 5, 2002; idem, "Pendleton Parties Brought the Rich and Famous," *Green Valley News and Sun*, June 7, 2002.

3. Kenneth J. Slocum, "Furor in Florida: Land Sales Practices of Gulf American Corp. Touch Off Controversy," *Wall Street Journal*, June 28, 1967, 1.

4. Albert Winnikoff, *The Land Game*, quoted in Pew 1971.

5. Slocum, "Furor in Florida," 1.

6. Ibid.

7. "Gulf American Named in Alleged Try at Blackmail," *Wall Street Journal*, Oct. 16, 1967, 3.

8. Slocum, "Furor in Florida," 19.

9. Ibid., 1.

10. *New York Times*, June 25, 1967.

11. "Gulf American Says It Has Paid $700,000 to Assuage Customers," *Wall Street Journal*, Oct. 17, 1967.

12. "Public Hearing Sought for Gulf American," *Arizona Daily Star*, Aug. 9, 1967, 2.

13. *Wall Street Journal*, Oct. 16, 1967, 3; Kenneth G. Slocum, "Florida Land Furor: State Officials Amplify Blackmail Charge Tied to Gulf American Case," *Wall Street Journal*, Nov. 9, 1967, 1, 22.

14. "Williams, Land Firm Meet," *Arizona Daily Star*, Aug. 1, 1967, B1; "Acting Without the Evidence," *Arizona Daily Star*, Aug. 2, 1967.

15. "Baca Float Ranch Bought for Reported $3.5 Million," *Arizona Daily Star*, July 1, 1967, A1.

16. "Gulf American Wins Nogales Zone Change," *Arizona Daily Star*, Aug. 25, 1967, A4.

17. "Rio Rico Rezoning Approved," *Arizona Daily Star*, Sept. 9, 1967, 2B.

18. Art Ehrenstrom, "Rico Rico Plans Moving Ahead," *Arizona Daily Star*, Oct. 11, 1967, B1.

19. "Gulf American's Stock Sale Halts," *Arizona Daily Star*, Oct. 14, 1967.

20. "Gulf American Now Facing Delay In Getting License," *Arizona Daily Star*, Oct. 15, 1967, A1.

21. "Gulf American Urged to Air Florida Issue," *Arizona Daily Star*, Nov. 1, 1967, A2.

22. "Gulf American Pleads Guilty On 5 Charges," *Arizona Daily Star*, Nov. 11, 1967, A1.

23. "Gulf American, County Reach Land Compromise," *Arizona Daily Star*, Nov. 7, 1967, A2; "County OKs Subdivision at Nogales," *Arizona Daily Star*, Nov. 16, 1967, B1.

24. "Land Firm Details Promised," *Arizona Daily Star*, Dec. 7, 1967, A2.

25. "Florida Firm Files to Sell Rio Rico Sites," *Arizona Daily Star*, Dec. 21, 1967, B12.

26. "State Official 'Cautious' On Gulf American Filing," *Arizona Daily Star*, Dec. 21, 1967, A3.

27. "Developer Resuming Fla. Sales," *Arizona Daily Star*, Jan. 11, 1968, B1.

28. "Gulf American Corp. to Resume Land Sales as Suspension Ends," *Wall Street Journal*, Jan. 10, 1968.

29. "Florida Official Urges Ban on Gulf American," *Arizona Daily Star*, Jan. 12, 1968, A4.

30. "Florida Agency Intends to Expand Investigation of Gulf American Corporation," *Wall Street Journal*, Jan. 22, 1968, 6.

31. Ibid.

32. "Gulf American Corp. Sues Dow Jones and Co., 4 Others for $16 Million," *Wall Street Journal*, Jan. 29, 1968, 4.

33. "Land Firm Named In Lawsuits," *Arizona Daily Star*, Feb. 3, 1968, A2; "Suit Against Land Firm," *Wall Street Journal*, Feb. 5, 1968, 5.

34. "Florida Agency Intends to Expand Investigation of Gulf American Corporation," *Wall Street Journal*, Jan. 22, 1968, 6.

35. "Gulf American Chief and Brother May Sell Control of Company," *Wall Street Journal*, Jan. 25, 1968, 10.

36. "Gulf American Results Declined in First Half," *Wall Street Journal*, April 5, 1968, 12.

37. "Gulf American Names Herzfeld as Chairman," *Wall Street Journal*, July 16, 1968, 24.

38. "Gulf American's Profit in Nine Months Fell 75% from Fiscal 1967," *Wall Street Journal*, July 17, 1968, 12.

39. "Rosens to Lose Power at Gulf American if GAC Bid Is Voted," *Wall Street Journal*, Jan. 27, 1969.

40. "GAC to Acquire Gulf American in Swap of Stock," *Wall Street Journal*, July 18,1968, 4.

41. "Gulf American Posts Deficit of $1.6 Million in Year Ended Aug. 31," *Wall Street Journal*, Oct. 23, 1968.

42. "Gulf American Holders Vote Merger of Firm into GAC," *Wall Street Journal*, Feb. 10, 1969, 12; "GAC Stockholders Back Gulf American Purchase, Offer for Equitable S and L," *Wall Street Journal*, Feb. 11, 1969, 4

43. "New Ownership Looms For Rio Rico Project," *Arizona Daily Star*, Jan. 28, 1969, A1.

44. "State Okays Land Sales by Gulf American Corp.," *Arizona Daily Star*, Jan. 29, 1969.

45. Ken Burton, "Gulf American Corp. Begins Sale of Lots at Rio Rico," *Arizona Daily Star*, May 20, 1969, B1.

46. Ibid.

47. Art Ehrenstrom, "Rio Rico Twin City Bid Pushed," *Arizona Daily Star*, July 28, 1969, B1.

48. "GAC Says Land Unit Will Have 1969 Earnings of Up to $25 Million," *Wall Street Journal*, Dec. 30, 1969.

49. "Rio Rico Inn Opening Set for Sunday," *Arizona Daily Star*, Oct. 29, 1970, C11; Art Ehrenstrom, "Rio Rico Prepares To Grow Big," *Arizona Daily Star*, Dec. 18, 1970, B8.

50. "Gulf American Wants Huge Empire Ranch," *Arizona Daily Star*, Oct. 30, 1969, B1; "GAC Purchases 2,000 Acres of Hammond Ranch," *Arizona Daily Star*, Feb. 20, 1970, B5.

51. "Empire-Sonoita Plan Premature," *Arizona Daily Star*, June 28, 1970, C2.

52. David O'Hern, "Planners Postpone Action on Empire Ranch Project," *Arizona Daily Star*, July 1, 1970, B1.

53. David O'Hern, "GAC Plan Called Peril to City Water Supply," *Arizona Daily Star*, July 11, 1970, B1.

54. David O'Hern, "GAC Zoning Bid Delayed; Effect on Land Studied," *Arizona Daily Star*, July 16, 1970, A1.

55. "Sonoita Area Residents Protest Plans by GAC," *Arizona Daily Star*, July 21, 1970, A9.

56. "Stew Udall Joins Group against GAC," *Arizona Daily Star*, Nov. 14, 1970, A15.

57. "Empire Ranch Water Plentiful, GAC Says," *Arizona Daily Star*, Aug. 1, 1978, B1; "GAC Water Franchise Decision Is Postponed," *Arizona Daily Star*, Sept. 22, 1970, A13.

58. "Historical Society to Receive Gifts," *Arizona Daily Star*, Nov. 15, 1970, A4.

59. "Empire Plan Is Good," *Arizona Daily Star*, Nov. 14, 1970.

60. Betty Beard, "GAC May Scrap Empire Ranch Plan Because of Two Zoning Restrictions," *Arizona Daily Star*, Dec. 8, 1970, A1.

61. Ibid.

62. "GAC Properties Accused of Selling Lots at Inflated Prices," *Arizona Daily Star*, June 18, 1970.

63. "GAC Wants Venue Change for Its Property Tax Suit," *Arizona Daily Star*, Nov. 3, 1970, B1.

64. Art Ehrenstrom, "GAC Developing On Deficit Basis," *Arizona Daily Star*, Jan. 31, 1971, B7.

65. According to Steve Auslander, who covered GAC and Rio Rico for the *Arizona Daily Star*, Franklin was one of the first to see through Gulf American and GAC's hard sell. Interview by author with Steve Auslander, Jan. 9, 2004.

66. "Developers of Rio Rico Face Hearing," *Arizona Daily Star*, Sept. 23, 1971, D9.

67. "FTC, Rhode Island Probing GAC," *Arizona Daily Star*, Oct. 3, 1971.

68. "GAC Offers Adjustment or Refund in R.I. Case," *Arizona Daily Star*, Nov. 9, 1971.

69. "GAC Ordered To Halt Sales in Rhode Island," *Arizona Daily Star*, Dec. 24, 1971.

70. Steve Auslander, Al Bradshaw Jr., and John Rawlinson, "Land Development in Arizona: Empty Promises?" (five-part series in *Arizona Daily Star*): "Land Development in Arizona: Empty Promises," Dec. 26, 1971, 1A, 8A; "Big Developers Sell Land, Delay Improvements," Dec. 27, 1971, 1A, 2A; "Promises of Salesman Not Binding on Developer," Dec. 28, 1971, 1A, 7A; "Arizona's Beauty Big Sales Pitch with Developers," Dec. 29, 1971, 1A, 7A; "Legislature to Consider Toughening Land Law," Dec. 30, 1971, 1A, 9A.

71. Ibid., Dec. 30, 1971, A9.

72. Ibid., Dec. 29, 1971, 1A. Former reporter Steve Auslander stated that developer William Franklin—the same Franklin quoted by Pew—was the one who drew his attention to the bond prospectus. "He was the one paying attention. He was my basic source," Auslander said. Auslander interview with author, Jan. 9, 2004.

73. Ibid., Dec. 29, 1971.

74. "Investors Cautioned on Dealing with GAC," *Arizona Daily Star*, Feb. 8, 1972, A3.

75. "GAC President Calls Critical Report Fair," *Arizona Daily Star*, Feb. 10, 1972, A7.

76. "GAC Lists '71 Loss Totaling $65.4 Million," *Arizona Daily Star*, Feb. 12, 1972, B9

77. "GAC Sued For $100 Million," *Arizona Daily Star*, April 21, 1972, A1, A6.

78. "Rio Rico Hit by Lawsuit," *Arizona Daily Star*, July 19, 1972, A2.

79. *Arizona Daily Star*, Sept. 10, 1972, C3.

80. Steve Auslander, "Article Says Resale Lot Value Lower than Original Price," *Arizona Daily Star*, Sept. 11, 1972, B1.

81. Steve Auslander, "Developers Accused of Fraud, Lies," *Arizona Daily Star*, Nov. 15, 1992, A1.

82. "GAC Plans Empire Ranch Sale," *Arizona Daily Star*, June 28, 1973, B1.

83. "Financial Troubles Halt Sales of Rio Rico Lots," *Arizona Daily Star*, Oct. 15, 1975, A1.

84. "GAC Faces Suspension of Right to Sell Land," *Arizona Daily Star*, Dec. 12, 1973, A1.

85. Ibid.

86. "U.S. Official Disputes Statement by GAC," *Arizona Daily Star*, Dec. 13, 1973, B1.

87. "Refund by GAC Possible," *Arizona Daily Star*, Mar. 27, 1974, A10.

88. "GAC Buyers Offered Settlement," *Arizona Daily Star*, July 10, 1974, A1.

89. Ernie Heltsley, "Subsidiary of GAC Is Bankrupt," *Arizona Daily Star*, Dec. 19, 1975.

90. "Hearing Is Faced by Talley," *Arizona Daily Star*, July 24, 1974.

91. "Real Estate Aide Backs Talley," *Arizona Daily Star*, July 31, 1974, A11.

92. "Talley Dies at Age 70; Suffered Heart Ailment," *Arizona Daily Star*, Nov. 4, 1974.

93. "Financial Troubles Halt Sales of Rio Rico Lots," *Arizona Daily Star*, Oct. 15, 1974, A1; Chuck St. Cyr, "Payment Due Nov. 15 Could Bankrupt Rio Rico Developer," *Arizona Daily Star*, Nov. 7, 1975, B1.

94. "GAC Shaken by Subsidiary's Default," *Arizona Daily Star*, Nov. 18, 1975, B1.

95. John Rawlinson, "GAC Files as Bankrupt in Florida," *Arizona Daily Star*, Dec. 30, 1975, A1.

96. "The Cash Flow Dries Up," *Arizona Daily Star*, Jan. 2, 1976, E10.

97. Ibid.

9 Buried Landscapes

1. Description of Rio Rico by Nogales-Santa Cruz County Chamber of Commerce http://www.nogaleschamber.com/rio_rico.htm, accessed July 27, 2004.

2. According to Officer (1987:295), there were fourteen Spanish or Mexican land grants in southern Arizona. United States authorities eventually confirmed eight of these. Because of Apache hostilities, all but Tumacácori had been abandoned by the late 1830s or early 1840s.

3. Ernie Hetlsley, "Homes Really Are on Menu at Rio Rico," *Arizona Daily Star*, Feb. 17, 1997, 1D.

4. "Bankrupt Firm Offers Plan to Swap Undeveloped Lots," *Arizona Daily Star*, Jan. 4, 1977, B1.

5. Bob Svejcara, "Rio Rico Offering New Homes and Promises," *Arizona Daily Star*, Aug. 12, 1978.

6. Heltsley, "Homes Really Are on Menu."

7. Ibid.

8. Macario Juarez Jr., "Rio Rico Looks to Future," *Arizona Daily Star*, Feb. 27, 2000, 1D.

9. Ibid.

10. Macario Juarez Jr., "Santa Cruz County Resorts Sold," *Arizona Daily Star*, Oct. 26, 2002, D1.

11. Description of Avatar Holdings (AVTR) http://finance.yahoo.com/q/pr?s=avtr, accessed July 27, 2004.

12. Form 10-Q for Avatar Holdings (quarterly report filed with Security and Exchange Commission) http://biz.yahoo.com/e/040506/avtr10-q.html, accessed on May 6, 2004.

13. Mitch Tobin, "Saving a Stream," *Arizona Daily Star*, Nov. 24, 2003, B1.

14. "Moving up: The Changing Face of Tucson Business," *Arizona Daily Star*, Jan. 7, 2004, D2.

15. Michael Marizco, "Trade Pact Reshapes Once-sleepy Rio Rico," *Arizona Daily Star*, May 23, 2004, I21.

16. Tim Steller, "NAFTA Road to Riches: Label Them True Believers," *Arizona Daily Star*, May 23, 2004, I27.

17. Triggered by the listing of the cactus ferruginous pygmy owl as a federally endangered species in 1997, Pima County in 1998 decided to pursue a Multi-Species Habitat Conservation Plan under Section 10(a)(1)(B) of the Endangered Species Act, which allows "incidental take" as long as the plan avoids, minimizes, and mitigates resulting impacts by preserving critical habitat of the species in question. Biologists identified fifty-five "priority vulnerable species," nine of which were federally listed. The Sonoran Desert Conservation Plan (SDCP) seeks

not only to secure a Section 10 permit by preserving critical habitat for the fifty-five species, but also to control the growth of metropolitan Tucson by preventing development within the Conservation Land System through acquisition or conservation easements. In May 2004, Pima County voters approved $174 million in open space bonds to make the SDCP a reality.

18. Arizona has 9,471,000 acres of State Trust Lands, more than any other state in the nation. These lands are managed by the State Land Department for fourteen beneficiaries, the largest of which are K-12 public schools. According to Arizona's Enabling Act and Constitution, these lands must be managed for "highest and best use," currently defined as the maximization of revenues. Most of the State Trust Lands are leased by ranchers, but they can and are being sold to developers, particularly around the urban fringes of Phoenix and Tucson (Sheridan 2003).

19. Tony Davis, "Historic Sopori Ranch Sold for $22M," *Arizona Daily Star*, Oct. 29, 2004, A1, A10.

20. Of that $174 million, at least $112 million had to be spent on land designated as Habitat Protection Priorities, the most biologically sensitive lands within the Conservation Lands System established by the Sonoran Desert Conservation Plan.

21. Davis, "Historic Sopori Ranch."

22. Tony Davis, "Board OKs buying Rancho Seco," *Arizona Daily Star*, Feb. 23, 2005, B1, B4.

Glossary of spanish Terms

acequia. An irrigation canal or ditch.

alcalde mayor. The principal municipal official of a city or district.

alcaldía mayor. The administrative jurisdiction of an alcalde mayor.

alférez. The lowest-ranking commissioned officer, roughly equivalent to an ensign or second lieutenant in the army.

arroba. A common unit of weight equal to twenty-five *libras* (pounds).

asesor. The legal counsel or advisor attached to official government offices.

audiencia. A judicial and legislative council administering royal affairs over a substantial geographic area. Judicially, it was subordinate only to the Council of the Indies. In a legislative role, it acted in conjunction with the viceroy.

auto. A judicial or administrative decree.

cacique. An Indian chief or leader.

capitán a guerra. The head of military operations in an area smaller than a province—usually on a frontier subject to Indian attacks.

cédula. A royal decree or order.

compañía volante. A military unit on detached or roving duty; a "flying company."

convento. The living quarters for religious personnel.

criollo. A Spaniard (without recognized Indian or African ancestry) born in the New World.

cuera. A leather jacket, usually sleeveless and consisting of several layers.

dictamen. An informed opinion or judgment.

encomendero. A person granted an *encomienda* who agreed to provide for the Indians' welfare and instruction in Christianity.

encomienda. A grant to extract tribute from an Indian community.

estancia. A landed property; a livestock ranch.

fanega. A common unit of dry weight that varied according to the produce being measured. It equaled about 55.5 liters or 1.575 bushels.

fiscal. An attorney; official of lower rank (highly variable).

frey. The title for members of mendicant religious orders.

gente de razón. Literally, "people of reason," a term used by Spanish speakers to distinguish themselves from Indians.

gentiles. Indians not converted to Christianity.

hacienda. Literally, a "doing," which might refer to a ranch, factory, or investment; commonly, a large, privately owned estate, usually in a rural setting.

jacal. A hut, usually made of brush.

junta de guerra. A council of war.

justicia mayor. A judge; member of a cabildo, or town council, who acted as the governor's deputy.

legua. A measure of distance equaling 5,000 varas or 4.19 kilometers.

manta. A blanket; mantelet; ordinary cotton cloth.

peso. (1) A Spanish colonial monetary unit; there were several types of pesos, but the most common was the silver peso, valued at eight *reales*. (2) A unit of weight.

pueblo. An unchartered settlement, unlike a *ciudad* or *villa*, including Indian settlements associated with missions.

ranchería. A native encampment or Indian settlement in which dwellings usually were not permanent and were scattered some distance from one another.

real. (1) Any place flying the royal banner, including mining districts; a military force or any place it or its assets might be stationed; (2) a monetary unit worth one-eighth of a silver peso.

real de minas. A town or district specializing in mining.

reglamento. A body of regulations or ordinances.

sargento mayor. A military position overseeing forces in a specified area.

soldado. Literally, a "soldier"; the lowest rank among presidial forces, equivalent to "private."

vara. A common unit of linear measure approximately equal to thirty-three inches.

vecindario. A community of *vecinos*.

vecino. Members of a community, with access to the settlement's commons.

villa. A chartered settlement with royally defined privileges; town.

visita. (1) An official visit or inspection; (2) a visiting station, church, or settlement on the circuit of a priest or missionary.

References

Abbey, Edward

1977   The BLOB Comes to Arizona. *The Journey Home: Some Words in Defense of the American West.* New York: E. P. Dutton.

Abbott, Carl

1993   *The Metropolitan Frontier: Cities in the Modern American West.* Tucson: University of Arizona Press.

Accomazzo, Betty

1985   Charles Corson Day. *Arizona National Ranch Histories of Living Pioneer Stockman [sic]*. Copy in Elizabeth R. Brownell Library, Tubac Historical Society, Tubac, Ariz.

Acuña, Rodolfo F.

1974   *Sonoran Strongman: Ignacio Pesqueira and His Times.* Tucson: University of Arizona Press.

Adams, F.

1929   Tucson in 1847: Reminiscences of Judge F. Adams—Description of the Fort and So Forth. *Arizona Historical Review* 1:83–85.

Almada, Francisco

1983   *Diccionario de Historia, Geografía y Biografía Sonorenses.* Hermosillo: Gobierno del Estado de Sonora.

Atondo Rodríguez, Ana María, and Martha Ortega Soto

1996   Entrada de Colonos Españoles en Sonora Durante El Siglo XVII. In *Historia General de Sonora*, Tomo II, *De la Conquista al Estado Libre y Soberano de Sonora*, 79–112. Hermosillo: Gobierno del Estado de Sonora.

Bahr, Donald M.

1983   Pima and Papago Medicine and Philosophy. *Handbook of North American Indians*, vol. 10, *Southwest*, ed. Alfonso Ortiz, 193–200. Washington, D.C.: Smithsonian Institution Press.

1988   Pima-Papago Christianity. *Journal of the Southwest* 30(2): 133–67.

Bahr, Donald M., Juan Gregorio, David I. Lopez, and Albert Alvarez

1974   *Piman Shamanism and Staying Sickness (Ká:cim Múmkidag).* Tucson: University of Arizona Press.

Bahr, Donald, Juan Smith, William Smith Allison, and Julian Hayden

1994   *The Short Swift Time of Gods on Earth: The Hohokam Chronicles.* Berkeley: University of California Press.

Barnes, Thomas, Thomas Naylor, and Charles W. Polzer, S.J.

1981 *Northern New Spain: A Research Guide*. Tucson: University of Arizona Press.

Bartlett, John Russell

1854 *Personal Narrative of Explorations and Incidents in Texas, New Mexico, California, Sonora, and Chihuahua, Connected with the United States and Mexican Boundary Commission during the Years, 1850, '51, '52, and '53.* Vols. 1 and 2. New York: Appleton; Glorieta, N.M.: Rio Grande Press, 1965.

Basso, Keith, ed.

1971 *Western Apache Raiding and Warfare: From the Notes of Grenville Goodwin*. Tucson: University of Arizona Press.

1979 *Portraits of "The Whiteman": Linguistic Play and Cultural Symbols among the Western Apache*. Cambridge, Eng.: Cambridge University Press.

Baugh, Timothy G., and Frank W. Eddy

1987 Rethinking Apachean Ceramics: The 1985 Southern Athapaskan Ceramics Conference. *American Antiquity* 52(4): 793–98.

Beardsley, Levi

1852 *Reminiscences: Personal and Other Incidents*. New York, n.p.

Beckett, Patrick H., and Terry L. Corbett

1992 *The Manso Indians*. Las Cruces: COAS.

Billington, Ray A.

1956 *The Far Western Frontier, 1830–1860*. New York: Harper and Row.

Blake, William P.

1859 Silver and Copper Mining in Arizona. *Mining Magazine and Journal of Geology*.

Bloch, Marc

1966 *French Rural History*. Berkeley: University of California Press.

Bolton, Herbert E.

1919 *Kino's Historical Memoir of the Pimería Alta*. Vols. 1 and 2. Cleveland: Arthur C. Clark.

1930 *Anza's California Expeditions*, 5 vols. Berkeley: University of California Press.

1984 *Rim of Christendom*. Tucson: University of Arizona Press. Originally published 1936. New York: Macmillan.

Boutmy, Emile

1891 *Studies in Constitutional Law: France-England-United States*. London: Macmillan.

Bradfute, Richard W.

1975   *The Court of Private Land Claims: The Adjudication of Spanish and Mexican Land Grant Titles, 1891–1904.* Albuquerque: University of New Mexico Press.

Brown, David E.

1985   *The Grizzly in the Southwest: Documentary of an Extinction.* Norman: University of Oklahoma Press.

1992   *The Wolf in the Southwest: The Making of an Endangered Species.* Tucson: University of Arizona Press.

Browne, J. Ross

1974   *Adventures in the Apache Country: A Tour Through Arizona and Sonora, 1864.* Tucson: University of Arizona Press.

Brownell, Elizabeth R.

1986   *They Lived in Tubac.* Tucson: Westernlore Press.

Burrus, Ernest, S.J.

1971   *Kino and Manje: Explorers of Sonora and Arizona.* Rome: Jesuit Historical Institute.

Chandler, Alfred D.

1980   Rise and Evolution of Big Business. In *Encyclopedia of American Economic History*, ed. Glenn Porter, 619–638. New York: Scribners.

Cochran, John A.

1971   *Money, Banking, and the Economy.* New York: MacMillan.

Cosulich, Bernice

1942   Three Generations of Tubac History. *Arizona Highways*, Oct., 14–19, 40–44.

Cronon, William

1983   *Changes in the Land: Indians, Colonists, and the Ecology of New England.* New York: Hill and Wang.

1991   *Nature's Metropolis: Chicago and the Great West.* New York: W. W. Norton.

Crosby, Alfred

1972   *The Columbian Exchange: Biological and Cultural Consequences of 1492.* Westport, Conn.: Greenwood Press.

Crosswhite, Frank

1981   Desert Plants, Habitat, and Agriculture in Relation to the Major Pattern of Cultural Differentiation in the O'odham People of the Sonoran Desert. *Desert Plants* 3:47–76.

Danson, Edward

1946   An Archaeological Survey of the Santa Cruz River Valley from the

Headwaters to the Town of Tubac in Arizona. Master's thesis, Department of Anthropology, University of Arizona, Tucson.

Deeds, Susan

1998   Indigenous Rebellions on the Northern Mexican Mission Frontier: From First-Generation to Later Colonial Responses. In *Contested Ground: Comparative Frontiers on the Northern and Southern Edges of the Spanish Empire*, ed. Donna Guy and Thomas Sheridan, 32–51. Tucson: University of Arizona Press.

Del Río, Ignacio

1981   A Pretexto de los Placeres y el Real de la Cieneguilla, Sonora. *Memoria del VI Simposio de Historia de Sonora*. Hermosillo: Instituto de Investigaciones Históricas.

Denevan, William

1992   The Pristine Myth: The Landscape of the Americas in 1492. *Annals of the Association of American Geographers* 82(3): 369–85.

DiPeso, Charles

1956   *The Upper Pima of San Cayetano de Tumacacori: An Archaeological Reconstruction of the Ootam of Pimería Alta*. Amerind Foundation Publication 7. Dragoon, Ariz.

1979   Prehistory: O'otam. In *Handbook of North American Indians*, vol. 9, *Southwest*, ed. Alfonso Ortiz, 91–99. Washington, D.C.: Smithsonian Institution Press.

Dobyns, Henry F.

1959   Tubac Through Four Centuries. Binders 1–3. Arizona State Parks Board.

1961   *Hepah, California! The Journal of Cave Johnson Couts from Monterey, Nuevo Leon to Los Angeles, California during the years 1848–1849*. Tucson: Arizona Pioneers' Historical Society.

1963   Indian Extinction in the Middle Santa Cruz River Valley, Arizona. *New Mexico Historical Review* 38:163–81.

1988   Piman Indian Historic Agave Cultivation. *Desert Plants* 9:49–53.

Doelle, William

1975   The Adoption of Wheat by the Gila Pima: A Study in Agricultural Change. Unpublished ms. in possession of author.

Doelle, William H., and Henry D. Wallace

1990   The Transition to History in Pimería Alta. In *Perspectives on Southwestern Prehistory*, ed. Paul Minnis and Charles Redman, 239–257. Boulder, Colo.: Westview Press.

Doyel, David

1979   The Prehistoric Hohokam of the Arizona Desert. *American Scientist* 67:544–54.

1991   The Transition to History in the Pimería Alta. In *Columbian Consequences, vol. 1, Archaeological and Historic Perspectives on the* Spanish Borderlands West, ed. David Hurst Thomas. Washington, D.C.: Smithsonian Institution Press.

Duany, Andres, Elizabeth Plater-Zyberk, and Jeff Speck

2000   *Suburban Nation: The Rise of Sprawl and the Decline of the American Dream*. New York: North Point Press.

Ebright, Malcolm

1994   *Land Grants and Lawsuits in Northern New Mexico*. Albuquerque: University of New Mexico Press.

Ellinwood, Sybil

1964   Calabasas. *Arizoniana* 5(4): 27–41.

Ellis, David M.

1969   *The Frontier in American Development: Essays in Honor of Paul Wallace Gates*. Ithaca, N.Y.: Cornell University Press.

Escandon, Patricia

1985   Economía y Sociedad en Sonora: 1767–1821. In *Historia General del Sonora: de la Conquista al Estado Libre y Soberano de Sonora*, vol. 2. Hermosillo: Gobierno del Estado de Sonora.

Etter, Patricia A.

1998   *To California on the Southern Route 1849: A History and Annotated Bibliography*. Spokane, Wash.: Arthur H. Clark.

Ewing, Russell C.

1934   The Pima Uprising, 1751–1752: A Study in Spain's Indian Policy. Ph.D. diss. Department of History, University of California, Berkeley.

Ezell, Paul

1961   *The Hispanic Acculturation of the Gila River Pimas*. American Anthropological Association Memoir 90. Menasha, Wisc.

1963   Is There a Hohokam-Pima Cultural Continuum? *American Antiquity* 29(1): 61–66.

Felger, Richard, Gary Paul Nabhan, and Thomas E. Sheridan

1976   Ethnobotany of the Río San Miguel, Sonora, Mexico. Centro Regional del Noroeste del Instituto Nacional de Antropología e Historia. Unpublished ms. in possession of author.

Fish, Suzanne K., Paul R. Fish, and John H. Madsen, eds.

1992   *The Marana Community in the Hohokam World*, Anthropological

Papers of the University of Arizona, no. 56. Tucson: University of Arizona Press.

Fontana, Bernard

1971   Calabazas of the Río Rico. *The Smoke Signal*, no. 24. Tucson: Tucson Corral of the Westerners.

1976   The Papago Indians. Parts 1–3. Sells, Ariz.: Indian Oasis Schools.

1996   The O'odham. In *The Pimería Alta: Missions and More*, ed. James Officer, Mardith Schuetz-Miller, and Bernard Fontana, 19–27. Tucson: Southwestern Mission Research Center.

Forbes, Jack D.

1960   *Apache, Navajo and Spaniard*. Norman: University of Oklahoma Press.

Foucault, Michel

1980   Questions on Geography. In *Power/Knowledge: Selected Interviews and Other Writings, 1972–1977*, ed. C. Gordon, 63–77. New York: Pantheon.

Fowler, Catherine

1983   Some Lexical Clues to Uto-Aztecan Prehistory. *International Journal of American Linguistics* 49:224–57.

Garate, Donald T.

1995   Basque ethnic connections and the expedition of Juan Bautista de Anza to Alta California. *Colonial Latin American Historical Review* [*CLAHR*] (winter): 71–93.

2003   *Juan Bautista de Anza: Basque Explorer in the New World, 1693–1740*. Reno: University of Nevada Press.

n.d.   Pedro de la Cruz, alias Chihuahua. Unpublished ms. in possession of author.

Gastelum, Luis A.

1995   Memories of My Youth at Tubac: From the Old Homestead to Adulthood. *Journal of Arizona History* 36(1): 1–32.

Gates, Paul W.

1996   *The Jeffersonian Dream: Studies in the History of American Land Policy and Development*, ed. Allan G. Bogue and Margaret Beattie Bogue. Albuquerque: University of New Mexico Press.

Gettings, M. E., and B. B. Houser

n.d.   Basin Geology of the Upper Santa Cruz Valley, Pima and Santa Cruz Counties, Southeastern Arizona. U.S. Department of the Interior, U.S. Geological Survey, Open-File Report 97–676. Southwest Field Office, U.S. Geological Survey, Tucson, Ariz.

Glannon, Thomas

1949   A Factual History of the Baca Location Number Three in Santa Cruz County. Typescript, Nogales, Tubac Historical Society, Tubac, Ariz.

González Rodríguez, Luis

1977   *Etnología y mission en la Pimería Alta, 1715–1740.* México: Universidad Nacional Autónoma de México.

Gray, Andre B., and Peter R. Brady

1963   *The A. B. Gray Report, and Including the Reminiscences of Peter R. Brady,* ed. L. R. Bailey. Los Angeles: Westernlore Press.

Gregg, Josiah

1954   *Commerce of the Prairies,* ed. Max Moorhead. Norman: University of Oklahoma Press.

Griffen, William B.

1969   *Culture Change and Shifting Populations in Central Northern Mexico.* Anthropological Papers of the University of Arizona, no. 13. Tucson: University of Arizona Press.

1979   *Indian Assimilation in the Franciscan Area of Nueva Vizcaya.* Anthropological Papers of the University of Arizona, no. 33. Tucson: University of Arizona Press.

1983   Southern Periphery: East. *Handbook of North American Indians,* vol. 10, *Southwest,* ed. Alfonso Ortiz. Washington, D.C.: Smithsonian Institution Press.

1988   *Apaches at War and Peace: The Janos Presidio, 1750–1858.* Albuquerque: University of New Mexico Press.

Griffith, James

1992   *Beliefs and Holy Places: A Spiritual Geography of the Pimería Alta.* Tucson: University of Arizona Press.

Griswold del Castillo, Richard

1990   *The Treaty of Guadalupe Hidalgo: A Legacy of Conflict.* Norman: University of Oklahoma Press.

Gumerman, George, and Emil Haury

1979   Prehistory: Hohokam. *Handbook of North American Indians,* vol. 9, *Southwest,* ed. Alfonso Ortiz. Washington, D.C.: Smithsonian Institution Press.

Guy, Donna J., and Thomas E. Sheridan, eds.

1998   *Contested Ground: Comparative Frontiers on the Northern and Southern Edges of the Spanish Empire.* Tucson: University of Arizona Press.

Hackbarth, Mark R.
1992   Population Density of the Pimería Alta, 1694–1701. Unpublished
            paper. Tempe: Northland Research.
Hadley, Diana
2000   San Ignacio de la Canoa Land Grant and Canoa Ranch History/
            Timeline. *SMRC-Newsletter* 34(123): 11–15. Tucson: Southwestern
            Mission Research Center.
Hadley, Diana, and Thomas E. Sheridan
1995   *Land Use History of the San Rafael Valley (1540–1960).* Rocky
            Mountain Forest and Range Experimental Station General Techni-
            cal Report RM-GTR-269. Fort Collins, Colo.: Rocky Mountain Forest
            and Range Experimental Station, U.S. Department of Agriculture.
Hale, Kenneth, and David Harris
1979   Historical Linguistics and Archeology. In *Handbook of North Ameri-
            can Indians*, vol. 9, *Southwest*, ed. Alfonso Ortiz, 170–77. Wash-
            ington, D.C.: Smithsonian Institution Press.
Hallenbeck, Cleve
1940   *Álvar Núñez Cabeza de Vaca: The Journey and Route of the First
            European to Cross the Continent of North America, 1534–36.* Glen-
            dale, Calif: Arthur H. Clark.
Halpenny, Leonard
1988   Review of the Hydrogeology of the Santa Cruz Basin in the Vicinity
            of the Santa Cruz-Pima County Line. Paper presented at the First
            Annual Conference of the Arizona Hydrological Society, Phoenix,
            Ariz., Sept. 16, 1988.
Halpenny, Leonard, and Philip Halpenny
1991   Renewable Urban Water Supplies, Nogales and the Microbasins of
            the Santa Cruz River: A Case of Natural Water Banking. Paper pre-
            sented at the Fifth Biennial Symposium on Artificial Recharge of
            Groundwater, "Challenges of the 1990s," Tucson, Ariz.
Harvey, David
1985   The Geopolitics of Capitalism. In *Social Relations and Spatial Struc-
            tures*, ed. Derek Gregory and John Urry. London: MacMillan. Re-
            printed in Harvey 2001:312–44.
1999   *The Limits to Capital.* London: Verso. Originally published 1982.
2001   *Spaces of Capital: Towards a Critical Geography.* New York: Rout-
            ledge.
Haury, Emil
1945   The Excavation at Los Muertos and Neighboring Ruins in the Salt
            River Valley, Southern Arizona. *Papers of the Peabody Museum in*

Archaeology and Ethnology 24. Cambridge, Mass.: Harvard University Press.

1950   *The Stratigraphy and Archaeology of Ventana Cave, Arizona.* Tucson: University of Arizona Press.

1976   *The Hohokam: Desert Farmers and Craftsmen. Excavations at Snaketown, 1964–1965.* Tucson: University of Arizona Press.

Hayden, Julian

1970   Of Hohokam Origins and Other Matters. *American Antiquity* 35(1): 87–93.

1987   The Vikita Ceremony of the Papago. *Journal of the Southwest* 29: 273–324.

Hickerson, Nancy

1988   The Linguistic Position of Jumano. *Journal of Anthropological Research* 44(3): 311–26.

Hinton, Richard J.

1878   *Handbook to Arizona: Its Resources, History, Towns, Mines, Ruins, and Scenery.* San Francisco: Payot, Upham.

Ingram, Helen, Nancy Laney, and David Gillilan

1995   *Divided Waters: Bridging the U.S.-Mexico Border.* Tucson: University of Arizona Press.

Jackson, Jack

1986   *Los Mesteños: Spanish Ranching in Texas, 1721–1821.* College Station: Texas A and M Press.

Jackson, Robert

1994   *Indian Population Decline: The Missions of Northwestern New Spain, 1687–1840.* Albuquerque: University of New Mexico Press.

Jordan, Terry G.

1993   *North American Cattle-Ranching Frontiers: Origins, Diffusion, and Differentiation.* Albuquerque: University of New Mexico Press.

Keller, Jane Eblen

2002   "They Have Everything!" George Simenon in Arizona. *Journal of the Southwest* 44(4): 449–516.

Kessell, John L.

1970   *Mission of Sorrows: Jesuit Guevavi and the Pimas, 1691–1767.* Tucson: University of Arizona Press.

1975   Friars, Bureaucrats, and the Seris of Sonora. *New Mexico Historical Review* 50(1): 73–95.

1976   *Friars, Soldiers, and Reformers: Hispanic Arizona and the Sonora Mission Frontier, 1767–1856.* Tucson: University of Arizona Press.

Kino, Eusebio Francisco
1989   *Las Misiones de Sonora y Arizona*. México: Editorial Porrúa, S.A.
Kroeber, Alfred
1934   Uto-Aztecan Languages of Mexico. *Ibero-Americana* 8. Berkeley:
            University of California.
Lamar, Howard R.
2000   *The Far Southwest, 1846–1912: A Territorial History*. Albuquerque:
            University of New Mexico Press.
Lefebvre, Henri
1991   *The Production of Space*. Trans. Donald Nicholson-Smith. Oxford:
            Blackwell.
Lockhart, Bill
1997   Protohistoric Confusion: A Cultural Comparison of the Manso,
            Suma, and Jumano Indians of the Paso del Norte Region. *Journal of
            the Southwest* 39(1): 113–49.
Logan, Michael
2002   *The Lessening Stream: An Environmental History of the Santa Cruz
            River*. Tucson: University of Arizona Press.
Luckingham, Bradford
1989   *Phoenix: The History of a Southwestern Metropolis*. Tucson: University of Arizona Press.
Martin, Albro
1980   Economy from Reconstruction to 1914. In *Encyclopedia of American Economic History*, ed. Glenn Porter, 91–109. New York: Scribners.
Marx, Karl
1969   *Theories of Surplus Value*, Parts 1 and 2. London: Lawrence and
[1861–63]   Wishart.
Matson, Daniel S., and Bernard L. Fontana
1996   *Before Rebellion: Letters and Reports of Jacobo Sedelmayr, S.J.* Tucson: Arizona Historical Society.
Mattison, Ray H.
1967   The Tangled Web: The Controversy over the Tumacácori and Baca
            Land Grants. *Journal of Arizona History* 8(2): 71–90.
McGuire, Randall
1991   On the Outside Looking In: The Concept of Periphery in Hohokam
            Archaeology. In *Exploring the Hohokam: Prehistoric Desert Peoples
            of the American Southwest*, ed. George Gumerman. Albuquerque:
            University of New Mexico Press.

McGuire, Thomas
1996   Towards a Political Ecology: Observation on the Social Science of
            Fleet Dynamics and Local Knowledge. Paper presented at sym-
            posium "Reinventing Fisheries Management," Fisheries Center,
            University of British Columbia.
Meinig, David
1993   *The Shaping of America: A Geographical Perspective on 500 Years of
            History*, vol. 2, *Continental America, 1800–1867*. New Haven: Yale
            University Press.
Menegus Bornemann, M.
1980   Ocoyoacac—Una Comunidad Agraria en el Siglo XIX. *Historia Mex-
            icana* 30(1): 33–78.
Merck, Frederick
1969   Foreword. In *The Frontier in American Development: Essays in
            Honor of Paul Wallace Gates*, ed. David M. Ellis, ix–xxx. Ithaca, N.Y.:
            Cornell University Press.
Meyer, Michael C.
1984   *Water in the Hispanic Southwest: A Social and Legal History, 1550–
            1850*. Tucson: University of Arizona Press.
Montejano, David
1987   *Anglos and Mexicans in the Making of Texas, 1836–1986*. Austin:
            University of Texas Press.
Moore, Geoffrey H.
1980   Business Cycles, Panics, and Depressions. In *Encyclopedia of Ameri-
            can Economic History*, ed. Glenn Porter, 151–56. New York: Scrib-
            ners.
Moore, James T.
1982   *Indian and Jesuit*. Chicago: Loyola University Press.
Moorhead, Max
1975   *The Presidio: Bastion of the Spanish Borderlands*. Norman: Univer-
            sity of Oklahoma Press.
Mowry, Sylvester
1859   *Geography and Resources of Arizona and Sonora: An Address before
            the American Geographical and Statistical Society*. Washington,
            D.C.: Henry Polkinghorn.
1864   *Arizona and Sonora: The Geography, History, and Resources of the
            Silver Region of North America*. New York: Harper.
Myers, Margaret G.
1970   *A Financial History of the United States*. New York: Columbia Uni-
            versity Press.

Myrick, David F.

1975   *Railroads of Arizona*, vol.1, *The Southern Roads*. Berkeley: Howell-North Books.

Nash, Gerald

1985   *The American West Transformed: The Impact of the Second World War*. Bloomington: Indiana University Press.

Naylor, Thomas H.

1981   Athapaskans They Weren't: The Suma Rebels Executed at Casas Grandes in 1685. In *The Protohistoric Period in the North American Southwest, AD 1450–1700*, ed. David R. Wilcox and W. Bruce Masse, 275–81. Arizona State University Anthropological Research Papers no. 24. Tempe: Arizona State University.

Naylor, Thomas H., and Charles W. Polzer, S.J., eds.

1986   *The Presidio and Militia on the Northern Frontier of New Spain*, Vol. I: *1570–1700*. Tucson: University of Arizona Press.

1988   *Pedro de Rivera and the Military Regulations for Northern New Spain, 1724–1729*. Tucson: University of Arizona Press.

Netting, Robert M.

1976   What Alpine Peasants Have in Common: Observations on Communal Tenure in a Swiss Village. *Human Ecology* 4(2): 135–46.

1981   *Balancing on an Alp: Ecological Change and Continuity in a Swiss Mountain Community*. Cambridge, Eng.: Cambridge University Press.

North, Diane M. T.

1980   *Samuel Peter Heintzelman and the Sonora Exploring and Mining Company*. Tucson: University of Arizona Press.

Oberly, James W.

1990   *Sixty Million Acres: American Veterans and the Public Lands Before the Civil War*. Kent, Ohio: Kent State University Press.

Oblasser, Bonaventure, O.F.M.

1931   Carnacion Tells Her Tale. *Arizona Historical Review* 3(4): 97–98.

Officer, James E.

1987   *Hispanic Arizona, 1536–1856*. Tucson: University of Arizona Press.

1991   Mining in Hispanic Arizona: Myth and Reality. In *History of Mining in Arizona*, vol. 2, ed. J. Michael Canty and Michael N. Greeley, 1–26. Tucson, Ariz.: Mining Club of the Southwest Foundation and the American Institute of Mining Engineers.

1993   Kino and Agriculture in the Pimería Alta. *Journal of Arizona History* 34(3): 287–306.

Officer, James, Mardith Schuetz-Miller, and Bernard Fontana

1996 *The Pimería Alta: Missions and More*. Tucson: Southwestern Mission Research Center.

Olson, Donald W., Marilynn S. Olson, Russell L. Doescher, Lance L. Lambert, David E. Lemke, Angela M. Carl, Ross Johnson, Sandra D. Smith, and Ken H. Trede

1997 Piñon Pines and the Route of Cabeza de Vaca. *Southwestern Historical Quarterly* 101(2): 175–86.

Pérez de Ribas, Andrés de

1999 [1645] *History of the Triumphs of Our Holy Faith Amongst the Most Barbarous and Fierce Peoples of the New World*. English translation based on 1645 Spanish original. Trans. Daniel T. Reff, Maureen Ahern, and Richard K. Danford. Tucson: University of Arizona Press.

Perry, Richard J.

1991 *Western Apache Heritage: People of the Mountain Corridor*. Austin: University of Texas Press.

Pew, Thomas W.

1971 Peddling the Great West. *Saturday Review*, Sept. 4, 1971, 48–51.

Pickens, Buford, ed.

1993 *The Missions of Northern Sonora: A 1935 Field Documentation*. Tucson: University of Arizona Press.

Pima County

2000 Our Common Ground: Ranch Lands in Pima County. Ranch Element. Sonoran Desert Conservation Plan. Tucson, Ariz.: Pima County.

Polzer, Charles W., and Thomas E. Sheridan, eds.

1997 *The Presidio and Militia on the Northern Frontier of New Spain*, vol. 2, part 1, *The Californias and Sinaloa-Sonora, 1700–1765*. Tucson: University of Arizona Press.

Povitch, Shirley

1988 Shirley Povitch on Walter Johnson. In *The Baseball Hall of Fame 50th Anniversary Book*, ed. Gerald Astor. New York: Prentice Hall Press.

Powell, H. M. T.

1931 *Santa Fe Trail to California, 1849–1852: The Journal and Drawings of H. M. T. Powell*, ed. Douglas S. Watson. San Francisco: Book Club of California.

Pumpelly, Raphael

1920 *Travels and Adventures of Raphael Pumpelly, Mining Engineer, Geologist, Archaeologist, and Explorer*. New York: Holt.

Radding, Cynthia

1997   *Wandering Peoples: Colonialism, Ethnic Spaces, and Ecological Frontiers in Northwestern Mexico, 1700–1850.* Durham: Duke University Press.

1998   The Colonial Pact and Changing Ethnic Frontiers in Highland Sonora, 1740–1840. In *Contested Ground: Comparative Frontiers on the Northern and Southern Edges of the Spanish Empire*, ed. Donna Guy and Thomas Sheridan, 52–66. Tucson: University of Arizona Press.

Ravelsoot, John C., and Stephanie M. Whittlesey

1987   Inferring the Protohistoric Period in Southern Arizona. In *The Archaeology of the San Xavier Bridge Site (AZ BB:13:14), Tucson Basin, Southern Arizona*, Arizona State Museum Archaeological Series 171, ed. John C. Ravesloot, 81–98. Tucson: University of Arizona.

Rea, Amadeo

1983   *Once a River: Bird Life and Habitat Changes on the Middle Gila.* Tucson: University of Arizona Press.

1997   *At the Desert's Green Edge: An Ethnobotany of the Gila River Pima.* Tucson: University of Arizona Press.

Reff, Daniel

1991   *Disease, Depopulation, and Culture Change in Northwestern New Spain, 1518–1764.* Salt Lake City: University of Utah Press.

1995   The "Predicament of Culture" and Spanish Missionary Accounts of the Tepehuan and Pueblo Revolts. *Ethnohistory* 63–90.

1998   The Jesuit Missionary Frontier in Comparative Perspective: The Reductions of the Río de la Plata and the Missions of Northwestern Mexico, 1588–1700. In *Contested Ground: Comparative Frontiers on the Northern and Southern Edges of the Spanish Empire*, ed. Donna Guy and Thomas Sheridan, 16–31. Tucson: University of Arizona Press.

1999   Critical Introduction: The *Historia* and Jesuit Discourse. *History of the Triumphs of Our Holy Faith Amongst the Most Barbarous and Fierce Peoples of the New World*, ed. Daniel T. Reff, Maureen Ahern, and Richard K. Danford, 11–46. Tucson: University of Arizona Press.

Río, Ignacio del

1996   El Noroeste Novohispano y la Nueva Political Imperial Española. In *Historia General de Sonora*, Tomo II, *De la Conquista al Estado Libre y Soberano de Sonora*. Hermosillo: Gobierno del Estado de Sonora.

Roberts, Leslie
1989   Disease and death in the New World. *Science* 246:1245–47.
Rome, Adam
2001   *The Bulldozer in the Countryside: Suburban Sprawl and the Rise of American Environmentalism.* New York: Cambridge University Press.
Rubert de Ventos, Xavier
1991   *The Hispanic Labyrinth: Tradition and Modernity in the Colonization of the Americas,* trans. M. A. Newman. New Brunswick, N.J.: Transaction.
Russell, Frank
1975   *The Pima Indians.* Tucson: University of Arizona. Originally published 1905.
Sacks, B.
1964   *Be It Enacted: The Creation of the Territory of Arizona.* Phoenix: Arizona Historical Foundation.
Sakolski, A. M.
1932   *The Great American Land Bubble: The Amazing Story of Land-Grabbing, Speculations, and Booms from Colonial Days to the Present Time.* New York: Harper.
Sargent, Charles, ed.
1988   *Metro Arizona.* Scottsdale, Ariz.: Biffington Books.
Sauer, Carl
1934   The Distribution of Indian Tribes and Languages in Northwestern Mexico. *Ibero-Americana* 3. Berkeley: University of California Press.
1935   Aboriginal Population of Northwestern Mexico. *Ibero-Americana* 10. Berkeley: University of California Press.
Sauer, Carl, and Donald Brand
1930   Pueblo Sites in Southeastern Arizona. *University of California Publications in Geography* 3(7): 415–58.
Schaus, Richard G.
1965   David John Cumming, 1889–. *Arizona Cattlelog,* June.
Schuetz-Miller, Mardith
2003   The Geometry of San Xavier del Bac and La Purísima Concepción de Nuestra Señora de Caborca. *Journal of the Southwest* 1, 2:263–88.
Scott, James
1985   *Weapons of the Weak: Everyday Forms of Peasant Resistance.* New Haven: Yale University Press.

1990   *Domination and Acts of Resistance: Hidden Transcripts*. New Haven: Yale University Press.

Seymour, Deni

1989   The Dynamics of Sobaipuri Settlement in the Eastern Pimería Alta. *Journal of the Southwest* 31(2): 205–22.

Shaul, David L.

n.d.   A Piman Voice. Unpublished ms. in possession of author.

Shaul, David L., and Jane H. Hill

1998   Tepimans, Yumans, and Other Hohokam. *American Antiquity* 63(3): 375–96.

Shaul, David L., and John M. Andreson

1989   A Case for Yuman Participation in the Hohokam Regional System. *The Kiva* 54(2): 105–26.

Sheridan, Thomas E.

1979   Cross or Arrow? The Breakdown in Spanish-Seri Relations, 1729–1750. *Arizona and the West* 21(4): 317–34.

1986   *Los Tucsonenses: The Mexican Community in Tucson, 1854–1941.* Tucson: University of Arizona Press.

1988a   Kino's Unforeseen Legacy: The Material Consequences of Missionization among the Northern Piman Indians of Arizona and Sonora. *The Smoke Signal*, Nos. 49 & 50. Tucson: Tucson Corral of Westerners.

1988b   *Where the Dove Calls: The Political Ecology of a Peasant Corporate Community in Northwestern Mexico.* Tucson: University of Arizona Press.

1992   The Limits of Power: The Political Ecology of the Spanish Empire in the Greater Southwest. *Antiquity* 66:153–71.

1995   *Arizona: A History.* Tucson: University of Arizona Press.

1996a   La Gente Es Muy Perra: Conflict and Cooperation over Irrigation Water in Cucurpe, Sonora, Mexico. In *Canals and Communities: Small-Scale Irrigation Systems*, ed. Jonathan Mabry, 33–52. Tucson: University of Arizona Press.

1996b   The O'odham (Pimas and Papagos): The World Would Burn Without Rain. In *Paths of Life: American Indians of the Southwest and Northern Mexico*, ed. T. Sheridan and N. Parezo, 115–40. Tucson: University of Arizona Press.

1998   From Black Robes to '49ers: The History of the Tinajas Altas Region before 1854. In *The Only Water for 100 Miles: The Ethnohistory and History of Tinajas Altas*. Phoenix: Luke Air Force Base.

1999   *Empire of Sand: The Seri Indians and the Struggle for Spanish Sonora, 1645–1803*. Tucson: University of Arizona Press.

2000   La Canoa: From Land Grant to Political Football. *SMRC-Newsletter* 34(123): 2–5.

2003   Archive and Laboratory Embedded in the Landscape: Future of the Santa Rita Experimental Range. In *Santa Rita Experimental Range: 100 Years (1903 to 2003) of Accomplishments and Contributions*, technical coordinators Mitchel McClaran, Peter Ffolliott, and Carleton Edminister, 101–10. USDA Forest Service Rocky Mountain Research Station Proceedings RMRS-P-30. Ogden, Utah: Rocky Mountain Research Station.

n.d.   Colliding Worlds: Southeastern Arizona at Contact. Unpublished ms. in possession of author.

Sheridan, Thomas E., and Nancy J. Parezo, eds.

1996   *Paths of Life: American Indians of the Southwest and Northern Mexico*. Tucson: University of Arizona Press.

Simenon, Georges

1954   The Bottom of the Bottle. *Tidal Wave*. New York: Doubleday.

Simpson, Ruth

1946   Those Who Have Gone Still Live: The Hohokam Since 1400 A.D. *The Masterkey* 20:73–80.

Smith, Fay Jackson, John L. Kessell, and Francis J. Fox, S.J.

1966   *Father Kino in Arizona*. Phoenix: Arizona Historical Foundation.

Soja, Edward W.

1989   *Postmodern Geographies: The Reassertion of Space in Critical Social Theory*. London: Verso.

Solórzano Pereira, Juan de

1930 [1647]   *Política Indiana*, 5 vols. Madrid: Compañía Ibero-Americana de Publicaciones.

Sonnichsen, C. L.

1974   *Colonel Greene and the Copper Skyrocket*. Tucson: University of Arizona Press.

1982   *Tucson: The Life and Times of an American City*. Norman: University of Oklahoma Press.

Spicer, Edward H.

1962   *Cycles of Conquest: The Impact of Spain, Mexico, and the United States on the Indians of the Southwest, 1533–1960*. Tucson: University of Arizona Press.

Stern, Peter, and Robert Jackson

1988   Vagabundaje and Settlement in Colonial Northern Sonora. *The Americas* 44(4): 461–81.

Stewart, Janet Ann

1974   *Arizona Ranch Houses: Southern Territorial Styles, 1867–1900*. Tucson: University of Arizona Press and Arizona Historical Society.

Swadesh, Frances L., Julián W. Vigil, and Marina Baldonado Ochoa

1975   *The Lands of New Mexico*. Santa Fe: Museum of New Mexico.

Teague, Lynn S.

1993   Prehistory and the Traditions of the O'odham and Hopi. *The Kiva* 58(4): 435–54.

Thompson, E. P.

1963   *The Making of the English Working Class*. New York: Vintage Books.

Treutlein, Theodore, ed. and trans.

1945   The Relation of Philipp Segesser: The Pimas and Other Indians [1737]. *Mid-America* 27 (July): 139–87; (Oct.): 257–60.

Turner, Christie

1993   Southwest Indian Teeth. *National Geographic Research and Exploration* 9:32–53.

Turner, Christie, and Joel Irish

1989   Further Assessment of Hohokam Affinity: The Classic Period Population of the Grand Canal and Casa Buena Sites, Phoenix, Arizona. In *Archaeological Investigations at the Grand Canal Ruins: A Classic Period Site in Phoenix, Arizona*, vol. 2, 775–92. *Soil Systems Publications in Archaeology* 12.

Underhill, Ruth M.

1938   *Singing for Power: The Song Magic of the Papago Indians of Southern Arizona*. Berkeley: University of California Press.

1939   *Social Organization of the Papago Indians*. Columbia University Contributions to Anthropology, vol. 30. New York: Columbia University Press.

1946   *Papago Indian Religion*. New York: Columbia University Press.

Underhill, Ruth M., Donald M. Bahr, Baptisto Lopez, Jose Pancho, and David Lopez

1997   *Rainhouse and Ocean: Speeches for the Papago Year*. Tucson: University of Arizona Press.

Vassberg, David

1974   The *Tierras Baldías*: Community Property and Public Lands in 16th Century Castille. *Agricultural History* 48(3): 383–401.

1980   Peasant Communalism and Anti-Communal Tendencies in Early Modern Castille. *Journal of Peasant Studies* 7(4): 477–91.

1984   *Land and Society in Golden Age Castille*. Cambridge: Cambridge University Press.

Voss, Stuart

1982   *On the Periphery of Nineteenth-Century Mexico: Sonora and Sinaloa, 1810–1877*. Tucson: University of Arizona Press.

Wagoner, Jay J.

1952   History of the Cattle Industry in Southern Arizona, 1540–1940. *University of Arizona Social Science Bulletin*, no. 20. Tucson: University of Arizona.

1970   *Arizona Territory 1863–1912: A Political History*. Tucson: University of Arizona Press.

1975   *Early Arizona: Prehistory to Civil War*. Tucson: University of Arizona Press.

Walker, Henry P., and Don Bufkin

1979   *Historical Atlas of Arizona*. Norman: University of Oklahoma Press.

Ward, Henry G.

1829   *Mexico*. 2 vols. London: H. Colburn.

Waters, Michael, and John Ravesloot

2003   Disaster or Catastrophe: Human Adaptation to High- and Low-Frequency Landscape Processes—A Reply to Ensor, Ensor, and Devries. *American Antiquity* 68(2): 400–5.

Weber, David

1982   *The Mexican Frontier, 1821–1846: The American Southwest Under Mexico*. Albuquerque: University of New Mexico Press.

1992   *The Spanish Frontier in North America*. New Haven: Yale University Press.

West, Robert C.

1949   The Mining Community in Northern New Spain: The Parral Mining District. *Ibero-Americana* 30. Berkeley: University of California Press.

1993   *Sonora: Its Geographic Personality*. Austin: University of Texas Press.

Wilcox, David R.

1981   The Entry of Athapaskans into the American Southwest: The Problem Today. In *The Protohistoric Period in the North American Southwest, AD 1450–1700*, 213–56, ed. David R. Wilcox and W. Bruce Masse. *Arizona State University Anthropological Research Papers*, no. 24. Tempe: Arizona State University.

1986   The Tepiman Connection: A Model of Mesoamerican-Southwestern Interaction. In *Ripples in the Chichimec Sea: New Considerations of Southwestern-Mesoamerican Interactions*, ed. Frances Joan Mathien and Randall H. McGuire. Carbondale: Southern Illinois University Press.

Willey, Richard R.

1979   La Canoa: A Spanish Land Grant Lost and Found. *The Smoke Signal*, no. 38. Tucson: Tucson Corral of Westerners.

Winter, Joseph

1973   Cultural Modifications of the Gila Pima: A.D. 1697–A.D. 1846. *Ethnohistory* 20(1): 67–77.

Wolf, Eric

1955   Types of Latin American Peasantry. *American Anthropologist* 57: 452–71.

1957   Closed Corporate Peasant Communities in Mesoamerica and Java. *Southwestern Journal of Anthropology* 13(1): 1–18.

Index

Acuña, Luis, 168

Adams, Helen and Roy, 188–189

Adams-Onís Treaty, 139, 140–41

agriculture, 41, 91, 182; O'odham, 34–35, 36–37, 39–40; use rights and, 63–64, 142

Aguilar, Francisco Alejandro de, 101, 102, 132, 133, 252–53n. 10

Aguilar-Gándara family, 134, 135, 254n. 30

Akimel O'odham. *See* O'odham

Allande, Pedro, 59

Allen, William, 188

Allison, George, 122, 253n. 14

Altar, 48, 88, 245n. 8

Alvarez Tuñón y Quirós, Gregorio, 42

American Exchange National Bank, 180, 185

American Exploration Company, 153

American Property Management, 230

Anaconda Copper Company, 216

Anamax Mining Corporation, 224

Anza, Juan Bautista de (elder), 42, 43, 87, 88, 143

Anza, Juan Bautista de (younger), 51, 56, 58, 64, 88, 92, 245–46n. 1; alliances of, 61–62; San Francisco and, 95, 190

Apaches, 6–7, 60, 61, 62, 82, 107, 118; attacks by, 26, 28–29, 51, 59, 81, 92, 103, 104, 120, 137, 147, 268n. 2; and Sonoita, 57, 250–51nn. 11, 12; Spanish and, 32, 47, 86, 89

Apodaca, Juan Nepomuceno, 66, 68

archaeology: Hohokam, 21–25

Arivaca, 44, 94, 161

Arizona Board of Property Tax Appeals, 217

Arizonac, 44, 86, 87, 92

Arizona Cattle and Improvement Company, 128–30

Arizona Cattle Growers Association, 215

Arizona Copper Estate, 153, 154

Arizona Daily Star (newspaper): on GAC, 215–16, 221, 223, 226

Arizona Department of Property Valuations, 217

Arizona Pioneers' Historical Society, 175, 215

Arizona Real Estate Board, 207

Arizona Real Estate Commission, 225

Arizona Real Estate Department, 212

Arizona Southern Railroad Company, 125, 127, 133

Arizona State Parks Department, 229, 231

Assalone, John, Jr., 220

Astiazarán, Dolores, 134, 254n. 30

Astiazarán, Joaquín, 98–99, 102–3

Atkinson, George, 134, 135, 155, 158, 159, 161, 164, 170

auctions: land, 101–2, 112, 135

Auslander, Steve, 223, 266n. 72

Avatar Holdings: Rio Rico, 229–31

Aztec Mining District, 122, 148, 150(map)

Babbitt, Bruce, 202
Baboquivari Peak, 79, 100–101
Bac, 32, 43, 49, 77, 86, 107
Baca family, 138, 143, 144, 146, 156–
  57, 167
Baca Float Mining and Cattle Company,
  180
Baca Float No. 3, 10, 12, 138, 143–44,
  149(map), 237; contested titles and
  locations for, 148, 151–67; home-
  steaders and, 167–71, 173–74; Pen-
  dleton and, 172–73, 184–86; sales
  of, 145–48, 176–77, 179–89
Baca Float Ranch, 172–73, 186, 195,
  201; as dude ranch, 187–88; sales
  of, 188–89
Baca Floats Mine Company, 178–79
Baes, Pedro, 68
Bailey, Josephine, 205
Bailey, Joseph W., 165, 180–81
Bailey, Sarah, 187–88, 189
Bailey, Weldon M., 167, 173, 176, 179,
  180, 181, 184–85
Bais, Juan Manuel, 88
Bartlett, John Russell, 110–11
Basques, 42, 87–88, 167
Beach, Don, 217
Belknap, A. T., 153
Bernstein, George, 224
Bertoch, Carl, 208–9
Black, John, 138
Black, Sarah, 138–39, 168, 170, 173
Blake, William P., 161
Boice, Henry, 177
Boice family, 213
Bolles, Don, 195, 202
bond issues: railroad, 128, 130–31
Bottom of the Bottle, 191, 192–94
Bouldin, David W., 151, 152, 177

Bouldin, James, 153, 180
Bouldin family: and Baca Float No. 3,
  153, 154, 166, 167, 172, 173, 175,
  176, 181, 185, 235; mining claims,
  177–79
Bourbon reforms, 58, 64, 93, 102
Brunckow, Frederick, 117
Buckeye, 138, 170
Buenavista, 48, 51, 60, 245n. 9, 246n.
  3; ranch at, 66, 68, 85, 86, 98
Burruel, Ramón, 173

Calabasas, 11, 12, 14, 56, 57, 62, 88,
  97, 158, 188, 228, 229, 235, 237–
  38; abandonment of, 100, 101, 132;
  and Baca Float No. 3, 145, 148,
  149(map), 164, 186; Gándara and,
  119–21; Pesqueira at, 120, 122;
  Sykes and, 124–28; and Tumacácori
  grant, 70, 72
Calabasas Land and Mining Company,
  12, 123, 133, 253n. 14; promotion
  of, 124–28
Calabasas, Tucson, and North Western
  Railroad Company, 128–31
Campbell, John Henry, 173–74, 178,
  179, 180, 181
Campos, Agustín de, 31, 32–33
Canoa Ranch, 5, 189–91, 195, 234,
  250n. 7
Carrera, Manuel Fernández de la, 66,
  68, 71, 247n. 13
cattle, 120, 168; colonial era, 38, 39,
  77, 82, 85–86, 89, 93, 98, 99; and
  drought, 182–83; Santa Gertrudis,
  172, 186; in Spain, 83–84
cattle companies, 128–30, 182
Christianization: Jesuits and, 44–45;
  of O'odham, 59, 73–76

Clark, Walter G., 178
colonial system. *See* Spanish empire
Colonization Law (1824), 141
Columbian Exchange, 33; O'odham
  and, 38–41
communities: Hohokam, 24–25; land
  grant, 143–44; mission, 59–60;
  peasant corporate, 9–10, 53, 62
Compañía de Pimas (de San Rafael de
  Buenavista), 60, 62, 63, 245n. 9
Compromise of 1877, 123
consumerism: post-war, 198–99
Contzen, Philip, 160–61
Coro, 26, 32, 96
creation myth, 79; O'odham, 19–21
Croix, Teodoro de, 60, 61
crops: Old and New World, 35, 38, 39–
  41
Cruz, Pedro de la, 47, 48, 245n. 7
Cumming, David John, 182, 183, 193,
  262n. 37
Curry, John, 123, 132

Davidson, Alexander, 164–65, 166
Davis, Dabney C. T., 154, 164, 165,
  166, 172, 181, 183, 185
Day, Charles, 187, 189, 192
Decree 89, 102
denuncias, 96, 98
depressions, 123, 130, 131, 182
diseases, 33, 122; O'odham and, 45,
  75–76, 248n. 31
Dougherty, F. M., 172, 184–86
drought, 63–64, 99, 182–83
Durrell, Russell, 177, 182

Earth Doctor, 19, 20
economy, 40, 108; homeownership
  and, 197–98; homesteaders, 168–

69; land speculation and, 113–14;
  livestock and, 85–86; mission, 53–
  54, 56, 77; Tubac-Tumacácori, 62–
  63; U.S., 112, 123–24
Edmunds, J. M., 145–46, 165
Elder Brother, 20, 75, 79
Eldredge, James, 152, 177, 257n. 22
Elías, José, 120, 136–37, 251n. 19
Elías family, 98, 251n. 17
Elías González family, 78, 93, 96, 98,
  103, 250n. 8, 251nn. 17, 19
Elizondo, Domingo, 50
El Paso, 28, 29, 175–76
El Tupo, 31, 32, 47–48
Empire Ranch, 116, 234; GAC and,
  213–16, 224, 226
Enclosure Law, 141, 142
environmentalism, 196, 216, 234
epidemics, 33, 45, 51, 76
estancias. See ranches
Estelric, Juan Bautista, 78, 97–98
Eureka mines, 177–78

Fairfield Homes, 234
Faxon, William, 133, 135
Faxon v. United States, 136, 254–55n.
  36
Federal Housing Administration, 197–
  98
Federal Trade Commission, 220, 224–
  25
finance: global, 108–10; U.S., 114–
  15
First United Realty, 229, 234–35
Florida: land fraud, 202–4, 207, 208–
  9, 211, 219–20, 221, 225
Franciscans, 6, 8, 55, 74, 76–77, 93,
  246n. 2, 249n. 4
Franklin, Selim, 175, 176

Franklin, William, 219, 266n. 72
Fronteras, 29, 61, 88

GAC, GAC Properties, 6, 12, 13, 211,
  223; and Empire Ranch, 213–16;
  land fraud and, 220–26; and Rio
  Rico, 212–13, 216–18, 224–25;
  sales tactics of, 218–20
Gándara, Manuel María, 72, 123, 132,
  134, 228, 251n. 23, 252–53n. 10;
  hacienda of, 119–21; land fraud,
  100–101, 102, 104, 136–37, 238
García Conde, Alejo, 64, 65–66, 71, 72
Garrucho, Joseph, 44, 47, 48
Gastellum family, 167, 168, 170–71
General Acceptance Corporation, 6.
  See also GAC
General Land Office, 147, 148, 151,
  152; and Baca Float, 157–64; homesteads, 164–71
Gil de Bernabé, Juan Chrisóstomo, 56–
  57
gold rush: California, 108–9
gold standard, 109–10
Gómez de Silva, Nicolasa, 88
González, Francisco, 99
grazing, 91, 92, 180, 182–83, 217;
  leases, 177, 217
Great Depression, 172, 185, 197
Green Valley, 5, 190, 196, 200, 232
Grund, A. R., 178, 179, 180
Guevavi, 10, 11, 14, 28, 43, 47, 51, 68,
  72, 86, 88, 100, 159, 233, 235; as
  cabacera, 32, 33; claims to, 133–34;
  as estancia, 65, 66, 70–71; Franciscans at, 56–57; 1751 rebellion and,
  48, 49, 50
Gulf American Corporation, 6, 12, 13,
  201; and GAC, 210–11; land fraud,
  202–4, 208–10, 219–20; in Santa
  Cruz County, 205–8
Gutiérrez, Narciso, 66, 76, 77, 78

Hacienda del Santa Rita, 122, 154
haciendas, 103; Gándara's, 102, 119–
  21, 154
Handbook of Arizona, 122
Hawani Mo'o, 50
Hawley, Christopher Eldredge, 152,
  156
Heintzelman, Samuel Peter, 116–17,
  118
Heintzelman Mine, 117, 118, 163
Herreros, Leon, 96, 97, 98
Higuera, Nicolás de, 29
Hitchcock, E. A., 157–59
Hohokam, 20, 23–25, 37, 52, 244n. 4;
  and O'odham, 21–22
homeownership, 197, 198–99
homesteaders, 12, 138, 240–41; on
  Baca Float No. 3, 157, 164–67, 173–
  74, 179, 180; Depression-era, 185–
  86; eviction of, 138–39, 167–71;
  12, 138; Tumacácori and, 174–75
Hoover, Herbert, 197
Howard, George Hill, 133, 134, 135
Hulsemann, Federico, 119, 120
Humari, 26

Ingalls, Frank, 160, 161, 162
Instructions of 1786, 61
interstate highways, 199, 231
investment: land, 11–12, 114, 122–
  28; mining, 116–18, 147; railroad,
  130, 131
Ireland, John, 152, 155, 156
irrigation systems, 24, 58, 59, 70, 90,
  182

Januske, Daniel, 30
Jesuits, 6, 8, 32–33, 42, 51, 53, 55, 93, 99, 249n. 4; O'odham and, 43–48; and livestock industry, 84, 85

Keller, Ignaz Xavier, 43, 47, 48, 49–50, 51, 245n. 7
King, Joseph, 122, 162, 252n. 8
King, Manuel, 173, 179, 185, 186
King, Wilbur H., 152, 155, 156
Kino, Eusebio Francisco, 26, 28, 32, 39, 40, 77, 85, 96, 244n. 6
Kirk, Claude, 204, 207, 208, 209, 211, 212

La Canoa, 90, 95–96, 250n. 7
land, 62, 64, 84, 89, 98, 196, 240–41, 246n. 5; auctions of, 135, 183; as commodity, 95–96; as commons, 10, 141–42; development of, 6, 124–25, 234; farm, 69–70; Mexican laws on, 101–2; O'odham and, 52, 228–29; rezoning, 205, 207; sales of, 172–73, 185–87, 188–89, 190, 195, 212–13, 218–20, 224–25, 230–31; social construction of, 11–12; surveys of, 96–97, 160–61, 247n. 16; and Tucson, 231–32; U.S. acquisition of, 112–14; use rights, 63–64, 72–73, 93, 136–37, 141–42; water and, 90–91
land booms, 114, 115–16, 201–2
land fraud, 10, 82, 211, 255n. 3; GAC's, 218–26; Gándara's, 100–101, 102, 104, 136–37, 238; Gulf American Corporation's, 202–10
land grants, 63, 89, 103, 107, 117, 246n. 5, 250nn. 6, 8, 252n. 3; community, 143–44; Mexican, 98–99,

140–41, 251nn. 17, 19, 252–53n. 10, 268n. 2; petitions for, 71–72; on Santa Cruz, 94–98; Tumacácori, 65–73, 99–101, 122, 123, 131–37, 246n. 6, 252–53n. 10. See also Baca Float No. 3
landscapes, 11, 15–16, 53, 239–40
land speculation, 6, 10, 11, 196, 201–2; Baca Float No. 3, 144–46, 152–54, 169–70, 172–73, 175–76, 179–81, 184–86; Rio Rico and, 12–13; sales tactics, 218–19; Sykes and, 122–28, 252–53n. 10; westward expansion and, 112–16. See also land fraud
land tenure, 52, 91, 97, 202, 252n. 4; and production, 72–73
Lane v. Watts, 166, 170
language: as resistance, 73, 74, 248n. 28
Legarra, Juan, 65, 69, 71, 246n. 6
León, Manuel de, 64, 66, 68, 70, 71, 96, 101
Liberós, Ramón, 78, 98, 99
Lim, Louis, 173
livestock, 73, 95; drought and, 182–83; Gándara's, 119–20; grazing and marketing, 83–84, 86–89, 92–93, 168; introduction of, 38–39, 82; mission, 53, 58, 77, 78, 85–86
Lower Pimas, 48, 50, 60
Luis of Pitic, 47, 48
Luque, María Josefa de, 88

Mallery family, 186–87
Manifest Destiny, 107, 110, 140
Manje, Juan Mateo, 26, 28, 244n. 6
Manning family, 190–91, 195
maquilas, 213, 230, 239

Martínez de Hurdaide, Diego, 84–85
massacres, 29, 31, 32, 86, 100–101
Mathews, Alexander, 153, 165
Mendez family, 174–75, 235
Merryweather, Hubert and Ann, 187, 192, 193, 201
Mexican-American War, 107, 139, 140
migrant workers, 170–71
militarization, 29, 48, 60–61, 93
military, 50, 88, 120; and Indian rebellions, 29–30, 31–32; Indians in, 46, 47, 48, 49; on Spanish frontier, 60–61
mineral rights, 117, 179, 180, 182
Mineral Segregation, 178, 185
mining, 5, 60, 83, 88, 124, 159, 248nn. 29, 30; on Baca Float, 162–63; investment in, 116–18; and land, 11–12; Spanish, 44, 86, 87; speculation in, 107, 122, 177–79
missionaries, 6, 8, 32–33, 43–44, 56–57, 73, 76
missions, 7, 8, 11, 39, 41, 58, 62, 246n. 2; economy of, 10, 53–54; influence of, 32–33; isolation of, 59–60; livestock industry, 85–86; and Mexican land grants, 98–99; and military, 60–61; O'odham opposition to, 43, 45; and rebellions, 30–32; Spanish politics and, 42, 46–47, 55–56
Mission Tumacácori. See Tumacácori
monetary standard, 109–10
Mototicachi massacre, 29, 32, 86
Mowry, Sylvester, 119, 125, 127

National Housing Act, 197
nature: social construction of, 15–16, 243n. 3

New Mexico, 143–44, 146, 147
New Mexico and Arizona Railroad, 127, 135
Nogales, 4, 15, 127, 233, 243n. 1
Nogales International Waste Water Treatment Facility, 14–15, 233
Núñez, Juan, 88

Oacpicagigua, Luis, 51, 245n. 7; as rebel leader, 46–48, 49–50
Oceguera family, 135, 254n. 30
O'Conor, Hugo, 58, 61
Oesting, Doris, 187, 188
Ohm, Henry, 174
O'odham, 6, 10, 12, 26, 28, 53, 56, 62, 63, 86, 100, 240–41; beliefs and rituals, 19–21, 41–42, 44–45, 73–75, 79–80, 243n. 1, 248nn. 29, 30, 31; Christianity and, 75–76, 80–81; Hohokam and, 21–22, 25; land tenure of, 27(map), 52, 228–29; language, 24, 244n. 3, 248n. 28; military companies, 48, 49, 60, 245n. 9; missions and, 32–33, 43–44; rebellions, 30–32; on Sonoita Creek, 98, 250n. 11; Spanish impact on, 7–8, 9, 29, 33–34, 38–41; subsistence, 34–38; and Tumacácori, 59, 65–73, 94, 99, 103–4, 107–8, 136–37, 238, 251n. 23
Opatas, 30, 48, 49, 60, 100, 167
oral tradition: O'odham, 21, 24
Ortiz, Agustín, 94, 249n. 6
Ortiz, Ignacio, 94–95, 99, 117, 250nn. 6, 7
Ortiz, Tomás, 94–95, 99, 249n. 6
Ortiz Parrilla, Diego, 46–47, 49
Otero, Sabino, 122, 138, 159, 168
Otero, Toribio, 63–64, 94

Pamplona, Ramón, 99
Panic of 1857, 117
Panic of 1884, 130
Panic of 1893, 131
Papagos. *See* Tohono O'odham
Papago War, 100, 251n. 23
Parker brothers, 189
Pauer, Francisco, 51, 96
Payeken, Hundhausen and Company, 119
peace policies: Spanish, 62, 81, 92
peasant corporate community, 9–10, 62
Peña Blanca hacienda, 143
Pendleton, Talbot T. "Tol," 12, 187, 201; and Baca Float, 172–73, 184–86, 188, 195; social life, 191, 192, 193, 194
Pendleton family, 187, 201
Pérez, Joseph, 73–74
Pérez de Ribas, Andrés, 84, 85
Pesqueira, Ignacio, 100, 102, 120, 122
Pesqueira, Ramona, 122
Pew, Thomas W., Jr., 218–20
Piatos, 50
Pima County, 176, 232, 268n. 17; land in, 196–97, 214, 216, 223
Pima County Board of Supervisors: land development and, 223, 234, 235; Sykes's railroad, 128, 130, 131
Piman languages, 22–23
Pimas. *See* O'odham
Pineda, Juan Claudio de, 69, 70
Pinkley, Frank, 175
Pintor, Francisco, 30
Pitic, 86, 88
Podenco, 26
Poston, Charles DeBrille, 117–18, 152, 159–60, 161
presidios, 6, 7, 29, 58, 61, 87–88,

245n. 8; Indian companies at, 48–49, 60, 245n. 9
private property, 11, 56, 58, 64, 93, 99, 141–42; land as, 96, 141–42, 246n. 5; and water rights, 90–91
property rights: under Treaty of Guadalupe Hidalgo, 140–41
Proto-River Yumans, 23–24, 25
Proto-Tepimans, 23–24, 25
Pueblo Revolt, 28
Pushaw, Charles P., 153, 177

Railroad Record (newspaper), 117
railroads, 124, 125, 127; Sykes's promotion of, 128–31
rancherías, 27(map), 28, 51
ranches, 6, 7, 11, 14, 54, 64, 68, 70–71, 82, 116, 122, 248nn. 29, 30; abandonment of, 51, 107; Baca Float, 12, 186–87; boundaries of, 66, 68; guest, 187–88, 189; earliest, 82–83; mission, 39, 53, 54; sales of, 188–89; on Santa Cruz, 44, 59, 86–89, 93; showcase, 189–91; Spanish traditions of, 83–85; after World War I, 182–83
Ratliff, John, 229
real estate, 6, 12–13, 235, 240; sales tactics, 212–13; speculation in, 114–15, 195–96, 202–10, 212–13, 220–26; taxes and, 217–18, 219
rebellions: Indian, 28–32, 46–48, 49–50
Regulations of 1772, 61
Regulations of 1828, 141
religion: O'odham, 73–75, 79–80. *See also* Roman Catholicism
resistance, 32, 248n. 28; O'odham forms of, 73–75

retirement communities, 5, 196, 200–201, 230
Reyes, Antonio de los, 59
Rio Rico, 3, 6, 227, 228; Avatar Holdings and, 229–31; GAC and, 212–13, 216–20, 221–25; Gulf American Corporation and, 205–8; land speculation at, 12–13; sales tactics, 212–13
Rio Rico Properties, 229, 230–31
Rio Rico Resort and Country Club, 15, 229, 230
ritual: Jesuit, 45; O'odham, 7, 30, 32, 36, 38, 45, 74–75, 80
Rivera Villalón, Pedro de, 42, 87–88
Robinson, John, 152–53
Robinson family, 175, 176, 177, 257n. 22
Robinson Land and Cattle Company, 176, 177
Roman Catholicism, 30, 79; missions, 32–33, 44–45; O'odham practice of, 74, 75–76, 80–81; space in, 8–9
Romero family, 64, 66, 68, 86, 98
Romo de Vivar, José, 82, 83, 86
Rosen, Leonard, 204, 205, 209, 210
Roskruge, George, 151, 154
Rubí, Marqués de, 58, 61, 245–46n. 1
Ruiz de Ael, Santiago, 47, 79

Saeta, Francisco, 30–31, 39
saguaro wine ceremony, 42, 44, 74–75, 79
Sahuarita, 5, 232–33
Salero, 117, 252n. 8
Salero Land and Cattle Company, 135
Salero Metals Corporation, 185
Salero Mine, 148, 161, 162, 179
Salero Ranch, 188–89

Samaniego, María Rosa, 88
San Cayetano Ranch, 187
Sandler, Ronald, 205, 207
San Ignacio, 31, 60, 101, 245n. 9
San Ignacio de Canoa, 95–96, 189, 195, 234, 250nn. 6, 7. See also Canoa Ranch
San José de Sonoita Grant, 160, 185
San José de Tumacácori, 8, 81, 243n. 2, 252n. 29; construction of, 76–79
San Lázaro, 82, 244n. 6
San Luís de Bacoancos, 39, 85
San Luís Valley, 44, 51, 59, 86
San Mateo, Rancho, 88
San Pedro River, 26, 35, 42, 49, 51, 61, 98, 127; land grants on, 95, 250n. 11
San Rafael del Valle grant, 98, 250n. 8, 251n. 17
San Rafael ranch, 116
San Rafael Valley, 13–14, 83, 182
Santa Anna, Antonio López de, 99–100, 108
Santa Bárbara, 51, 68, 86
Santa Cruz County: and Baca Float, 180, 181, 183; and Rio Rico, 205–8, 217–18
Santa Cruz Development Company, 153, 154
Santa Cruz River, 4, 35, 58, 88, 98; boundary commission and, 110–11; farmland on, 69–70; as navigable, 125, 127; water and, 13–14, 92
Santa Fe Railroad, 125, 127
Santa Fe Ring, 146, 147
Santa Gertrudis Lane, 173, 227; social life on, 191–93
Santa Rita Hotel, 127–28, 188
Santa Rita Land and Cattle Company, 133

Santa Rita Mining Company, 116–17, 133, 134, 147, 161

Santa Rita Mountains, 147, 148; mining in, 86, 117, 122, 161

San Xavier del Bac, 37, 43, 50, 95, 104, 110–11, 237, 252n. 29; church at, 76, 77; livestock introduction, 39, 40, 85

San Xavier Mining and Smelting Company, 123, 124

Schuchard, Charles, 117, 119

Schurz, W. H., 134–35

Sedelmayr, Jacob, 37, 48, 245n. 7

Segesser, Felipe, 40, 43

Seris, 31, 46, 48, 50, 57

shamans, 43, 44–45, 75, 248n. 31

Shankle, Joanna Fay, 187

sheep, 39, 83, 84, 85, 89, 119, 143; and missions, 77, 86, 99

Shute, G. W., 176

Sibubapas, 50

sickness: treatment of, 75–76, 248n. 31

Sicurisuta, Rancho, 88, 249n. 1

Siete partidas, Las, 90–91

Silo Land and Cattle Company, 175–77

silver, 44, 86, 117, 163

Simenon, George, 191, 192–94

Slocum, Kenneth, 209

Smith, Juan, 19–20

Smith, William Allison, 19

Sobaipuris, 26, 35, 39; resettlement of, 32, 34, 51; at Sonoita, 96, 250–51nn. 11, 12; Spanish military and, 29–30; trade and, 41–42

Solís, Antonio, 29–30

Sonoita, 50, 56, 57, 100, 215; Baca Float No. 3, 145, 164; land grant survey, 96–97; Sobaipuris at, 32, 51, 250–51nn. 11, 12

Sonoita and Santa Cruz Land and Water Company, 135

Sonoita Creek, 14, 68, 88, 92, 98, 228, 230

Sonoita Creek State Natural Area, 229, 231

Sonoita Creek Ranch, 229

Sonoita Valley, 127; Empire Ranch and, 213–15

Sonora, Río, 83, 85, 87, 96, 102

Sonora Exploring and Mining Company, 12, 116–18, 151, 160, 161

Sonoran Desert Conservation Plan, 196–97, 223, 232, 235, 268–69nn. 17, 20

Sonoran Expedition, 50

Sonora Railway, 127

Sópori, 49, 51, 99, 161

Sópori Ranch, 88, 235

Sorrells family, 181–82, 183

Sosa family, 88, 99

Soto, Manuela, 60

Southern Pacific Railroad, 131

space, 10; sacred, 8–9, 79; society and, 3–4; Spanish colonial, 7–8

Spain, 246n. 5; stock raising in, 83–84; water law in, 90–91

Spaniards, 63, 98

Spanish empire, 6, 11, 52, 93; conflict and, 28–29; missions and, 55–56; ranching in, 84–85, 86–89; space in, 7–10; water use in, 89–91

Spar, William A. J., 154–55

Species Circular of 1836, 115

squatters, 154; eviction of, 138–39; on Santa Cruz, 122, 138

State Trust Lands, 232, 269n. 18

Stiger, Gaspar, 43, 47
Strike Force on Organized Crime, 225
Strong family, 186, 188, 194
Suamca, 43, 49–50
suburbs, 198–99, 234
Suma Revolt, 28
Sun City, 196, 200
supernatural power: O'odham, 79–80
Sykes, C. P., 12, 228, 239; land and, 122–28; railroads and, 128–31; and Tumacácori grant, 132, 133, 135, 252–53n. 10
Syme, S. A. M., 153, 165, 177

Talley, J. Fred, 207, 208, 221, 225
taxes: property, 217–18, 219, 222
Taylor Grazing Act, 114, 182
Tepiman, 22–24, 243–44n. 2
Terrenate, 48, 49, 51, 61
Tobin, Guy, 230
Tobin, Leonard, 177–78
Tohono O'odham, 24, 25, 26, 50, 57, 237; at San Xavier, 110–11
Treaty of Guadalupe Hidalgo, 107, 120, 140–41, 144
Tresierra y Cano, Alonso, 71–72
Tubac, 5–6, 11, 14, 15, 44, 51, 57, 69, 92, 104, 117, 122, 138, 167, 168; abandonment of, 118–19; Baca Float No. 3, 145, 148, 180; land use at, 63–64; loss of garrison at, 58–59, 61; in 1850s, 110, 111; O'odham company at, 60, 62–63, 245n. 9; presidio at, 48, 88
Tubac Foothills Ranch, 229
Tubutama, 30, 77, 243n. 2
Tucson, 14, 51, 102, 124, 202, 214, 216; growth of, 231–32, 268–69n.

17; presidio move to, 58, 61; Sykes's railroad and, 130–31
Tumacácori, 3, 6, 7(fig.), 11, 12, 14, 57, 58, 86, 97, 110, 111, 158, 159, 179, 192; Baca Float and, 148, 164, 174–75; church at, 76–79; land auction, 101–2; land grant, 65–73, 94, 98, 99–100, 119–20, 122, 123, 132–37, 145, 149(map), 246n. 6, 252–53n. 10, 268n. 2; O'odham at, 28, 56, 103–4, 107–8; space use at, 8–10; and Tubac, 62–63; as visita, 32, 33
Tumacácori National Historical Park, 6, 10, 235–36, 237
Tumacácori National Monument, 175, 185, 235
Tuñón y Quirós, Gregorio Alvarez, 87, 88
Tyndall Mining District, 122, 148, 162

U.S. Court of Private Land Claims, 135, 141, 152, 158, 255n. 3
U.S. Department of Housing and Urban Development, 223, 224, 225–26
U.S. Department of the Interior, 237–38; and Baca Float No. 3, 10, 157–64, 166
U.S. District Court of Arizona, 166, 176–77
U.S. Forest Service, 175, 182
U.S. General Land Office, 134; Baca Float No. 3, 151, 163–64, 166
U.S. Supreme Court: land issues and, 10, 12, 133, 134, 136, 138, 139, 140–41, 146, 166, 245n. 6
U.S. v. Percheman, 140–41
Upper Pimas. *See* O'odham
Ures, 102, 251n. 27

Urrea, Bernardo de, 49, 88, 245n. 10
Urrea, José de, 100, 102, 251n. 23
Urrea family, 93

Velarde, Luis, 30, 33, 37–38, 40–41
Veteran Housing Administration, 198
Vildósola family, 88, 93
Virginia Lee mines, 177–78
Vroom family, 153, 160, 164, 165, 166

warfare, 20–21, 26, 48, 61–62
Warren, Ned, 202, 223, 225
Wasson, John, 132–33, 134, 151, 238
water, 10, 16, 97; access to, 89–91,
  186, 190; land development and,
  214, 215, 221; management of, 58,
  182, 249n. 3; population growth
  and, 232, 233; in Santa Cruz River,
  13–15
Watts, Cornelius, 154, 181, 183, 185
Watts, John, 12, 153; and Baca Floats,

144–46, 148, 151, 156, 159–60,
  162–63, 164, 165, 166, 167, 170
Watts, J. H., 151–52, 153, 165
Webb, Del, 195–96, 199–200
Webb, James, 216–17
Western Apaches, 6–7, 81, 107, 120
wheat, 39–40, 41, 73, 99
Williams, Jack, 205, 207, 208, 212,
  225
Wills, S. Hayward, 213, 217–18
Wise, Joseph E., 154, 155–57, 158,
  166, 167
Wise family, 154–57, 158, 166, 167
wool production, 85, 99, 119
Wooshkum, 20, 21
World War I, 12, 182
Wrightson, William, 12, 117, 146–47,
  148, 160, 252n. 8

Yaquis, 48, 60, 85, 100, 167
Yrun, Mario, 213

About the Author

Thomas E. Sheridan, Ph.D., holds a joint appointment as professor of anthropology at the Southwest Center and Department of Anthropology at the University of Arizona. He has conducted ethnographic fieldwork and ethnohistorical research in the southwestern United States and northern Mexico since 1971. From 1984 to 2003, he was Curator of Ethnohistory at the Arizona State Museum and served as Director of the Office of Ethnohistorical Research from 1997 to 2003.

Dr. Sheridan has written or co-edited twelve books and monographs, including *Los Tucsonenses: The Mexican Community of Tucson, 1854–1941* (Tucson: The University of Arizona Press, 1986), *Where the Dove Calls: The Political Ecology of a Peasant Corporate Community in Northwestern Mexico* (Tucson: The University of Arizona Press, 1988), and *Arizona: A History* (Tucson: The University of Arizona Press, 1995).

Dr. Sheridan is chairman emeritus of the Canoa Ranch Foundation, a member of Pima County's Canoa Advisory Committee, chair of the Ranch Conservation Technical Advisory Team of Pima County's Sonoran Desert Conservation Plan, and a member of Pima County's Conservation Acquisition Commission and Science Commission. He is past president of the Anthropology and Environment Section of the American Anthropological Association and currently serves on the board of the Altar Valley Conservation Alliance, a not-for-profit organization of ranchers dedicated to the conservation of open space, biodiversity, and working ranches in the Altar Valley southwest of Tucson. He received the Sonoran Institute's Faces of Conservation: Sustainable Communities Award in 2007.